User-Centered Design Strategies for Massive Open Online Courses (MOOCs)

Ricardo Mendoza-Gonzalez
Instituto Tecnologico de Aguascalientes, Mexico

A volume in the Advances in Educational Technologies and Instructional Design (AETID) Book Series

Information Science REFERENCE
An Imprint of IGI Global

Published in the United States of America by
Information Science Reference (an imprint of IGI Global)
701 E. Chocolate Avenue
Hershey PA, USA 17033
Tel: 717-533-8845
Fax: 717-533-8661
E-mail: cust@igi-global.com
Web site: http://www.igi-global.com

Library of Congress Cataloging-in-Publication Data

Names: Mendoza-Gonzalez, Ricardo, 1979- editor.
Title: User-centered design strategies for massive open online courses (MOOCs) / Ricardo Mendoza-Gonzalez, editor.
Description: Hershey, PA : Information Science Reference, [2016] | Includes bibliographical references and index.
Identifiers: LCCN 2015041967| ISBN 9781466697430 (hardcover) | ISBN 9781466697447 (ebook)
Subjects: LCSH: MOOCs (Web-based instruction) | User-centered system design.
Classification: LCC LB1044.87 .U83 2016 | DDC 371.33/44678--dc23 LC record available at http://lccn.loc.gov/2015041967

This book is published in the IGI Global book series Advances in Educational Technologies and Instructional Design (AE-TID) (ISSN: 2326-8905; eISSN: 2326-8913)

British Cataloguing in Publication Data
A Cataloguing in Publication record for this book is available from the British Library.

All work contributed to this book is new, previously-unpublished material. The views expressed in this book are those of the authors, but not necessarily of the publisher.

For electronic access to this publication, please contact: eresources@igi-global.com.

Advances in Educational Technologies and Instructional Design (AETID) Book Series

Lawrence A. Tomei
Robert Morris University, USA

ISSN: 2326-8905
EISSN: 2326-8913

Mission

Education has undergone, and continues to undergo, immense changes in the way it is enacted and distributed to both child and adult learners. From distance education, Massive-Open-Online-Courses (MOOCs), and electronic tablets in the classroom, technology is now an integral part of the educational experience and is also affecting the way educators communicate information to students.

The **Advances in Educational Technologies & Instructional Design (AETID) Book Series** is a resource where researchers, students, administrators, and educators alike can find the most updated research and theories regarding technology's integration within education and its effect on teaching as a practice.

Coverage

- Digital Divide in Education
- Social Media Effects on Education
- K-12 Educational Technologies
- Hybrid Learning
- Virtual School Environments
- Bring-Your-Own-Device
- Online Media in Classrooms
- E-Learning
- Educational Telecommunications
- Higher Education Technologies

IGI Global is currently accepting manuscripts for publication within this series. To submit a proposal for a volume in this series, please contact our Acquisition Editors at Acquisitions@igi-global.com or visit: http://www.igi-global.com/publish/.

The Advances in Educational Technologies and Instructional Design (AETID) Book Series (ISSN 2326-8905) is published by IGI Global, 701 E. Chocolate Avenue, Hershey, PA 17033-1240, USA, www.igi-global.com. This series is composed of titles available for purchase individually; each title is edited to be contextually exclusive from any other title within the series. For pricing and ordering information please visit http://www.igi-global.com/book-series/advances-educational-technologies-instructional-design/73678. Postmaster: Send all address changes to above address.

Titles in this Series

For a list of additional titles in this series, please visit: www.igi-global.com

Handbook of Research on Estimation and Control Techniques in E-Learning Systems
Vardan Mkrttchian (HHH University, Australia) Alexander Bershadsky (Penza State University, Russia) Alexander Bozhday (Penza State University, Russia) Mikhail Kataev (Tomsk State University of Control System and Radio Electronics, Russia) and Sergey Kataev (Tomsk State Pedagogical University, Russia)
Information Science Reference • copyright 2016 • 554pp • H/C (ISBN: 9781466694897) • US $235.00 (our price)

Handbook of Research on Active Learning and the Flipped Classroom Model in the Digital Age
Jared Keengwe (University of North Dakota, USA) and Grace Onchwari (University of North Dakota, USA)
Information Science Reference • copyright 2016 • 450pp • H/C (ISBN: 9781466696808) • US $300.00 (our price)

Handbook of Research on Applied Learning Theory and Design in Modern Education
Elena Railean (European University of Moldova, Moldova) Gabriela Walker (University of South Dakota, USA) Atilla Elçi (Aksaray University, Turkey) and Liz Jackson (University of Hong Kong, Hong Kong)
Information Science Reference • copyright 2016 • 866pp • H/C (ISBN: 9781466696341) • US $400.00 (our price)

Handbook of Research on Strategic Management of Interaction, Presence, and Participation in Online Courses
Lydia Kyei-Blankson (Illinois State University, USA) Joseph Blankson (Ohio Northern University, USA) Esther Ntuli (Idaho State University, USA) and Cynthia Agyeman (Ohio University, USA)
Information Science Reference • copyright 2016 • 611pp • H/C (ISBN: 9781466695825) • US $235.00 (our price)

Intelligent Design of Interactive Multimedia Listening Software
Vehbi Turel (Bingol University, Turkey)
Information Science Reference • copyright 2015 • 448pp • H/C (ISBN: 9781466684997) • US $215.00 (our price)

Utilizing Virtual and Personal Learning Environments for Optimal Learning
Krista Terry (Appalachian State University, USA) and Amy Cheney (Appalachian State University, USA)
Information Science Reference • copyright 2016 • 375pp • H/C (ISBN: 9781466688476) • US $185.00 (our price)

Handbook of Research on Individual Differences in Computer-Assisted Language Learning
Mehrak Rahimi (Shahid Rajaee Teacher Training University, Iran)
Information Science Reference • copyright 2015 • 571pp • H/C (ISBN: 9781466685192) • US $325.00 (our price)

Fuzzy Logic-Based Modeling in Collaborative and Blended Learning
Sofia J. Hadjileontiadou (Hellenic Open University, Greece) Sofia B. Dias (Universidade de Lisboa, Portugal) José A. Diniz (Universidade de Lisboa, Portugal) and Leontios J. Hadjileontiadis (Aristotle University of Thessaloniki, Greece)

Editorial Advisory Board Members

List of Reviewers

Table of Contents

Detailed Table of Contents

Collaborative learning facilitates the clarification of ideas, provides access to peer-feedback and promotes the sharing of diverse and alternate perspectives (Stacey, 2007). Guardia, Maina and Sangra (2013) identified collaborative learning as a key design principle for MOOCs and the interactions facilitated through this kind of learning are often considered to be as valuable as the direct instruction provided by the teacher (Stewart, 2013). This chapter explores a variety of technologies and pedagogical approaches that can be employed in a MOOC environment to promote collaboration and student interaction. Benefits and drawbacks of these strategies are considered in order to help guide decisions about the instructional design of MOOCs.

Several government programs oriented to contribute in reducing digital divide gaps have emerge in Mexico, particularly in States like Jalisco, Nayarit, Nuevo Leon, Veracruz, and Aguascalientes. However, current alternatives have certain weaknesses and issues that should be solved in order to provide appropriate literacy. To contribute in achievement of this goal, here is proposed an alternative to conform a strategy based on Massive Open Online Courses (MOOCs). First, a study was performed to establish the actual level of digital competences of current program users, and then obtained feedback was considered to structure the contents to offer through the MOOCs. This study was performed in the Aguascalientes state government program Vagones de Ciencia.

Massive Online Open Courses are a recent trend in distance learning promoted by several prestigious universities. They have drastically changed the way we learn as well as how we teach. The main aim of MOOCs is to provide new opportunities to a massive number of learners to attend free online courses from anywhere all over the world. MOOCs provide open learning. It has been found that the current model of open learning suffers from some limitations, and one of these limitations is the lack of personalization. A way to provide personalization into open learning is through learning style theory. The learning style theory is considered and, specifically, the Felder and Silverman model is selected to identify the learning styles and provide the required adaptation.

This work investigates the challenges and concerns faced when users set up and use web filtering systems for children, and identifies those changes, in the configuration interface and notifications, that could improve the users' experience and satisfaction. The findings of this study derived from the perception of one hundred parents on the usability of ten web filtering systems. The obtained results could represent a convenient starting point for further design-strategies oriented to facilitate the user-centered design in order to get web filtering systems easy to interpret and understand, thus helping to reduce configuration errors that create gaps in the safety of kids when using MOOCs and their integrated social tools.

The platforms edX, Coursera, and Udacity are pioneers in MOOCs distribution and access providing and their popularity among people grows daily. Prestigious universities, such as Massachusetts Institute of Technology, Harvard, Stanford, Princeton, among others, support their courses, which are conducted by the best Professors and academic staff. On the other hand, these platforms provide adequate interactions for users, focusing in encourage the appropriation of knowledge and competences related to specific topics. User Interfaces include video-lectures display; quizzes; forums; slides, code and many other resources. However, there are certain interaction features that are not common among these platforms

Due to its open and massive nature, with an adequate implementation, MOOCs can overcome inclusion barriers for the benefit of potential learners worldwide, both able and disabled. For evaluation, there are accessibility evaluation tools that identify accessibility problems in the content, semantic and structural elements of a website that can be used to evaluate the level of accessibility of MOOCs. Additional expert-based and user-based evaluations are always recommended in order to achieve valid results.

The concept of universal access to information society stands for the guaranteed access for all people in the world to internet services, online learning including. Blind users have been benefited by accessible tools such as screen readers, auditory interfaces, etc., nevertheless this kind of external software would not be required if the blind user's requirements were taking into account since the design process. This chapter presents a set of guidelines for designing hearing messages that help blind students to navigate in a MOOC's interface.

The intention of Massive Open Online Courses (MOOCs) is to extend online learning worldwide and to the most users as possible. Nowadays MOOCs have been used not only by undergraduate and hig-school students, but also by the elderly and the children. MOOCs have the potential to change the education in a better way to all people, including off course, the cognitive disabled people. From basic mathematics to specialized technical courses, MOOCs may enhance the opportunity to have better educational programs for cognitive disabled users, nevertheless, there are many things to do, about accessibility to guarantee a delightful user experience. This chapter introduces a new perspective to design inclusive MOOCs' interfaces.

The aim of this chapter is to present an exam preparation system designed to generate exams for propositional logic. The main challenge was to determine a filter to single out relevant problems. An expert assessment

This process allowed them to know the four aspects considered as essential for the PIBA implementation which are 1) Users approximation, 2) Session Development, 3) Therapist strategies, and 4) Contradictory speeches. It was found that they mainly describe how users are, which mainly are sent by schools. And how well the session and developing therapeutic channeling strategies worked over the users. This is important because therapists seemed to have used, as main MOOC strategies, technology techniques to promote readiness to change among adolescents.

Preface

Since its appearance in 2008, Massive Open Online Courses (MOOCs) had been capturing attention from researchers, learning experts, even government emerging all kind of opinions, some emphazise their features and others its disadvantages. Despite of said heterogeinity, tens of MOOCs options emerge every day and thousands of people sign up for registration in available courses mainly motivated by the free of charge and because the contents are commonly offered by prestigious Universities including Harvard; Massachussets Institute of Technology; Stanford; University of California; among others. Additionally, multidisciplinary research-teams from Universities arround the world daily focus their efforts in finding new alternatives for access and distribution of content in MOOCs in order to provide enhancements for better learning experiences for large number of students/users.

Brief History of MOOCs and Main Features

Probably the most significant events in MOOCs' history were a) The launch of the well known on-line course "Connectivism & Connected Knowledge", AKA CCK08, created by George Siemens and Stephen Downes in 2008. This course was originally thought as an alternative to offer an open-online learning experience for a small group of people, but unexpectedly it evolve to a massive learning experience having more than 2,200 registered students (Xin, Barnett & Stephens, 2015; Moe, 2015); and b) The appearance of the course "Introduction to Artificial Intelligence" in 2011. The course was offered by Peter Norvig and Sebastian Thrun, having more than 160,000 registered students from 190 countries (Xin, Barnett & Stephens, 2013).

This phenomenon motivates to many worldwide but particularly to Sebastian Thrun, which created Udacity in 2012. Udacity is an organization that provides lifelong learning options particularly in Computer Science and Math. Udacity was the first platform for MOOCs storage and management. After that, platform edX emerged from headquarters of Harvard and The Massachussets Institute of Technology, joining them The University of California in Berkeley shortly after. edX covers a wide number of knowledge areas including Music, Social Sciences, Artes, and many others. Additionally edX is a non-profit alternative (Dasarathy, et al., 2014).

In the same year, Professors Andrew Ng and Daphne Koller from Stanford University launched Coursera, having collaboration from The University of Michigan, Princeton, and The University of Pennsilvania. Currently Coursera have even two million of students, collaborates more than 40 Universities with this project and the American Council on Education authorized several courses to provide university credits (Moe, 2015).

Even if experts have not agree yet in a standard definition for MOOCs they converge in the idea that said historical facts, particularly to render learning for a large number of people (Massiveness), could provide background for future learning theories and approaches based on distance learning (Balakrishh-nan, et al., 2014). Additionally, these facts allowed experts from different fields to visualize the need of technological requirements in order to guarantee good learning experiences in MOOCs. In this vein, technological advances for MOOCs include several strategies based on Computer Sciences approaches such as distributed systems, artificial intelligence, machine learning, and mobile technologies, intended to improve supporting distribution, storage, access and management of content; user accounts; and individual performance statistics, all for a large number of students (Moe, 2015).

The fact of providing learning alternatives for masses is considered one of MOOCs' virtues, but the fuel for massiveness is openness, which offer people free registration and access to MOOCs' content; the possibility for sharing with others knowledge, perspectives, an experience on specific topics; even to collaborate in order to improve the platform. Oppeness also encourages other benefit from MOOCs, connectivism. This aspect fosters autonomy; diversity; and interactivity among participants including students and staff. The connectivist approach in MOOCs enable students to be facilitators for other students, that could derives in "the social learning" which according to (Brinton et al., 2013) is the hidden strength of MOOCs and represents the key for scalable learning in them. Social learning could expands learning experiences and contribute to reduce massive desertion by increasing interest and engagement in students. There are several studies, such as presented in (Lim, et al., 2014; Collazos, González, & García, 2014; Brinton, et al., 2013; Nelimarkka, & Vihavainen, 2015), where authors analyze collaboration between students through small discussion groups, could inspire several ideas and possibilities in order to take advantage from collaborative activities inherent in MOOCs to achieve an adequate social learning.

Main Challenges

MOOCs' have a high potential however its full exploitation represents big challenges -mainly focused in massiveness, openness, and connectivism- that should be tackled from different angles through multidisciplinary approaches. Ciber-social ecology of MOOCs could benefit collaboration not only among students but also institutions being able to conform learning-paths for students allowing customized curriculums selecting MOOCs from different institutions according to their learning preferences and needs (Dasarathy, et al., 2014). Another important requirement for inter-institutional collaboration is the MOOCs formalization. In this way, formal MOOCs could be part of the campus-student curriculum or conform a set of courses to obtain a diploma on-line. An example of this scenario could be found in the specialization "Mobile Cloud Computing with Android" which is hosted by Coursera (Porter, Schmidt, & White, 2014).

This collaborative environment also demands advances in software and hardware in order to support coordination among people communities caring of organized participations and measurable individual performances (Brinton, et al., 2013). MOOCs encourages grow of learning communities, and digital infrastructure systems that support MOOCs should evolve to the new needs emerged said people groups, by example fostering interactions between local and global learning communities (Dasarathy, et al., 2014).

MOOCs should adequately integrate current advances in social media in order to reinforce learning experiences helping staff and faculty to communicate with students as close as possible to traditional classroom-lectures. Setting up adequate collaborative environments becomes particularly complex in MOOCs because of the large number and variety of students with multiple learning styles being a challenge to tailor the learning environment to fit the need of each student (Xin, Barnett & Stephens, 2013). Some strategies based on machine learning and artificial intelligence had been studied in order to simulate those communication ways used between students and faculty in large lecture courses at many universities, nevertheless the it is necessary to find an adequate correlation between interaction and machine learning (Schmidt & McCormick, 2013; Xin, Barnett & Stephens, 2013).

Accordingly to (Desarathy et al., 2014) MOOCs could help improving crowd-sourcing multi-institutional degrees and competency-based education, however it is crucial to increase effectiveness of education through MOOCs by improving quality and personalization in the student experience. Similarly, (Rose et al., 2015) emphasize the need of exploring new possibilities (e.g. incorporating tools that encourages collaborative activities such as structured brainstorming; whole group feedback; group reflections, among others) to foster and maintain desirable connections support and direction throughout the course looking for more positive experiences for students.

The adequate collaborative learning environment in MOOCs should also support a reliable scheme for students' performance assessment. Besides of complexity by massiveness and reliability, assessment in MOOCs should face plagiarism, one of the widely discussed challenges in online education (Cooper & Sahami, 2013). In this vein, MOOCs should maintain improving openness, massiveness, and affordability but preserving academic rigor pursuing students' success (Xin, Barnett & Stephens, 2013).

An important piece at the puzzle is to achieve well-designed interfaces that provide good learning experiences and interaction for students / users. In this way good designs could be crucial (Dow, et al., 2012). Good designs help people to do those things that we care about and complete wide tasks in our daily life (Dix, et al., 2003). When an interface offers a good design, it encourages a good user experience since interfaces become intuitive or automatic for users by a combination of well-designed interactions and practice (Hartson, & Pyla, 2012). In his MOOC of Human Computer Interaction hosted by Coursera, Professor Scott Klemmer states that intuitivity in interfaces means "*To shifts attention from manipulating an interface to accomplishing a task*".

To achieve great designs is not easy; it demands a lot of hard work and creativity however Human-Computer Interaction provides specific techniques, methods, approaches, and tools to design, implement and evaluate user interfaces. Another essentially is the User Centered Design approach, which according to (Lowdermilk, 2013) is a multidisciplinary design approach based on the active involvement of users to improve the understanding of user and task requirements.

WHAT ABOUT THIS BOOK?

The main intention of this book is to provide a set of strategies based on principles and approaches from Human-Computer Interaction and User Centered Design aimed to contribute in improving designs of interactions in MOOCs. Here are described meaningful insights focused in aspects that could benefit massiveness, openness, and connectivism in MOOCs. In this vein, the book concentrates proposals oriented to fostering social learning and its implication for collaborative spaces; design strategies; inclusion of diverse users; assessment for a large number of users; and some envisions, ideas, approaches and applications to explore as future work.

Organization of the Book

The book is organized into sixteen chapters. A brief description of each of the chapters follows:

Chapter 1 explores a variety of technologies and pedagogical approaches that can be employed in a MOOC environment to promote collaboration and student interaction. These alternatives are aimed to foster the clarification of ideas, provide access to peer-feedback and promote the sharing of diverse and alternate perspectives. This chapter discuss benefits and drawbacks of said technologies in order to help guide decisions about the instructional design of MOOCs. The chapter emphasize collaborative learning as a key design principle for MOOCs considering that interactions facilitated through this kind of learning are as valuable as the direct instruction provided by the teacher.

Chapter 2 present the findings obtained from the implementation of a MOOCs strategy to reinforce a government program to reduce digital divide in Aguascalientes, Mexico.). The proposal is oriented to Foster connectivism and social learning in order to achieve a vast digital competencies distribution and appropriation. Study's results suggested an increment in digital competencies among participants and a good acceptance of contents.

Chapter 3 emphasizes one of the principal issues in current model of open learning the lack of personalization. This chapter discuss a particular perception on the importance of to provide personalization in MOOCs suggesting an alternative based on the consideration of the multiple learning styles, which is oriented to preserve openness, massiveness and connectivism in MOOCs.

Chapter 4 review the basic challenges and concerns faced when users set up and use web filtering systems for children, emphasizing those features for interactive elements at user interfaces that could improve the users' experience and satisfaction, which could finally derive in adequate protection for kids when using MOOCs and their integrated social tools.

Chapter 5 highlights those interactive elements offered by the current most popular MOOCs providers; edX, Coursera, and Udacity, in order to establish a first draft of basic interactions for MOOCs. The main objective is to provide designers a starting point on which interactions should be included as basics in every MOOC scaffolding those particular interactions needed to offer a complete learning experience for users, e.g. chemistry virtual lab.

Chapter 6 describes a study aimed to investigate the learning elements which would offer students a sense of connection and deeper understanding of concepts by means of online community-based practices. This chapter reports on the findings from surveying 3,000 students that enrolled in free online offerings at Open2Study. The findings of this chapter may contribute to reduce important gaps in MOOCs often criticized for having very low completion rates, not contributing much to the development of higher order thinking skills, and lacking academic rigor.

Chapter 7 presents a proposal to design notifications conveyed from MOOCs to users. The strategy is based on the three basic types of interaction/communication in MOOCs: User-User; User-Platform (content); User-group which helped to extracting the essential notifications from MOOCs and then specify them into a pattern-based structure which could be easily incorporated into the systems life cycle. The main target of this proposal is to contribute both to facilitate designers to create well designed notifications for MOOCs and to enhance user experience through its final application.

Chapter 8 reveals specific accessibility requirements that need to be considered in the design, implementation and evaluation of Massive Open Online Courses (MOOCs) to ensure they are inclusive. Authors emphasize the particular needs, preferences, skills and situations of diverse learners which should be considered in MOOCs to provide good learning experiences. Additionally, authors analyze some accessibility evaluation tools and approaches that identify accessibility problems in the content, semantic and structural elements of a website that can be used to evaluate the level of accessibility of MOOCs.

Chapter 9 presents a set of guidelines for designing hearing messages that help blind students to navigate in a MOOC's interface and contents. Authors bring to the front the importance of considering concepts of universal access from the earliest stage in the design process of MOOCs particularly those used by blind people. They concluded that even if external accessible tools -such as screen readers and auditory interfaces- are useful, could not be required if blind users requirements were taking into account by design.

Chapter 10 introduces a new perspective to design inclusive interfaces for MOOCs in order to ensure massive access to online learning worldwide. The chapter emphasizes the fact that MOOCs have been used not only by undergraduate and high school students, but also by Elder people and even children. Said diversity represents one of the principal challenges in MOOCs' accessibility in order to guarantee a delightful user experience by offering better educational programs for cognitive disabled users. This chapter is aimed to contribute in this big effort.

Chapter 11 describes an evaluation approach for MOOCs using an exam preparation system designed to generate exams for propositional logic. The expert assessment tool was used to generate initial learning data for Markov Logic Network and then the result was analyzed in terms of evaluation conducted on students. Authors found that there was no significant difference between problems prepared by a human examiner and problems generated by the proposed tool.

Chapter 12 proposes a platform called SPLAShED: Software Platform for Large-Scale Assessment of Software-Development for Education-at-a-Distance, that uses Linux containers to provide OS-level virtualization. SPLAShED platform applies recent advances in Linux container deployment automation, resources isolation, portability, and usability. The Authors explores assignments as a case study showing how the SPLAShED platform will able to accommodate and facilitate advanced Software Development courses with features and abilities currently not available.

Chapter 13 clarify - from a theoretical perspective - the interaction role in MOOCs and increased emphasis on utilization the virtual worlds as tools to create a constructive process where the learner should be actively involved. Authors presents an interaction model based on collaboration, so as to elucidate the major design differences between current MOOCs environments and those envisioned implementing virtual worlds emphasizing the changing role of formal learning in an open education era where the MOOCs could allow access for all, in many cases free of charge.

Chapter 14 highlights the importance of integrating new interactive elements in MOOCs. Specifically, the Author focuses in the benefits of introducing Gamification elements in order to commitment the learners for completing the courses, with willingness and pleasure. The chapter presents a whole context on the gamification concept including a theoretical background of combined with the principles of user experience (UX); a description of design guidelines for the MOOCs' interfaces and their involvement of learning theories; and game-based learning theory. All this knowledge is then putting together into a design proposal for the interface of MOOCs that will engaged UX with elements of Gamification.

Chapter 15 explains the importance of use Augmented Reality in MOOCs in order to improve its inherent advantages. This study further shows the development tools, application areas, and results obtained through augmented reality in the education, as a support tool to achieve the primary objective of education, which is learning through the use of MOOCs.

Chapter 16 analyzes possible benefits of integrating MOOCs specific supervision techniques used traditionally for therapy. The idea is to incorporate a sending-reports strategy in order to inform counselors about the performance of students. Authors describe the findings obtained from a study case using Moodle platform where 95 clinical psychologists participated in order to analyze reports from students enrolled in an addiction prevention course.

Ricardo Mendoza-González
Instituto Tecnológico de Aguascalientes, Mexico

REFERENCES

Brinton, C. G., Chiang, M., Jain, S., Lam, H., Liu, Z., & Wong, F. M. F. (2013). Learning About Social Learning in MOOCs: From Statistical Analysis to Generative Model. *IEEE Transactions on Learning Technologies*, *7*(4), 346–359. doi:10.1109/TLT.2014.2337900

Collazos, C. A., González, C. S., & García, R. (2014). Computer Supported Collaborative MOOCs: CSCM. *Proceedings of the IDEE Conference* (pp. 1-5), Albacete, Spain. ACM Press.

Cooper, S., & Sahami, M. (2013). Education reflections on Stanford's MOOCs: New possibilities in online education create new challenges. *Communications of the ACM*, *56*(2), 28–30. doi:10.1145/2408776.2408787

Dasarathy, B., Sullivan, K., Schmidt, D. C., Fisher, D. H., & Porter, A. (2014). The Past, Present, and Future of MOOCs and their Relevance to Software Engineering. *Proceedings of The FOSE Conference*, Hyderabad, India (pp. 212-224). ACM Press. doi:10.1145/2593882.2593897

Dix, A., Finlay, J., Abowd, G. D., & Beale, R. (2003). *Human Computer Interaction* (3rd ed.). New York, USA: Pearson-Prentice Hall.

Dow, S. P., Fortuna, J., Schwartz, D., Altringer, B., Schwartz, D. L., & Klemmer, S. R. (2012). Prototyping dynamics: sharing multiple designs improves exploration, group rapport, and results. In H. Plattner, C. Meinel, & L. Leifer (Eds.), *Design Thinking Research: Measuring Performance in Context* (pp. 47–70). Berlin, Heidelberg: Springer. doi:10.1007/978-3-642-31991-4_4

Hartson, R., & Pyla, P. (2012). *The UX Book: Process and Guidelines for Ensuring a Quality User Experience*. Burlington, MA: Morgan Kaufman.

Lim, S., Coetzee, D., Hartmann, B., Fox, A., & Hearst, M. A. (2014). Initial Experiences with Small Group Discussions in MOOCs. *Proceedings of the L@S Conference*, Atlanta, GA, (pp. 151-152). ACM Press. doi:10.1145/2556325.2567854

Lowdermilk, T. (2013). *User Centered Design: A Developer's Guide to Building User-Friendly Applications*. Sebastopol, CA: O'Reilly.

Mao, J., Vredenburg, K., Smithh, P. W., & Carey, T. (2005). The State of User-Centered Design Practice. *Communications of the ACM*, *48*(3), 105–109. doi:10.1145/1047671.1047677

Moe, R. (2015). The Brief & Expansive History (and Future) of the MOOC: Why two divergent models share the same name. *Current Issues in Emerging eLearning*, 2(1), 2-24.

Nelimarkka, M., & Vihavainen, A. (2015). Alumni & Tenured Participants in MOOCs: Analysis of Two Years of MOOC Discussion Channel Activity. *Proceedings of the L@S Conference*, Vancouver, BC, (pp. 85-93). ACM Press. doi:10.1145/2724660.2724671

Porter, A., Schmidt, D. C., & White, J. (2014). *Mobile Cloud Computing with Android, Coursera Specialization*. Retrieved from www.coursera.org/specialization/mobilecloudcomputing/2

Rose, C. P., Ferschke, O., Tomar, G., Yang, D., Howley, I., Aleven, V., & Baker, R. et al. (2015). Challenges and Opportunities of Dual-Layer MOOCs: Reflections from an edX DeploymentStudy. *Proceedings of the 11th International Conference on Computer Supported Collaborative Learning* (Vol. 2). Gothenburg, Sweden: International Society of the Learning Sciences

Schmidt, D. C., & McCormick, Z. (2013). Creating and Teaching a MOOC on Pattern-Oriented Software Architecture for Concurrent and Networked Software. *Proceedings of the WaveFront Forum at the SPLASH 2013 conference*, Indianapolis, IN.

Xin, C., Barnett, D. R., & Stephens, C. (2013). Fad or Future: The Advantages and Challenges of Massive Open Online Courses (MOOCs). *Proceedings of the 32nd Research-to-Practice Conference in Adult and Higher Education*, St. Charles, Mo., Lindenwood University Press.

Acknowledgment

The editor would like to acknowledge the help of all the people involved in this project and, more specifically, to the authors and reviewers that took part in the review process. Without their support, this book would not have become a reality.

First, the editor would like to thank each one of the authors for their contributions. My sincere gratitude goes to the chapter's authors who contributed their time and expertise to this book.

Second, the editor wish to acknowledge the valuable contributions of the reviewers regarding the improvement of quality, coherence, and content presentation of chapters.

Ricardo Mendoza-González
Instituto Tecnologico de Aguascalientes, Mexico

Section 1

Fostering Social Learning with MOOCs:

Perspectives and MOOCs Applications Oriented to Promote Social Learning Among People

Chapter 1
Facilitating Student Interaction and Collaboration in a MOOC Environment

Stein Brunvand
University of Michigan-Dearborn, USA

ABSTRACT

Collaborative learning facilitates the clarification of ideas, provides access to peer-feedback and promotes the sharing of diverse and alternate perspectives (Stacey, 2007). Guardia, Maina and Sangra (2013) identified collaborative learning as a key design principle for MOOCs and the interactions facilitated through this kind of learning are often considered to be as valuable as the direct instruction provided by the teacher (Stewart, 2013). This chapter explores a variety of technologies and pedagogical approaches that can be employed in a MOOC environment to promote collaboration and student interaction. Benefits and drawbacks of these strategies are considered in order to help guide decisions about the instructional design of MOOCs.

INTRODUCTION

When Lev Vygotsky (1978) first posited his theory of socially constructed knowledge it isn't likely he was envisioning a day when 100,000 students would sign-up for a single Massive Open Online Course (MOOC) (Breslow et al, 2013). Yet Vygotsky's findings on the social nature of learning can directly inform the design of MOOCs and the opportunities to collaborate inherent within these types of learning environments. MOOCs are intended to emphasize socialized learning and promote peer-to-peer interactions through different forms of social media and technology (Conole, 2013). This is particularly true in the design of connectivest MOOC courses or cMOOCs (Milligan et al, 2013), which adhere to connectivism (Siemens, 2006) and social constructivism (Vygotsky, 1978) theoretical guidelines.

The theory of social constructivism suggests that, "knowledge is generated through social intercourse" (p. 3, Kanuka & Anderson, 1998) and that the construction of this knowledge is ongoing as social interactions persist and evolve (Young, 1998). Online learning environments such as MOOCs add a new layer

DOI: 10.4018/978-1-4666-9743-0.ch001

of complexity to the social construction of knowledge because of the fact that online communication is often mediated through text rather than in face-to-face, synchronous settings (Gunawardena, 1995). The lack of non-verbal cues can make it difficult to interpret tone, inflection and emotion, which are all characteristics that would be present in a face-to-face interaction. In addition, learners must negotiate the technological interface of their learning environment, which can impact their ability to successfully construct knowledge (Hillman et al, 1994). Siemens (2006) offers an alternative theory to social constructivism known as connectivism, which posits that, "learning is a process that occurs within nebulous environments of shifting core elements" (p. 3). Within the framework of connectivism, learning is dependent upon the correct information or knowledge being connected to the appropriate people or learners at the right time. This theory seems tailor made for the online environment where vast amounts of information is available by the click of a mouse and that informational landscape is being continually updated and revised.

At the core of both social constructivism and connectivisim is the notion that learning exists when individuals collaborate to share ideas, engage in problem solving, brainstorm, produce artifacts and wrestle with difficult concepts. Collaborative learning facilitates the clarification of ideas, provides access to peer-feedback and promotes the sharing of diverse and alternate perspectives (Stacey, 2007). Guardia, Maina and Sangra (2013) identified collaborative learning as a key design principle for MOOCs and the interactions facilitated through this kind of learning are often considered to be as valuable as the direct instruction provided by the teacher (Stewart, 2013). This chapter explores a variety of technologies and pedagogical approaches that can be employed in a MOOC environment to promote collaboration and student interaction.

BACKGROUND

The advent of MOOCs can be traced back to 2008 when George Siemens and Stephen Downes granted open enrollment to their Connectivism and Connective Knowledge course at the University of Manitoba (Fini, 2009). This course was designed as a connectivest or cMOOC in that students were expected to learn largely through making connections with each other as well as the content of the class (Siemens & Downes, 2008). By 2012 prestigious institutions such as MIT, Harvard and Stanford started to experiment by offering a style of MOOC known as xMOOC, which takes a more behaviorist approach to instruction (Daniel, 2012). The xMOOC defers from the cMOOC structure in that more emphasis is placed on providing access to course content and allowing students to work independently rather than encouraging or facilitating collaboration. A primary goal of creating MOOCs of either kind is to provide access to educational opportunities to a population of students who would not otherwise be able to take college level courses for any number of reasons. However, due to the nascent nature of MOOCs, it has yet to be determined if they offer a viable educational experience for students.

MOOCs and other similar types of online learning environments present a different set of instructional challenges for the instructor. Traditional pedagogical strategies that work in a face-to-face setting don't translate well to an online class with an enrollment of 5,000 students and the sheer size of enrollment within most MOOCs decentralizes the teacher's role (Stewart, 2013). Therefore, it is important to utilize social pedagogies that encourage student interaction, promote social learning and leverage the openness of the MOOC environment (Stacey, 2014). These peer-to-peer interactions and social learning opportunities have been shown to positively impact student satisfaction within MOOCs (Khalil & Ebner,

2013). However, students don't routinely take advantage of these opportunities to interact partly because participation in a MOOC is voluntarily and there aren't negative financial or academic consequences for dropping out or failing to participate fully (Martin-Monje, Barcena & Venture, 2013). This makes it particularly important to create high quality and relevant opportunities to interact and collaborate so that students see the value in engaging with their peers. The following sections further explore the design and use of collaborative pedagogies within a MOOC environment.

MAIN FOCUS OF THE CHAPTER

Issues, Controversies, Problems

One of the advantages of an online course such as a MOOC is the convenience of being able to engage in the class from any geographic location and on a schedule that suits the learner. Having students spread across the globe in different time zones doesn't present much of a problem when the learning is facilitated asynchronously and online. However, the lack of face-to-face engagement can lead to isolation and cause students to feel disconnected from their peers within the class (Willging & Johnson, 2009). As a result, participants in an online setting can tend to feel more like they are taking an independent study rather than being active members of a community of learners (Lave & Wenger, 1991). One way to combat this sense of isolation is through the use of interactive technologies, which can enhance collaboration as well as knowledge construction (Comeaux & Mckenna-Byington, 2003). This section explores a variety of pedagogical strategies for promoting collaboration in a MOOC environment and highlights the benefits, and occasional pitfalls, of these different strategies.

Providing students with opportunities to communicate about course topics, assignments and readings can help promote deeper understanding of relevant content (Dewiyanit, Brand-Gruwel, Jochems & Broers, 2007; Young, 2008). By communicating with their peers, either synchronously or asynchronously, students are forced to articulate their ideas and perspectives while also gaining exposure to viewpoints different, and possibly in contradiction, to their own. Asynchronous communication facilitated through technologies such as discussion boards, blogs and social media tools like Facebook and Twitter can be beneficial because it allows students time to reflect on what they want to say and revise and edit their comments before making them publicly available to their peers (Richardson & Swan, 2003). There is also evidence that students tend to contribute more in an asynchronous communication environment than they do in face-to-face sessions because they have more control over when a how they contribute (Angeli, Valanides & Bonk, 2003). The face-to-face environment can inhibit individual comments as students wait for their turn to speak or lack the confidence to share their thoughts publicly. However, McInnerney & Roberts (2004) found that synchronous communication can be an effective way to create a sense of community within an online learning environment particularly when clear communication guidelines are established. A key component to any mode of communication interaction is the degree to which students are able to establish social presence (Short, Williams & Christie, 1976), which essentially is measured as the degree to which a person is perceived to be real within a technology mediated interaction. Social presence has been shown to have a positive impact on student satisfaction within an online course environment (Gunawardena & Zittle, 1997) and can be a predictor of student learning (Richardson & Swan, 2003). Students need to feel that their voice is credible and that their presence is validated even if it is virtual.

There are a variety of ways to structure and design opportunities for students to communicate in order to encourage collaboration and facilitate the social construction of knowledge. A more traditional example is a discussion forum that is used to reflect on assigned course readings. Most discussion forum tools allow for threaded replies, which means students can easily reply to a main posting as well as individual posts and replies created by their classmates. This type of discussion can be an effective way to get students talking to each other rather than just replying to a main topic. Blogs can used to engage students in conversations about relevant topics and are more commonly used when the main purpose is to get a response to an initial idea rather than generate a threaded discussion. Social media such as Twitter and Facebook can be used to facilitate less structured types of communication. Conversations hosted through these types of tools tend to develop more organically based on the interest and postings of the individual students rather than being guided by an initial post provided by the instructor. The use of social media for communication has also been shown to increase collaboration as students get more immediate feedback from their peers while also allowing them to engage with experts and other relevant resources from outside the course (Brady, Holcomb & Smith, 2010). This can provide more freedom to the students to explore perspectives and topics based on individual interests. It also allows students to customize their learning experience by choosing the mediums and technologies for communication that make the most sense to them based on their individual learning preferences.

Peer assessment is another commonly used strategy to promote collaboration in MOOCs (Suen, 2014). The sheer size of most MOOCs can make peer assessment difficult to manage since it is nearly impossible to monitor the feedback being given and determine if it is credible and accurate. However, there is evidence that the feedback given by peers is equivalent in accuracy to that given by instructors (Bouzidi & Alain, 2009). In order to be effective, Suen (2014) suggests that peer feedback should be simple to understand, efficiently implemented and limited in scope so as not to occupy too much of an individual student's time. Following this framework, instructors could have students engage in peer-assessment of writing projects by providing a rubric that clearly articulated the relevant criteria. Encouraging students to engage in ongoing revisions and regularly collaborate on pieces of writing can help them develop a shared understanding of what a coherent and well-written final product should look like. Rubrics can be created for other types of assignments as well and students could even be included in the development of these rubrics in order to ensure they are given a voice in how they are assessed. Involving students in the development of the learning criteria that will be used to assess their work is an effective way to enhance their overall performance (Stiggins, 1999) and get them actively thinking about how they will be assessed (Skillings & Ferrell, 2000).

Students also provide one another with informal feedback when they engage in discussion boards and the many other types of communication interactions outlined earlier. Sharing alternate perspectives, asking clarifying questions and addressing misconceptions are some of the many ways students can provide feedback to their colleagues through these interactions. These informal assessments are often less about determining an exact right or wrong answer but instead focused on arriving at a shared understanding of a relevant topic. In order for these interactions to be productive, students need to have an opportunity to get to know each other and establish agreed upon guidelines for how they will communicate (Murphy & Cifuentes, 2001). This is particularly important in a MOOC environment where students could be coming together from a wide range of cultures and geographic areas. Providing opportunities for students to get to know each other through orientation sessions and virtual ice-breaking activities can help ensure more respectful communication within the group. Encouraging students to draft an explicit set of communication guidelines is another way to allow them to share their preferences and expectations up front and provide them with a chance to exert some control over their learning.

Any student who has gone through a formal, or even informal, educational system has likely participated in some kind of groupwork project or assignment. From an early age, children are assigned to work in groups to create posters, presentations, skits and many other artifacts to represent their learning. Evidence of these types of projects can be found throughout K-12 classrooms and undergraduate and graduate courses at the post-secondary level as well. This emphasis on group work isn't surprising as evidence indicates employers see the ability to work as a team as a valuable character trait (Markow & Pieters, 2011). Of course, there are several common pitfalls with group work and these include "freeloaders" who let the rest of the group do all the work, inflated grades for individuals who get credit for knowledge demonstrated by the group and a potential lack of experience with all aspects of the project, which can result from tasks being divided up amongst group members (Chapman, 2006). Some of these issues might be less prevalent in a MOOC considering the volunteer nature of this kind of class, but it's still imperative to be mindful of the design of group projects within a MOOC.

In order for there to be a group project assignment there first needs to be an assignment of students into groups. The two primary ways to assign groups is randomly or to allow students to self-select their groups. There are pros and cons to both methods but evidence does suggest that being able to select their own groups positively impacts students' satisfaction and academic performance (Mahenthiran & Rouse, 2000). Self-selection seems to be particularly useful in a MOOC setting where there could likely be students speaking different native languages and placing them together in a group would make communication and collaboration challenging. Once groups are created, there are many different projects in which students could engage. For instance, students could work together on a variety of writing assignments including research papers, position statements, design proposals and business plans to name a few. Groups could also be presented with case studies or design challenges that require them to develop a series of solutions to real-world problems. The online environment also makes it possible for groups to collaborate on the creation of different digital artifacts such as websites, concept maps, presentations, videos and other forms of multimedia. The following section provides an overview of some of the many tools and technologies that can be used to help facilitate this kind of group work.

SOLUTIONS AND RECOMMENDATIONS

Collaborative Technologies

The technologies reviewed in this section can be used in a variety of ways to foster collaboration and interaction between participants in a MOOC. However, it's important to note that the specific tools reviewed may only enjoy a short existence considering the frequency with which digital technologies, and the companies that produce them, come and go. While certain names may seem dominate today, think Google which will be referenced on multiple occasions in the following paragraphs, there is no guarantee that these same companies will survive and continue to provide the services they offer indefinitely. It is acknowledged that some of the specific technologies referenced in this chapter may not be available in the near future for any number of reasons, but it is reasonable to expect that the features and capabilities they provide will continue to be relevant so these types of tools will persist even if the individual names change. Therefore, the reader is encouraged to focus on the capabilities of the different tools and consider how they can help promote collaborative learning rather than concentrating solely on the specific names that are shared.

Communication Tools

A key to successful collaboration is being able to engage in both synchronous and asynchronous communication with your peers and colleagues. Research has demonstrated that students who are actively engaged in their learning through communication and collaboration with their peers tend to exhibit higher academic achievement than their colleagues who are more passive (Nurmela et al., 2003). Tools such as Skype (http://www.skype.com/en/), Google Hangouts (https://plus.google.com/hangouts), BlueJeans (http://bluejeans.com/) and basic chat rooms can be used to facilitate synchronous communication. Students can choose to use these tools to communicate by typed text, audio, video or a combination of these mediums. Blogs, discussion forums, e-mail, Twitter (https://twitter.com/) and social networking sites such as Facebook (https://www.facebook.com/) or Celly (https://cel.ly/) can be used for asynchronous communication. In addition to facilitating communication, all of these tools can be used to share resources such as links, files and multimedia that might be relevant to the topics of the course. Giving students a range of choices for how they communicate allows them to customize the learning experience and select the modes of communication that works best for them. Encouraging students to keep their interactions in a public or semi-public environment will allow individuals to more easily police the comments made by their peers. For instance, having students engage in a small group online discussion rather than one-to-one chat session makes all comments visible to the entire group and will likely decrease the chances of a personal attack or disrespectful comment. Should a rude or inappropriate posting appear, the group can work to mediate the situation and come to a shared understanding of decorum and expectations for all communication sessions rather than a single participant being left to defend him or herself.

To facilitate conversations around multimedia such as videos and animations you could direct students to a tool like Vialogues (https://vialogues.com/), which allows you to either upload a video, or access one already available online, and create a discussion around it by adding comments, discussion prompts and questions. These discussions could revolve around videos created by the students themselves or video content found online that relates to the topic of the course. Similar conversations could be facilitated with a basic online discussion tool, blog or social networking site such as Facebook where links to videos can be shared and comments can be added. A tool such as Vialogue simply creates a more purposeful and structured environment for this type of discussion.

Writing Tools

Oneof the more commonly used tools for collaborative writing is Google Docs (https://docs.google.com) but sites like Zoho Docs (http://www.zoho.com/docs/) and Etherpad (http://etherpad.org/) offer a similar range of features and capabilities. The value of these types of tools is that they are web-based, which makes them easy to access regardless of the operating system you are running or the type of device you might be using. They also allow individuals to write, revise, comment and collaborate in real-time or asynchronously. In addition, since the documents are stored online, rather than on each individual user's computer or device, students always see the most up to date version of whatever file they are revising.

It is also possible to track individual contributions since each edit is attributed to the specific author, which makes it possible for an instructor to assess each student based on his or her contributions to a given piece of writing. Similar to the "Track Changes" feature in Microsoft Word, these online writing tools allow you to suggest changes, edits and revisions that can be reviewed by fellow authors before being rejected or accepted. This makes it easier to track revisions as they happen and promotes an open dialogue among the authors as they articulate their rationale for suggested changes and likewise defend the artistic choices they make throughout a given piece of writing.

Students can use tools such as Zotero (https://www.zotero.org/) and Mendeley (http://www.mendeley.com/) for more in-depth research reports and writing that requires the use of citations. These are bibliographic tools that have a web interface as well as a desktop application. Both tools allow you to create a library of references to use in your writing and they also help format your citations and find relevant sources to add to your library. You can create groups and shared libraries in order to facilitate collaborative writing and citing of references. This is particularly powerful as students look to do literature reviews and work collectively to pull together relevant references. Authors are able to easily share references and cite sources contributed by their peers rather than having to rely solely on the citations they find independently.

Wikis can also be used to facilitate collaborative writing and could be appropriate when the final product doesn't necessarily need to be a traditional word processing document. Wikispaces (http://www.wikispaces.com/) is one of the more popular wiki platforms currently available. The wiki environment is different from something like Google Docs in that users create an actual webpage to edit and write on rather than a stand alone document, which creates opportunities for different kinds of writing. For instance, students could be assigned different sections of a wiki to develop around a specific topic such as was done here: http://edt514tpack.wikispaces.com/. In this case, students were grouped by content area (math, science, social studies etc.) and tasked with writing and developing a page on the class wiki related to that specific subject matter. This particular example was not taken from a MOOC, but it demonstrates how wikis could be used for collaborative writing.

Presentation Tools

There are a variety of tools students could use to create collaborative presentations online. Google Presentation (https://docs.google.com/presentation), Prezi (https://prezi.com) and Zoho Show (https://www.zoho.com/docs/show.html) are three examples in this category. Much like their writing tool counterparts, these are all web based and allow for real-time editing and collaboration. Likewise, they don't require users to have the same operating system or a specific piece of software installed to work since they are browser based. Students can split up portions of a presentation and work independently on their sections while still editing the same presentation file. This makes it easier for each individual to track the progress of his/her peers and ensure that each section is fitting together coherently. Sharing of completed presentations is easy to facilitate and can be done by providing a direct link to anyone who might want to view the finished product. This is generally easier than having to send around a specific presentation file that may or may not display properly or even open depending on the operating system and available software on the machine of each individual trying to view it.

VoiceThread (http://voicethread.com/) is another option that could be used for collaborative presentations. This tool is hard to classify in just one category as it could also be used as a communication tool. One of the easiest ways to learn more about this tool is to view the introductory VoiceThread (http://

voicethread.com/#q.b409.i848804) created by the developers. To create an individual VoiceThread, users can upload any combination of images, documents (i.e. Word, PDF, Excel or PowerPoint) and video clips and arrange these elements into a slideshow. You can then add comments to each slide in the VoiceThread by several different methods including typed text or recorded voice or video. A VoiceThread can be made public, allowing anyone to add their own comments to the slides, or set to private, restricting comments to only invited users. Through this process, you can facilitate conversations around a series of images, videos or an entire PowerPoint style presentation and create opportunities for students to share their voice, literally, in presentations and discussions.

Students can use a tool such as WeVideo (https://www.wevideo.com/) to create videos and slideshows collaboratively online with their peers. WeVideo is a robust, browser based video editing tool that allows you to upload movie clips and images from any device. Users can create groups in order to share clips and photos and also engage in collaborative editing of an individual project. Students can create videos for a variety of purposes including demonstrating understanding, presenting information and synthesizing research. This is particularly well suited for MOOCs and other online courses since it allows students who might be separated geographically to work collaboratively on a multimedia artifact much like Google Docs facilitates cooperative writing projects.

Social Networking Tools

Social networking tools are becoming increasingly popular as ways to connect with friends, colleagues and even strangers. These tools also allow users to share information, resources, images, videos and a host of other content. While social in nature, they do provide opportunities for educational collaboration and knowledge construction and these tools come in many different varieties. Diigo (https://www.diigo.com) could be classified as a social-bookmarking tool as it allows users to create web archives of the sites and online resources they bookmark. These archives can be made public and shared with specific individuals and groups. You can choose to "follow" another Diigo user, which means you will get notifications when that person bookmarks a new website. In addition to bookmarking sites, Diigo also has a set of annotation tools that make it possible to mark up websites and online articles by attaching virtual sticky notes, highlighting text and adding shapes and arrows in order to draw attention to different pieces of content. These annotations can be seen by other Diigo users, which can make the practice of reading and viewing information online a more social and collaborative experience.

There are a variety of other tools that can be used to facilitate "social" reading among students. For instance, booklikes (http://booklikes.com/) has an interface similar to a blog that allows readers to share books and book reviews with groups. eMargin (http://emargin.bcu.ac.uk/) is similar to Diigo in that it allows you to collaboratively annotate articles and other pieces of writing as you read. Students can post notes and start discussions around different passages in order to come to a shared understanding of the text. Highlighter (http://highlighter.com/) is another collaborative annotation tool that is a bit more robust in it's feature set than eMargin. You can highlight Word documents, PDFs and Power Point files as well as eBooks and websites on any device. Groups can be created so that students can collaborate privately with a specified set of peers. Social reading tools such as these allow students to come together virtually to make meaning out of the text they are reading. It takes the often-solitary act of reading and turns it into a more collaborative and interactive experience for students.

Twitter and Facebook have already been mentioned as communication tools but they certainly warrant inclusion in any discussion of social media or social networking. Students can use Twitter to create hashtags (i.e #quantumphysics, #electromagnetics, #MOOCgroup16) specific to the entire course or just for a small group. Communication and the sharing of ideas, resources and information is facilitated by group members "tweeting" with the specified hashtag and "following" each other's tweets. Facebook groups can also be created to give students a chance to come together in this popular online social environment. One benefit of a Facebook group is that students can "like" the group without having to "like" or "friend" individual members within the group. This makes it possible for everyone to retain some privacy by not being forced to open up their personal Facebook profiles and postings to their classmates. Members of a group can share links, resources, videos and postings through the status update feature in Facebook. One benefit of using popular, or at least commonly known, tools such as Twitter and Facebook is that students are more likely to be familiar and comfortable with these technologies, making them easier to adapt and use in a MOOC or other online class setting.

Brainstorming Tools

Students can utilize an array of tools to engage in collaborative brainstorming. Some of the tools that have already been mentioned such as Google Docs and Wikispaces could be used to capture text-based brainstorming sessions. There is also an option within Google Drive to create drawings so students could work collectively to produce visual representations of their understanding through imagery and doodling. Online whiteboards such as Realtime Board (https://realtimeboard.com/), Magnoto (http://www.magnoto.com/), Padlet (https://padlet.com/) and ScribLink (http://www.scriblink.com/) provide users with a blank canvas on which they can draw freehand or insert images, text, maps and other visual elements to annotate and mark-up. These tools allow you to build a virtual "wall" and can be used to capture brainstorming sessions similar to what would be done in a traditional classroom with a physical whiteboard or bulletin board. Walls can be saved and shared through a direct link as well.

In addition to online whiteboard tools, there are also several sites such as Creately (http://creately.com/), Gliffy (http://www.gliffy.com/) and bubbl.us (https://bubbl.us/) that can be used to collaboratively create concept maps, flowcharts, schematic diagrams and other types of graphic organizers. Much like the virtual walls created with the online whiteboard tools, the finished products created with these online diagramming tools can be exported as stand alone images or shared via a link.

FUTURE RESEARCH DIRECTIONS

MOOCs are still fairly new and there is much to be learned about the design and efficacy of these types of learning environments. It remains to be seen if they can be viable and cost-effective alternatives to more traditional forms of face-to-face and online courses. While many different avenues could be explored in future research, the author would recommend investigating drop-out/participation rates and the comparison between instances of socially constructed knowledge in a MOOC setting versus a more guided face-to-face or online course setting.

The high drop rate in MOOCs is well documented (Clow, 2013; Daniel, 2012) and can be directly attributed to the fact that students are voluntarily participating in these courses. While there is a basic understanding of why students drop out of MOOCs, it would be interesting to learn more about the students who choose to complete MOOC courses and the motivation behind doing work in a class where college credit is not granted. Are there common design elements in MOOCs that enjoy greater participation and completion rates? Is there a commonality among the students who complete various courses? Learning more about the students who complete MOOCs and their rationale for doing so will help inform the design and use of these learning environments going forward.

As articulated earlier in this chapter, MOOCs rely heavily on the social construction of knowledge and having students interact with each other as well as the content of a given course. It has also been pointed out that the large enrollment typical of a MOOC makes it difficult, if not impossible, for an instructor to effectively guide the social interactions that might lead to knowledge construction. In a traditional face-to-face course or a closed online class where enrollment is capped the instructor can actively monitor student interactions and provide guidance, insight and redirection when necessary. Since the construction of knowledge that occurs in a MOOC environment is void of this monitoring and guidance, it would be worthwhile to investigate how this learning experience is similar to and different from that in which an instructor plays a more integral role. Can the learning experiences be equivalent with regards to the depth of knowledge explored? Does the presence of the instructor aid or inhibit students in their exploration of different viewpoints and perspectives? Exploring these kinds of questions will help to make determinations about the academic efficacy of MOOCs.

CONCLUSION

MOOCs make it possible for universities and other institutions to make coursework available to a wide range of learners regardless of geographic region, economic status or academic ability. They also present instructors with an array of challenges not the least of which is learning how to facilitate a class structured around student centered teaching (Swan, 2001). Learning how to successfully leverage the opportunities for student collaboration in order to promote the respectful and productive construction of knowledge is another significant challenge. One thing is for certain though. The opportunities to collaborate and the technologies that support collaboration are nearly limitless and students learning in this digital age expect there to be a social element to their learning. Ensuring that they have the chance to interact and engage with their classmates should be a design staple of any MOOC.

REFERENCES

Angeli, C., Valanides, N., & Bonk, C. (2003). Communication in a web-based conferencing system: The quality of computer- mediated interactions. *British Journal of Educational Technology*, *34*(1), 31–43. doi:10.1111/1467-8535.00302

Bouzidi, L., & Jaillet, A. (2009). Can online peer assessment be trusted? *Journal of Educational Technology & Society*, *12*(4), 257.

Brady, K. P., Holcomb, L. B., & Smith, B. V. (2010). The Use of Alternative Social Networking Sites in Higher Educational Settings : A Case Study of the E-Learning Benefits of Ning in Education. *Journal of Interactive Online Learning*, *9*(2), 151–170.

Breslow, L., Pritchard, D. E., DeBoer, J., Stump, G. S., Ho, A. D., & Seaton, D. T. (2013). Studying learning in the worldwide classroom: Research into edX's first MOOC. *Research & Practice in Assessment*, *8*(1), 13–25.

Clow, D. (2013, April). MOOCs and the funnel of participation. *Proceedings of the Third International Conference on Learning Analytics and Knowledge* (pp. 185-189). ACM. doi:10.1145/2460296.2460332

Comeaux, P., & McKenna-Byington, E. (2003). Computer-mediated communication in online and conventional classroom: Some implications for instructional design and professional development programmes. *Innovations in Education and Teaching International*, *40*(4), 348–355. doi:10.1080/1470329032000128387

Conole, G., (2013). MOOCs as disruptive technologies: strategies for enhancing the learner experience and quality of MOOCs. *RED - Revista de Educación a Distancia, 39*, 1-17.

Daniel, J. (2012). Making Sense of MOOCs: Musings in a Maze of Myth, Paradox and Possibility. *Journal of Interactive Media in Education*, *2012*(3), 18. doi:10.5334/2012-18

Dewiyanti, S., Brand-Gruwel, S., Jochems, W., & Broers, N. J. (2007). Students' experiences with collaborative learning in asynchronous computer-supported collaborative learning environments. *Computers in Human Behavior*, *23*(1), 496–514. doi:10.1016/j.chb.2004.10.021

Fini, A. (2009). The technological dimension of a massive open online course: The case of the CCK08 course tools. *International Review of Research in Open and Distance Learning*, *10*(5), 1–15.

Guàrdia, L., Maina, M., & Sangrà, A. (2013). MOOC Design Principles. A Pedagogical Approach from the Learner's Perspective. *eLearning Papers, 33*(May), 1–6.

Gunawardena, C. (1995). Social Presence Theory and Implications of Interaction and Collaborative Learning in Computer Conferencing. *International Journal of Educational Telecommunications*, *1*, 147–166.

Gunawardena, C. N., & Zittle, F. J. (1997). Social presence as a predictor of satisfaction within a computer-mediated conferencing environment. *American Journal of Distance Education*, *11*(3), 8–26. doi:10.1080/08923649709526970

Hillman, D. C., Willis, D. J., & Gunawardena, C. N. (1994). Learner-interface interaction in distance education: An extension of contemporary models and strategies for practitioners. *American Journal of Distance Education*, *8*(2), 30–42. doi:10.1080/08923649409526853

Kanuka, H., & Anderson, T. (1998). Online Social Interchange, Discord, and Knowledge Construction. *Journal of Distance Education*, *13*(1), 57–74.

Khalil, H., & Ebner, M. (2013, June). How satisfied are you with your MOOC?-A Research Study on Interaction in Huge Online Courses. *Proceedings of the World Conference on Educational Multimedia, Hypermedia and Telecommunications* (Vol. 1, pp. 830-839).

Lave, J., & Wenger, E. (1991). *Situated learning: Legitimate peripheral participation. Learning in doing* (p. *95*, p. 138). Retrieved from http://books.google.com/books?id=CAVIOrW3vYAC&pgis=1

Mahenthiran, S., & Rouse, P. J. (2000). The impact of group selection on student performance and satisfaction. *International Journal of Educational Management*, *14*(6), 255–264. doi:10.1108/09513540010348043

Markow, D., & Pieters, A. (2011). *The MetLife Survey of Preparing Students for College and Careers.*

Martin-Monje, E., Barcena, E., & Ventura, P. (2013). Peer - to - peer interaction in Professional English MOOCs: A proposal for effective feedback. *The European Conference on Language Learning*. Retrieved from http://www.iafor.org/offprints/ecll2013-offprints/ECLL2013_Offprint_0220.pdf

McInnerney, J. M., & Roberts, T. S. (2004). Online learning: Social interaction and the creation of a sense of community. *Journal of Educational Technology & Society*, *7*(3), 73–81.

Milligan, C., Littlejohn, A., & Margaryan, A. (2013). Patterns of Engagement in Connectivist MOOCs. *MERLOT Journal of Online Learning and Teaching*, *9*(2), 149–159.

Murphy, K. L., & Cifuentes, L. (2001). Using web tools, collaborating, and learning online. *Distance Education, 22*(2), 285-305. Retrieved from http://search.proquest.com/docview/217782583?accountid=14667

Nurmela, K., Palonen, T., Lehtinen, E., & Hakkarainen, K. (2003). Developing tools for analyzing CSCL process. In B. Wasson, S. Ludvigsen, & U. Hoppe (Eds.), *Designing for change in networked learning environments* (pp. 333–342). Dordrecht, The Netherlands: Kluwer. doi:10.1007/978-94-017-0195-2_41

Richardson, J. C., & Swan, K. (2003). Examing social presence in online courses in relation to students' perceived learning and satisfaction.

Short, J., Williams, E., & Christie, B. (1976). The social psychology of telecommunications.

Siemens, G. (2006). Connectivism. Retrieved from http://www.elearnspace.org/Articles/connectivism.htm

Siemens, G., & Downes, S. (2008). *Connectivism & connective knowledge*. Retrieved from http://ltc.umanitoba.ca/connectivism

Skillings, M. J., & Ferrell, R. (2000). Student-generated rubrics: Bringing students into the assessment process. *The Reading Teacher*, 53(6), 452–455.

Stacey, E. (2007). Collaborative learning in an online environment. *International Journal of E-Learning & Distance Education, 14*(2), 14–33.

Stacey, P. (2014). Pedagogy of MOOCs. *INNOQUAL-International Journal for Innovation and Quality in Learning, 2*(3).

Stewart, B. (2013). Massiveness + Openness = New Literacies of Participation? *MERLOT Journal of Online Learning and Teaching*, *9*(2), 228–238.

Stiggins, R. J. (1998). *Classroom Assessment for Student Success. Student Assessment Series.* NEA Professional Library.

Suen, H. K. (2014). Peer assessment for massive open online courses (MOOCs). *International Review of Research in Open and Distance Learning*, *15*(3), 312–327.

Swan, K. (2001). Virtual interaction: Design factors affecting student satisfaction and perceived learning in asynchronous online courses. *Distance Education*, *22*(2), 306–331. http://search.proquest.com/docview/217782729?accountid=14667 doi:10.1080/0158791010220208

Vygotsky, L. S. (1978). Mind and society: The development of higher mental processes.

Willging, P. A., & Johnson, S. D. (2009). Factors that Influence Students' Decision to Dropout of Online Courses. *Journal of Asynchronous Learning Networks*, *13*(3), 115–127.

Young, A. (2008). Structuring asynchronous discussions to incorporate learning principles in an online class: One professor's course analysis. *MERLOT Journal of Online Learning and Teaching*, *4*(2), 218–224.

Young, G. (1997). *Adult development, therapy, and culture: A postmodern synthesis*. Springer Science & Business Media. doi:10.1007/978-1-4757-9015-3

ADDITIONAL READING

Bonk, C., Lee, M. M., Reeves, T., & Reynolds, T. (2014). MOOCs and Open Education around the World: Recapping the Past Year, Mapping the Road Ahead. *Proceedings of World Conference on E-Learning in Corporate, Government, Healthcare, and Higher Education* (pp. 238-241). Chesapeake, VA: Association for the Advancement of Computing in Education (AACE)

Breslow, L. B., Pritchard, D. E., DeBoer, J., Stump, G. S., Ho, A. D., & Seaton, D. T. (2013). Studying learning in the worldwide classroom: Research into edX's first MOOC. *Research & Practice in Assessment* (pp. 13-25).

Brinton, C., Chiang, M., Jain, S., Lam, H., Liu, Z., & Wong, F. (2013). Learning about social learning in MOOCs: From statistical analysis to generative model. *IEEE Transactions on Learning Technologies*, *7*(4), 346–359. doi:10.1109/TLT.2014.2337900

Fasihuddin, H. A., Skinner, G. D., & Athauda, R. I. (2013). Boosting the Opportunities of Open Learning (MOOCs) through Learning Theories. *Journal on Computing*, 3(3), 112-117.

LeClair, J., & Ferrer, T. (2014) A case for MOOCs. *Proceedings of the ASEE Gulf-Southwest Conference*, New Orleans, Louisiana, United States, American Society for Engineering Education.

Mak, S., Williams, R., & Mackness, J. (2010). Blogs and Forums as Communication and Learning Tools in a MOOC. *Proceedings of the 7th International Conference on Networked Learning* (pp. 275-284).

Martin, F. (2012). Will Massive Open Online Courses change how we teach?: Sharing recent experiences with an online course. *Communications of the ACM*, *55*(8), 26–28. doi:10.1145/2240236.2240246

Neubaum, G., Wichmann, A., Eimler, S., & Krämer, N. (2014). Investigating Incentives for Students to Provide Peer Feedback in a Semi – Open Online Course: An Experimental Study. *Proceedings of International Symposium on Open Collaboration*. Berlin, Germany. ACM press. doi:10.1145/2641580.2641604

Núñez, M. M., Oriol, G., & Ángel, B. (2014). Social community in MOOCs: practical implications and outcomes. *Proceedings of the Second International Conference on Technological Ecosystems for Enhancing Multiculturality*. ACM press.

Riel, A., & Lawless, K. A. (2014). Massive Open Online Courses (MOOCs) and the Technologies That Support Learning with Them. In M. Khosrow-Pour (Ed.), *Encyclopedia of Information Science and Technology* (3rd ed., pp. 7529–7535). Hershey, PA: IGI Global Publishing.

Rodriguez, C. (2012). *MOOCs and the AI-Stanford like courses: Two successful and distinct course formats for massive open online courses*. Retrieved from http://www.eurodl.org/?p=archives&year=2012&halfyear=2&article=516

KEY TERMS AND DEFINITIONS

Collaborative Learning: Is a situation in which two or more people learn or attempt to learn something together. Unlike individual learning, people engaged in collaborative learning capitalize on one another's resources and skills (e.g. asking one another for information, evaluating one another's ideas, monitoring one another's work, etc.). Specifically, collaborative learning is based on the model that knowledge can be created within a population where members actively interact by sharing experiences and take on asymmetry roles.

E-Learning: Electronic educational technology, also called *e-learning*, has become an important part of society today, comprising an extensive array of digitization approaches, components and delivery methods. [4]For example, m-learning emphasizes mobility, but is otherwise indistinguishable *in principle* from educational technology.

Learner Engagement: A Also known as Student Engagement, this term refers to the degree of attention, curiosity, interest, optimism, and passion that students show when they are learning or being taught, which extends to the level of motivation they have to learn and progress in their education. Generally speaking, This concept is predicated on the belief that learning improves when students are inquisitive, interested, or inspired, and that learning tends to suffer when students are bored, dispassionate, disaffected, or otherwise disengaged. Stronger student engagement or improved student engagement are common instructional objectives expressed by educators.

Social Constructivism: Social constructivism is closely related to social constructionism in the sense that people are working together to construct artifacts. However, there is an important difference: social constructionism focuses on the artifacts that are created through the social interactions of a group, while social constructivism focuses on an individual's learning that takes place because of their interactions in a group.

Social Media: Social media are computer-mediated tools that allow people to create, share or exchange information, ideas, and pictures/videos in virtual communities and networks. Social media is defined as "a group of Internet-based applications that build on the ideological and technological foundations of Web 2.0, and that allow the creation and exchange of user-generated content".

Chapter 2
Users' Digital Competences Study to Design MOOCs for Digital Literacy in Mexico

Ricardo Mendoza-Gonzalez
Instituto Tecnológico de Aguascalientes, Mexico

Laura C. Rodríguez-Maríinez
Instituto Tecnológico de Aguascalientes, Mexico

Mario A. Rodríguez-Díaz
Instituto Tecnológico de Aguascalientes, Mexico

ABSTRACT

Several government programs oriented to contribute in reducing digital divide gaps have emerge in Mexico, particularly in States like Jalisco, Nayarit, Nuevo Leon, Veracruz, and Aguascalientes. However, current alternatives have certain weaknesses and issues that should be solved in order to provide appropriate literacy. To contribute in achievement of this goal, here is proposed an alternative to conform a strategy based on Massive Open Online Courses (MOOCs). First, a study was performed to establish the actual level of digital competences of current program users, and then obtained feedback was considered to structure the contents to offer through the MOOCs. This study was performed in the Aguascalientes state government program Vagones de Ciencia.

INTRODUCTION

Nearly from three decades developed countries from Europe, Asia, and North America had been addressing resources and government policies to preserve a long-term vision and plans towards reduce the digital divide creating inclusive programs that penetrates the social layers mainly covering to those most unprotected (Suba Rao, 2010; Binghamton University, 2011; Grillo et al., 2007; Gustafson et al., 2005; Chauveau & Vergara Sanchez, 2009; Zhou, Singh & Kaushik, 2011; ASRLO, 2007; PPE, 2013, CSIP, 2013; IDRC, 2002). Mexico and many other Latin-American countries were added to these ef-

DOI: 10.4018/978-1-4666-9743-0.ch002

forts emerging several proposals such as (ICDL, 2011) where proposed programs for certification of people are as Digital Citizens. Similar efforts have been proposed in Mexico, where States like Jalisco and Nayarit had been referenced points for other States such as Aguascalientes where an efficient and effective Digital Agenda was implemented (IJTI, 2013). Said plan consisted of several programs that encourage the IT universal access. Each of these state alternatives is supported by the Digital Policy from Mexican Federal Government.

Particularly, the Aguascalientes Government creates in 2009 the program "Vagones de Ciencia y Tecnologia" (IDSCEA, 2015). Said alternative is oriented not only to approaching IT to people, but also to training them on usage and appropriation of IT. This program provides people -including senior citizens and students from basic education- an interactive space for science and technology divulgation. The program "Vagones de Ciencia y Tecnologia" has two railcars adapted as IT classrooms including forty PCs each and Wi-Fi internet service where are carry out playful activities, experiments, conferences, talks about IT for society, video projections, among other learning and training activities oriented to provide basics on IT usage and digital competences appropriation. These aspects was perceived as the difference against previous programs in the State and the country that just provide technology to people but do not launched any training program, in this vein several experts state that "Access is not enough" (Suba Rao, 2010; Shulman et al. 2002).

The program "Vagones de Ciencia y Tecnologia" is complemented by sister alternative called "Casas de la Ciencia y la Tecnologia", which helps to extend benefits of the program to the most of towns in the State. This extension offer people free interactive spaces to approching them to IT and Science fostering and increment in their interest on technology. This program is also offered to training workers at local industry on IT and Internet usage.

The whole alternative is then oriented to contribute to reduce digital divide in the State of Aguascalientes providing free IT and Internet training to people fostering both adequate access and usage to be applied later for personal benefits, academic, or labor.

As digital literacy strategy, this program could be classified as a non-formal educative program, understanding that non-formal education is that organized and planed educational activity provided out of the official educative system. Non-formal education could be provided at diverse places including cultural centers, libraries, among others. In this way, training sessions at the program "Vagones de Ciencia y Tecnologia" promotes several aspects from tacit knowledge encouraging learning from own experiences and acquiring knowledge from others as a result to live in society including values, attitudes, and abilities.

It is important to mention that through this research was corroborated the excellent labor of the people that operates and manage the program "Vagones de Ceincia y Tecnologia" in their commitment to improve the current alternatives for digital literacy for people in Aguascalientes. However, some pain points were identified by means of this study. From this feedback emerged some alternative solutions that were structured in collaboration with program staff and managers and users of the current program. The most adequate solution was selected to be described in this chapter.

BACKGROUND

As mentioned before the first step on this research was to perform a study about the actual level of digital competences among the users of the program "Vagones de Ciencia y Tecnologia". To perform this study was used a questionnaire with thirty five items (closed questions, Likert scale style) closely associate to a set of digital competences worldwide valid obtained from (Mossberger, et al. 2008; Ribble et al., 2004; TECDLF, 2014; NFK, 2008) and classified in levels basic, intermediate, and advanced. Likert scale used had five elements, 1) not domain, 2) under domain, 3) middle domain, 4) good domain, and 5) total domain. Obtained data derived in knowledge about those digital competences covered by the program contents, the current level of appropriation of digital competences in program's users, and demographics.

The implemented instrument is divided in the three levels of competence mentioned above, reserving the first set of fifteen items for those digital competences in the basic level, including tasks from the turning on of the computer to simple search and surfing in internet. The second set of questions, sixteen to twenty for, includes digital competences from the intermediate level, such as social interaction through internet social applications, searching information in foreign language sites, among others. The last eleven questions of the instrument suppose the complete appropriation of IT in favor or help of the people, including fostering ecology through the IT usage, using IT to complete daily tasks and activities, among other advanced level competences.

The questionnaire was validated by the Crombach Alpha obtaining a 97% of fidelity, and its application at "Vagones de Ciencia y Tecnologia" and "Casas de Ciencia y Tecnologia" helps to identify which digital competences were covered and which need to be reinforced or considered in the contents offered to people.

The findings of the study revealed that the program just covered a part of digital competences classified as basics in literature (Mossberger, et al. 2008; Ribble et al., 2004; TECDLF, 2014; NFK, 2008) highlighting details reported by UNESCO in (UNESCO, 2005). Therefore, it was necessary to reinforce basic level competences and encourage the appropriation of the added competences among people. Additionally was necessary to extend digital competences coverage at least to those classified into the intermediate level.

As part of the study several demographics from users was considered, in this case fifty participants provide data through the questionnaire. Findings, revealed that 82% (f = 41) of the users were women and just the 18% (f = 9) men. As mentioned before, the program is addressed to attend people from children to older people, in this scenario Table 1 shows the frequency ages provided by participants, it is possible to observe that the higher frequency belongs to the group of ages from 13 to 19 years old (f = 21, 42%), followed by age groups 36 to 45 and 46 to 60 (f = 9, 18%, each). It also highlight that just the 4% of the users belongs to the age group from 61 or elders.

Table 1. Frequency of ages among participants

Age Group	Frequency	Percentage	Cumulative Percentage
13-19	21	42%	42%
20-25	4	8%	50%
26-35	6	12%	62%
36-45	8	16%	78%
46-60	8	16%	94%
61-	2	4%	98%
Not answer	1	2%	100%

Schooling level of participants mostly was secondary school (48%, f = 24), followed by high school level (34%, f = 17). Just 2%, (f = 1) had college level.

Previous information helps to complement a whole idea to suggest as alternative solution mainly based on data obtained from the thirty five items of the questionnaire related to digital competences. In this context, participants reflected domain levels on digital competences between 2) under domain and 3) middle domain, even some higher but less than 4) good domain. Just one item of the questionnaire was qualified 5) total domain by most of the participants (82%). This item was classified under basic level and relates to those advantages for information storage offered by computers. Meanwhile, most of the participants (70%) do not had abilities to surfing internet and search information in a foreign language, use online games, or restrict content from browser, e.g. adult content.

Feedback obtained by the instrument reveals specific pain points to tackle, solutions and strategies were supported by previous successful experiences from other countries in Latin America reported in literature, such as "TecnoBus" from Costa Rica (Grillo et al., 2007), and the chilenean project "Escuelas Rurales de IT y Ciudadania Digital" (Chauveau & Vergara Sanchez, 2009), which integrates several features and objectives similar to "Vagones de Ciencia y Tecnologia" and "Casas de Ciencia y Tecnologia". Additionally, for this research the concept Digital Divide represented the base construct of this research understanding said term as the differentiated access that have members from different communities to IT services, as well as those differences of digital competences that allow people to have a significant usage of that tools in favor of their personal growth and social progress (Suba Rao, 2010; Shulman et al., 2002).

MAIN FOCUS OF THE CHAPTER

Issues, Controversies, Problems

As mentioned before, the program "Vagones de Ciencia y Tecnologia" and "Casas de Ciencia y Tenologia" represents a great contribution from state Government to reduce gaps in Digital Divide in Aguascalientes and its towns, the performed study revealed several aspects that should be reinforced to better achieve original objectives of the program. Bearing in mind that the main goal of the program is to "contribute in reducing digital divide in Aguascalientes providing people with free training in proper use of IT and Internet access, encouraging appropriation of digital competences in benefit of their own personal, academic, and labor purposes". Essence of this goal and its relation with the enhancement point found through the study are summarized in the following Conceptual Hypothesis strongly related to the digital divide construct described above, and supported by literature (Jan & Van, 2006; Wei & Hindman, 2011; Notten et al., 2009; Van & Hacker, 2003; Vie, 2008; Sylvester & McGlynn, 2010; DDN, 2015):

1. **Access:** It refers to the existence or inexistence of the adequate technological infrastructure in the people environment to exercise their right to free access to IT services and Internet in a responsible manner.
2. **Person:** Is the individual that appropriates the necessary abilities to develop the entire set of cognitive, emotional, and social competences in a digital context needed to participate and be active part of the technological culture that prevails in his or her society.
3. **Communities with Digital Disadvantages:** This term may refer to specific individuals in a community and not the whole community. Includes contexts where prevails the low or even no access to It services for people of a community, for both the remoteness of the IT services, or the lack of digital abilities which contributes the exclusion from the digital society.

4. **Information and Communications Technology (ICT):** Represent technological and digital media that allow people to convey voice, data, texts, videos, images, and other kind of digital information. Additionally, facilitate searching, manage, and access information; encourage socialization and communication among people around the world; creation of social networks; among other important aspects related to sharing information.
5. **Digital Competences:** Is the set of cognitive, personal, and social abilities that allow people a significant usage of ICT transcending the instrumental use of the technological tool to produce from this, a contextualized and functional implementation for the fulfillment of their rights, satisfying their needs and scope of their aspirations.
6. **Significant use of ICT:** A significant use of ICT occur when people integrates ICT to their lives as tool to help them to complete their daily activities and tasks. Additionally identify ICT as a media to create knowledge or products that contribute in their own benefit by using ICT as a gate to create new cognitive, emotional and social competences.
7. **Symbolic Inclusion:** It refers to the inclusion that experiment people from communities with digital disadvantages, because of lack in technological competences needed to have a significant usage of ICT and the resources that generates a technological culture.
8. **Digital Culture:** Is the set of knowledge, routines, practices, and experiences that allow people decode the language and interpret rules that govern the context of ICT, starting from the suppose that ICT bring a particular way to be related with the environment and to establish diverse expressions of humans links.
9. **Constructive Inclusion:** Counter to Symbolic Inclusion, constructive inclusion is perceived when people integrate to the Technological Culture that experience a specific population or society, which is recognized by itself and by others like a participative and active community in digital world, with significant use of the resources offered by ICT.

As mentioned above, the fulfillment of these nine conceptual hypothesis by the program "Vagones de Ciencia y Tecnologia" and "Casas de Ciencia y Tecnologia" strongly depends of mitigate the following pain points found from the study performed:

1. Insufficient promotion and divulgation of the program.
2. Digital literacy process without documentation or defined structure.
3. Low alternatives of courses to offer.
4. Available courses do not include a specification of the digital competences to convey and their contents are not enough to ensure appropriation of knowledge by users.
5. Courses have not a structure that facilitates track of its topics or their digital competences related.
6. Courses topics are currently based on the requested from users and not to a set of specific digital competences to cover.
7. The scope of the course is not well defined.
8. Most of the teachers / facilitators do not appropriate the digital competences needed to achieve the main goal of the program.
9. Nature of the program makes it susceptible to changes in operation and staff when government administration changes.

The urgency to solve these issues increases in parallel with the interest in people to appropriate basic and intermediate digital competences since are required in almost all the job offers and admission to high schools in the State, and even in many daily activities of people, e.g. withdrawal money from ATM machine. For this reason was necessary to design and implement several strategies addressed to contribute reduce gaps taking advantage from the virtues of the program redesigning them from an organizational and structural vantage point to be congruent to the Conceptual Hypothesis and to the original goal of the program maintaining as low as possible the implementation costs.

It is important to mention that this research focused in the achievement of reinforce basic level digital competences and to integrate those competences from intermediate level to the program. This decision was taken together with the authorities of the program which delimitate the scope of the strategy according to State budget and study data.

SOLUTIONS AND RECOMMENDATIONS

Bering in mind study findings, was structured an intervention model based on Massive Open Online Courses (MOOCs) addressed to reinforce the current digital literacy strategy of the program. In this vein the following objectives were set:

1. Establish a collection of contents in a set of MOOCs specifically oriented to foster the appropriation of those identified digital competences from basic and intermediate levels.
2. To create an educative model to facilitate the integration of new contents and digital competences to the program as needed.
3. Encourage and ensure the adoption of the contents from MOOCs for facilitators and staff of the program.
4. Enhance the MOOCs contents and interaction with feedback from staff and facilitators of the program.
5. Training staff and facilitators to get the ability to propose and integrate additional contents to the MOOCs or create new ones according to the current digital competences.
6. Establish a flexible catalogue of digital competences that allow facilitators and staff to integrate new digital competences parallel to the advances in ICT.
7. Convey first version of MOOCs to advanced program users to get feedback and improve content and interaction before the release to a massive population.
8. Impulse diversification of program users to increase the number of people interested in the program particularly men and young people from rural towns.

Previous objectives were distributed in four main components which integrate the digital literacy model proposed; 1) Staff Training; 2) People Access; 3) Literacy; and 4) Tracing. Each component is described in the following subsections.

Staff Training

It is crucial that program staff appropriates digital competences to convey by the MOOCs and ensure as possible an adequate training to program users. In this way the program "Vagones de Ciencia y Tecnologia" and "Casas de Ciencia y Tecnologia", has two principal roles, Facilitator and Assistant. Broadly speaking, Facilitators are state employees that coaching sessions with users explaining them practices, contents, and several playful activities. While Assistants are mostly Young high school students that are incorporated to the program by social service support. They help Facilitators solving concerns and questions among users and occasionally give preventive maintenance to the PCs in classrooms. In order to preserve this structure, were identified specific competences for each role which were structured according to the requirements of the program authorities as well as the findings suggested by the study, reinforced by the ICT Competences Standards for Teachers (UNESCO, 2008) and the National Standards of ITC for Teachers in United States (ISTE, 2008) which encourage an adequate convey of the digital competences to people and are oriented to increment the interest of users, and facilitates the activities and tasks management for Facilitators. The competences for Facilitators and Assistant of the program "Vagones de Ciencia y Tecnologia" and "Casas de Ciencia y Tecnologia" are the following:

- **Facilitator Competences**
  - Didactical Competences: All facilitator should appropriate the needed abilities to instruct people, encourage autonomy in ICT usage; adapt explanations according to the program users literacy levels; implement or develop group activities; asses appropriation of knowledge in an egalitarian way and in some cases compensatory; and to foster the auto-evaluation among program users.
  - Instrumental Competences: Facilitators should domain and appropriate all the digital competences suggested by the study; to have the basic abilities to correct simple issues with hardware and software.
  - Group and classroom management competences: Facilitators should appropriate competences to ensure discipline; motivation; and respect among the program users after, during and before the sessions, ensuring also the group control.
  - Sociocultural competences: Facilitators should be able to guide program users in developing specific transversal competences such as the team work; ethical use oif the information; among others; to convey the importance of a good appropriation of ICT usage, and its incorporation to the daily activities of people; motivate people to face technological challenges; encourage the continuous training among users; and even to advise program users in personal situations that involve the use of ICT to complete tasks or specific activities.
  - Curricula management competences: Facilitators should be capable to manage and adapt contents in a logical and sequential manner according to the program users literacy level; select new contents and incorporate them to the current model in line to their original purpose; determine if the current topics in a MOOC are congruent to the spected impact on digital competences appropriation by users; and integrate new topics or even MOOCs to increase pertinence and relevance to the training.
- **Assistant Competences**
  - Didactical competences: Assistants should have those abilities needed to mediate among people and contents fostering auto-evaluation.
  - Instrumental competences: As Facilitators, Assistants should domain and appropriate all the digital competences suggested by the study; to have the basic abilities to correct simple issues with hardware and software.

- Group and classroom management competences: To assist and help Facilitators to ensure discipline; motivation; and respect among the program users after, during and before the sessions, ensuring also the group control.
- Sociocultural competences: Facilitators should be able to guide program users in developing specific transversal competences such as the team work; ethical use oif the information; among others; to convey the importance of a good appropriation of ICT usage, and its incorporation to the daily activities of people; motivate people to face technological challenges; encourage the continuous training among users; and even to advise program users in personal situations that involve the use of ICT to complete tasks or specific activities.
- Sociocultural competences: Assistants should be able to motivate program users to face technological challenges; encourage the continuous training among users; and even to advise program users in personal situations that involve the use of ICT to complete tasks or specific activities. And help Facilitators to developing specific transversal competences such as the team work; ethical use oif the information; among others; to convey the importance of a good appropriation of ICT usage, and its incorporation to the daily activities of people.
- Technical competences: This subset of competences could be the most distinctive between Facilitators and Assistants. It is important to mention that these competences were specifically suggested by program authorities to be integrated as improvement of the program. It is expected that an Assistant should has those abilities that allow him or her to diagnose failures in PCs, printers, mouses, keyboards, and other devices used during normal sessions in the program; to provide preventive maintenance to software and hardware including memory and storage media cleaning, software updates, use of tools for diagnose and correction of basic issues, among other activities; and to offer technical support to the program users.

People Access

In order to better organize the incorporation of users to the program was proposed a simple scheme for people access. This scheme included a set of simple requirements oriented to provide more control of the people needs and to provide better tracing of users progress in digital competences appropriation. In the same way the program was reinforced by the incorporation of a users placement-test in order to place users in the most convenient level of the digital training according to their needs and current digital competences appropriation. In order to provide a wide context these components are following described:

- **Access Requirements:** Even if the program continues offering free access for all citizens it was proposed a simple procedure for people access which consisted in provide name, address, phone number, birth date; age; and Id citizen number (called CURP in Mexico). After that, interested people answer a brief questionnaire about their purposes to enroll the program and their current knowledge on ICT usage. If this last part of the questionnaire is affirmative then interested people may choose answer the placement test or start digital training from the beginning.
- **Placement Test:** This is a brief and simple quiz that integrates the three levels of competences considered for this research. It has 15 items that includes simple tasks such as create a new folder in the operating system of the PC, open an existing file, to complete a search in internet, and to

use a service offered by a government web-site. All interested people should incorporate at least to one level of digital training independently of the result given by the test. The activities and tasks included in the first version of the placement test could be changed bay program staff as they consider it convenient according to the current digital competences.

Literacy

The axial component of the proposed strategy was the set of digital competences detected by the study performed. This set of competences is not exhaustive and it was suggested to staff and program authorities its continue update in line to the ICT advances and the current digital competences.

From this initial competences set, was proposed two main Massive Open Online Courses:

- **The Basic Digital Competences MOOC:** The contents of this course focus on reinforce basic digital competences covered by the original program, and convey and assurance of the appropriation of the complete set of currently valid basic level digital competences.
- **The Intermediate Course:** This course integrates those contents oriented to foster appropriation of digital competences from intermediate level, and represents the natural advance for the current contents offered by the program "Vagones de Ciencia y Tecnologia" and "Casas de ciencia y Tecnología".

Both MOOCs have the following general features:

- Both integrate a set of contents specially selected according to the set of digital competences identified for the basic and intermediate levels considered as valid internationally by literature (Mossberger, et al. 2008; Ribble et al., 2004; TECDLF, 2014; NFK, 2008) ensuring their pertinence.
- Contents of each MOOC includes practices, exercises, instructions, and theory addressed to ensure a significant usage of ICT, encouraging its appropriation by people suggesting incorporate it to their lives and daily activities as cultural and technological tools to create and recreate knowledge or products that reflect their own personal and social growth.
- The contents of both MOOCs are free and a pilot version is available at http://ccc.ccbas.uaa.mx/moodle/.
- The contents were structured to facilitate program staff to future adaptations to subjects and topics according to the current digital competences in order to encourage the continuous update of content.
- Each course was structured to cover all its content in 40 hours distributed in blocks of 6 hours by week (2 hours every other day) according to the operational schedule of the program.

To facilitate the management of proposed MOOCs it was structured a simple curriculum that integrates both courses. Each course consisted of several topics to a group of specific digital competences according to the level of literacy (basic or intermediate). Curriculum also includes the number of theoretical and practical hours for each topic. All this information was structured into a format including the following sections; Course level, course name, author of the content, activities and tasks to complete for each topic, main concepts, and evaluation.

In the same way, the content from each topic was structured to facilitate the appropriation of the digital competences associated; every topic includes the following sections:

1. **Presentation:** Contents information on the topic and the author of the content.
2. **Content:** Show a summary of the topic and the available resources through the lesson.
3. **Activities:** Describe the set of activities related to the content and resources available for the lesson.
4. **Evaluation:** For the first version of the MOOCs, evaluations for each topics consisted just of questionnaires but there are several ways to evaluate knowledge available.

Tracing

Tracing require all people involved Facilitators and Assistants and program users, and initially will be performed using two instruments for feedback specifically designed for each competency level basic and intermediate. These instruments will be showed to users at the end of each course automatically through each MOOC. As initial scheme was proposed a midterm test in order to compare with the initial test and to have a reference for advance of each user at the end of the course. This proposal is under review by program authorities. Other alternative under consideration is to offer users (just those that have covered intermediate level competences) a certification test at the end of the intermediate level in order to give official validity to the competences appropriated and be useful as reference for work. Currently program authorities evaluate some alternatives provided by national institutions.

FUTURE RESEARCH DIRECTIONS

This project is currently in process and one of the first improvements to be implemented is the reinforcement of the digital competences of Facilitators and Assistants. To achieve this purpose it was established a training program that integrates several topics related to the set of digital competences and that were incorporated to the MOOCs proposed. This strategy will allow obtaining feedback from Facilitators and Assistants to improve contents and interactions from MOOCs. Facilitators and Assistants will take lessons structured into 20 theoretical hours and complemented by 20 practical hours including a diversity of tasks such as sending an email, and make some calculations with formulae in an Excel document, the basic operation of the browser, and searching specific information in the internet. Training will ends by the presentation of a final project that reflects appropriation of digital competences, the project will consist in developing a topic that helps to convey one or more digital competences among the program users.

Findings from the study revealed some weaknesses in technical knowledge from Facilitators and Assistants specifically in basic maintenance of PCs and other computational equipment, in this way it will be necessary to focus a second part of training in technical topics for corrective and preventive maintenance to avoid and mitigate common failures in software and hardware. It is important to mention that this part of staff training are not considered as digital competences but authorities of the program believe that it is important to cover these lack of technical knowledge among the program staff members.

The technical competences workshop will be perform with help of undergraduate advanced students from diverse Universities of the State as social service. In fact, this will provide the basis to a parallel strategy to future incorporation of undergraduate students as Assistants to the program as part of their social service in order to help current Assistants and Facilitators in their activities and to training them.

It is expected that all current Facilitators and Assistants of the program "Vagones de Ciencia y Tecnologia" and "Casas de ciencia y Tecnologia" participate in the whole training strategy including the technical workshop and uses the feedback tools provided by the MOOCs including chat and forums, and for specific topics, predefined videoconferences and video chats to solve concerns and doubts related to the use of the MOOCs interactions and contents or with the presentation of the final project.

Currently, initial perceptions from program staff was favorable, all of them accept well the MOOCs contents, resources, and interactions. Even some of them uses the MOOCs with some most advanced program users obtaining good comments and feedback that will be applied in the next stage of the strategy.

Additionally through a presentation of the pilot version of MOOCs to the authorities of the program the "Instituto para el Desarrollo de la Sociedad del Conocimiento del Estado de Aguascalientes (IDSCEA) (IDSCEA, 2015)" agreed with the model for digital literacy, the training strategy for the staff, the set of competences, the contents to offer and the MOOCs structure and benefits auguring a great acceptance of people.

CONCLUSION

Digital divide reduction in Aguascalientes through strategies such as program "Vagones de Ciencia y Tecnologia" and "Casas de Ciencia y Tecnologia"directly depends on the coverage of the nine conceptual hypotheses which are closely related to specific pain points such as detected in this study. The solution of these issues is essential to achieve objectives of these alternatives.

In a favorable way, it could be inferred by the first results of the strategy proposed that this particular alternative could help to contribute in reducing gaps from Digital Divide in the State, and the suggestions could be applied in other States of the country that have similar programs. Bearing in mind the nine pain points identified in section issues and controversies, during the pilot presentation to the authorities of the "Instituto para el Desarrollo de la Sociedad del Conocimiento del Estado de Aguascalientes (IDSCEA) (IDSCEA, 2015)" make them to get new interest in the program and contribute to the assignment of additional resources to reinforce it according to the strategy explained.

On the other hand, one of the most important advances and improvements to the program was to structure courses and contents, and the incorporation of several instruments for assessment and tracing of the digital literacy advances from users.

All contents are now in the two MOOCs proposed; content consisted in seven teen topics which could be adapted in content and activities to offer a better learning experience to program users. Facilitators could easily integrate new practices and activities for each topic in order to ensure a better appropriation of the content by program users. Additionally, MOOCs contents were structured to facilitate management and sequence of their topics including activities, resources, exercises and practices. This structure helps to organize and convey information in an adequate way, but the most useful improvement for both program staff and program users, was the association between contents and digital competences which encourages digital competences appropriation which in the near future will derive in the significant use of ICT by people. These aspects will contribute to give a precise framework for the program "Vagones de Ciencia y Tecnologia" y "Casas de Ciencia y Tecnologia" focusing on their main goal "reducing the digital devide in Aguascalientes".

Other crucial aspect was the reinforcement of the program staff by integrating undergraduate advanced students as part of the Assistants team to provide technical training to the current staff and to help them with their daily activities in the program.

Initial results obtained by this pilot application of the MOOCs strategy suggest a great future for this alternative that could be maturate to a digital literacy model basic but reliable and flexible that allow to be adapted to the new requirements and digital competences from the natural advances in ICT, fostering its continue renovation and improvement encouraging its continuity even if some changes in government administration occurs.

REFERENCES

Austrian Science and Research Liaison Office (ASRLO). (2007). *Bridging the Digital Divide in South-Eastern Europe (SEE)*. Retrieved from www-it.fmi.uni-sofia.bg/cist/bridge/index.htm

Binghamton University. (2011). *Bridging the Digital Divide Project*. Retrieved from www.binghampton.edu/cce/digitaldivide/home.html

Chauveau Brañes, D., & Vergara Sánchez, E. (2009). Proyecto piloto de Escuelas Rurales de Informática y Ciudadanía: un modelo de transformación social en Chile (Technical Report). Ministerio de Agricultura, y Comité para la Democratización de la Informática, Santiago, Chile.

Colombia, I. C. D. L. (2015). *Ciudadano Digital*. Retrieved from www.ciudadanodigital.org.co

Digital Divide Network (DDN). (2015) *Digital Divide*. Retrieved from www.digitaldivide.net

Grillo, M., Zúñiga, M., Esquivel, W., González, M., & Fonseca, E. (2007). *Modelo TecnoBus Inducción en la Cultura Tecnológica para Adolescentes de Comunidades en Desventaja Social. Una intervención costo efectiva y replicable para enfrentar la brecha digital que afecta a su población meta, Paper presented in the X Reunión de la Red de Popularización de la Ciencia y la Tecnología en América Latina y el Caribe (RED POP - UNESCO), IV Taller "Ciencia*. San José, Costa Rica: Comunicación y Sociedad.

Gustafson, D. H., Mc Tavish, F. M., William, S., Ballard, D., Jones, E., Julesberg, K., & Hawkins, R. et al. (2005). Reducing the Digital Divide for Low-incomeme Women with Breast Cancer: A Feasibility Study of a Population-Based Intervention. *Journal of Health Communication: International Perspectives*, *10*(1), 173–193. doi:10.1080/10810730500263281 PMID:16377607

IDSCEA. (2015) *Instituto para el Desarrollo de la Sociedad del Conocimiento del Estado de Aguascalientes*. Retrieved from http://www.aguascalientes.gob.mx/idscea/vagones.aspx

Instituto Jaliscience de Tecnologías de la Información (IJTI). (2013). Agenda Digital Jalisco 2013. Retrieved from http://www.bajacalifornia.gob.mx/agendadigitalbc/doctos/AGENDA_DIGITAL_JALISCO.pdf

Instituto para el Desarrollo de la Sociedad del Conocimiento del estado de Aguascalientes. (n. d.).

International Development Research Center (IDRC). (2002) *Bridging the Digital Divide: Electronic Networking for Rural Asia/Pacific (ENRAP)*. Retrieved from www.ifad.org/evaluation/public_html/eksyst/doc/profile/pi/enrap.htm

International Society for Technology in Education (ISTE). (2008). *National Educational Technology Standards for Teachers* (2nd ed.). United States: ISTE.

Jan, A. G. M., & Van, D. (2006). Digital Divide Research, Achievements, and Shortcomings. *Poetics*, *34*(4-5), 221–235. doi:10.1016/j.poetic.2006.05.004

Mossberger, K., Tolbert, C. J., & McNeal, R. S. (2008). *Digital Citizenship*. Cambridge, Massachusetts: MIT Press.

Nasjonalt Fagorgan for Kompetansepolitikk (NFK). (2008). The Digital Citizen: An analysis of digital competence in the Norwegian population. Oslo, Norway.

Notten, N., Peter, J., Kraaycamp, G., & Valkenburg, P. M. (2009). Digital Divide Across Borders –A Cross-National Study of Adolescents' Use of Digital Technologies. *European Sociological Review*, *25*(5), 551–560. doi:10.1093/esr/jcn071

Piemonte, C. S. I. (CSIP) (2013) Satellite systems to Slash Digital Divide in Europe, Retrieved from www.csipiemonte.it/en/newsroom/497-satellite-systems-to-slash-digital-divide-in-europe.html

Public Policy Exchange (PPE). (2013). *Europe 2020: Bridging the Digital Divide: Securing Equal Access to High-Speed Internet*. Retrieved from www.publicpolicyexchange.co.uk

Ribble, S. M., Gerald, D., Bailey, D., & Ross, T. W. (2004). Digital Citizenship, addressing appropriate technology behavior. *Learning and Leading with Technology*, *1*(32), 6.

Shulman, S., Beisser, S., Larson, T., & Shelley, M. (2002). Digital Citizenship: Lessons Learned as Service-Learning Meets the Digital Divide. *Proceedings of the Annual Conference on Digital Government Research,* Santorini, Greece, ICPS (pp. 1-7). ACM press.

Subba Rao, S. (2005). Bridging the Digital Divide: Efforts in India. *Telematics and Informatics*, *22*(4), 361–375. doi:10.1016/j.tele.2005.01.007

Sylvester, D. E., & McGlynn, A. J. (2010). The Digital Divide, Political Participation and Place. *Social Science Computer Review*, *28*(1), 64–74. doi:10.1177/0894439309335148

The European Computer Driving Licence Foundation (TECDLF). (2014). *Syllabus Guide e-Citizen*. Retrieved from http://www.icdl.org.za/ktml2/files/uploads/Syllabus%20Guide%20SWGP1eC1.pdf

UNESCO. (2005). *Hacia las Sociedades del Conocimiento*. Ediciones UNESCO.

UNESCO. (2008). *Estándares de Competencia en TIC para Docentes*. Retrieved from www.eduteka.org/pdfdir/UNESCOEstandaresDocentes.pdf

Van, D., & Hacker, K. (2003). The Digital Divide as a Complex and Dynamic Phenomenon. *The Information Society*, *19*(4), 315–326. doi:10.1080/01972240309487

Vie, S. (2008). Digital Divide 2.0: Generation M and Online Social Networking Sites in the Composition Classroom. *Computers and Composition*, *25*(1), 9–23. doi:10.1016/j.compcom.2007.09.004

Wei, L., & Hindman, D. B. (2011). Does the Digital Divide Matter More? Comparing Effect of New Media and Old Media Use on the Education-Based Knowledge Gap. *Mass Communication & Society*, *14*(2), 216–235. doi:10.1080/15205431003642707

Zhou, Y., Singh, N., & Kaushik, P. D. (2011). The Digital Divide in Rural South Asia: Survey Evidence from Bangladesh, Nepal, and Sri Lanka. *IIMB Management Review*, *23*(1), 15–19. doi:10.1016/j.iimb.2010.12.002

ADDITIONAL READING

Carey, K. (2012). Into the future with MOOCs. *The Chronicle of Higher Education*, *59*(2), 29.

Christopher, B., Mung Chiang, Jain, S., Lam, H., Zhenming Liu, & Wong, F.M.F. (2013). Learning about social learning in MOOCs: From statistical analysis to generative model, *IEEE Transactions on Learning Technologies, 7*(4), 346-359.

Dimitriadou, C., Palaiologou, N., & Nari, E. (2014). E-Learning Training Courses on Multicultural Education: An Example from Greece. In V. Zuzevičiūtė, E. Butrimė, D. Vitkutė-Adžgauskienė, V. Vladimirovich Fomin, & K. Kikis-Papadakis (Eds.), *E-Learning as a Socio-Cultural System: A Multidimensional Analysis* (pp. 102–116). Hershey, PA: Information Science Reference. doi:10.4018/978-1-4666-6154-7.ch006

Greene, J. (2014). Introductory Study Using MOOCs for Homeless Education. *Proceedings of World Conference on E-Learning in Corporate, Government, Healthcare, and Higher Education* (pp. 724-728). Chesapeake, VA: Association for the Advancement of Computing in Education (AACE).

LeCounte, J. F., & Johnson, D. (2015). The MOOCs: Characteristics, Benefits, and Challenges to Both Industry and Higher Education. In F. Nafukho & B. Irby (Eds.), *Handbook of Research on Innovative Technology Integration in Higher Education* (pp. 228–247). Hershey, PA: Information Science Reference. doi:10.4018/978-1-4666-8170-5.ch011

Ronkowitz, K., & Ronkowitz, L. C. (2015). MOOCs: Evolution and Revolution. In E. McKay & J. Lenarcic (Eds.), *Macro-Level Learning through Massive Open Online Courses (MOOCs): Strategies and Predictions for the Future* (pp. 183–211). Hershey, PA: Information Science Reference. doi:10.4018/978-1-4666-8324-2.ch011

Thrun, S. (2013). MOOCs: The Future Is Here. *The Journal of Nursing Education*, *52*(1), 3–4. doi:10.3928/01484834-20121227-10 PMID:23293938

Tømte, C., Fevolden, A., & Olsen, D. S. (2014). To MOOC or not to MOOC?: A Case Study of Norway. In V. Zuzevičiūtė, E. Butrimė, D. Vitkutė-Adžgauskienė, V. Vladimirovich Fomin, & K. Kikis-Papadakis (Eds.), *E-Learning as a Socio-Cultural System: A Multidimensional Analysis* (pp. 210–223). Hershey, PA: Information Science Reference. doi:10.4018/978-1-4666-6154-7.ch012

Tu, C. H., & Sujo-Montes, L. E. (2015). MOOCs. In R. Papa (Ed.), *Media Rich Instruction* (pp. 287–304). New York: Springer International Publishing.

Valentin, C. (2015). MOOCs Global Digital Divide: Reality or Myth? In F. Nafukho & B. Irby (Eds.), *Handbook of Research on Innovative Technology Integration in Higher Education* (pp. 376–397). Hershey, PA: Information Science Reference. doi:10.4018/978-1-4666-8170-5.ch019

Zheng, S., Rosson, M., Shih, P., & Carroll, J. (2015) Designing MOOCs as Interactive Places for Collaborative Learning, *Proceedings of the 2nd Annual ACM Conference on Learning at Scale* (pp.343-346), Vancouver, BC, Canada, ACM Press. doi:10.1145/2724660.2728689

KEY TERMS AND DEFINITIONS

Digital Competences: The set of skills that allow people to use ICT in favor of their own benefits for life, work, and socialization.

Digital Literacy: Is the knowledge, skills, and behaviors used in a broad range of digital devices such as smartphones, tablets, laptops and desktop PCs, all of which are seen as network rather than computing devices.

Usability: Ease of use, efficiency, and learnability of a technology (software or hardware) which derives in helping users to complete a task (satisfaction of use).

User Centered Design: Process to create technology (not restricted to software) based in incorporate users into each stage of the design process by obtaining and implementing feedback to refine design ideas.

User eXperience: It involves a combination of several aspects from emotional to cognitive when a person uses a device or a tool to complete a task.

Chapter 3
MOOCs and Multiple Learning Styles

Sandra Jiménez González
Universidad Politécnica de Aguascalientes, Mexico

Ricardo Mendoza-González
Instituto Tecnologico de Aguascalientes, Mexico

Laura C. Rodriguez-Martinez
Instituto Tecnológico de Aguascalientes, Mexico

Mario Rodríguez-Díaz
Instituto Tecnológico de Aguascalientes, Mexico

ABSTRACT

Massive Online Open Courses are a recent trend in distance learning promoted by several prestigious universities. They have drastically changed the way we learn as well as how we teach. The main aim of MOOCs is to provide new opportunities to a massive number of learners to attend free online courses from anywhere all over the world. MOOCs provide open learning. It has been found that the current model of open learning suffers from some limitations, and one of these limitations is the lack of personalization. A way to provide personalization into open learning is through learning style theory. The learning style theory is considered and, specifically, the Felder and Silverman model is selected to identify the learning styles and provide the required adaptation.

INTRODUCTION

Online learning is an evolutionary learning approach that keeps evolving and changing due to the continuous evolution of technology. Open leaning is a new phenomenon of online learning that allows learning materials to be freely available on the Internet for anyone who is interested; this new phenomenon becomes a tangible reality due to the newly emerged cloud computing technology.

Recently, various prestigious learning institutions, such as Harvard, MIT, and Stanford, have utilized cloud computing to provide learning materials in an open approach. Coursera (Coursera, 2012), edX (edX, 2012), Udacity (Udacity, 2012), and many others are examples of this inventive open learning style. Courses that are provided through these open learning environments are termed Massive Open Online Courses (MOOCs).

DOI: 10.4018/978-1-4666-9743-0.ch003

The concept and format of MOOCs have been invested with hopes for radical changes in higher education, due to their potential to make high quality teaching accessible to everyone with broadband Internet access and motivated to invest their time into concentrated learning. While all MOOCs share the goal of bringing together thousands of learners into a common event, they largely differ with respect to the underlying concept of openness (Rodriguez O., 2013). Minimally MOOCs are open because access is not restricted by cost, affiliation, or any other type of privilege.

With no cost to entry or exit, MOOCs attract learners with a wide range of backgrounds and intentions, as well as personal or technical constraints to participation. Given the heterogeneity of the population, we would be remiss to make a priori assumptions about the appropriate characteristics or behaviors around which to categorize learners, or which pathways and outcomes are more or less valuable for their learning.

Analogous challenges can be found in research on community colleges-the closet brick-and-mortar analogue to MOOCs in terms of the diversity of educational objectives among their students (Goldrick-Rab, 437-469) and on unstructured virtual inquiry environments, where there is not a clear notion of "correct" pathways through the available resources. Using unsupervised clustering techniques, community college researchers have developed meaningful typologies of students based on longitudinal enrollment patterns (Bahr, 2010) and survey measures of engagement (Saenz, Hatch, Bukoski, Kim, Lee, & Valdez, 2011).

Despite the popularity of MOOCs and the fact they attract an enormous number of learners (Breslow, Pritchard, DeBoer, Stump, Ho, & Seaton, 2013), there are some limitations that still need to be considered and managed to enhance such an open model of learning. These limitations relate to different aspects of the courses, such as teaching and learning methods; learning content; assessments; identity authentication; accreditation; and learners´ varying needs, among others. All of these limitations raise different concerns about the sustainability of open learning. The authors believe that there is a need to enhance the current model of open learning, and based on the suggestion in (Williams, 2013), they find that this can be done efficiently by considering cognitive science and learning principles. The authors have previously introduced some learning theories that can be considered to enhance the presentation and organization of learning materials in open learning environments, and also to personalize the learning experience and adapt to individual learners´ needs and preferences (Fasihuddin, Skinner, & Athauda, 2013). The focus of this chapter is talk about MOOCs based on the theory of learning styles.

Students learn in many ways –by seeing and hearing; reflecting and acting; reasoning logically and intuitively; memorizing and visualizing and drawing analogies and building mathematical models; steadily and in fits and starts. Teaching methods also vary. Some instructors lecture, others demonstrate or discuss; some focus on principles and others on applications; some emphasize memory and others understanding. How much a given student learns in a class is governed in part by that student´s native ability and prior preparation but also by the compatibility of his or her learning style and the instructor´s teaching style.

Learning style refers to the way a learner receives and processes information; therefore, every learner had a different learning style (Felder & Silverman, 1988).

A student´s learning style may be defined in large part by the answer to five questions: 1) what type of information does the student preferentially perceive: sensory (external) –sights, sounds, physical sensations, or intuitive (internal) –possibilities, insights, hunches? 2) Through which sensory channel is external information most effectively perceived: visual (pictures, diagrams, graphs, and demonstrations) or auditory (words, sounds)? 3) With which organization of information is the student most comfortable: inductive—facts and observations are given, underlying principles are inferred or deductive—principles are given, consequences and applications are deduced? 4) How does the student prefer to process information: actively— through engagement in physical activity or discussion, or reflectively— through introspection? 5) How does the student progress toward understanding: sequentially—in continual steps, or globally—in large jumps, holistically?

Teaching style may also be defined in terms of the answers to five questions: 1) what type of information is emphasized by the instructor: concrete— factual, or abstract—conceptual, theoretical? 2) What mode of presentation is stressed: visual—pictures, diagrams, films, demonstrations, or verbal—lectures, readings, discussions? 3) How is the presentation organized: inductively—phenomena leading to principles, or deductively— principles leading to phenomena? 4) What mode of student participation is facilitated by the presentation: active—students talk, move, reflect, or passive—students watch and listen? 5) What type of perspective is provided on the information presented: sequential—step-by-step progression (the trees), or global—context and relevance (the forest)?

Among different existing models of learning styles, the Felder and Silverman Learning Style Model (FSLSM) has been considered in different studies to provide adaptive learning environments.

The Felder-Silverman model explores three issues: (1) the aspects of learning style that is significant in engineering education, (2) the learning styles most preferred by students and the teaching styles most favored by educators; and, (3) strategies that will reach students whose learning styles are not addressed by regular engineering education methods (Felder & Silverman, 1988)

The model proposes the hypothesis that engineering instructors who adapt their teaching style to include both poles of each of the given dimensions (for example both visual and verbal) should be close to providing an optimal learning environment for most of the students in any given class (Felder & Silverman, 1988).

According to Felder and Spurlin (2005), each of the dimensions (sensing or intuitive, visual or verbal, active or reflective, sequential or global) has parallels in other learning style models. The combinations, however, are unique to Felder's model. The first dimension – sensing/intuition – is one of four dimensions of Jung's theory of psychological types, and the third dimension – active/reflective – is a component of Kolb's learning style. The second dimension – visual/verbal – is analogous to the visual-auditory-kinesthetic formulation of modality theory and is rooted in cognitive studies of information processing. The fourth dimension – sequential/global – has numerous references.

In the Felder-Silverman model, the visual dimension refers to internal processing (such as visualization), rather than sensory input. Felder and Spurlin (2005) also point out that Silverman in a 2002 article, presents evidence from brain hemisphere research and clinical observations that show that global learners are more likely to be visual processors and sequential learners are more likely to be verbal processors.

Since the 1988 publication of Learning & Teaching Styles in Engineering Education, Felder has made two significant changes to his model. The first change is the deletion of the inductive/deductive dimension, because of confusion with educators between using the inductive or deductive method of instruction. The second change was renaming the visual/auditory category to visual/verbal. Felder made this change to allow both spoken and written words to be included in the verbal category (Felder, 2002)

Felder and Spurlin (2005) summarize that learning styles reflect preferences and tendencies; they are not infallible indicators of strengths or weaknesses in either the preferred or the less preferred categories of a dimension. They conclude that the Index of Learning Styles has two principle applications: to provide guidance to instructors on the diversity of learning styles within their classes and to help them design instruction that addresses the learning needs of all their students; and, to give individual students insights into their possible learning strengths and weaknesses.

The FSLSM has been considered in different studies to provide adaptive learning environments. Some of these studies were based on using the Index of Learning Styles (ILS) (Felder & Silverman, 1988), which is a questionnaire developed by Felder and Soloman to identify the learning style in order to provide learning objects that suit each learner's learning style.

The ILS is a self-scoring web-based instrument that assesses preferences on the Sensing/Intuiting, Visual/Verbal, Active/Reflective, and Sequential/Global dimensions. It is available free to individuals and instructors who wish to use it for teaching and research on their own classes, and it is licensed to companies and individuals who plan to use it for broader research studies or services to customers or clients.

The authors found that the literature-based approach, firstly introduced by Graf in (Graf, 2007) and mainly based on monitoring the learners´ behaviors on some determined patterns based on the FSLSM, had higher accuracy results in detecting learning styles. Therefore, it has been proposed to apply this approach to automatically identify learning styles and personalize open learning environments.

BACKGROUND

The evolution of technology leads to continual change and development in online learning approaches, and recently, open learning has emerged as a new form on online learning based on the utilization of cloud computing capabilities. In open learning, resources are freely available on the Internet to be accessed by anyone who is interested. These resources are provided by different learning provides who could be academics representing learning institutions or individuals who have appropriate knowledge and expertise. The provided resources have been defined by UNESCO as "Technology-enabled, open provision of educational resources for consultation, use and adaptation by a community of users for non-commercial purposes. They are typically made freely available over the Web or the Internet. Their principal use is by teachers and educational institutions to support course development, but they can also be used directly by students. Open Educational Resources include learning Objects such as lecture material, references and readings, simulations, experiments and demonstrations, as well as syllabi, curricula and teachers´ guides" (UNESCO, 2002).

Recently, many academics have changed their practice by publishing their learning materials online, this allowing their expertise to be accessed in open educational resources. This practice has gradually refined into what are known as Massive Open Online Courses (MOOCs).

Massiveness. MOOCs easily accommodate large number of students. More than a million people in the world have taken MOOCs (Carr, 2012). "From a pragmatic perspective MOOCs provide access to large numbers of people who might otherwise be excluded for reasons ranging from time, to geographic location, to formal prerequisites, to financial hardship" (McAuley, Stewart, Siemens, & Cormier, 2010). The artificial intelligence course developed and conducted by Stanford faculty Sebastian Thrun and Peter Norving is an example of massiveness as 160,000 enrolled in the course (Martin, 2012).

Openness. Opennes involves several key concepts: software, registration, curriculum, and assessment; communication including interaction, collaboration, and sharing; and learning environments (Rodriguez C. O., 2012). Rodriguez (2012) further discussed that the software used is open-source, registration is open to anyone, and the curriculm is open (perhaps loosely structured and it can even change as the course evolves), the sources of information are open, the assessment process (if they exist) are open, and the learners are open to a range of different learning environments. In sum, McAuley et al. (2010) reitered the concept of openness as any learner can take a MOOC and, as are result, exclusion from higher education opportunities is not an issue.

MOOCs offer free university-level courses online and have two key features –open access and scalability (Yuan & Powell, 2013). These two features allow MOOCs to be taken online by anyone and enable the courses to be designed to support an indefinite or even infinite number of participants. They are learner-centered courses, so learners are able to work and learn at their own pace, which gives learners able to work and learn at their own pace, which gives learners the opportunity to maintain their peak cognitive level and ability as they are able to access learning resources repeatedly until they meet their learning needs.

MOOCs are current point of controversy, and their success cannot yet be determined. There are some limitations of MOOCs that make them a point of contention. These limitations relate to various factors including accreditation, authentication, teaching methods and subjects that can be taught in such a way (Roberts & O´Loughlin, 2013). Moreover, it has been claimed that MOOCs place less emphasis on providing interactive and dynamic approaches to learning, as there is no creativity in delivering learning content, only the use of traditional approaches that lack support for learners' variable needs (Parr, 2013).

Based on the highlighted dilemmas, the authors believe that there is no clear frontrunner in terms of a model for MOOCs or open learning environments. Rather, MOOCs and other open learning initiatives are in their early stages of evolution. Different aspects and research questions still need to be considered and addressed in order to achieve a valid model (Fasihuddin, Skinner, & Athauda, 2013). However, there is the possibility that a single model might not be a solution to all learning needs and environments, and a plethora of models and systems may emerge catering to differing learning needs and environments.

The development of open learning environments is a critical and sensitive field due to the implications they have on learners, instructors, and the learning process. Therefore, scientific principles for learning should be considered in the development of MOOCs in order to achieve the desired learning goals. It is stated in (Williams, 2013) that tailoring general learning principles and working with cognitive scientist is one approach that needs to be considered to enhance MOOCs and provide the best outcomes for learners. Bases on this the authors consider the theory of learning styles (Felder & Silverman, 1988) to introduce an approach for personalizing open learning environments. This is believed to increase learners´ satisfaction and lead to better learning outcomes.

MAIN FOCUS OF THE CHAPTER

Issues, Controversies, Problems

Numerous studies have investigated the impact of learning styles in community college courses (Jones, Reichard, & Mokhtari, 2003; Terry, 2001), for educators in public schools (Lemire, 2002), and pre-service student teachers (Raschick, Maypole, & Day, 1998). Very little research, however, has focused on the relevance of learning styles to internet-based courses in higher education. Simpson and Du (2004) recently investigated the relationship of learning styles to self-reported enjoyment in students enrolled in online classes. The researchers found that learning style was correlated with students' perceptions of class enjoyment. Students with the converging style reported the greatest amount of enjoyment followed by those with diverging, accommodating, and assimilating styles. Although the authors did not analyze the distribution of learning styles, they did report the number of participants who were considered divergent, convergent, assimilative, or accommodative. Evaluating this distribution, most students were characterized by either the convergent or assimilative style. In their conclusions, the authors suggest the relevance of Kolb's (1984) learning styles theory for designing online distance education courses.

According to Kolb (1984), there are four learning environments that support the various learning styles and their associated modes. These include the affective, symbolic, perceptual, and behavioral learning environments. It should be noted that Kolb (1984) did not make a direct correlation or causal relationship between learning environments and learning styles.

The affective learning environment emphasizes concrete experiences so that students actually experience what it might be like to be a professional in a given field of study. Affective learning tasks include activities such as practical exercises, simulations, or field experiences. Information is usually peer oriented and delivered informally. The instructor is considered as a role model and an exemplar for the particular field of study. Activities are noncompetitive, and feedback should not be comparative but personalized to the individual student's goals and needs (Kolb, 1984).

The symbolic learning environment is one in which learners are involved in trying to solve problems for which there is usually a right answer or a best solution. Information is abstract and usually presented in readings, data, pictures, and lecture formats. Characteristic activities may include lecture, homework, and theory readings. The instructor is acknowledged as the expert, enforcer of rules, regulator of time, and taskmaster. This instructional format is typically didactic with a top-down, hierarchical class structure (Kolb, 1984).

According to Kolb and Fry (1975), the perceptual learning environment is one in which the main goal is to identify and understand relationships among concepts. Unlike activities in the symbolic environment, the perceptual environment emphasizes the process of problem solving rather than coming up with the best solution. Learners are required to collect relevant information for researching questions and are expected to attack a problem situation through different perspectives (own opinion, expert opinion and literature) by listening, observing, writing, discussing and personal pondering. In this environment, the teacher's role is to act as a facilitator of the learning process, to be nonevaluative, and to act as mirror by reflecting back student observations and comments. Learning processes may include reflective exercises such as keeping journals, writing reflective essays, or engaging in dialogue with other students. Such practices are incorporated into each class session, which emphasizes the importance of reflection on learning.

Finally, the behavioral learning environment emphasizes actively applying knowledge or skills to a practical problem. Although correct answers for activities are not necessary for success in this environment, activities should be structured so that learners gain intrinsic rewards and values. The teacher acts as a coach or guide but only when the student initiates or solicits help. Small group work, interactive projects that apply theory to real-world settings, and peer feedback are prime examples of student activities in this environment. Measurement is in the form of "how well something worked, feasibility, sellability, client acceptance, cost, testing results, aesthetic quality" (Kolb, 1984).

Effective online distance education courses should be based on instructional design decisions that will have the most impact on student learning. These may include decisions related to structure of course delivery, teacher-student communication, appropriate assignments and activities that are conducive to online learning, and effective use of online resources. Consistent with Maddux et al., (2002) and Thiele,

(2003), we suggest that it is important to design courses, which accommodate student learning styles. Accordingly, we suggest that Kolb's learning styles theory holds promise for providing a solid framework for accomplishing this goal.

Various studies have considered the variety of learning styles and the importance of incorporating them into learning environments. Some of these studies were concerned with introducing models and approaches to incorporate the FSLSM into the adaptive systems based on the attributes that were used. These methods differ based on the attributes that were used for detecting learning styles (personality factors, behavior factors), the underlying techniques (literature-based, data-driven) and the underlying infrastructure (Learning Management Systems (LMSs), special user interface).

Felder (1996) indicates that the Felder-Silverman model classifies students as fitting into one of the following four learning style dimensions.

- *Sensing Learners* (concrete, practical, oriented towards facts and procedures) or intuitive learners (conceptual, innovative, oriented towards theories and meanings);
- *Visual Learners* (prefer visual representations of presented material – pictures, diagrams, flow charts) or verbal learners (prefer written and spoken explanations);
- *Active Learners* (learn by trying thins out, working with others) or reflective learners (learn by thinking things through, working alone);
- *Sequential Learners* (linear, orderly, learn in small incremental steps) or global learners (holistic, systems thinkers, learn in large leaps) (Felder, 1996, p. 19).

Felder and Silverman (1988) explain that sensing and intuition are two ways in which people tend to perceive the world. Sensing involves observing and gathering data through the senses; intuition involves indirect perception by way of the unconscious: speculation, imagination, and hunches. Although learners will use both of these faculties, most will prefer using one to the other (p. 676).

Sensors like facts, data, experimentation, and solving problems by standard methods, but dislike surprises. They are patient with detail, but do not like complications. Sensors are good at memorizing facts, and tend to be careful and slower in completing their work (Felder & Silverman, 1988).

Intuitors prefer principles, theories, and innovation, but dislike repetition. Detail may bore them, and they welcome complications. Intuitors are good at grasping new concepts, and they tend to complete tasks quickly, which on occasion, may lead to carelessness (Felder & Silverman, 1988).

According to Felder and Silverman (1988), an important distinction between intuitors and sensors is that intuitors are more comfortable with symbols. Since words are symbols, translating them into what they represent comes naturally to intuitors and is more of a struggle for sensors.

Felder and Silverman (1988) indicate the way people receive information may be divided into three categories or modalities: (1) visual – sights, pictures, diagrams, symbols; (2) verbal – sounds and words; and, (3) kinesthetic – taste, touch, and smell. They explain that visual and auditory learning both have to do with learning processes that perceive information, and kinesthetic learning has to do with both perception such as taste, touch, and smell, and information processing such as moving, relating, or doing something active.

Visual learners remember best what they see: pictures, diagrams, flow charts, time lines, films, demonstrations. They may forget information that is communicated to them verbally (Felder & Silverman, 1988).

Verbal learners remember much of what they hear and even more of what they hear and then say. They remember and learn well from discussions, prefer verbal explanation to visual demonstration, and learn effectively by explaining things to others (Felder & Silverman, 1988).

Felder and Silverman (1988) state that the complex mental processes that convert perceived information into knowledge consist of two categories: active experimentation and reflective observation. Active experimentation involves doing something with information in the external world, such as discussing it, explaining it, or testing it in some way. Reflective observation involves examining and manipulating the information introspectively.

Active Learners do not learn much from lectures because they require them to receive information passively. They work and learn better in situations that allow for group work and hands on experimentation (Felder & Silverman, 1988).

Reflective Learners require situations that provide opportunity to think about the information being presented. They work well alone or in a one-on-one situation with another person and when given the opportunity to devise theories (Felder & Silverman, 1988).

Felder and Silverman (1988) postulate that the opposite of active is passive, not reflective. This consideration is within the context of student participation in class. They explain that active signifies that students are doing something other than listening and watching in class, and that active student participation will encompass the learning processes of both active experimentation and reflective observation.

Sequential learners are comfortable with mastering material presented in a logically ordered progression, learning it as the educator presents it. They follow linear reasoning processes when solving problems, and can work with material even when they only have a partial or superficial understanding of it. They may be strong in convergent thinking and analysis, and learn best when educators present material in a steady progression of complexity and difficulty (Felder & Silverman, 1988).

Global learners tend to learn in bits and pieces: they may feel lost for days or weeks unable to solve simple problems or show the most rudimentary understanding, until suddenly them "get it" – the light bulb flashes and the entire puzzle finally comes together. And as a result, they may understand the material well enough to apply it to problems that leave most of the sequential learner's baffled (Felder & Silverman, 1988).

Global learners may have difficulty working with material that they only have a partial or superficial understanding of. They tend to make intuitive leaps and then have difficulty explaining how they came up with solutions. They tend to do better at divergent thinking and synthesis and have the ability to move directly to more complex and difficult material (Felder & Silverman, 1988).

SOLUTIONS AND RECOMMENDATIONS

Currently, open learning environments are based on the "one size fits all" approach. There is no personal support or consideration of individual needs and preferences. As open learning environments target a massive number of learners with different background, preferences, and cognitive abilities, adaptability to the variability of learners´ needs and preferences is crucial. Brusilovsky described adaptive systems as the system´s ability to provide personalized learning support to the learner throughout their interaction with the system based on the goals, preferences, and knowledge of each individual learner (Brusilovsky, 2001). It has been found that adaptive learning systems lead to better learning outcomes, reduce time and effort required, and increase learners´ satisfaction (Graf & Kinshuk, 2014). Adaptive systems can adapt to user data, usage data and environments data (Brusilovsky, 2001). User data refer to various characteristics of the users, such as learning styles and cognitive traits. Usage data refers to user interaction with the systems.

Environment data refers to the adaptation to user context, including location or platform. Providing adaptability based on the considered factors has been classified into two different areas- adaptive presentation and adaptive navigation support (Brusilovsky, 2001). Adaptive presentation comprises text and multimedia adaptation technologies, while adaptive navigation support comprises links sorting hiding, annotation, and multimedia adaptation technologies, while adaptive navigation support comprises links sorting, hiding, annotation, and direct guidance.

Learning style refers to the way a learner receives and processes information. Therefore, different learners have different learning styles (Felder & Silverman, 1988). Considering learning styles in the courseware design has been found effective and beneficial in learning. It has been stated that providing learners with learning materials and activities that suit their preferences and learning styles make learning easier for them (Graf & Tzu-Chien, Supporting Teachers in Identifying Students' Learning Styles in Learning Management Systems: An Automatic, 2009). This statement has been proven by many studies that found that students can achieve better learning outcomes and higher scores (Bajraktarevic, Hall, & Fullick, 2013), and can also master the learning materials in lees time.

The Felder and Silverman Learning Style Model (FSLSM) classify learning styles into four dimensions and identify two types of learners for each dimension. The dimensions are perception, input, processing, and understanding. Firstly, the perception dimension defines the type of information that learners prefer to receive and learn by; intuitive learners prefer meaning and theories, while sensory learners prefer learning by examples and practice. The second dimension is input, which defines the approach the learners prefer to learn with; visual learners prefer pictures, diagrams, and flowcharts, while verbal learners prefer written or spoken explanations. The processing dimension indicates how learners prefer to process and practice their learning; active learners prefer working with others, while reflective learners prefer thinking and working alone. Finally, the understanding dimension indicates how learners progress toward understanding; sequential learners learn in continual small steps, while global learners learn holistically in large jumps. Table 1 represents these learning styles and their associated types.

Systems that are adaptive to learning styles need to identify learner´s learning style first and then adapt to the learner´s preferences. Adaptation methods of adaptive systems have been classified into two different approaches – collaborative and automatic (Brusilovsky, 1996). In the collaborative approach, learners are asked to provide their preferences explicitly by taking a test or filling out a questionnaire, such as the ILS questionnaire (Soloman & Felder, 2013), in order to build their adaptable models. On the other hand, in the automatic approach, the learners´ adaptable models are built automatically by the adaptive systems through intelligent and machine learning techniques that exploit learners´ interactions and behaviors while they are using the systems for learning.

Table 1. Learning Styles (Soloman & Felder, 2013)

Dimension	Preferred Learning Style	
Perception	Sensory	Intuitive
Input	Visual	Verbal
Processing	Active	Reflective
Understanding	Sequential	Global

In the literature, two different methods for identifying learning styles based on the FSLSM were used the data-driven method (Graf & Kinshuk, Adaptive Technologies, 2014). Both methods rely on some identified patterns to detect the learning style of the learner. These patterns are based on monitoring the provided learning objects in such a way that they adhere to the FSLSM. The data-driven method aims to build a mode that imitates the ILS questionnaire and uses sample data to construct a model. Some of the techniques used to apply this method are neural network, decision tree, Hidden Markov Model, fuzzy clustering, and Bayesian network. The literature based method uses the behavior of students and actions with the systems while they are learning in order to identify their learning style preferences. It is entirely literature-based, as patterns are identified based on findings of learners´ preferences and behaviors for each specific learning style. This method uses only simple rule-based methods to calculate learning styles. A study has been conducted to compare the efficiency of these two methods in detecting learning styles and has found that the literature-based method gives more accurate results than the data-driven method (Graf, 2007). Although the literature-based method has been found to be efficient, it has been claimed in (Ahmad, Tasir, Kasim, & Sahat, 2013) that this method´s point of weakness is embodied in the possibility of not considering all the potential patterns that could affect the detection of learning styles.

The authors have observed the provided learning objects in some of the well-known MOOCs, such as edX, Coursera and Udacity. The identified learning objects include course overviews, outlines, video lectures that are supported with scripts in some MOOCs such as in edX, number of learning objects that vary between textual-based and visual-based, discussion forums, examples exercises, quizzes with immediate feedback, and additional reading materials. Monitoring the learners´ interactions and behaviors with these different learning objects leads to identifying the learning styles and consequently provide and organize the learning materials based on the learners´ preferences.

Felder and Silverman have presented a good explanation for the FSLSM in terms of learners´ preferences and the corresponding learning and teaching styles (Felder & Silverman, 1988). Considering this and other literature (Cha et. al, 2006; Gaf, Kinshuk, & Tzu-Chien, 2008; Atman, Inceoğlu, & Aslan, 2009; Graf & Viola, 2009; Ahmad et. al, 2013), the authors have determined patterns to identify learning styles in open learning environments; these patterns consider the previously listed learning objects.

To identify the preferred learning styles for each dimension, certain patterns of behaviors need to be monitored. Following are descriptions of these patterns behaviors. First, in terms of learners´ perception, sensing learners prefer facts, data and experimentation, while intuitive learners prefer principles and theories, so annotating the learning objects to specify their types and the learners´ access to these objects and the time spent on them can be used as a pattern. In addition, sensing learners like to solve problems by standard methods and do not like surprises, while intuitive learners like to invent new ways to solve problems. Based on this, sensing learners are expected to access more examples and spend more time on them, while intuitive learners spend more time on the learning materials. These can be considered other patterns to distinguish between sensors and intuitors. Sensing learners are patient with details, careful but slow, while intuitive learners tend to be quick and careless; therefore, sensing learners spend more time on quizzes while intuitive learners spend less time.

In regards to the Input dimension, visual learners remember what they see well than what they listen to or are told, while verbal learners remember more of what they hear than what they see. Visual learners learn better by diagrams, flowcharts, pictures, and demonstrations, while verbal learners prefer verbal explanation rather than visual demonstration. Therefore, annotating the learning object to distinguish whether they are visual or verbal, and the access and time spent on them, can be considered a pattern.

In regards to the processing dimension, active learners like to try out and learn by practice, while reflective learners prefer to think and reflect about what they learn, so they learn better by observation. Based on this, active learners tend to access more examples and exercises and spend more time on them. In addition, active learners like to work in groups, while reflective learners prefer to learn alone; therefore, active learners access the discussion forums and posts more than the reflective learners.

Finally, in regards to the understanding dimension, sequential learners like to learn in a sequential process and prefer learning materials to be organized and presented in a steady progression of complexity and difficulty. Global learners do not like the linear approach and might jump directly to the more complex materials. Based on this, the behavior of accessing the learning materials can be considered ad a pattern. In addition, global learners like to be provided with the overall picture of the provided topic; therefore, they access and spend more time on the overview and outline.

Moreover, global learners are expected to access the knowledge maps of the learning concepts more than the sequential learners, so the time spent on accessing the knowledge maps is another pattern. Furthermore, the findings of (Spada, Sánchez-Montañés, Paredes, & Carro, 2008) can lead to another pattern to distinguish between the global and sequential learners. This study has found that the mouse maximum vertical speed for global learners is higher than for sequential learners. Table 2 summarizes all the mentioned patterns to identify learning styles in open learning environments like MOOCs.

As mentioned, sensing learners prefer to learn from concrete materials, so these types of learning objects need to be shown before the abstract materials. The opposite needs to be done for intuitive learners, abstract materials need to be shown to them first. In addition, sensing learners prefer to learn by examples and real life applications, so examples need to be shown to them before the explanation, while intuitive learners prefer the reverse.

Table 2. Patterns for identifying learning styles in open learning environments

Sensing learners	Intuitive learners
• Example access (+) • Example time (+) • Exercise access (+) • Exercise time (+) • Details and concrete learning objects time (+) • Abstract learning objects time (-) • Additional reading access (+) • Quiz time (+)	• Example access (-) • Example time (-) • Exercise access (-) • Exercise time (-) • Details and concrete learning objects time (-) • Abstract learning objects time (+) • Additional reading access (-) Quiz time (-)
Visual learners	**Verbal learners**
• Visual learning objects access (+) • Visual learning object time (+)	• Visual learning objects access (-) • Visual learning object time (-)
Active learners	**Reflective learners**
• Exercise access (+) • Exercise time (-) • Example access (-) • Example time (-) • Forum access (+) • Forum post (+)	• Exercise access (-) • Exercise time (+) • Example access (+) • Example time (+) • Forum access (-) • Forum post (-)
Sequential learner	**Global learners**
• Outline access (-) • Outline time (-) • Access the topic knowledge map (-) • Linear access for learning concepts (+)	• Outline access (+) • Outline time (+) • Access the topic knowledge map (+) • Linear access for learning concepts (-)

Moreover, sensing learners prefer to get mote examples and exercises, so all the available examples and exercises need to be recommended to them, while just some can be recommended to intuitive learners. In terms of the input dimensions, textual-based learning objects can be recommended to verbal-based learners, while the visual-based objects can be recommended to the visual learners.

For the processing dimension, active learners prefer to learn by doing, so more exercises will be provided to them in between the learning material. They also like to invent their own approaches to solving problems, therefore, fewer examples will be shown to them. The reverse approach needs to be taken for reflective learners, so more examples will be shown in between the learning objects and less exercises. In regards to the understanding dimension, sequential learners prefer to learn by a linear approach, so learning objects involving examples and exercises need to be organized in a linear increase of complexity, and the course conclusion and knowledge map are to be shown last.

FUTURE RESEARCH DIRECTIONS

Future work involves developing a prototype that simulates open learning environments in terms of offering open online courses that learners can take and learn at their own pace. This prototype will be dynamically adaptable to learners' learning styles based on the presented patterns, and will also provide individual navigational support. In addition, evaluations of the precision of identifying learning styles and the learners' satisfaction about the provided adaptability will be done.

CONCLUSION

This chapter introduces an approach to enhance the learning experience in open learning environments, where Massive Open Online Courses (MOOCs) are provided for free and taken by learners at their own pace. It has been found that many aspects still need to be considered and addressed in order to achieve an effective sustainable model of MOOCs; one of these aspects is the lack of personalization and adaptability. Based on this, the theory of learning styles, and particularly the FSLSM, has been selected for application to provide personalized learning.

Also this chapter presents the FSLSM as an approach to personalizing open learning environments. The literature-based method has been found to give better results in identifying the learning styles (Graf & Tzu-Chien, 2009), and therefore it was proposed to take this method.

REFERENCES

Ahmad, N., Tasir, Z., Kasim, J., & Sahat, H. (2013). Automatic Detection of Learning Styles in Learning Management Systems by Using Literature-based Method. *Procedia: Social and Behavioral Sciences* (Vol. *103*, pp. 181–189). doi:10.1016/j.sbspro.2013.10.324

Atman, N., Inceoğlu, M., & Aslan, B. (2009). Learning styles diagnosis based on learner behaviors in web based learning. *Computational Science and Its Applications*, LCNS (Vol. 5593, pp. 900-909).

Bahr, P. (2010). The bird's eye view of community colleges: A behavioral typology of first-time students based on cluster analytic classification. *Research in Higher Education, 51*(8), 724–749. doi:10.1007/s11162-010-9180-5

Bajraktarevic, N., Hall, E., & Fullick, P. (2013). *Incorporating learning styles in hypermedia environment: Empirical evaluation.*

Breslow, L. B., Pritchard, D. E., DeBoer, J., Stump, G. S., Ho, A. D., & Seaton, D. T. (2013). Studying learning in the worldwide classroom: Research into edX's first MOOC. *Research & Practice in Assessment* (pp. 13-25).

Brusilovsky, P. (1996). Methods and techniques of adaptive hypermedia. *User Modeling and User-Adapted Interaction, 6*(2-3), 87–129. doi:10.1007/BF00143964

Brusilovsky, P. (2001). Adaptive hypermedia. *User Modeling and User-Adapted Interaction, 11*(1/2), 87–110. doi:10.1023/A:1011143116306

Brusilovsky, P., & Millán, E. (2007). User models for adaptive hypermedia and adaptive educational systems. *The adaptive web*, LCNS (Vol. 4321, pp. 3-53).

Carr, N. (2012). *The crisis in higher education. MIT Technology Review.* Retrieved from http://www.technologyreview.com/featuredstory/429376/the-crisis-in-higher-education/

Cha, H., Kim, Y., Park, S., Yoon, T., Jung, Y., & Lee, H. (2006). Learning Styles Diagnosis Based on User Interface Behaviors for the Customization of Learning Interfaces in an Intelligent Tutoring System. *Intelligent Tutoring Systems*, 513-524.

Choi, S., Lim, C., & Leem, J. (2002). Effects of Different Types of Interaction on Learning Achievement, Satisfaction and Participation in Web-Based Instruction. *Innovations in Education and Teaching International*, 39(2), 153-162.

Christopher, B., Mung Chiang, Jain, S., Lam, H., Zhenming Liu, & Wong, F.M.F. (2013). Learning about social learning in MOOCs: From statistical analysis to generative model, *IEEE Transactions on Learning Technologies, 7*(4), 346-359.

Coursera. (2012). *Coursera.* Retrieved from https://www.coursera.org/

edX. (2012). *edX.* Retrieved from http://www.edxonline.org/

Fasihuddin, H. A., Skinner, G. D., & Athauda, R. I. (2013). Boosting the Opportunities of Open Learning (MOOCs) through Learning Theories. *Journal on Computing*, 3(3), 112-117.

Felder, R. M. (2002). Author's preface to learning and teaching styles in engineering education. *Engr. Education*, Volume, 674–681.

Felder, R. M., & Silverman, L. K. (1988). Learning and teaching styles in engineering education. *Engr. Education*, Volume, 674–681.

Felder, R. M., & Spurlin, J. (2005). Applications, reliability, and validity of the index of learning styles. *International journal of Engineering Education,* 21(1), 103-112.

Gaf, S., Kinshuk, & Tzu-Chien, L. (2008). Identifying Learning Styles in Learning Management Systems by Using Indications from Students' Behaviour. *Proceedings of the 8th IEEE ICALT '08* (pp. 482-486).

Glance, D., Frosey, M., & Riley, M. (2012). *The pedagogical foundation of massive online courses*. First Monday Journal.

Goldrick-Rab, S. (2010). Challenges and opportunities for improving community college student success. *Review of Educational Research*, *80*(3), 437–469. doi:10.3102/0034654310370163

Graf, S. (2007). *Adaptivity in Learning Management Systems Focusing on Learning Styles* [Ph.D. Thesis]. Vienna University of Technology.

Graf, S. (2014). *Kinshuk. Adaptive Technologies. Handbook of Research on Educational Communications and Technology* (pp. 771–779).

Graf, S., & Kinshuk, K. (2007). Providing Adaptive Courses in Learning Management Systems with Respect to Learning Styles. *Proceedings of the World Conference on E-Learning in Corporate, Government, Healthcare, and Higher Education.*

Graf, S., & Tzu-Chien, L. (2009). Supporting Teachers in Identifying Students' Learning Styles in Learning Management Systems: An Automatic. *Journal of Educational Technology & Society*, 12(4), 3–14.

Graf, S., & Viola, S. (2009). Automatic student modelling for detecting learning style preferences in learning management systems. *Proceedings of the International Conference on Cognition and Exploratory Learning in Digital Age* (pp. 172-179).

Guardia, L., Maina, M., & Sangrá, A. (May de 2013). *MOOC Design Principles. A Pedagogical Approach from the Learner's Perspective*. Retrieved from http://elearningeuropa.info/sites/default/files/asset/Indepth_33_4_0.pdf

Jones, C., Reichard, C., & Mokhtar, K. (2003). Are students' learning styles discipline specific? *Community College Journal of Research and Practice*, *27*(5), 363375. doi:10.1080/713838162

Kolb, D. A. (1984). *Experiential learning: Experience as the source of learning and development*. Upper Saddle River, New Jersey: Prentice Hall.

Kolb, D. A., & Fry, R. E. (1975). Toward an applied theory of experiential learning. In C. Cooper (Ed.), *Theories of group processes*. London: Wiley Press.

Lemire, D. (2002). Brief report: What developmental educators should know about learning styles and cognitive styles. *Journal of College Reading and Learning*, *32*(2), 177–182. doi:10.1080/10790195.2002.10850296

Mak, S., Williams, R., & Mackness, J. (2010). Blogs and Forums as Communication and LearningTools in a MOOC. *Proceedings of the 7th International Conference on Networked Learning* (pp. 275-284).

Martin, F. G. (2012). Will massive open online courses change how we teach? *Communications of the ACM*, *55*(8), 26–28. doi:10.1145/2240236.2240246

McAuley, A., Stewart, B., Siemens, G., & Cormier, D. (2010). Massive Open Online Courses Digital ways of knowing and learning. *The MOOC model For Digital Practice.*

McAuley, A., Stewart, B., Siemens, G., & Cormier, D. (2010). *The MOOC model for digital practice.* Retrieved from http://www.elearnspace.org/Articles/MOOC_Final.pdf

Thiele, J. E. (2003). Learning patterns of online students. *The Journal of Nursing Education, 42*(8), 364–367. PMID:12938899

Parr, C. (2013). *Mooc Creators Criticise Courses' Lack of Creativity.* Retrieved from http://www.timeshighereducation.co.uk/news/mooc-creators-criticisecourses-lack-of-creativity/2008180.fullarticle

Raschick, M., Maypole, D. E., & Day, P. A. (1998). Improving field education through Kolb's learning theory. *Journal of Social Work Education, 34*(1), 31–42.

Roberts, J. J., & O'Loughlin, J. (2013). The Season of the MOOC. *Universitas*, 8.

Rodriguez, C. (2012). *MOOCs and the ai-standord like courses: Two successful and distinct course formats for massive open online courses.* Learning.

Rodriguez, C. O. (2012). MOOCs and the AI-Stanford like courses: Two successful and distinct course formats for massive open online courses. *European Journal of Open, Distance and E-Learning*, 2012.

Rodriguez, O. (2013). *The concept of opennes behind a and x-moocs (massive open online courses).* Open Praxis.

Saenz, V., Hatch, D., Bukoski, B., Kim, S., Lee, K., & Valdez, P. (2011). Community college student engagement patterns a typology revealed through exploratory cluster analysis. *Community College Review, 39*(3), 235–267. doi:10.1177/0091552111416643

Siemens, G. (2005). Connectivism: A Learning Theory for the Digital Age. *International Journal of Instructional Technology & Distance Learning* .

Siemens, G. (2013). Massive Open Online Courses: Innovation in Education? *Commonwealth of learning, Perspectives on Open Educational Resources: Innovation, Research and Practice*, 5.

Simpson, C., & Du, Y. (2004). Effects of learning styles and class participation on students' enjoyment level in distributed learning environments. *Journal of Education for Library and Information Science, 45*(2), 123–136. doi:10.2307/40323899

Soloman, B. A., & Felder, R. M. (2013). *Index of Learning Styles Questionnaire.* Retrieved April 20, 2015 from:

http://www.engr.ncsu.edu/learningstyles/ilsweb.html

Spada, D., Sánchez-Montañés, M., Paredes, P., & Carro, R. (2008). Towards Inferring Sequential-Global Dimension of Learning Styles from Mouse Movement Patterns. *Adaptive Hypermedia and Adaptive Web-Based Systems* (pp. 337-340).

Terry, M. (2001). Translating learning style theory into university teaching practices: An article based on Kolb's experiential learning model. *Journal of College Reading and Learning, 32*(1), 68–85. doi:10.1080/10790195.2001.10850128

Udacity. (2012). *Udacity.* Retrieved April 20, 2015 from http://www.udacity.com/

UNESCO. (2002). *UNESCO*. Retrieved from http://www.unesco.org/education/news_en/080702_free_edu_ress.shtml

Waard, L. (2011). *Explore a New Learning Frontier – MOOCs*. Retrieved from http://www.cedmaurope.org/newsletter%20articles/eLearning%20Guild/Explore%20a%20New%20Learning%20Frontier%20-%20MOOCs%20(Jul%2011).pdf

Williams, J. J. (2013). Improving learning in MOOCs with Cognitive Science. *Proceedings* of *AIED 2013 Workshops* (p. 49).

Yuan, L., & Powell, S. (2013). MOOCs and Open Education: Implications for Higher Education. *Proceedings of CETIS JISC*, 2013.

ADDITIONAL READING

Bass, S. A.BassScott. (2014). Simple Solutions to Complex Problems—MOOCs as a Panacea? *The Journal of General Education*, *63*(4), 256–268. doi:10.1353/jge.2014.0023

Cook, J. A., Edwards, S. V., & Lacey, E., A., Guralnick, R. P., Soltis, P. S., Soltis, D. E., … Ickert-Bond, S. (2014). Natural History Collections as Emerging Resources for Innovative Education. *Oxford Journals Science & Mathematics BioScience*, *64*(8), 725–734.

Davidson, C. N. (2014). Why Higher Education Demands a Paradigm Shift. *Public Culture*, *26*(1), 3–11. doi:10.1215/08992363-2346313

Flynn, J. (2013). MOOCS: Disruptive innovation and the future of higher education. *Christian Education Journal*, *10*(1), 149–162.

Hara, N. (2014). (Re) Inventing the Internet: Critical Case Studies. *New Media & Society*, *16*(1), 173–175. doi:10.1177/1461444813507877a

Kumbhar, R. M. (2014). Academic Library's Responses to the Emerging Trends in Higher Education. *DESIDOC Journal of Library & Information Technology*, *34*(6), 477–485. doi:10.14429/djlit.34.6.6878

Milligan, C., & Littlejohn, A. (2014). Supporting Professional Learning in a Massive Open Online Course. *International Review of Research in Open and Distance Learning*, *15*(5), 197–213.

Parkes, T., Jones, C., Randall, D., Crow, G., Pryke, M., & Jones, R. (2013) *The Potential of Virtual Learning and Virtual Learning Environments for Advanced Doctoral Training in the UK*. Retrieved from http://esrcsocietytoday.esrc.ac.uk/_images/Virtual-Learning-report_tcm8-29850.pdf

Tekdal, M., Cagatay Baz, F., & Catlak, S. (2015). Current MOOC Platforms at Online Education. *International Journal of Scientific and Technological Research*, *1*(2), 144–149.

Zemsky, R. (2014). With a MOOC MOOC here and a MOOC MOOC there, here a MOOC, there a MOOC, everywhere a MOOC MOOC. *The Journal of General Education*, *63*(4), 237–243. doi:10.1353/jge.2014.0029

KEY TERMS AND DEFINITIONS

Adaptive Learning Environment: Environments that personalizing the instructional process on different instructional parameters as: sequence of tasks and task difficulty, time and type of feedback, pace of learning speed, reinforcement plan and others.

Cognitive: Concerned with the act or process of knowing, perceiving, etc.; Relating to the mental processes of perception, memory, judgment, and reasoning.

Intuitor: Is a website promoting creative learning as both a method of enlightenment and a cultural theme in its own right.

Learner-Centered Learning: Refers to a wide variety of educational programs, learning experiences, instructional approaches, and academic-support strategies that are intended to address the distinct learning needs, interests, aspirations, or cultural backgrounds of individual students and groups of students.

Learning Environments: Refers to the diverse physical locations, contexts, and cultures in which students learn. Since students may learn in a wide variety of stings, such as outside-of-school locations and outdoor environments, the term is often used as a more accurate or preferred alternative the classroom, which has more limited and traditional connotations.

Learning Styles: Refer to a range of competing and contested theories that aim to account for differences in individuals' learning.

MOOC: A course of study made available over the internet without charge to a very large number of people.

Open Learning: Learning based on independent study or initiative rather than formal classroom instruction.

Prototype: An original or first model of something from which other forms are copied or developed.

Section 2

Designing Interactions for MOOCs:

Strategies, Studies and Methods to Define Starting Points for Well Designed MOOCs' Interactions

Chapter 4
Identifying Parent's Security Requirements for Web Filtering in MOOCs for Kids

Juanita Avila Sánchez
Procuraduría General de Justicia de Aguascalientes, Mexico

Ricardo Mendoza González
Instituto Tecnológico de Aguascalientes, Mexico

ABSTRACT

This work investigates the challenges and concerns faced when users set up and use web filtering systems for children, and identifies those changes, in the configuration interface and notifications, that could improve the users' experience and satisfaction. The findings of this study derived from the perception of one hundred parents on the usability of ten web filtering systems. The obtained results could represent a convenient starting point for further design-strategies oriented to facilitate the user-centered design in order to get web filtering systems easy to interpret and understand, thus helping to reduce configuration errors that create gaps in the safety of kids when using MOOCs and their integrated social tools.

INTRODUCTION

Nowadays Massive Open Online Courses are widely available around the world offering an ocean of subjects and topics from thousands areas of knowledge. Primarily, these information technologies for learning were thought for advanced students (e.g. Undergraduate students or even High school students). Nevertheless, MOOCs face several issues as reported in this scenario as mentioned in research works such as (LeClair & Ferrer, 2014; Baggaley, 2014; Bonk, et al., 2014) including individual peer feedback convey for massive students, the massive desertion of courses, or the need of most adequate assessment mechanisms and procedures, among other barriers. Nevertheless there are great opportunities in other scenarios to use MOOCs as a complement of education or instruction not necessarily academic. One of these scenarios is the use of MOOCs for kids.

DOI: 10.4018/978-1-4666-9743-0.ch004

Currently, this topic it have been less explored than others and there are some counter opinions about this such as the comment posted by (Finn Jr., 2012) that makes interesting and true observations about using MOOCs for children academic education. In spite of that MOOCs could be a great support tool for training and learning in several academic and non-academic aspects, e.g. those aspects related to behavior and manners. In this way (Huerta, 2014) suggested the following three great reasons to foster integration and use of MOOCs through children education:

1. **MOOCs Could Enrich and Challenge:** Many children perceive school boring because activities do not represent a challenge to them. For this type of child, a challenge or an intellectually stimulating activity might be a solution. Parents or teachers could get child registered in an emotionally and intellectually appropriate MOOC according to a particular topic. This could encourage enhancements learning and classroom behavior, even spark excitement. It could also challenge children, build confidence, and jumpstart his love for learning. MOOCs could be developed by the own school and offer college credit.
2. **MOOCs Could Encourage Independent Learning:** In some cases, children do not have the skills to actively learn the materials provided by teachers to support or complement the conceptual explanation of specific topics. Additionally, many kids do not know how to be independent learners, it means to find some key aspects from a concept and associate them to particular situations or even solving problems. Commonly this association process becomes from teachers' materials. The MOOC, by its design, encourages students to work independently, provides online assignments that frame the information in such a way that students process and apply knowledge to more global problems. Some MOOCs include discussion threads where kids can post assignments and receive immediate feedback from the MOOC instructor and from other students taking the MOOC. Particularly, social tools from MOOCs could contribute to increase interest in subjects and foster independence in learning. Imagine how excited a child might be to receive feedback from a student in Singapore? Another consideration. If a child can teach what he or she knows to someone else, if he or she can explain a concept, that child is actively learning and integrating knowledge. It's what's known in education as metacognition, which is a "must" in learning goals.
3. **MOOCs Could Supplement Weak Students:** Some children simply cannot learn in a traditional classroom where the instructor lectures and the student is responsible for passively taking notes. In many cases, particular topics are complex or tedious and some children cannot keep up with the lectures, they could not figure out how to summarize or pick the most important details for note taking. If a child is not an auditory learner (one who learns through listening) or if a child has a processing disorder, material delivered through lectures can be lost. MOOCs break down material into short lectures on videotape. The student learns basic concepts through the lectures and then practices these new concepts through interactive assignments or games.

Agree with these assumptions, learning could be reinforced for children by using MOOCs and take advantage from the virtues from these technologies such as social learning. This chapter focuses on contribute in this particular area suggesting the incorporation of Web filtering applications to MOOCs (e.g. like plugins, or services provided by third parties) configured by parents in order to protect children against social deviations when they surfing a MOOC platform or uses social tools available on it, such as blogs, chat rooms, or instant messages communication.

There are many powerful applications oriented to combat social deviations are available, being one of the most popular option the web filtering systems, which analyze the content of a website (including blogs, chats, e-mail, and social networks) before submitting it to the user. They ensuring that the content do not disclose information related to bullying, pornography, violence, racism, among others, and prompting the user to not accessing the site or even blocking access to the website or content (Baguma et al., 2009; Turati et al., 2009; Guermazi, Hammani, & Ben Hamadou, 2007). In this sense, parents had opted to use these systems as protecting kids from the dangers when they surfing internet. However, to prevent kids from viewing certain graphic material or access to certain websites is not enough. Today, children interact with each other through social networks, blogs, and applications to exchange messages. The dangers that exist in these venues are particularly problematic because, unlike websites that draw a general audience, they point directly at the individual child. While adult predators are always a concern, cyberbullying among kids has become one of the most disturbing and potentially dangerous online developments (Dadvar, & deJong, 2012; Dadvaret al., 2012; Bosse, & Stam, 2011). Such protection often requires configuration settings, which can be perceived as complex for inexperienced users (Mendoza-Gonzalez, Muñoz-Arteaga, & Alvarez-Rodriguez, 2010). This situation could lead to mistakes and misunderstandings causing vulnerabilities that would result in damages to the kids.

It is essential that web filtering systems have well-designed and friendly interfaces, easy to understand even by novice users. This image is share by various authors concerned with achieving a balance between security and usability (Möckel, 2011; Kainda, Flechais, & Roscoe, 2010) whose contributions can help lessen this problem. However, the available alternatives have many gaps since they are not specific for filtering systems.

Accordingly, the main purpose of this research is to create a starting point for the generation of a strategy to strengthen the process of designing interfaces for web filtering systems, through the integration of usability and user-centered design. Thus, contribute to bridge the gap between security and usability, and undermine the possibilities of risk for kids to the dangers on the Internet.

BACKGROUND

For this study, one hundred parents used ten popular web filtering systems for one week, in order to conduct a comparison test following the specifications of previous methods and guides (Følstad, Lai-Chong Law, & Hornbæk, 2010; Rubin & Chisnell, 2008). This method, also include a personal interpretation of previous concept for conducting usability studies in a public space (Karam, 2010). The perceptions of the participants constitute the essence of the analysis, and the following subsections describe in detail the aspects in obtaining this information. It is appropriate to mention that the authorities of Instituto Tecnológico de Aguascalientes review and approve the methodology proposed for this usability study.

1. **Staff:** The staff for this research consisted in thirty five students from the Computer Science and IT careers of the Instituto Tecnológico de Aguascalientes. In order to ensure a decent job, the recruitment was highly specific, addressed to selected dedicated and diligent students. Students enrolled in the career of Computer Science are close to graduating (9th semester), while the IT students are in 6th semester. Staff members ranged in age from 21 to 29, and they are native Spanish speak-

ers but with a good proficiency of English. Obviously, all were regular computer users who were comfortable with security applications such as web filtering systems. The staff members had two main tasks:

a. To invite two or more parents (may be their own parents, uncles, among other acquaintances with kids) to use a web filtering system for a week. During this task, the staff members carry a personal ID, and give a brief description of the research.
b. To serve as technical assistance, installing the software on the participants' family-computer and solving technical doubts (without influencing on the usability perception) through daily conversations via messenger

2. **Participants:** Each member of the research staff did recruit an average of three parents/families, which were truly interested in participating; thus, hundred families participated in this study. All families were upper-middle class and had the basic digital skills and competences (see e.g. VOX Norway, 2012). Among the families four were not Mexican families, one was German, two were Japanese, and one more was Canadian. All of this subgroup had an acceptable level of Spanish and English languages. Mexican parents had a basic level of English but sufficient to managing the selected web filtering systems, and understanding the questionnaire used in this study. The parents ranged in age from 40 to 58, and the vast majority (eighty nine parents) was father and mother, ten was just a mother (including the German and Canadian families), and one was just a father. After recruitment, the participants assisted to an informative meeting held in an auditorium of the Institute, in order to present them the purposes and importance of the research, achieving tremendously positive acceptance of the participants. Ninety parents attended to the meeting.
3. **Aparatus:** For this study considered the free trial versions of ten popular web filtering systems, eight of which are in the "2012 Best Internet Filter Software Reviews and Comparisons" list from the well-known web systems ranking site Top-Ten Reviews (Top-Ten Reviews, 2012). The last two filtering tools (K9 Web Protection and VIMA Web Filter) did not belong to this ranking. The following list present a brief description of each web filtering systems emphasizing their technical virtues revealed by Top-Ten Reviews site (Top-Ten Reviews, 2012).

a. **Net Nanny Parental Controls 6.5:** This web-filtering tool combines cutting-edge technology with non-technical settings and reports for informed, proactive parents who may or may not be computer or internet savvy. According to Internet-Filter-Review this web filtering system stay at the forefront of internet filtering, offering some unique and compelling features not found in other programs. This system was awarded "Gold Award, Excellence Award" by Top Ten Reviews and was rated as the 2011 best web filtering system.
b. **Safe Eyes 6.0.241:** Safe Eyes is a very popular web-filtering tool because offering coverage on multiple computers. In addition, provides the flexibility to treat different user groups differently in terms of internet privileges. This approach makes it much easier to manage filtering needs for multiple people in a family or business. This system was awarded "Silver Award, Excellence Award" by Top Ten Reviews, and was rated as the 2011 second best web filtering system.
c. **McAfee Family Protection:** McAfee Family Protection is internet filter software for Windows PCs, Macintosh computers and Android devices. It wins the Top-Ten Reviews Bronze Award for internet filter software. It effectively filters websites, video, music, instant messaging,

web-based games, social networking, email and time. It alerts users according to parameters that they decide. This system was awarded "Bronze Award, Excellence Award" by Top Ten Reviews and was rated as the 2011 third best web filtering system.

d. **PureSight PC:** This internet filter software is among the best ranked. As internet threats against children have evolved, PureSight PC internet filter software has placed particular emphasis on protecting kids while using chat and instant messaging programs. Filtering of objectionable websites is central to any worthwhile internet filter software and PureSight PC has this issue covered with multiple layers. PureSight PC internet filter software is primarily a cloud-based application. The client that is resident on any protected computer is small and nimble.
e. **CYBERSitter 11:** CYBERsitter offers excellent ways to track and monitor surfing on the computer discreetly. The program creates reports about visited sites and records of messenger conversations. It emails all of the information to the parent administrator on a daily basis. This software offer a kind of discreet monitoring, the parents can monitor the program from a remote location (anywhere with an internet connection) and change the settings on the filter from outside their homes. For this study CYBERsitter 10.7 was used because free trial of the 11th version is not available. Version 10.7 is very similar to 11th version nevertheless some features like password protection are disabled.
f. **CyberPatrol 7.7:** This web-filtering system is relatively easy to use, quite customizable, and effective. CyberPatrol offers a host of good features and filtering settings, but lacks a few advanced features found in some of the higher-performing internet filter solutions. Additionally, this web-filtering tool offers a quality internet filtering program with some compelling features.
g. **Profil Parental Filter 2:** Is internet filter software from Profil Technology, a subsidiary of the company that publishes BitDefender security software, which protects children while they're on the internet. After all, internet security is important. This internet filter software lets parents control what their children see by categorizing content and giving them several ways to filter.
h. **ImView:** Uses an approach to internet filter software that is different from the other selected softwares. The program monitors and records a child's internet activity so that parents can view it after the fact. It records most online activities such as websites visited, keywords searched and instant message and email correspondence. ImView is a complete keystroke recorder. The parents can block specific websites and websites that contain certain keywords in the URL, and can remotely access all reports, screenshots and activity. This application includes lists of suggested keywords to block. It also allows you to enter new keywords. This internet filter software operates in stealth mode without the user's knowledge.
i. **K9 Web Protection:** The web filtering technology used by this tool divides Internet content into 60 distinct categories. These categories are stored in a master database called "Blue Coat", through which webmasters maintain and update more than 15 million ratings of websites and domains. A Web site will fall into one or more of these categories, based on the content of the site. This system allows the software configuration to block or allow specific categories.
j. **VIMA Web Filter:** This tool analyze images on more than 150 parameters, the VIMA WebFilter objectionable image and website filtering software can carry out effective real-time and/or off-line filtering of pornographic content and websites. Because of the extent of the analysis it

performs, VIMA WebFilter is able to differentiate between a nude picture on a pornographic site and a nude picture in a work of art, among other things. This particular feature is one that is inadequate or completely lacking in other filters. This web-filtering system also minimizes the number of objectionable images that get through to the user, while also maximizing the amount of acceptable material that does get through. In addition, VIMA WebFilter offers tremendous flexibility and can be customized and personalized to meet different filtering criteria.

In this fact, all participants received software, achieving evaluate ten times each web filtering system by different participants

1. **Tasks:** After the software installation and the brief introduction (basic application tour) given to the participants by the staff members, parents only had to start the assigned web filtering system and freely use it (according to their preferences and needs) by seven calendar days. The total number of days did not include the software installation nor brief introduction day. The use of the web filtering systems consisted in the following interaction tasks:
    a. **System Configuration:** Participants selected types of users and roles for each family member, e.g. Dad, user type = Administrator; role = super user. They could indicate features including restrictions, permissions, roles, definition of the internet usage schedule, and configurations of the frequency, modality of system's reports, among others. The set up of the web filtering systems depended on their capabilities. The participants could change the system configuration at any time.
    b. **Heeding and Follow the System's Feedback:** Participants addressed the web filtering systems notifications and navigation-activity reports, following the instructions presented on it, and adapting the system configuration according to their needs.
    c. **System Navigation and Design:** Parents just followed the natural flow through the design of the different screens of the systems' interfaces.

Participants could daily ask for help to the staff members in order to resolve technical issues via messenger or e-mail. They also completed a final post-task questionnaire entirely based on the widely known seven-point Likert items Computer System Usability Questionnaire (CSUQ) of IBM, characterized by its generalizability of results and wide applicability (Lewis, 1993). The applied questionnaire aims to capture the participant's perception on the usability of the web filtering systems. Each element of this questionnaire is a statement which includes a rating on the following seven-point scale, complemented by an additional section for comments:

1. Strongly Disagree.
2. Disagree.
3. Moderately Disagree.
4. Neither Agree Nor Disagree.
5. Moderately Agree.
6. Agree.
7. Strongly Agree.

The original CSUQ (Lewis, 1993) was slightly adapted for this is study as follows:

1. Overall, I am satisfied with how easy it is to use this web filtering system.
2. It is simple to use this web filtering system.
3. I can effectively complete my work using this web filtering system.
4. I am able to complete my work quickly using this web filtering system.
5. I am able to efficiently complete my work using this web filtering system.
6. I feel comfortable using this web filtering system.
7. It was easy to learn to use this web filtering system.
8. I believe I will take the most this web filtering system quickly.
9. The web filtering system gives error messages that clearly tell me how to fix problems.
10. Whenever I make a mistake using this web filtering system, I recover easily and quickly.
11. The feedback (such as online help, on-page messages, and other documentation) provided by the system is clear.
12. It is easy to find the help-information I need.
13. The feedback provided with the system is easy to understand and follow.
14. The feedback is effective in helping me complete my tasks.
15. The information shown on this web filtering system screens is well organized.

Note: The interface includes those items that you use to interact with the web filtering system. For example, some components of the interface are the keyboard, the mouse, the screens (including their use of graphics and language).

16. The interface of this web filtering system is pleasant.
17. The interface of this web filtering system allows an agile and flowing navigation.
18. I like using the interface of this web filtering system.
19. This web filtering system has all the functions and capabilities I expect it to have.
20. Overall I am satisfied with this web filtering system.

According to the interaction tasks for this research, the questionnaire were dividing as follows:

- **Statements2-8**: Activities related to system configuration.
- **Statements 9 to 14**: Tasks associated with monitoring and feedback system notifications.
- **Statements 15 to 19**: Tasks related to navigation and interface design.
- **Statements 1 and 20**: These elements were treated separately because are oriented to find the general perception of the participants on usability and satisfaction of systems.

These statements-groups were applied to get the perception of the interaction of participants with the web filtering systems from three perspectives: System configuration, feedback, and navigation and design. The orientation of the original questionnaire's items allowed this separation of components almost automatically.

It is pertinent to mention that participating parents had at their disposal a Spanish version of this questionnaire properly traduced by the staff of the Department of Languages of the Instituto Tecnológico de Aguascalientes; nevertheless, all of the participants decided to answer the English version of the questionnaire.

Three different approaches have used to classify the main findings of this research: Configuration, Feedback, and Navigation and Design; which coincide to the three types of interaction tasks assigned to participating parents, and its corresponding set of questionnaire statements (as described above). In this vein, the presentation of findings begins with the aggregate results in order to provide an overview of the usability level of the web filtering systems, finalizing this section with the general perception on usability and users' satisfaction.

Results: Three different approaches have used to classify the main findings of this research: Configuration, Feedback, and Navigation and Design; which coincide to the three types of interaction tasks assigned to participating parents, and its corresponding set of questionnaire statements. In this vein, the presentation of findings begins with the aggregate results in order to provide an overview of the usability level of the web filtering systems, finalizing this section with the general perception on usability and users' satisfaction.

MAIN FOCUS OF THE CHAPTER[1]

Issues, Controversies, Problems

Unexpectedly, the participants perceived the web filtering systems as particularly poor in usability. The results widely contrasted with the review presented in the site Top-Ten Reviews (Top-Ten Reviews, 2012), where although their analysis covers various factors, rate the first eight selected systems with high scores in usability. In fact, the site TopTen Reviews awarded the systems "Net Nanny", "Safe eyes", and "McAfee Familly Protection" with the "Excellence Award" (Top-Ten Reviews, 2012); nevertheless, these systems got scores remarkably low in this usability study (see Figure 2). Figure 1 depicts the aver-

Figure 1. Average score for each questionnaire's statement. This Figure shows the average scores for each statement of the IBM CSUQ questionnaire

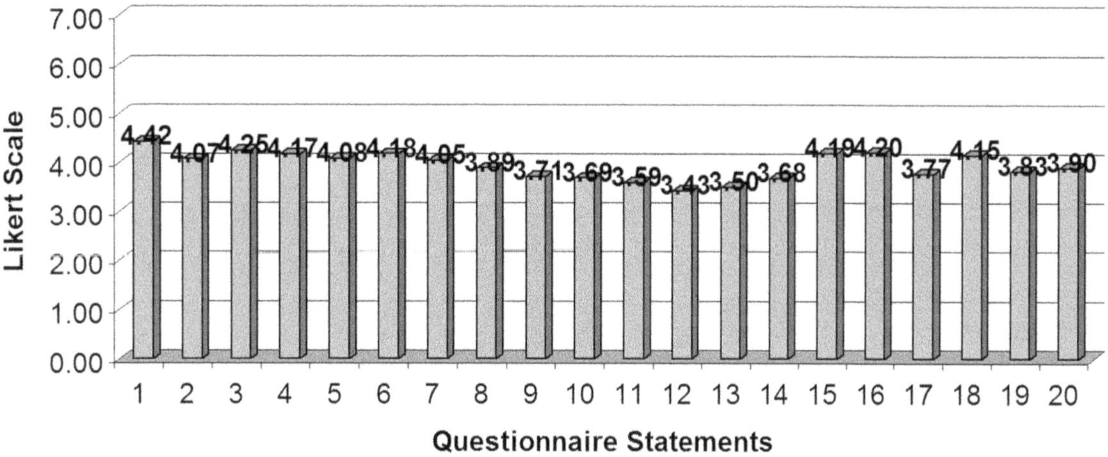

Figure 2. Global usability perception for each perspective

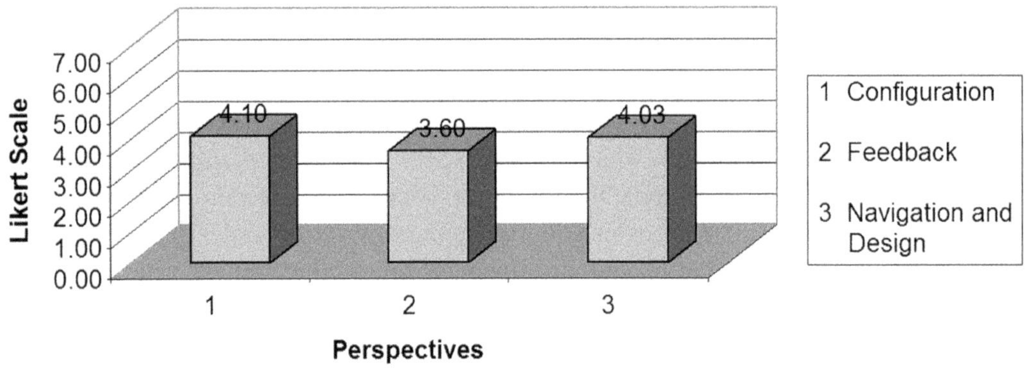

age score for each statement of the version of the Computer System Usability Questionnaire (CSUQ) (Lewis, 1993) used in this study. In the same way, Figure 2 shows the overall average reached by the web filtering systems for each of the three classification approaches, also reflecting low overall averages.

Figure 3 shows the global average (considering the average from the three approaches) achieved by each web filtering system. In this case, "PureSight PC" reached the highest rating (5.21). However, this score reaches only "Moderately Agree" on the Likert scale considered for this research. Other highlights include systems "CyberPatrol 7.7" and "Profil Parental Filter 2", with averages of 4.53 and 4.37 respectively reaching perceptions that range from indifferent "Neither Agree Nor Disagree" to low "Moderately Agree".

Figure 2 shows the average scores for each perspective considering the global collected data.

Figure 3 shows the average scores for each of the selected system taking into account the Likert scale established for the questionnaire used in this study.

In terms of interaction tasks "System configuration", participants gave low scores to the vast majority of the analyzed systems, perceiving them as perplexing to configure due to the amount and/or complexity of configuration options. Only the web filtering system "Pure Sight PC" exceeded the Likert scale's negative barrier, obtaining an average score into perception "Moderately Agree" (5.23). See Figure 4.

Figure 3. Average ratings given by participants

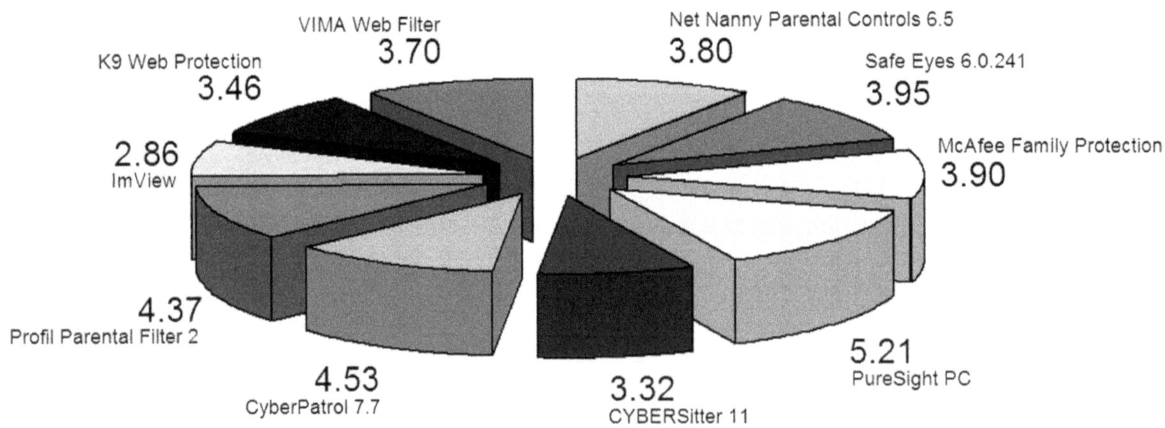

Figure 4. Average ratings given by participants on system configuration usability

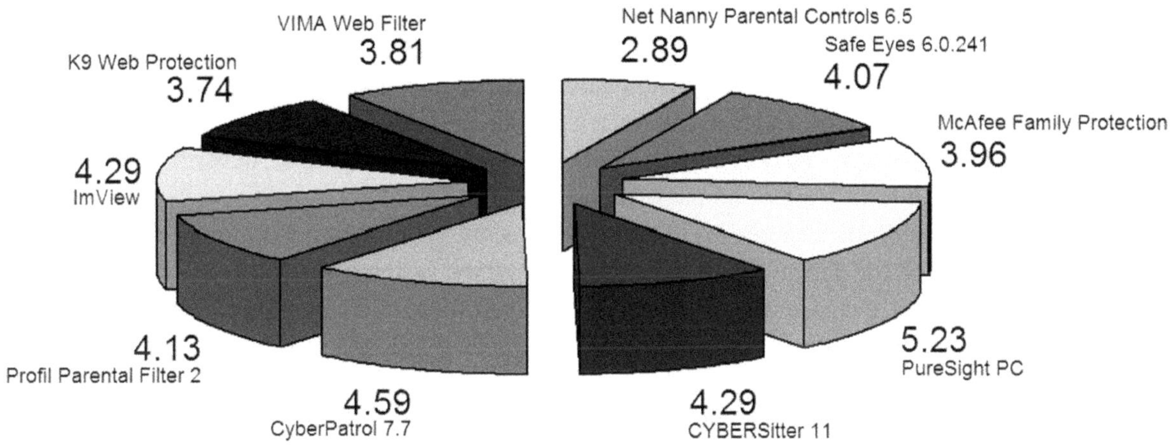

Figure 4 shows the average scores for each of the selected system considering the perception of the participating parents on how usable and understandable were the options to configure the systems.

Findings on Usability Level of Feedback

Second interaction tasks correspond to considered activities "Heeding and follow the system's feedback". The perception of the participants in this approach was extremely low (see Figure 5). Although the informative nature of the web filtering systems suggests that they will receive high scores in this area, the obtained results revealed the opposite. This situation is noteworthy since often the proper functioning of a system depends on adequate feedback (usable and effortless possible), but is essential in any security system. In Figure 5 can be observed that highest average mark in this approach corresponds to web filtering system "Profil Parental Filter 2" (4.57). Nevertheless, this score barely exceeding the level "Neither Agree Nor Disagree" in the Likert scale considered for this study. Figure 5 also highlights the lowest score achieved by the system "ImView" which practically does not provide feedback to users.

Figure 5. Average ratings given by participants on system feedback usability

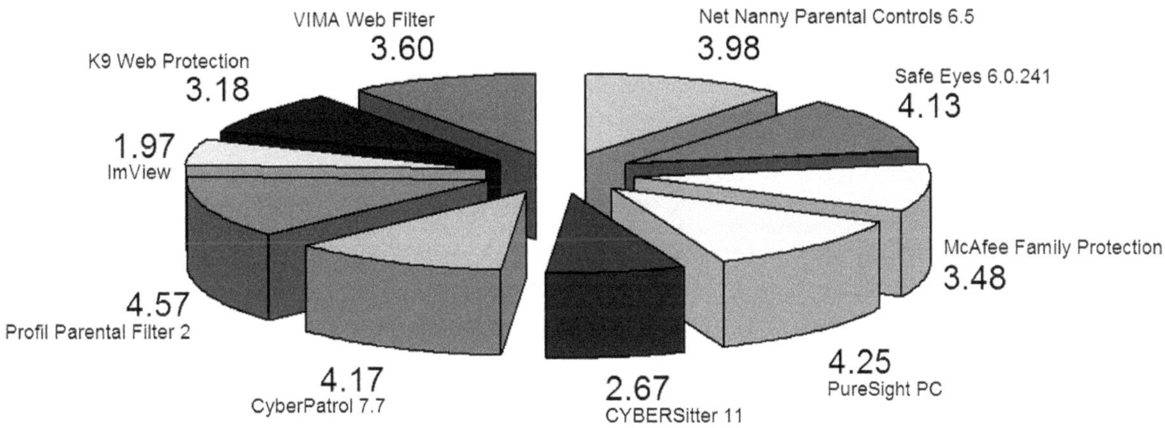

Figure 5 depicts the average scores for each of the selected systems reflecting the usability and usefulness of the system's feedback according to the data provided by the participating parents.

The third set of interaction tasks included activities related to the "*System navigation and design*" in order to obtain the perception of the participants on the organization of system's interface and its different screens, interface look and feel, interface usability, and display and affordability of functions and capabilities of the system. The low averages dominated again (see Figure 6), nevertheless one of the tested systems reached level "Agree" on the Likert scale "PureSight PC" (6.14).

Figure 6 shows the average scores for each of the selected systems based on the perception of the participating parents on the design and navigability through the systems' interfaces.

As mentioned before, the generality of questionnaire used allows analyzing them separately in order to capture the general perception of the participants on the usability and satisfaction. The analysis reveals that user satisfaction increases almost proportionally to the usability level of the observed systems regardless of its security features (see Figure 7). As evident in Figure 7, the bigger discrepancy with this assumption appear for evaluation of web filtering system "ImView" (8), which although is easy to use, lacks many of the functions of other systems. In fact, this system aims to help more as a "gossip system" on the activity of members of a family on the internet, than a content-filtering system, which could be the main reason of this discrepancy.

Figure 7 graphically depicts the average scores for each of the selected systems comparing its level of usability and the corresponding user satisfaction with that system.

SOLUTIONS AND RECOMMENDATIONS

The conducted study reveals some flaws in web filtering systems which influencing not only the adoption intentions for users, but also the fail or success of that systems. Undoubtedly, an appropriate design

Figure 6. Average ratings given by participants on system configuration usability

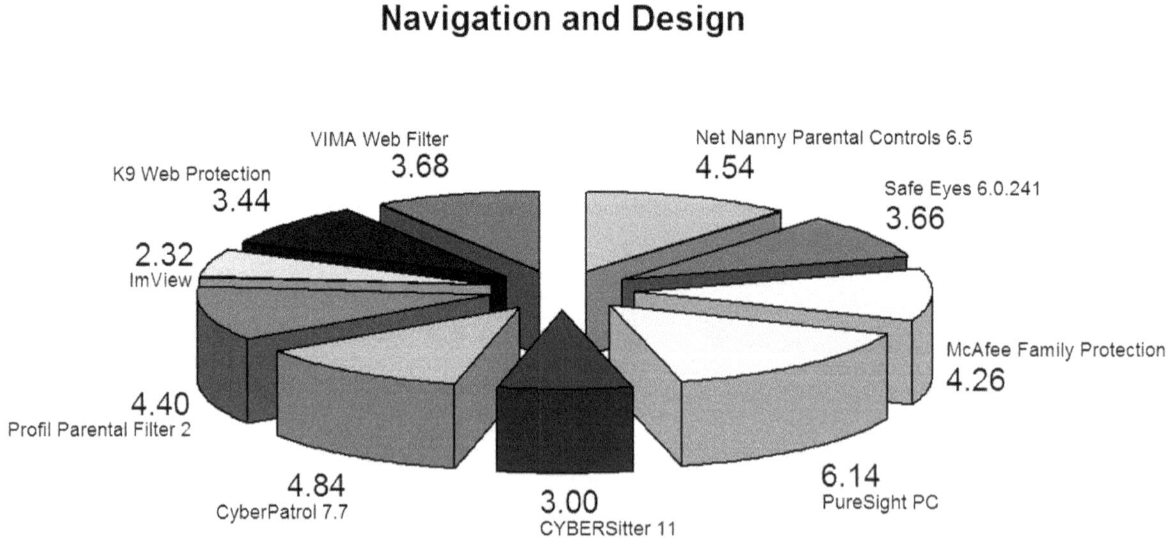

Figure 7. Average ratings given by participants on overall system's usability and user's satisfaction

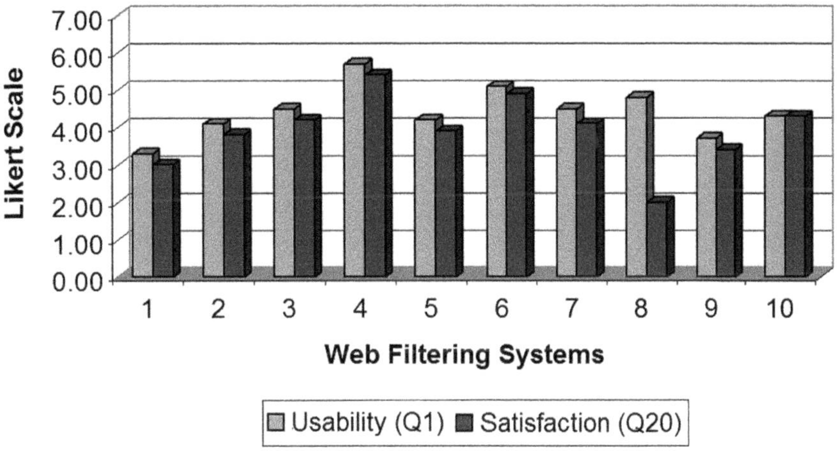

could improve some of these issues, such as Easiness of configuration and use, adaptability, ease of learning, fostering a trustworthy environment (particularly difficult). Nevertheless some others require more than technology, e.g. achieve a culture of use among users.

In this way, it is possible to interpret the design flaws detected as a number of aspects that parents would like to see reflected in a web filtering system, since this information derives from the perception of participants.

As mentioned above, the collected data keep a strong relationship with the perception extracted from the interpretation of the parent's wishes on web filtering systems. Three tables summarize this information, each of which includes three columns the detected issues, their current situation, and the improvements desired by users (see Tables 1 to 3). Particularly, Table 1 focused on the approach "Configuration", while Table 2 concentrates on approach "Feedback" and Table 3 shows what corresponds to the approach "Navigation and Design".

Regarding the configuration usability perceived by participating parents (Figure 4) was possible to identify some issues, one of these is the time required for configuration, see Table 1. In this fact, the conducted study reveals that most evaluated systems do not have an adequate distribution of configuration options, and often are too much for novel users. Usually, a big number of options lead to excessive

Table 1. Summarized issues and requirements for usable configuration of web filtering systems

<table>
<tr><th>Issues</th><th>Discovered Requirements</th></tr>
<tr><td>• Configuration time.
• Complex configuration.</td><td rowspan="3">• Well-described and justified automatic configuration.
• Just in case, the option for advanced configuration (with assistance and internet facilities).
• Possibility of adapting the form to deliver reports (e-mail, directly in the system as a log, graphically, by user, or a combination), and the periodicity of reports (daily, every other day, weekly, bi weekly and monthly).
• Availability of multiple user profiles with predefined content-restrictions, but with options to modify.
• Ease of creating new user profiles with different levels of content-restriction.</td></tr>
<tr><th>Current status</th></tr>
<tr><td>Too many configuration options and, in many cases, too complex for novel users.</td></tr>
</table>

Table 2. Summarized issues and wishes for usable feedback of web filtering systems

Issues	Discovered Requirements
• Lack of feedback. • Ineffective feedback. • Technical terms embedded in feedback.	• Feedback available during normal operation and configuration of the system. • Effective feedback to mitigate errors or problems. • Feedback for assistance and guidance available when needed. • Feedback easy to understand and follow. • Reports of online activity by user or profile defined complemented by graphics and concise explanation. • Immediate notifications (by e-mail, or maybe by cell phone messages) about the access to specific websites.
Current status	
In many cases, feedback is negligible in the web filtering systems, especially during the set up process. Similarly, the notifications during the monitoring/filtering process (online usage) are unattractive, seem like developers are focused on the technical functionality and overlook the design of feedback and notifications.	

Table 3. Summarized issues and wishes for usable Navigation and Design of web filtering systems

Issues	Discovered Requirements
• Lack of well organized interfaces. • Inconsistent design. • Poor interface design.	• Structuring options and facilities of the system within a design as simple as possible to understand and use. • Maintain a friendly look-and-feel throughout the system. • A neat and consistent design even if system need requires third parties. • A sequence of interfaces easy to model mentally. • To include interface elements that provide an agile navigation between the screens and through them, e.g. tabbed panes, tree directories style, among others. • Provide themes of notifications for each profile, e.g. General, for children, and for teenagers. This is to make attractive messages.
Current status	
In many cases the systems interfaces do not reflect the interest that should be taken in its design and development. It seems that designers and developers concentrate on the guts of the system and forget that systems will be used by ordinary people who have few digital skills.	

configuration time causing neglect and indifference in configuration options that may be essential for proper filtering.

Although it is necessary to reduce the number of configuration options, users tended to distrust the quality of those web filtering systems that offered only a few configuration options. Another closely related issue is the complexity of settings, which directly affects the proper functionality of the system and, therefore, user satisfaction (even knowing that they had certain responsibility). A desirable solution to these dilemmas could be to provide auto configuration options, which cover the key features for a reliable filtering process, complemented with options for advanced settings. These configuration options must possess certain characteristics, for example, for automatic configuration should be clearly presented to the user the advantages, disadvantages and features of this option, avoiding at all costs including technical terms. The description should be prepared in a accurate and concise manner using a friendly and respectful dialogue. This information will be necessary to promote a trustworthy environment with the user. It is crucial to maintain high levels of usability for advanced configuration also, since it is likely that any novice user may require this option to configure your system. Therefore, the interface should include elements to expedite and facilitate the process such as dropdown lists, select options, tabbed panes, and configuration assistance, complemented to clear descriptions of each option.

As can be seen in Figure 5, the participants perceived usability of the web filtering systems as too low. Certainly, design flaws such as poor feedback or feedback absence may cause this perception. During the study, it was common to note that some of the best web filtering systems does not provide any feedback through the configuration process and shows vague and poorly designed notifications for online usage.

The ineffectiveness of feedback to orienting users to reduce errors, resolve security issues, or explain system reports, represents another significant concern. Closely related to this last aspect is to provide adequate guidance to the user in performing tasks such as the location of help topics, and the appropriate fulfillment of configuration tasks. This means that the feedback system should serve as an assistant for the user throughout the session with the system. On the other hand, all feedback should be as intuitive as possible for the user. A good strategy for the designer is to incorporate real-world metaphors, figures, or even humor to try to make easier for the user the correct interpretation of feedback and decisively avoid the use of technical terms, see e.g. (Mendoza-Gonzalez, Muñoz-Artega, & Alvarez-Rodriguez, 2010; Muñoz et al., 2009) Additionally, the reports should provide view options of the online activities of users either together or separately. The reports must include graphics complemented by brief and clear textual description.

According to data collected (see Figure 6) perception of participants on system navigation and design (bearing in mind aspects like appearance, access to resources and options of system, composition and structure of the interface elements and interfaces themselves) was uncommonly low. The vast majority of the evaluated systems lacked proper organization of its interfaces, which directly affected the navigability making it complicated. Added to this, the systems evaluated tended to have screens with varying designs hindering the flow of navigation to be particularly distracting to users. The appearance of the interface is clearly a fundamental aspect. However, the results show that a "friendly interface" was not in the plans of developers and designers of the systems evaluated. Poor designed interfaces significantly influenced the participants' decision in adoption of systems. The exception was the system "PureSight PC". This system received the highest score in this approach, in fact, the highest score recorded throughout the study. The design of this web filtering system as well as its organization and sequence of screens are particularly suitable. One of the most significant aspects is the online notifications which have a pleasant look-and-feel highly suitable for kids. Additionally, the reports are truly comprehensive and easy to understand, however, do not include graphical views of the online activity of users. Table 3 concentrates these perceptions.

Perhaps the wishes discovered seem to be basic, however, the study showed that the best web filtering systems lack these basics, or just consider them superficially. This situation directly influences their acceptance by the user.

Regardless of technological robustness, user satisfaction of web filtering system depends largely on usable and well-designed user interfaces.

This study reveals an interesting phenomenon, specifically with the web filtering system "ImView", whose situation seems to contradict the previous statement (see software 8 in Figure 7). Although this application is easy to use, it has a number of technological limitations. This situation could negatively impacted to user satisfaction on this application since the purposes and functions expected by participants for a web filtering system at baseline.

Although the features and functions of the application "ImView" does not correspond exactly to a web filtering system, it appears in site Top-Ten Reviews(Top-Ten Reviews, 2012) as one of the best "filtering" applications, and its inclusion in the study was in order to be consistent with the "Benchmark" selected.

FUTURE RESEARCH DIRECTIONS

There are several venues for future work most of the related to specific issues that this research faced. One of the main barriers for this study is certainly the large number of web filtering systems available. In this fact, the selection of the sample focused to those systems whose had already been assessed in some way or another. In this vein, the web systems ranking site Top-Ten Reviews (Top-Ten Reviews, 2012) provide a convenient source; nevertheless, omitted details on the evaluation method, especially in the area of usability, e.g. It was unclear if people who reviewed the filters in Top-Ten Reviews were IT or usability "experts" and not "regular" users (parents). Furthermore, assessments in (Top-Ten Reviews, 2012) prioritized technological and functional aspects, rather than the interaction with users, nevertheless included an individual section for review of the systems usability.

Another limitation in this study lies in the set of common tasks, particularly established to be easily carried by the participants in any application alike. Conceivably, the analysis of additional or complementary tasks reveals more meaningful information.

Other barrier was the lack of proper statistical evaluations. This analysis did not carry out due to time and purposes on this stage of the research. Nevertheless, statistics and other traditional (but important) usability testing represent one of the overriding subsequent steps in this research work. Another aspect that could be seen as a limitation is the choice of the evaluation method; however, the selected method allowed an easy adaptation to the needs of this research. Additionally, several studies indicate the robustness of the questionnaire such as described in (Tullis & Stetson, 2004).

Another future research consists in compare the present results against those observed through other studies, which consider populations with different demographics; perhaps other nationalities, customs, or even beliefs. These aspects could reveal surprising conclusions; by example, it may be likely that religious beliefs will influence the perception of people on these applications considering not only usability but also its usage.

Other aspect considered as future work, consist of establishes the creation of a set of design patterns for web filtering system interfaces, considering the results of this research and following a formal strategy such as suggested in . Mentioned contribution could considerably facilitate, to developers and designers, the generation process of usable interfaces for web filtering systems.

CONCLUSION

The findings of this research revealed several flaws in the design of the interfaces of Web Filtering Systems that should be fixed before to be suggested as plugins or services provided by third parties in MOOCs. Additionally, each of these flaws represents opportunities to improve the usability of these applications, and increase proper use. This aspect is particularly significant because there is a lack of alternatives that encourage well-designed interfaces for these applications.

Similarly, this research highlights the importance of inherently maintain a user-centered design, demonstrating that even today developers and designers focus on the technical and functional aspects (back end), neglecting the interaction with the user forgetting the idea that "The best system in the world is useless if users does not know how to use it". Surely, user-centered design is critical in security systems whose capabilities depend, almost directly, on the users; but, it has an additional importance in applications (such as web filtering systems) designed for serious social purposes, including to reduce those vulnerabilities which expose kids to cyber bullying, pornography, pedophilia, among other social deviations.

On the other hand, the "Discovered Whishes" on usable web filtering systems, could be adapted (slightly) to extend its use in order to improve the interface design of other security systems, such as privacy systems, identity management systems, firewalls, and antivirus, often manipulated by inexperienced users.

Additionally, it is indispensable also to strengthen the relevance of this research work by performing full statistical reviews of microdata, e.g. involving significance tests. Similarly, classical measurements of usability, such as time for task completion, error rates among others, could reinforce these findings with valuable information on usability.

REFERENCES

Baggaley, J. (2014). MOOCs: Digesting the facts. *Distance Education*, *35*(2), 159–163. doi:10.1080/01587919.2014.919710

Baguma, R., Stone, R. G., Lugega, J. T., & van der Weide, Th. P. (2009). A Framework for Filtering Web Accessibility Guidelines. *Proceedings of International Cross-Disciplinary Conference on Web Accessibility W4A'09*, Madrid, Spain (pp. 46-49). ACM Press. doi:10.1145/1535654.1535663

Bonk, C., Lee, M. M., Reeves, T., & Reynolds, T. (2014). MOOCs and Open Education around the World: Recapping the Past Year, Mapping the Road Ahead. *Proceedings of World Conference on E-Learning in Corporate, Government, Healthcare, and Higher Education 2014*, Chesapeake, VA (pp. 238-241). Association for the Advancement of Computing in Education (AACE).

Bosse, T., & Stam, S. (2011). A Normative Agent System to Prevent Cyberbullying. *Proceedings of the IEEE/WIC/ACM International Conferences on Web Intelligence and Intelligent Agent Technology*, Lyon, France (pp. 425-430). IEEE Computer Society Press. doi:10.1109/WI-IAT.2011.24

Dadvar, M., & de Jong, F. (2012). Cyberbullying Detection: A Step Toward a Safer Internet Yard *Proceedings of the World Wide Web Companion WWW*, Lyon, France (Vol. *12*, pp. 121–125). ACM Press.

Dadvar, M., de Jong, F., Ordelman, R., & Trieschnigg, D. (2012). Improved Cyberbullying Detection Using Gender Information. *Proceedings of the 12th -Dutch-Belgian Information Retrieval Workshop DIR'12*, Ghent, Belgium.

Flinn, C.E., Jr. (2012). *MOOCs in Size Small, Please*. Retrieved from http://educationnext.org/moocs-in-size-small-please/

Følstad, A., Lai-Chong Law, E., & Hornbæk, A. (2010). Analysis in Practical Usability Evaluation: A Survey Study. *Proceedings of the ACM SIGCHI Conference on Human Factors in Computing Systems CHI'12*, Austin, Texas, USA (pp. 2127-2136). ACM Press.

Guermazi, R., Hammami, M., & Ben Hamadou, A. (2007). Combining Classifiers for Web Violent Content Detection and Filtering. *Proceedings of the 7th International Conference on Computational Science*, LCNS (Vol. 4489, pp. 773-780). Springer. doi:10.1007/978-3-540-72588-6_126

Huerta, M. (2014). Why your Kids Should MOOCs. Retrieved from http://www.kars4kids.org/blog/why-kids-should-mooc/

Kainda, R., Flechais, I., & Roscoe, A. W. (2010). Two Heads are Better Than One: Security and Usability of Device Associations in Group Scenarios. *Proceedings of the Symposium on Usable Privacy and Security SOUPS'10*, Redmond, Washington, United States. ACM Press. doi:10.1145/1837110.1837117

Karam, M. (2010). The Coffee Lab: Developing a Public Usability Space. *Proceedings of the ACM SIGCHI Conference on Human Factors in Computing Systems CHI'10*, Atlanta, Georgia, USA (pp. 2671-2680). ACM Press. doi:10.1145/1753846.1753850

LeClair, J., & Ferrer, T. (2014). A case for MOOCs. *Proceedings of the ASEE Gulf-Southwest Conference,* New Orleans, Louisiana, USA (pp. 1-8). American Society for Engineering Education.

Lewis, R. J. (1993). *IBM Computer Usability Satisfaction Questionnaires: Psychometric Evaluation and Instructions for Use.* Boca Raton, FL: Human Factors Group.

Mendoza-González, R., Muñoz Arteaga, J., & Álvarez Rodríguez, F. J. (2010). Designing Usable Security Feedback for Web Filtering Systems. In M. Vargas Martin, M. García-Ruíz, & A. Edwards (Eds.), *Technology for Facilitating Humanity and Combating Social Deviations* (pp. 230–248). Hershey, PA: IGI Global. doi:10.4018/978-1-60960-094-5.ch013

Möckel, C. (2011). Usability and Security in EU E-Banking Systems - Towards an Integrated Evaluation Framework. *Proceedings of the 2011 IEEE/IPSJ International Symposium on Applications and the Internet SAINT'11*, Munich, Germany, (pp. 230-233). IEEE Computer Society. doi:10.1109/SAINT.2011.42

Muñoz, J., Mendoza, R., Vargas Martin, M., Vanderdonckt, J., & Álvarez, F. J. (2009). A Methodology for Designing Information Security Feedback Based on User Interface Patterns. *Advances in Software Engineering*, *40*(12), 1231–1241. doi:10.1016/j.advengsoft.2009.01.024

Nieuwenhuijsen, E. (2014). *Using game based learning as an approach for teaching kids how to program* (Forum).

Rubin, J., & Chisnell, D. (2008). Handbook of Usability Testing: How to Plan, Design, and Conduct Effective Tests (2nd ed.). Indianapolis, IN: Wiley Publishing.

Taibi, T. (2006). Formalising design patterns composition. *IEE Proceedings. Software Engineering*, *153*(3), 127–136. doi:10.1049/ip-sen:20050072

Top-Ten Reviews. (2012). Internet Filter review. Retrieved from http://internet-filter-review.toptenreviews.com/

Tullis, T., & Stetson, J. (2004, June). *A Comparison of Questionnaires for Assessing Website Usability.* Paper presented at the Usability Professionals Association Conference, Minneapolis, MN.

Turati, A., Cerizza, D., Celino, I., & Della Valle, E. (2009) Analyzing User Actions within a Web 2.0 Portal to Improve a Collaborative Filtering Recommendation System. *Proceedings of the IEEE/WIC/ACM International Conference on Web Intelligence and Intelligent Agent Technology WI '09*, Milan, Italy (pp. 65-68). IEEE Computer Society. doi:10.1109/WI-IAT.2009.232

VOX Norway. (2012). The Digital Citizen: An analysis of digital competence in the Norwegian population. Retrieved from http://www.vox.no/PageFiles/15123/The_Digital

ADDITIONAL READING

Dimitriadou, C., Palaiologou, N., & Nari, E. (2014). E-Learning Training Courses on Multicultural Education: An Example from Greece. In V. Zuzevičiūtė, E. Butrimė, D. Vitkutė-Adžgauskienė, V. Vladimirovich Fomin, & K. Kikis-Papadakis (Eds.), *E-Learning as a Socio-Cultural System: A Multidimensional Analysis* (pp. 102–116). Hershey, PA: Information Science Reference. doi:10.4018/978-1-4666-6154-7.ch006

Greene, J. (2014). Introductory Study Using MOOCs for Homeless Education. *Proceedings of World Conference on E-Learning in Corporate, Government, Healthcare, and Higher Education* 2014 (pp. 724-728). Chesapeake, VA: Association for the Advancement of Computing in Education (AACE).

Johnson, M. C., & Graham, C. R. (2015). Current Status and Future Directions of Blended Learning Models. In M. Khosrow-Pour (Ed.), *Encyclopedia of Information Science and Technology* (3rd ed., pp. 2470–2480). Hershey, PA: Information Science Reference. doi:10.4018/978-1-4666-5888-2.ch240

Kilgore, W., & Lowenthal, P. R. (2015). The Human Element MOOC. In R. Wright (Ed.), *Student-Teacher Interaction in Online Learning Environments* (pp. 373–391). Hershey, PA: Information Science Reference.

LeCounte, J. F., & Johnson, D. (2015). The MOOCs: Characteristics, Benefits, and Challenges to Both Industry and Higher Education. In F. Nafukho & B. Irby (Eds.), *Handbook of Research on Innovative Technology Integration in Higher Education* (pp. 228–247). Hershey, PA: Information Science Reference. doi:10.4018/978-1-4666-8170-5.ch011

Ronkowitz, K., & Ronkowitz, L. C. (2015). MOOCs: Evolution and Revolution. In E. McKay & J. Lenarcic (Eds.), *Macro-Level Learning through Massive Open Online Courses (MOOCs): Strategies and Predictions for the Future* (pp. 183–211). Hershey, PA: Information Science Reference. doi:10.4018/978-1-4666-8324-2.ch011

Thrun, S. (2013). MOOCs: The Future Is Here. *The Journal of Nursing Education*, *52*(1), 3–4. doi:10.3928/01484834-20121227-10 PMID:23293938

Tømte, C., Fevolden, A., & Olsen, D. S. (2014). To MOOC or not to MOOC?: A Case Study of Norway. In V. Zuzevičiūtė, E. Butrimė, D. Vitkutė-Adžgauskienė, V. Vladimirovich Fomin, & K. Kikis-Papadakis (Eds.), *E-Learning as a Socio-Cultural System: A Multidimensional Analysis* (pp. 210–223). Hershey, PA: Information Science Reference. doi:10.4018/978-1-4666-6154-7.ch012

Tu, C. H., & Sujo-Montes, L. E. (2015). MOOCs. In R. Papa (Ed.), *Media Rich Instruction* (pp. 287–304). New York: Springer International Publishing.

Valentin, C. (2015). MOOCs Global Digital Divide: Reality or Myth? In F. Nafukho & B. Irby (Eds.), *Handbook of Research on Innovative Technology Integration in Higher Education* (pp. 376–397). Hershey, PA: Information Science Reference. doi:10.4018/978-1-4666-8170-5.ch019

KEY TERMS AND DEFINITIONS

Cognitive Load: It refers to the mental effort used to complete a task or activity using a device or tool.

Interface Feedback: Is all the communications provided from the system to the users through the user interfaces, the most common Interface Feedback are notifications.

Usability: Ease of use, efficiency, and learnability of a technology (software or hardware) which derives in helping users to complete a task (satisfaction of use).

Usability Test: Usability testing is a method by which users of a product are asked to perform certain tasks in an effort to measure the product's ease-of-use, task time, and the user's perception of the experience.

User Centered Design: Process to create technology (not restricted to software) based in incorporate users into each stage of the design process by obtaining and implementing feedback to refine design ideas.

User eXperience: It involves a combination of several aspects from emotional to cognitive when a person uses a device or a tool to complete a task.

Web Filtering Applications: Software that can screen an incoming Web page to determine whether some or all of it should not be displayed to the user.

Web Plugins: Applications that adds specific functions to an existing software in order to complement it or to integrate additional features or extensions. When an application supports plug-ins it could be perceived as customizable.

Chapter 5
Finding the Design Basic for MOOCs:
Analyzing the UIs of edX, Coursera, and Udacity

Sandra G. Jiménez-González
Universidad Politécnica de Aguascalientes, Mexico

Huizilopoztli Luna-García
Universidad Autónoma de Zacatecas, Mexico

Ricardo Mendoza-González
Instituto Tecnologico de Aguascalientes, Mexico

ABSTRACT

The platforms edX, Coursera, and Udacity are pioneers in MOOCs distribution and access providing and their popularity among people grows daily. Prestigious universities, such as Massachusetts Institute of Technology, Harvard, Stanford, Princeton, among others, support their courses, which are conducted by the best Professors and academic staff. On the other hand, these platforms provide adequate interactions for users, focusing in encourage the appropriation of knowledge and competences related to specific topics. User Interfaces include video-lectures display; quizzes; forums; slides, code and many other resources. However, there are certain interaction features that are not common among these platforms and undoubtedly could improve the user experience. The objective of this chapter is to highlight those interactive elements and provide an alternative for well-designed user interfaces for MOOCs including generic interactions which able users to properly perform their activities and achieve their learning goals. The findings will be discussed and then reflected in a prototype.

DOI: 10.4018/978-1-4666-9743-0.ch005

INTRODUCTION

Nowadays, the teaching and learning demand is growing inordinately around the world; this phenomenon suggests the need of radical changes and innovative strategies oriented to reinforce currently available techniques.

Additionally, new learning proposals should encourage lifelong learning, besides factors such as society, professional life, among others. In this way the process should be customized, adapting itself to the student requirements and abilities. Similarly it should consider student's free time, other activities and the acquired knowledge through both cultural and educational life of the student (Christopher, 2013).

There is a need that can be fulfill with a tool that gives the possibility to be used in different times and places, a tool host in the cloud that allows the self-taught person easy access to the information and tuition during the learning process. This tool that gives solution to this requirement is a MOOC.

The main goal of the MOOCs is mostly focused on provide access to the people who are looking for get their education completed, or even the people who want to extend their education, but in some way cannot do that in Universities in classroom (Dasarathy, Sullivan, Schmidt, Fisher, & Porter, 2014).

The MOOCs are developed based on the great experience of the biggest Universities in the subject of distance education and open resources or free distribution resources.

The MOOCs are accessible, and the high quality courses allow to the students to develop knowledge to support their own learning goals (Al-Zoube, 2009). The main attribute or strength of these courses is their scalability, meaning that, a course which has been already developed can be reach globally, allowing to the big amount of students to be part of the specific topic.

The biggest achievements of the MOOCs include the capability of get together some of the finest academic people of the best Universities through the world in order to develop the material and resources, and the more special one are to offer free courses. The MOOCs are often known as supercharged distance education courses.

Currently the MOOCs are in growing and consolidation process, they are found in many subjects, such as, math, sciences, computing, social sciences, economics, finance, and business.

Thanks to the increasing amount of the information sources through network, the MOOCs have been better structured, having in account with some rules which are integrating them into the formal education, the courses have initial date and deadline, in which the students can register and now, the courses have forums, wikis, and a big quantity of tools which help to make formal the education through MOOCs.

Different ideologies have driven MOOCs in distinct pedagogical directions, but the two most important are: the connectivist MOOCs (cMOOCs) which are based on a connectivism theory of learning with networks developed informally; and content-based MOOCs (xMOOCs), which follow a more behaviorist approach.

cMOOCs emphasise connected, collaborative leaning and the courses are built around a group of like-minded "individuals" who are relatively free from institutional constraints. cMOOCs provide a platform to explore new pedagogies beyond traditional classroom settings and, as such, tend to exist on the radical fringe of higher education. On the other hand, the instructional model (xMOOCs) is essentially an extension of the pedagogical models practiced within the institutions themselves, which is arguably dominated by the "drill and grill" instructional methods with video presentations, short quizzes and testing.

There are many platforms that host MOOCs, these platforms provide the user interface (UI).

UI is the space where interactions between humans and computers occur. The goal of this interaction is to allow effective operations and control of the computer from the human end, whilst the computer simultaneously feeds back information that aids the users decision making process. The user interface can arguably include the total "user experience," which may include the aesthetic appearance of the device, response time, and the content that is presented to the user within the context of the user interface.

The most known platforms that host MOOCs are Coursera, Udacity and Edx. Coursera was founded in 2012 Stanford affiliates, computer science professors Andrew Ng and Daphne Koller. It is a for-profit company, though it currently does not generate any revenue. Coursera have the most diverse course selection of all the MOOC providers and currently have over 4 million students and 410 courses from 83 partner institutions. Partners include the University of California, University of British Columbia, Oxford University and Princeton.

Udacity was founded by Sebastian Thrun, who is a former professor of computer science at Stanford University and the creator of the artificial intelligence system behind Google´s self-driving cars. He left Stanford to spearhead this new venture soon after the huge success of his online artificial intelligence course in 2011, which attracted over 160,000 students from more than 190 countries. Udacity's focus is on college-level courses for building and applying your knowledge of STEM (Science, Technology, Engineering, and Mathematics) disciplines.

EdX, unlike the other organizations, is a venture spearheaded by universities themselves and was conceived as a platform to provide an MIT to anyone who wants it. EdX grew out of the MIT initiative –the brainchild of MIT President L. Rafael Reif (then MIT´s provost) and Professor Anant Agarwal. It was branded as an open platform that other universities could join and leverage for their own residential education purposes. Since its inception, the University of California, Berkeley has become a part of the venture. EdX is financed mostly by its member institutions and the courses and certifications are currently free.

Social learning is a key part of MOOC platforms. It holds the promise of scalable peer-based learning and is often the dominant channel of teacher-student interactions (Christopher, 2013).

The social learning theory proposed by Albert Bandura has become perhaps the most influential theory of learning and development. While rooted in many of the basic concepts of traditional learning theory, Bandura believed that direct reinforcement could not account for all types of learning.

While the behavioral theories of learning suggested that all learning was the result of associations formed by conditioning, reinforcement, and punishment, Bandura's social learning theory proposed that learning can also occur simply by observing the actions of others.

His theory added a social element, arguing that people can learn new information and behaviors by watching other people. Known as observational learning, this type of learning can be used to explain a wide variety of behaviors.

However, the issues associated with distance education are: poor quality of the material, the interaction between people involved in the process, named student-student or student-teacher, the high cost of the premium courses and the difficulties of accreditation or certification of the taken course.

This chapter is about a comparison between platforms mentioned above identifying the advantage that each of them has and also the ones that have in common, also compare the weakness and the solutions to this, then, creating a platform prototype, one that integrates the most important elements of the social learning that creates a learning environment that favors the users experience and the interaction between them.

BACKGROUND

Distance education has a long history, with correspondence courses making use of reasonable cost universal postal services for the delivery of study material to learners and for submission/ return of assignments by students (Casey, 2008). Further developments of distance education have appeared with each new communication technology: radio, television, video recorders, home computing. The latest development that of the internet has similarly been adopted by many existing higher education providers but has also supported the emergence of a new model dubbed massive open online courses (MOOCs), the term coined in 2008 to describe an open online course to be offered by the University of Manitoba in Canada. A range of both topics and platforms have since emerged and the term was describing as "the educational buzzword of 2012" by Daniel (2012) reflecting widespread interest in the concept. MOOCs are widely discussed across a range of media, including blogs and specialist and popular press; however this includes "thinly disguised promotional material by commercial interests, and articles by practitioners whose perspective is their own MOOC courses" according to Daniel (2012).

The promise of MOOCs is that they will provide free access, cutting edge courses that could drive down the cost of university-level education and potentially disrupt the existing models of Higher Education (Future learn, 2013).

One area that has been identified as an important factor affecting students´ learning experiences in MOOCs is student interaction (Mak, Williams & Mackness, 2010). Many educators pointed out the importance of interaction in high quality MOOCs (Mcauley, Stewart, Siemens & Cormier, 2010; Waard, 2011). They confirmed the role of interaction and communication in MOOCs as learners construct their own knowledge and develop their personal learning network from the nodes and connections in the digital environment. Mak Williams and Mackness (2010) indicated that interaction in MOOCs helps students to develop their own ideas, express themselves, establish a presence and make thoughtful long-term relationships. In addition, Chamberlin & Parish (2011) pointed out the importance of interaction in MOOCs, saying that "all the work within the MOOC should be shared with everyone else: readings, discussions, repurposing of material, among others. The idea is that the more you engage within the course and with other participants, the more you will learn."

Interaction has been recognized as one of the most important components of learning experiences both in conventional education and distance education (Choi, Lim & Leem, 2002). Moore (1989) was one of the first who concentrate on interaction issues in distance education. He classifies interaction into student to student, student to instructor, and student to content. According to him, student to student interaction refers to the exchange of information and ideas amongst students with or without the real-time presence of an instructor. Student to instructor interactions refers to the interaction between student and expert which establish an environment that encourages students to understand the content better. Student to content interaction is a defining characteristic of education and without it there cannot be education.

There is some evidence that interaction between students and students, students and content, students and instructors in MOOCs may influence performance and retention (Navarro & Shoemaker, 2000). Northrup (2002) pointed out that since interaction has been found to be a part of overall student satisfaction, interaction should be considered in retention efforts.

Adelskold (1999) suggested that interaction among students could have grater effects on learning in a problem solving situation than other types of interaction whereas Kanuka and Anderson (1998) noted that interaction between students and instructor could contribute to student satisfaction and frequency of interaction in online learning. While Moore (1989) and Murray (2012) pointed out that student to content interaction results in changes of student´s understanding, student´s perceptions, or even cognitive structures of student´s mind.

In her research work, Khalil (2013) concluded that student to student is the most interesting type of interaction that is used in MOOCs. Also the study found out that there is a big lack on student to instructor interaction in MOOCs. This, there is a big need for instructors activities and strategies to enhance interaction in future MOOCs.

Khalil (2013) found that one reason that may cause students drop-out or withdraw of their MOOCs is feelings of isolation and the lack of interactivity in MOOCs. Palloff &Pratt (2003) believe that feelings of isolation are the inherent result poor course design. Physical isolation can be overcome by focusing more on social interactions.

MAIN FOCUS OF THE CHAPTER

Issues, Controversies, Problems

Boettclher (1999) defines online learning as an educational philosophy for designing interactive, responsive, and valid information and learning opportunities to be delivered at a time, place, and in appropriate forms convenient to the learners. Porter (1997) finds that the online environment, sometimes called the "virtual classroom," is not radically different from a traditional classroom and that any effective "classroom" includes six important elements: appropriate tools for learning are either provided or their location and access instructions are explained; there is an expectation of an environment conducive to learning; learners are brought together with educators to share information and exchange ideas; learners have opportunities to apply what they have learned and are free to experiment and make errors; there is a mechanism for evaluating performance; and the environment is safe for learning.

One of the major differences between traditional classroom instruction and online education is the amount of face-to-face contact students have with their teacher and with other students. Learning is a social process, and the support of teachers and classmates forms an important element of the learning that occurs. Although online learning environments provide the means for increased interaction, communication and collaboration, online students "often bring a range of expectations and backgrounds that have been set by the patterns of traditional classroom pedagogy: an active and present instructor; instructor directed activities and discussions; and a passive or merely responsive role for students" (Zapalska, 2004).

With a growing number of courses offered online, there is a considerable interest in concerns and problems associated with online education, particularly as it relates to the quality of online instruction. Traditional or face-to face instructional environments have been criticized because they encourage passive learning, ignore individual differences and needs of the learners, and do not pay attention to problem solving, critical thinking, or other higher order thinking skills (Hannum & Briggs, 1982). For online education to be effective in addressing these issues, the online instructors must be flexible in constantly shifting between a number of roles such as lecturer, tutor, facilitator, mediator and co-learner.

Alley and Jansak (2001) have identified 10 keys to quality online learning. The authors suggested that online courses will be high quality when they are student-centered and when:

- **Knowledge Construction:** The authors note that educational theory suggests that all knowledge is based and constructed upon prior knowledge. They then suggests that problem based learning through internet based exercises can effectively make use of this educational principle.
- **Student Responsibility:** In order to encourage student responsibility, a clear web based roadmap and targeted competencies are highlighted.
- **Student Motivation:** Distance education provides significant challenges for student motivation as much external motivation is not directly visible as in a classroom setting.
- **Reflection:** In order to internalize concepts and understand ideas, students need time to reflect. The nature of distance education if properly structured allows time to work through material at the student´s own pace, reviewing items that are unclear, and skipping over already known sections. Time to internalize can be effectively accomplished via distance education.
- **Learning is Unique:** Different students learn in different ways, at different times, and at different levels. Good distance education can allow for unique and individualized educational experiences.
- **Learning Requires Actual Experience:** Best learning is accomplished when students actually do and use the information imparted. Good distance education assignments recognize this factor and incorporate "doing" into the learning process. The authors suggest two options: learn then do but also do then learn, experimenting in the realm without prior knowledge.
- **Learning is Social and Private:** There is both a social aspect to learning where individuals can learn from both the instructor and from each other. But also there is time to read and study and comprehend the full material. This is often best accomplished in solitude.
- **Preconceptions Can Impact Learning:** The authors suggest that preconceived notions can have a significant negative impact on learning and proposes methods for students to self-discover these notions and forego false assumptions.
- **Iterative Learning:** As with systems development, rarely does learning progress in a one directional straight line. There are many iterations and spirals in both systems development and education.
- **The Unclean Aspect of Pure Learning:** Though there are many successful concepts, there are many extraneous factors that can impact the success or failure of an online course. Most of us have had the experience of using the same techniques that were successful in one class but fail miserably and inexplicably in another. We must be mindful of the dynamic nature of learning and always be ready to alter our strategies to achieve our ultimate goals.

The online setting provides a level of flexibility and convenience not provided by traditional classroom courses. Effective teaching and learning in this setting requires responsible, motivated students whose aims are to learn and not to simply get passing grades. Many elements of an online environment can lead students to frustration, overloading, procrastination, passivity, isolation and finally disengagement. Instructors should not take for granted that students have the ability to use effectively the online component or have the required previous knowledge on the content subject or are willing to participate in meaningful discussions and knowledge shearing. In order for students to be motivated self-learners and learn on their own, instructors have to design an environment that promotes interaction, communication and problem solving, as means to encourage, motivate and engage students in the learning experience.

Interaction is a key factor for students' satisfaction, motivation, retention and higher level of academic achievement. Chickering & Gamson (1987) suggested that the concept of interaction is a core element of the seven principles of good practice in education. These practices include: encouraging students / faculty contact; developing cooperation among students; engaging in active learning; providing quick feedback; emphasizing the amount of time dedicated to a task; communicating high expectations; and respecting diverse talents and ways of learning.

Moore (1989) described three classical forms of interaction in distance education: interaction between students and teachers, interaction between students, and the interaction of students with content. Hillman, Willis, & Gunawardena (1994) described another type of interaction, the student-interface interaction, which focuses on the access, skills, and attitudes necessary for successful mediated interaction. Wagner (1994) defines interactions as "reciprocal events that require at least two objects and two actions. Interactions occur when these objects and events mutually influence one another. An instructional interaction is an event that takes place between a learner and the learner's environment. Its purpose is to respond to the learner in a way intended to change his or her behavior toward an educational goal. Instructional interactions have two purposes: to change learners and to move them toward achieving their goals".

The concept of interaction, as it applies to online learning, is more complicated than it has been treated in traditional classroom teaching, depending upon students personality, age or cognitive/learning styles, the type of media (real-time or asynchronous) used, the support and timely feedback, the sense of belonging in the learning community and students' perceptions of their learning experiences including "how well" or "how much" they have learned (Kearsley, 1995; Picciano, 2002). Since effective online instruction requires an active learner, a carefully designed course should involve interactions of all four types in order to promote control, feedback, participation, online presence, motivation and social exchange.

"Student to instructor" interaction involves direct communication between the learner and the instructor through the use of email, discussion boards, online chats, instant messaging, voice over IP, and virtual classrooms (Bigus, 2004). In this process, the instructor assists students as they come to understand the course content and apply their knowledge, assesses students' comprehension or progress with the content, and offers the learner counseling, encouragement, and motivational support.

"Student to student" interaction, is defined as interaction between one learner and other learners, alone or in groups, with our without the real-time presence of the instructor. Team projects, debates, role playing, small-group discussions, requirements to post and respond to other postings on a discussion board, and chats used for discussion and brainstorming are all instructional components that can be used in online courseware to ensure learner-learner interaction (Bigus, 2004). It is important to mention that inside MOOCs interaction between students encourages the social learning.

In "student to content" interaction, the student interacts with the materials being studied. Current technologies provide a wide variety of media alternatives for creating content for student interaction: sound, text, graphics, video, and virtual reality. To be successful interacting with the selected media, students must have the skills to extract information and learn from the media. Instructor may enhance motivation through clarifying how learning the material will fulfill the student's needs, illustrating how the material is important, stating that the tests will be based on the material.

"Student to interface" interaction demands instructional design strategies that will facilitate students´ acquisition of skills needed to participate effectively in our project workspace. In this context it is important to take into account issues such as appropriate layout, including the positioning of different elements on the screen, for instance, accessibility issues, and what tools and resources are available. In a typical online workspace there are a number of ways to foster active engagement with material and encourage collaborative learning, creating an active, dynamic class structure. The design of the environment is important since it affects the ease with which different activities can be carried out. The platform interface and the interaction that it offers make the learning environment for the students, which are closely related to the instructional interaction.

Padavano & Gould (2005) presented a useful set of interactions that encounters all these issues from the beginning of the course.

Online interactions student to instructor:

- List contact information on the syllabus
- Set up communication guidelines and expectations
- Provide office hours in person or virtually using instant messenger tools or chat rooms
- Set up a weekly optional chat for students
- Provide prompt and detailed feedback on assessments and discussion responses
- Call students to clear up misunderstandings
- Make frequent announcements to the class

Online interactions student to student:

- Set up group or team projects within the course
- Create a thread for class members and instructor to make an introduction
- Create a weekly thread where students can ask each another questions
- Encourage group chats and email
- Set up guidelines for students to students communication and response expectations
- Set up a thread where the student facilitates the learning

Online interactions student to content:

- Develop an interactive course road map
- Interactive syllabus with links and details
- Create a quiz about where to find content within course
- Set up a location with important content links
- Create questions threads for weekly content questions
- Detail what is expected in multiple locations
- Create virtual labs for students to practice tasks

Online Interactions student to interface:

- Provide an orientation to the online environment or content management tool
- Give detailed instructions to students about where things are located in the course, use links
- Give detailed instructions to students on how to submit assignments
- Provide a grade book and post feedback
- Provide a thread for students to ask questions about how to use the course management tool
- Provide a help desk for student questions

SOLUTIONS AND RECOMMENDATIONS

For students studying in an online environment, social interaction with peers and educators can often be an exercise in frustration. If such frustration is to be minimized, much thought needs to be given to the methods of communication that will be utilized, so that the online environment fulfills the human desire for social interaction. Asynchronous communication may not give the immediacy that is requires for successful social interaction. The lapsed time that can occur between question and answer may not assuage the tyrannies of distance, time zones, and isolation from which learners may suffer.

The inability to interact freely with other students may exacerbate feeling of aloneness, and provide a less-than-ideal environment for successful study. Techniques such as the incorporation of protocols and guidelines for social interaction into the learning concepts of the online environment (Curry, 2000) can be utilized to minimize the feelings of aloneness that affect many students.

Synchronous and Asynchronous communication are often required for the successful operation of an online course.

Synchronous Communication

In an online classroom environment many of the learning activities and expectations are similar to those found in a traditional classroom. These learning environments offer meaningful interactions in a face-to-face setting and are most commonly referred to as synchronous learning activities (Hrastinski, 2008; Harris, 2009, Simonson, 2012). Lectures, discussions, and lesson presentations occur at a specific point in time with the expectation that all students will be available to participate. Synchronous learning environments support learning and teaching and offer students and teachers with multiple ways of interacting, sharing, and the ability to collaborate and ask questions in real-time through synchronous learning technology types include videoconferencing, webcasts, interactive learning models, and telephone conferences.

Student Engagement

In addition to videoconferencing, webcasts and telephone conferences other examples of synchronous technology types include virtual words and chats rooms. In Order to successfully participate in these environments students must be engaged in student-learning, which is the most important learner characteristic a student can demonstrate.

Synchronous Collaboration

Studies show that the higher learner perceives the level of collaboration the more satisfied they are with e-learning overall (Diaz & Entonado, 2009). In both the traditional and online classroom environments, interaction and collaboration are identified as a major factor in successful learning outcomes (Bonk & Zhang, 2006; Martinez-Caro, 2011). In an online learning environment the teacher´s role become more about facilitating, guiding, and motivation the learner (Diaz & Entondado, 2009) and can be successfully achieved through feedback and collaboration.

Instructional Pacing

Online learning environments provide flexibility and offer students personalized learning opportunities (Lorenzo & Ittelson, 2005). Students learning online have the opportunity to express their thoughts without judgment or interruptions .Online learning experiences can be developed to provide advanced educational opportunities for the learning needs of individual students.

Asynchronous Communication.

In an asynchronous learning environment students are able to actively participate in their own learning, giving them the opportunity to interact with their peers, provide peer feedback, and reflect on the status of their personal learning goals and outcomes (Harris, 2009; Simonson et al., 2012). In many learning environments there are learning activities and expectations that require students to create, synthesize, explain, and apply the content or skills being taught (Harris, Mishra, & Koehler, 2009; Simonson et., 2012). Asynchronous technologies support learning and allow more time for student reflection, collaboration, and student-to-student interactions (Bonk & Zhang, 2006; Skylar, 2009; Meloni, 2010).

According to Meloni (2010) asynchronous communication and learning is by far the more popular learning type many of the learning tools are free, require minimal hardware, and are used at the student´s pace. Just as with synchronous learning, the growing increase in IT and online connections has expanded the online learning opportunities available. A number of educational benefits can be observed from the use of asynchronous technologies in an online learning environment including: enriched student products and portfolios, student and teacher collaboration and learner specific pacing geared to the individual student needs.

Student Portfolios

Electronic portfolios (e-folios) demonstrate a student´s skill and knowledge level over a specific topic. Online learners of the create e-folios that combine text, images, presentations, video, audio, links, and a discussion space to demonstrate mastery of a specific content area or subject matter (Mason, Pegler, & Weller, 2004; Lorenzo & Ittelson, 2005; eLearners.com, 2012). Many institutions have begun viewing e-folios as a replacement for traditional classroom high stake assessments (Lorenzo & Ittelson, 2005). E-folios help facilitate the exchange of ideas, discourse, and subject area feedback between student and teacher creating meaningful learning experience for the student (Lorenzo & Ittelson, 2005). Due to the success of these e-folios some higher education institutions have also started using them to document and archive student´s academic careers.

Asynchronous Collaboration

As with synchronous collaboration, studies have shown that collaboration increases overall student learning in online learning environments (Diaz & Entonado, 2009). A sense of community is necessary to sustain the educational experience over time and this can be achieved through collaborative learning communities (Garrison & Kanuka, 2004). In this learning environment the teacher's role is still about developing and facilitating a student´s learning experiences (Dias & Entonado, 2009). This facilitation can be successfully achieved through asynchronous collaboration, allowing students to thoughtfully consider learning objectives because they have the time to critically synthesize their learning (Garrison & Kanuka, 2004; Bonk & Zhang, 2006).

Individualized Pacing

Asynchronous learning technologies have been defined as personalized learning tools (Lorenzo & Ittelson, 2005). With these tools, the teacher can assess what students understand and adapt future course assignments to facilitate a higher level and more in-depth understanding of the content (Bonk & Zhang, 2006; Hrastinski, 2008). These online learning environments create an opportunity for online students to become highly self-reflective (Bonk & Zhang, 2006). Perhaps most significantly, what is facilitated through the use of asynchronous tools provides a learning space where participant can confront debatable ideas and faulty thinking in more objective and reflective ways (Garrison & Kanuka, 2004).

Types of Communication in MOOCs

Moore (1989) describes three types of interaction in distance education: interaction between students and teachers, interaction between students, and the interaction of students with content. These types of interaction can occur either synchronously or asynchronously.

The ways in which the "Student to student" interaction, "Student to instructor" interaction and "Student to content" interaction take place are:

In "Student to student" interaction Social networks are widely used in MOOCs. Twitter allows a quick exchange of resources and thoughts. Facebook helps learners to share resources on the web that can be retrieved later on. Blogs can give students a social presence, self-expression, self-indulgence, rich and critical distribution of information Wikis allow students themselves to easily add, remove, or otherwise edit and change some available content, sometimes without the need for registration. Discussion groups are the next most commonly used tool in "students to student" interaction. They enhance networking opportunities and increase opportunities for consultation as well as collaboration with others while other percent of students to student interaction happened through meet up tools.

Most of "student to instructor" interactions take place through announcements. This is because announcements can be used in a variety of ways to push important information to students in MOOCs. In addition they help instructors to "write once so many can read." This allows MOOCs instructors to provide general information from a single location with the assurance that all students are receiving the information. While only a limited number of instructors used the tools "guides", "participate in online discussion with students", and "ask and answer questions" to interact with their students.

The most commonly interaction way that was used for "student to content" interaction is according to homework assignments. They help students to apply information previously learned in online classes. Homework assignments are short tasks that provide students immediately with feedback. In the same way, quizzes and tests are used widely in "student to content" interaction. With quizzes and tests, students take the entire assignment without feedback or the assistance of learning aids. Unlike homework assignments, a student can only receive feedback on a test or quiz once after its submission (Dorsey, 2011).

They allow students to keep up with the material and provide them with valuable formative feedback on what concepts they need to review. Moreover, these online quizzes and tests allow students to see how the concepts they are learning in lectures apply in the real world. Due to the lack of the instructor's role, using various strategies and instructional activities to deepen the learner´s understanding of the subject matter, little of "student to content" interaction in MOOCs happened through activities and submitting projects.

Student to student interaction is probably an absolute necessity for maximal achievement, socialization, and healthy development. It can foster learning through student collaboration and knowledge sharing (Sher, 2004). Blake (2009) discovered that students' interaction in online environment had significantly higher gains than those in a control environment with no "student to student" interaction.

Faust and Courenay (2002) assert that interactions between students fell into one of two categories: social interactions or course focused interactions. Based on their findings, four conclusions pertaining to "student to student" interactions include:

1. The structure of the course influences student participation and "student to student" interaction.
2. The interaction tools that are available in the course enhance participation.
3. Discussion patterns established early hinder some students' participation.
4. The social climate affects participation.

This finding is in line with a recent study by Murray, Giest and Hedrick (2012) who suggested that interaction between students is considered fundamental in MOOCs. It provides students with the feedback they need to determine when they are mastering the content of the course. Additionally it makes students become more actively engaged in the learning process, even leading to higher levels of learning.

MOOCs Platforms

Many place offer MOOCs, and many more will. But Coursera, Udacity and edX are the leading providers.

Coursera

Coursera is the most popular MOOC platform today. What makes Coursera unique is the wide range of subjects they cover. They have courses in Arts, Economics, Life Sciences, Law, Computer Science, Chemistry and many more, all taught by leading educators throughout the world. This great variety gives you incredible flexibility to explore as many topics as interest you, no matter how diverse your interests are.

Coursera does not produce the courses on their platform themselves, but rather allows universities to create them under a set of guidelines and a common structure, generally consisting of weekly short video lectures, content quizzes and assignments and also including a midterm and final exam but this varies between courses. Some have only quizzes and videos whilst others have only a final exam. Also, computing courses generally have automated coding assignments while humanities courses usually use peer-reviewed essay assignments.

Most courses offer free completion certificates (although not all) and some are eligible for Coursera's Signature Track.

Udacity

Udacity is another Stanford-born MOOC platform. Unlike Coursera, the emphasis was mainly on Computer Science but they have since expanded to include Mathematics, Physics, Business and Psychology courses to its catalog.

Also unlike Coursera, which has many introductory courses, Udacity courses are divided into three levels: beginner, intermediate and advanced. Each course also has requirements and follow-up courses, making it easy to plan a more structured, "degree-like" curriculum.

Udacity create all of their courses themselves and they follow their own unique pedagogy style with strict quality control. The team of instructors, teaching assistants and video editors work closely together to create courses that are well designed and highly polished.

edX

edX offered Engineering, Computer Science and Science courses but they now offer courses on Humanities and Liberal Arts too.

The nature of edX courses is much more similar to offline college courses than with the other platforms but there is a feeling of great polish and quality for each one, especially with their Computer Science assignments which are very in-depth and interactive. Unlike Udacity, courses are not self-paced and unlike Coursera, the courses usually last between 10-12 weeks as opposed to Coursera's shorter 5-8 week average.

Table 1 shows a comparative between the types of interaction and the necessary elements that promote this interaction in the platforms of Coursera, Udacity and edX.

MOOC platforms, as they are designed currently, do not reflect the new hybrid pedagogies necessary to teach within, through and about a digital environment. Many of their features have been simply lifted from various classroom methodologies.

Online communication tools, from e-mail and discussion boars to chat, instant messaging and web conferencing, provide powerful platforms to set up discussions among student, implement collaborative assignments, foster peer tutoring and review, and encourage greater communication between students and instructors. Asynchronous discussions, allowing time for reflection by the student, can produce greater depth of learning than the synchronous environment alone (Donaldson & Conrad, 2004). The nature of

Table 1. Interaction in the platforms Coursera, Udacity and edX

Type of Interaction	Description	Platforms
Face to Face interaction.	These platforms have elements like video chats or video calls that promote the face to face interaction.	None of the three
Synchronous distributed interaction.	These platforms have external elements like social networks or Meetup external platforms that promote synchronous distributed interaction.	Coursera, Udacity
Asynchronous interaction.	These platform have elements like announcements, videos, courses notes, documents and practices/ exercises evaluations that promote asynchronous communication.	Coursera, Udacity, edX
Asynchronous distributes interaction.	These platforms have elements like discussion forums among students, discussion forums between students and staff members and wikis that promote asynchronous distributes interaction.	Coursera, Udacity, edX

threaded discussion "allows all voices to be heard because (a) students are usually required to respond and their participation can be easily documented and (b) those who may be intimidated by speaking in front of their peers or those who need more response time are more easily able to participate" (Black, 2005). Certain situations best lend themselves to synchronous communications. Such activities include group meetings or activities requiring group consensus or simultaneous response. Synchronous discussions are especially useful for brainstorming or replicating the face to face situation and tend to be more successful when utilized by small groups. While both synchronous and asynchronous discussions have advantages and disadvantages, their use together in a blended learning situation is critical to the development of the online learning community. Asynchronous, threaded discussions "complemented by the synchronous use of virtual white boards and chat rooms, allow student teams to collaborate on group projects, coupling real-time learning activities with opportunities to communicate at their convenience" (McCracken, 2002).

Teaching in any environment involves providing content and "leading the student to analyze, synthesize, and exercise critical judgments. These advanced skills require a high amount of interactivity between professor and student, as well as collaboration among students" (Weiss, 2000). Interaction implies active students participation in the learning process, through intense and effective communication with the members of the learning community. Since it should not be assumed that students know how to communicate or behave online, instructors need to have not only the technical competence but, more important, they need to understand the dynamics of online communication and interactions and use effective ways of moderating and facilitating online dialogs. Moderating involves: encouraging students to participate, ensuring that some students do not dominate, keeping discussion focused, bringing out multiple perspectives and summarizing highlights of the discussion. Facilitating involves: providing information to help students complete assignments, suggesting ideas or strategies to help students pursue course work, getting students to reflect on their response and work (Kearsley, 2000).

FUTURE RESEARCH DIRECTIONS

Create groups of students in the different platforms with the objective of having a feedback of the elements that are needed to incentive the many types of interactions inside MOOCs and based on this feedback improve the prototype of interaction propose in this chapter.

CONCLUSION

Because the number of MOOCs in higher education grows continuously (Markoff, 2013), one are that has been identified as an important factor affecting students´ learning experiences in students´ interaction. Interaction in learning settings is a necessary and fundamental process for knowledge acquisition and cognitive development (Murray, 2012). Three main types of interaction are identified and focused. According to Moore (1989) the study deals with "student to student", "student to instructor", and "student to content" interaction. Although interaction id often viewed as necessary and important factor affecting students´ learning experiences in MOOCs, there is no clear strategy or hints of how online interaction should happen in MOOCs best so far. As a result, the present document shows the most important elements required to have good relationships in the different types of interaction.

REFERENCES

Adelsköld, G., Alklett, K., Axelsson, R., & Blomgren, G. (1999). Problem- based distance learning of energy issues via computer network. *Distance Education*, *20*(1), 129–143. doi:10.1080/0158791990200110

Al-Zoube, M. (2009). E-Learning on the Cloud. *Int. Arab J. e-Technol, 1*(2), 58-64.

Chamberlin, L., & Parish, T. (2011). MOOCs: Massive Open Online Coursesor Massive and Often Obtuse Courses? *E- learn Magazine*, 2011(8).

Choi, S., Lim, C., & Leem, J. (2002). Effects of Different Types of Interaction on Learning Achievement, Satisfaction and Participation in Web-Based Instruction. *Innovations in Education and Teaching International*, 39(2), 153-162.

Christopher, B. (2013). Learning about social learning in MOOCs: From statistical analysis to generative model.

Cruz, P. V. (2013). *SCOPEO*. Obtenido de SCOPEO: Retrieved from http://scopeo.usal.es/wp-content/uploads/2013/06/scopeoi002

Dasarathy, B., Sullivan, K., Schmidt, D. C., Fisher, D. H., & Porter, A. (May de 2014). The past, present, and future of MOOCs and their relevance to software. *Proceedings of the on Future of Software Engineering* (pp. 212-224). doi:10.1145/2593882.2593897

Dorsey, M. (2011). *Pearson Assignments: Quizzes, Tests, and Homework Explained*. Retrieved from http://www.myaccountinglabcommunity.com/custom/scripts/google-search-init.js

Future Learn. (2013). *Future learn launches*. Retrieved from http://futurelearn.com/feature/futurelearn-launches

Kanuka, H., & Anderson, T. (1998). Online social interchange, discord, and knowledge construction. *Journal of Distance Education*, *13*(1), 57–74.

Khalil, H., & Ebner, M. (2013). Interaction Possibilities in MOOCs – How Do They Actually Happen? *International Conference on Higher Education Development* (pp. 1-24).

Mak, S., Williams, R., & Mackness, J. (2010). Blogs and Forums as Communication and Learning Tools in a MOOC. *Proceedings of the 7th International Conference on Networked Learning* (pp. 275-284).

McAuley, A., Stewart, B., Siemens, G., & Cormier, D. (2010). Massive Open Online Courses Digital ways of knowing and learning. *The MOOC model For Digital Practice.*

Moore, M. G. (1989). Editorial: Three types of interaction. *American Journal of Distance Education*, *3*(2), 1–6. doi:10.1080/08923648909526659

Murray, M., Pérez, J., Geist, D., & Hedrick, A. (2012). Student Interaction with Online Course Content: Build It and They Might Come. *Journal of Information Technology Education*, *11*(1), 125–142.

Navarro, P., & Shoemaker, J. (2000). Performance and perceptions of distance learners in cyberspace. *American Journal of Distance Education*, *14*(2), 15–35. doi:10.1080/08923640009527052

Northrup, P. T. (2002). Online learners' preferences for interaction. *The Quarterly Review of Distance Education, 3*(2), 219–226.

Waard, L. (2011, July). *Explore a New Learning Frontier – MOOCs*. Retrieved from http://www.cedma-europe.org/newsletter%20articles/eLearning%20Guild/Explore%20a%20New%20Learning%20Frontier%20-%20MOOCs%20(Jul%2011).pdf

KEY TERMS AND DEFINITIONS

Asynchronous Communication: Is the exchange of messages, such as among the hosts on a network or devices in a computer, by reading and responding as schedules permit rather than according to some clock that is synchronized for both the sender and receiver or in real time. It is usually used to describe communications in which data can be transmitted intermittently rather than in a steady stream.

Good Design: It helps people to do things that we care about. It applied to Hardware and Software. Good Design has a tremendous impact on both the individual's ability to accomplish specific tasks and societies.

Human Computer Interaction: Is the study of how people interact with computers and to what extent computers are or are not developed for successful interaction with human beings.

MOOC: A course of study made available over the internet without charge to a very large number of people.

Online Learning Environments: Is a set of teaching and learning tools designed to enhance a student's learning experience by including computers and the Internet in the learning process.

Platforms: Is a raised stage, or a forum in which an idea can be shared, or a standard for computer hardware that determines what types of software it can run, or is a series of beliefs of a political group.

Social Interaction: Is the process by which we act and react to those around us. Let's examine the different types of social interaction and test your knowledge with a quiz.

Social Learning: Process in which individuals observe the behavior of others and its consequences, and modify their own behavior accordingly.

Synchronous Communication: Is the transmission of data, generally without the use of an external clock signal, where data can be transmitted intermittently rather than in a steady stream.

User Centered Design: The development is driven by the people´s tasks, goals, and values. It allows to work with users throughout the process and to assess decisions from their vantage point; their work; and their ecology including their abilities and situations. User centered Design focuses in developing technology to help people to do those that we care about.

User Experience: A person's perceptions and responses that result from the use or anticipated use of a product, system or service. User experience includes all the users´ emotions, beliefs, preferences, perceptions, physical and psychological responses, behaviors and accomplishments that occur before, during and after use.

Chapter 6

Online Community-Based Practices for Massive Open Online Courses (MOOCs) at Open Universities Australia: A Case Study

Mandi Axmann
Open Universities, Australia

Ren Atkins
Open Universities, Australia

ABSTRACT

Free online offerings or massive open online courses (MOOCs) have caused much controversy in the higher education sector. MOOCs are often criticized for having very low completion rates, not contributing much to the development of higher order thinking skills, and lacking academic rigor. This study aimed to investigate the learning elements which would offer students a sense of connection and deeper understanding of concepts by means of online community-based practices. This chapter reports on the findings from surveying 3,000 students that enrolled in free online offerings at Open2Study. Preliminary findings indicated that the learning elements of interaction and complexity rated highest for student motivation and learner engagement within free online offerings.

INTRODUCTION

Open Universities Australia launched the first of many Massive Open Online Courses (MOOCs) during April 2013. These courses, named as the Open2Study initiative, aimed to provide the following:

- Instruction from top instructors from leading universities, TAFEs and businesses;
- Ample choice of high-demand subjects available;
- High quality videos, simulators, short quizzes, auto-graded assessments and discussion forums to support learner engagement;

DOI: 10.4018/978-1-4666-9743-0.ch006

- A variety of tools and methods to support peer connection and collaboration;
- Flexible online study that fits around the learner's schedule; and
- Free subject offerings to the general public.

Currently, the Open2Study free online courses have 145,234 enrolled students from 217 countries across 49 courses, as illustrated by Figure 1. Courses range from Agriculture, Physics, Astronomy, Financial Literacy all the way to Anthropology and Chinese Language and Culture.

Each course comprises four modules with an overall course duration of four weeks. The courses consist of a series of short videos totaling approximately four hours, quizzes related to the video content, a weekly auto-graded assessment, additional resources and readings, and an online discussion forum.

A small team of Online Learning Facilitators posts between four and seven discussion points or questions in each Open2Study course to encourage students to connect with one another and engage in dialogue relevant to the course material. Social media platforms such as Google+, Twitter and Facebook are also utilized by the facilitators to provide students with additional opportunities to work together on weekly challenges and to share resources with one another. Additional connection and collaboration tools provided on the platform include a 'connect' feature (similar to the Facebook 'friend' feature), direct messaging and synchronous chat functions.

Course grades are calculated from the weekly assessments, with a pass achieved by attaining an average of 60% or above. Students who pass a course are awarded a Certificate of Achievement.

Retention rates are often cited as a concern for MOOCs (Koller, Ng, Do, & Chen, 2013). According to the Ontario Online Learning Portal for Faculty and Instructors, Contact North (2013), a total MOOC enrolment in 2013 is estimated at between 3.6 million and 5 million learners. The average completion rate is usually quoted at being below 10%. However, completion rates do not always reflect learner intent.

Figure 1. Open2Study community dashboard

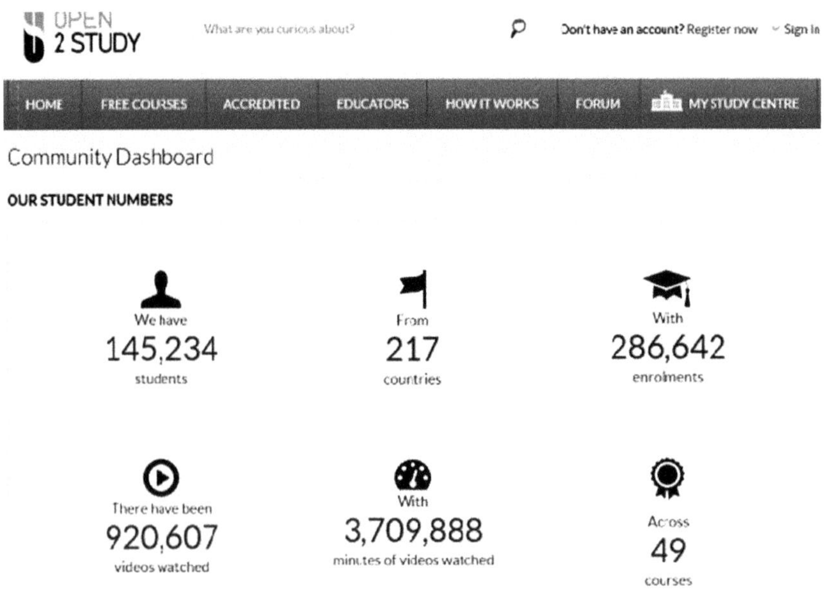

In an analysis of a business strategy MOOC offered via the Coursera MOOC platform, Gilliani (2013) found that the majority of the most active discussion forum participants achieved an overall course grade below 50%, indicating that many active MOOC students are more interested in connecting with other students and engaging in meaningful dialogue than in meeting the requirements to pass the course.

Initial research analysis reported the average completion rate for Open2Study over the first 4 cohorts for 2013 as 26%, which sets it at a higher completion rate than the average. Case study research excels at bringing us to an understanding of a complex issue or object, and may provide contextual analysis of a limited number of events or conditions and their relationship (Zikmund, 2003). This study investigates which learning elements may offer students a sense of belonging to and real connection with and within a group. It also sets out to discover how students would find meaning and deepen their understanding of concepts through well designed online community activities.

BACKGROUND

Much attention has been given to the creation of online learning communities, including asynchronous (anytime) learning such as online discussion forums, wikis and blogs, to develop and sustain social interaction (Bruckman, 2004; Jones, 2007). However, Kehrwald (2008) underlines that: '...since the identification of a social presence as a key component of online learning, a single, shared understanding of social presence has not yet emerged' (p. 89).

During 2008, George Siemens and Stephen Downes offered the first massive open online course (MOOC), and thereby offering free online materials to thousands of students (Siemens, 2012). This sent waves of repercussions throughout the higher education environment, and compelled higher education institutions to rethink their own teaching and learning strategies.

Cognitivism and constructivism are prominent learning theories implemented within the design and development of instructional environments (O'Donnel, Mulwa, Sharp, & Wade, 2013). According to Siemens (2012) these theories were developed in a time when learning was not as heavily influenced by technology as today. In many fields the life of knowledge is now measured in months and years, instead of decades or centuries (Downes, 2012), and this impacts on the design of online education environments.

The potential exists to create robust courses that are responsive to knowledge and information evolution, and also create learning networks and social support infrastructure for students (Francisco, 2013). However, connectivism is a modernist approach and not without critique. One of the main issues is privacy and student learning management, as many of the more popular social media lies outside of the existing learning management systems (Rodriguez, 2012). A further criticism is that learner engagement and support becomes a near impossible task with hundreds of students enrolled in a course (Palmer & Holt, 2012).

MAIN FOCUS OF THE CHAPTER

Issues, Controversies, Problems

Making use of a more traditionalist instructional approach, developing and designing learning objects learning pathways and specific learning activities can be a very laborious and time-consuming task (Chen,

Pedersen, & Murphy, 2011). However, by making use of a connectivism approach, existing learning networks and social media infrastructures could be leveraged to cut down on instructional design time (Downes, 2012).

This would also create avenues where the most recent and updated knowledge and information can be readily accessed, without having to continuously redesign course content. Figure 2 illustrates a classroom on the Open2Study platform.

Figure 2. Open2Study: Foundations in Psychology

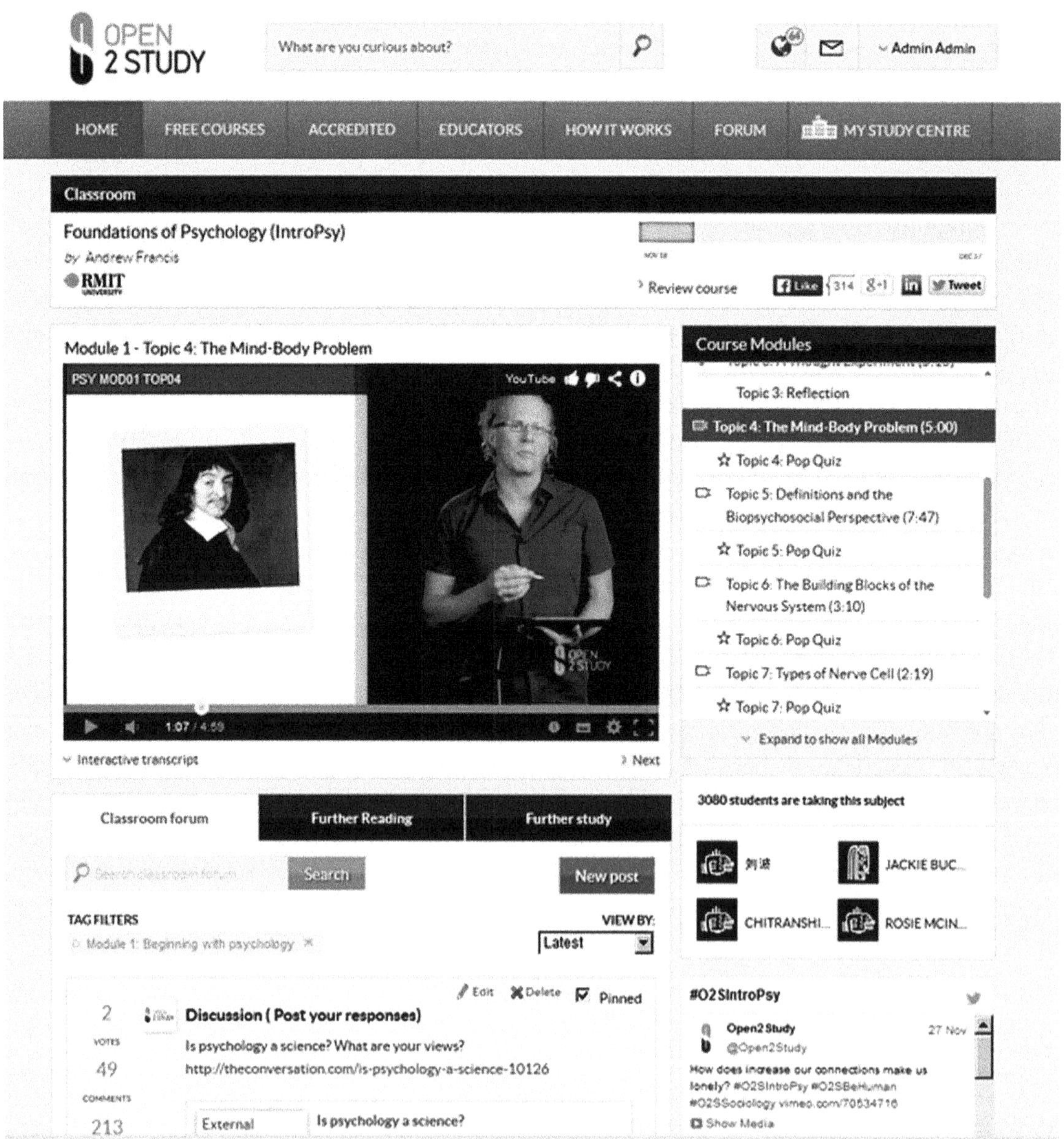

A study conducted by some of the major founders of Coursera (Koller, et al., 2013) offers a detailed look at learner intent as a critical factor in retention. In total, roughly 5% of students who signed up for a Coursera MOOC earned a credential signifying official completion of the course. This equals between 2,000 and 3,000 completions.

Due to different motivations and levels of interest, many students start a MOOC with no intention of completing the assignments. Students are most often university graduates who are following their own interest levels, and retention should be considered in the context of learner intent.

According to Koller et al (2013), committed learners, who tend to stay engaged throughout most or all of a MOOC class, can be divided into at least three partially overlapping groups: passive participants, active participants, and community contributors:

- Passive participants engage with a MOOC predominantly through watching lecture videos, have limited participation on course forums, and typically attempt few assignments and quizzes (but may interact with in-video questions as needed to progress through the video content).
- Active participants engage in course content by completing homework assignments, quizzes, exams, and time-intensive programming or peer-graded assessments; they include the subset of "course completers" who do all the work necessary to earn a Statement of Accomplishment.
- Community contributors also actively participate in courses, but their specific means of interaction is through generation of new content, such as engaging in forum discussions or contributing foreign language subtitles.

This study set out to discover which elements would contribute to encouraging students from passive to active participants that also become community contributors. The Open2Study platform was viewed as a case study and a sample of students were surveyed to this aim.

Project Aim

The goal of education is to provide students with the skills they need to achieve their own life goals, not to retain individuals in a classroom (Griffin, Care, Bui, & Zoanetti, 2013). The aim of the study was to

- Explore which learning elements offer students a sense of belonging to and real connection with and within a group.
- Discover how students would find meaning and deepen their understanding of concepts through well designed online community activities.

Given the broad range of motivations in the population of students who participate in MOOCs, the true challenge of online education will be to identify what students want to get from their virtual classroom experience and help them achieve those goals.

Methodology

A survey of 17 test items was compiled, asking respondents about the following elements presented in Table 1.

Table 1. Elements considering during survey

Elements	Aspects
Confidence	• Studying online • Previous completed studies
Motivation	• Levels of motivation • What motivated them to enroll in the course? • What motivated them to complete the course? • Time preference • Learner expectations
Enjoyment	• What they enjoyed most? • If they could change one thing about the course?
Interaction	• Social media pages • Online collaboration
Growth	• Rate on a scale of 1-10 your understanding before the course • Rate on a scale of 1-10 your understanding after the completion of the course
Demographic data	• Age • Highest level of education • Most recent attempt at study • Online study experience

A sample population of 3,000 students was selected as possible participants, adhering to the following criteria (see Table 2):

The survey was made available from 29 January to 6 February 2014. A total of 442 (n=442) responses were received, a total percentage of 14.73% of the total population. This is considered a substantial percentage for online survey responses.

Of the 442 survey respondents, 62.7% were aged 40 or above, 66.3% had a bachelor, postgraduate or doctoral degree, and 61.5% reported having studied online before. Just over half of the respondents (50.5%) reported that prior to commencing their course with Open2Study, they felt 'very confident' in their ability to succeed.

Analysis

A great deal of data was collected, and the preliminary analysis of the data revealed the following trends. For the purpose of this chapter, the qualitative analysis conducted in NVivo, a qualitative research analysis software package (Richards, 2002), of the open-ended type questions focused on the elements that motivated students to be engaged and to complete the course.

Table 2. Criteria for Students' selection

Survey Invitation Sent	Category	Selection Criteria
1,000 invitations	Passed Participated in community forum	Achieved a passing grade of 60% or higher and participated at least three times in the classroom discussion forums
1,000 invitations	Passed Did not participate in community forum	Achieved a passing grade of 60% or higher but did not participate in the forums
1,000 invitations	Incomplete Did not participate in community forum	Did not meet the requirements to pass their course and did not participate in the classroom discussion forums

Recommendations for Courses

Students attached the most value to the variety of choice of courses, the navigation of the courses and the ability to self-pace. Requests were also made for language availability (Spanish, French), accreditation of the efforts, and more information on courses. It was also important for students to be able to see the full course from the beginning, and not have selective release of the course content (Figure 3).

Specific comments made by students were as follows:

- Certificates verification (free recommended) would further enhance the value of it.
- The certificate must be certified by experts so it can be used to enhance the personal profile.
- To create a series, where one could continue to learn in the subject that one is interested in. For example, I really enjoyed Early Childhood Education and would love to continue to study that subject because I learned very helpful information.
- I wish courses were self paced, because sometimes even if you're motivated to finish a course but since you don't have enough time you are forced to abandon the course half way.
- Unlock the course from the beginning, making available all the exams and modules from the start of the course ... allowing end before if possible.

Recommendations for Online Communication

In terms of the various online collaboration activities available, students were not rating so much a specific type of tool (such as online discussion, Twitter, Facebook), but rather demanded the interaction between lecturer and student and student to student, regardless of the type of tool.

Of the 442 respondents, 68.6% reported being frequent social media users who used a social media platform at least once a day. Many students engaged with the social elements of the Open2Study courses, with 75.1% of respondents reporting that they made use of the online discussion forum, one of the dedicated Open2Study social media accounts, chat, direct messaging, connections, or a combination of two or more activities.

Figure 3. Qualitative analysis of the recommendations for courses

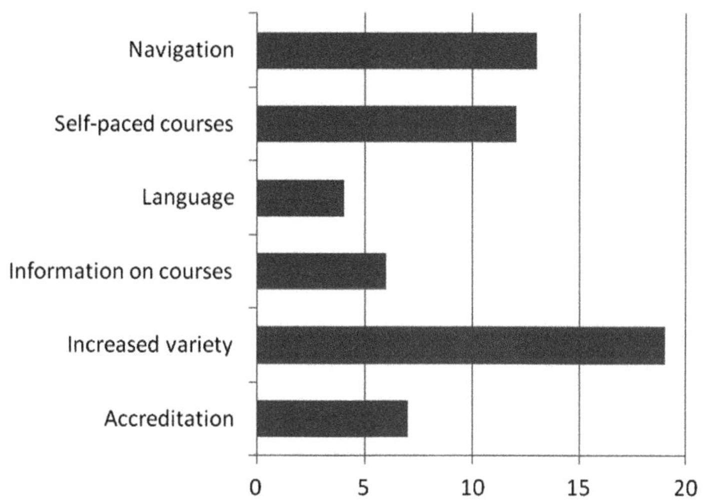

However, many students felt that they were not motivated or encouraged enough to participate with other course participants. It seemed interesting that the students required some specific activity around this, and that it could not merely be left to chance or informal interaction.

Students want the navigation around the discussion forum to be easy and accessible (Francisco, 2013). Students also required specific topics and examples to discuss. By necessity for reasons of scale, MOOCs are generally designed to be run and re-run with minimal or no input from the instructor, instead relying on facilitators or the concept of "teachers on the side" (Rodriguez, 2012). Although the Open2Study facilitators posted at least four questions or discussion points in each course, it is noteworthy that more than one survey respondent commented that the course instructors were expected to be more involved with discussion, and pose specific questions or topics (Figure 4).

Specific comments made by students were as follows:

- There was nothing motivating me to contact others taking the course. I ticked all the boxes, and saw no reason to use the forum or chat with others.
- More examples and topics to encourage discussion
- Some involvement of staff in discussions.
- I would like the discussion forums to be easier to use. I found it hard to navigate around the forum and I don't remember there being a lot of discussion topics. Maybe you could have teaching assistants to help by posting questions and answering.
- Discussion forums were fairly quiet. Perhaps the instructor could pose a question for discussion for each unit.

Recommendations for Course Content

Students appear to be motivated by detailed discussion, in-depth exploration of the subject area and a variety of media (Boyle & Ravenscroft, 2012). In courses where the quizzes and assessment tasks were perceived as too easy, students requested an increased level of complexity.

Figure 4. Qualitative analysis of the recommendations for online communication

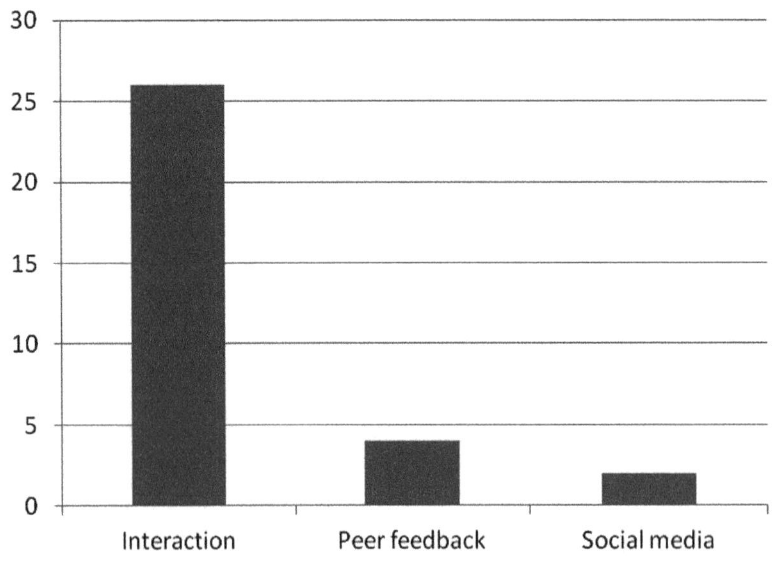

The main element for learner motivation and engagement was not the videos, quizzes, content or assessment, but rather the complexity related to these content items. Students want to be challenged and have opportunities for application of their knowledge (Osman-Schlegel, Fluker, & Cheng, 2011). Students also requested a challenge question related to the subject matter, and disliked the quiz answers being too easy or too obvious.

This finding also correlates with Vygotsky's zone of proximal development (Vygotsky, 1978) namely that students require tasks which are not too easy, but requires for them to stretch out of their comfort zone (Figure 5).

Specific comments regarding course content made by students were as follows:

- Don't be so easy.
- More detailed discussions and study.
- Explore more depth on the subject or create more courses for further study.
- There needs to be more variety in presenting the information other than video. There needs to be more in-depth questions.
- Make the assessments more challenging, more in depth.
- Make it a bit harder. Or add a challenge question that requires more research etc.
- Increase the level of complexity.
- More challenging courses about written correspondence and tender writing.
- More opportunities to apply the knowledge.
- Do not make quiz question answers too obvious.

Figure 5. Qualitative analysis of the recommendations for course content

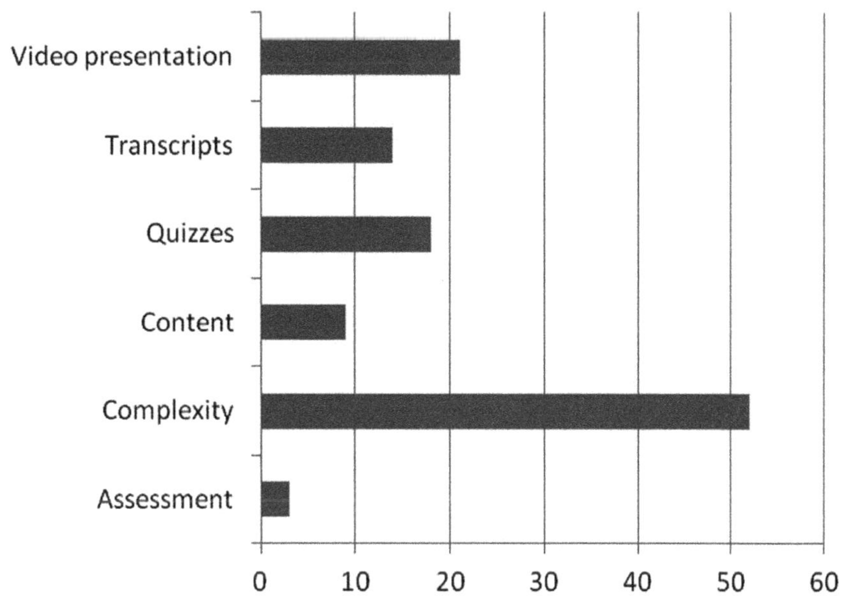

Findings

When designing learner engagement within online free offerings, there are certain aspects to take into account. These aspects could be equally important for higher education paid online programs. Recommendations from the qualitative analysis of the open-ended type questions can be summarized as follows (see Table 3).

The true challenge of online education is to identify what students want to get from their virtual classroom experience and help them achieve those goals (O'Donnel, et al., 2013). Students attach value to their time spent on learning, and want to obtain the most from their learning experience even if in a free online offering.

SOLUTIONS AND RECOMMENDATIONS

Students seem to be most interested in a variety of learning offerings. Students are motivated by structured interaction, to be challenged and to feel that they have achieved a greater level of competence by increasing levels of complexity (Oreilly, Lefoe, Philip, & Parrish, 2010).

Many online courses include multi-media objects such as quizzes and videos. However, these objects by themselves do not allow the online course to be interactive or even engaging (Könings, Brand-Gruwel, & Merriënboer, 2010). For student engagement and motivation, learning activities such as projects need to be designed based on the multi-media objects.

Table 3. Recommendations from the qualitative analysis of the open-ended type questions

Elements	Aspects
Courses	- Provide a variety of courses with the ability to self-pace; - Have translations of courses available where possible; - Do not have selective release within the courses, but rather have all content available to students - Make available a variety of multi-media objects available (not just quizzes and videos, but also scenarios, case studies and projects) - Award some sort of certificate of attendance - Create a series of courses that are linked and related to each other.
Online communication	- Regardless of the types of online communication tools available (Google apps, twitter, Facebook, discussion), provide specific activities for students to engage with related to the content; - Provide an intuitive and accessible navigational structure for the discussion forum; - Make available topics, examples and case studies for students to engage with; - Encourage interaction with other group members with collaborative projects or peer reviews; - The instructor or community manager needs to be present in the online discussion, posting thought-provoking questions or topics for debate; - Offer online support from the instructor or community manager when students are experiencing difficulties with the course content, this can also be in the form of a virtual assistant. - Afford reasons for students to make use of the discussion forum or chat to others.
Course content	- Motivate students by providing opportunities for in-depth exploration of the study area; - Increase the level of complexity for assessment types and quizzes through the duration of the course; - Challenge students by providing problems related to the subject matter; - Make available opportunities to apply knowledge; - Present information in a variety of different formats to keep students interested and engaged.

The same concept applies to online communication tools. Simply providing students with avenues for communication (such as Google chat, Twitter, Facebook, discussion forum) does not make for meaningful interaction (Bradley, 2010). Structured activities need to be provided to encourage students to engage in the learning process.

FUTURE RESEARCH DIRECTIONS

Massive open online courses are gradually changing perceptions about the nature of online learning (Gilliani, 2013). A plethora of small, competency-based free online offerings are saturating the further education market, and students are expecting rapid learning within sleek, sophisticated online learning environments.

Students are more prepared than ever to learn within online, self-paced environments. The rise of social media created further expectations of online communication and collaboration (Oreilly, et al., 2010). Students are also becoming more discerning and sophisticated online learners, and are more demanding of multi-media objects, video presentations and the complexity of the learning design. This will in the future heavily impact on the expectations set on higher education.

CONCLUSION

This chapter reported on the findings from surveying 3,000 students that enrolled in free online offerings at Open2Study. Preliminary findings indicated that the learning elements of interaction and complexity rated highest for student motivation and learner engagement within free online offerings.

A small team of Online Learning Facilitators encourage students to connect with one another and engage in dialogue relevant to the course material. Gilliani (2013) found that the majority of the most active discussion forum participants achieved an overall course grade below 50%, indicating that many active MOOC students are more interested in connecting with other students and engaging in meaningful dialogue than in meeting the requirements to pass the course.

Due to different motivations and levels of interest, many students start a MOOC with no intention of completing the assignments. Students are most often university graduates who are following their own interest levels, and retention should be considered in the context of learner intent.

This study set out to discover which elements would contribute to encouraging students from passive to active participants that also become community contributors. The Open2Study platform was viewed as a case study and a sample of students were surveyed to this aim.

Students attached the most value to the variety of choice of courses, the navigation of the courses and the ability to self-pace. In terms of the various online collaboration activities available, students were not rating so much a specific type of tool (such as online discussion, Twitter, Facebook), but rather demanded the interaction between lecturer and student and student to student, regardless of the type of tool.

Students appear to be motivated by detailed discussion, in-depth exploration of the subject area and a variety of media (Boyle & Ravenscroft, 2012). In courses where the quizzes and assessment tasks were perceived as too easy, students requested an increased level of complexity. Students want to be challenged and have opportunities for application of their knowledge (Osman-Schlegel, et al., 2011). These increases in student expectation, learner engagement and student motivation may in the future heavily impact on the expectations set on higher education.

REFERENCES

Boyle, T., & Ravenscroft, A. (2012). Context and deep learning design. *Computers & Education*, *59*(4), 1224–1233. doi:10.1016/j.compedu.2012.06.007

Bradley, J. (2010). Promoting and Supporting Authentic Online Conversations - Which Comes First - The Tools or Instructional Design? *International Journal of Pedagogies*, *5*(3), 20–31. doi:10.5172/ijpl.5.3.20

Bruckman, A. (2004). Co-Evolution of Technological Design and Pedagogy in an Online Learning Community. In S. Barab, R. Kling, & J. Gray (Eds.), *Designing Virtual Communities in the Service of Learning (Learning in Doing: Social, Cognitive and Computational Perspectives)*. Cambridge: Cambridge University Press. doi:10.1017/CBO9780511805080.013

Chen, C. Y., Pedersen, S., & Murphy, K. L. (2011). Learners' perceived information overload in online learning via computer-mediated communication. *Research in Learning Technology*, *19*(2), 101–116. do i:10.1080/21567069.2011.586678

Downes, S. (2012). *Connectivism and connective knowledge: essays on meaning and learning networks*. Canada: National Research Council.

Francisco, J. M. (2013). Learning in collaborative settings: Students building on each other's ideas to promote their mathematical understanding. *Educational Studies in Mathematics*, *82*(3), 417–438. doi:10.1007/s10649-012-9437-3

Gilliani, N. (2013). Learner Communications in Massively Open Online Courses. Retrieved from http://oxcheps.new.ox.ac.uk/MainSite%20pages/Resources/OxCHEPS_OP53.pdf

Griffin, P., Care, E., Bui, M., & Zoanetti, N. (2013). Development of assessment design and delivery of collaborative problem solving in the assessment of teaching of 21st century skills project. In E. McKay (Ed.), *ePedagogy in online learning: new developments in web mediated human computer interaction* (pp. 55–73). Hershey, PA: IGI Global. doi:10.4018/978-1-4666-3649-1.ch004

Jones, S. (2007). Online Discourse: Encourage active student participation in large classes. In E. McKay (Ed.), *Enhancing learning through Human-computer interaction*. Hershey: Idea Group Reference. doi:10.4018/978-1-59904-328-9.ch005

Kehrwald, B. (2008). Understanding social presence in text-based online learning environments. *Distance Education*, *29*(1), 89–106. doi:10.1080/01587910802004860

Koller, D., Ng, A., Do, C., & Chen, Z. (2013). Retention and intention in massive open online courses: In depth. *EDUCAUSE Review*.

Könings, K. D., Brand-Gruwel, S., & Merriënboer, J. J. G. (2010). An approach to participatory instructional design in secondary education: An exploratory study. *Educational Research*, *52*(1), 45–95. doi:10.1080/00131881003588204

North, C. (2013). Ontario Online Learning Portal for Faculty and Instructors. Retrieved from http://contactnorth.ca/home

O'Donnel, E., Mulwa, C., Sharp, M., & Wade, V. (2013). Web mediated education and training environments: a review of personalised interactive eLearning. In E. McKay (Ed.), *ePedagogy in online learning: new developments in web mediated human computer interaction* (pp. 188–208). Hershey, PA: IGI Global. doi:10.4018/978-1-4666-3649-1.ch012

Oreilly, M., Lefoe, G., Philip, R., & Parrish, D. (2010). Designing for user engagement: The ALTC Exchange for higher education. *International Journal on E-Learning*, *9*(2), 251.

Osman-Schlegel, L., Fluker, G., & Cheng, S. T. (2011). Working collaboratively in a group assignment using MediaWiki for an architecture and construction management undergraduate unit. *Paper presented at the Ascilite*.

Palmer, S., & Holt, D. (2012). Trajectories of engagement: A repeated cross-sectional investigation of student perceptions of an online learning environment. *Research in Learning Technology*, *20*(3), 253–265.

Richards, L. (2002). Rigorous, rapid, reliable and qualitative? Computing in qualitative method. *American Journal of Health Behavior*, *26*(6), 425–430. doi:10.5993/AJHB.26.6.3 PMID:12437017

Rodriguez, C. O. (2012). MOOCs and the AI-Stanford like Courses: Two Successful and Distinct Course Formats for Massive Open Online Courses. *European Journal of Open, Distance and E-Learning*, 2012.

Siemens, G. (2012). George Siemens on Massive Open Online Courses (MOOCs) and recent useful resources. Retrieved from http://facultyecommons.org/george-siemens-on-massive-open-online-courses-moocs-and-recent-useful-resources/

Vygotsky, L. S. (1978). *Mind in society: The development of higher psychological processes*. Cambridge, MA: Harvard University Press.

Zikmund, W. G. (2003). *Business Research Methods* (7th ed.). Mason, Ohio: Thomson Learning.

ADDITIONAL READING

Boyle, T., & Ravenscroft, A. (2012). Context and deep learning design. *Computers & Education*, *59*(4), 1224–1233. doi:10.1016/j.compedu.2012.06.007

Dainoff, M. J. (2009). Can't We All Just Get Along? Some Alternative Views of the Knowledge Worker in Complex HCI Systems. *International Journal of Human-Computer Interaction*, *25*(5), 328–347. doi:10.1080/10447310902864944

Dick, W., & Carey, L. (2006). *The Systematic Design of Instruction* (6th ed.). NY: HarperCollins College Publishers.

Dix, A., Finlay, J., Abowd, G., & Beale, E. (1993). *Human-computer interaction*. New York: Prentice Hall.

Ellis, R. A., Jarkey, N., Mahony, M. J., Peat, M., & Sheely, S. (2007). Managing quality improvement of eLearning in a large, campus-based university. *Quality Assurance in Education*, *15*(1), 9–23. doi:10.1108/09684880710723007

Fleischmann, K. R. (2009). Sociotechnical Interaction and Cyborg-Cyborg Interaction: Transforming the Scale and Convergence of HCI. *The Information Society*, *25*(4), 227–235. doi:10.1080/01972240903028359

Gagné, R. M., & Merrill, M. D. (1990). Integrative goals for instructional design. *Educational Technology Research and Development*, *38*(1), 23–30. doi:10.1007/BF02298245

Graham, C. R., & Dziuban, C. (2008). Blended learning environments. In J. M. Spector, M. D. Merrill, J. V. Merrienboer, & M. P. Driscoll (Eds.), *Handbook of research on educational communications and technology* (3rd ed., pp. 269–275).

Gregory, J., & Jones, R. (2009). 'Maintaining competence': A grounded theory typology of approaches to teaching in higher education. *Higher Education*, *57*(6), 769–785. doi:10.1007/s10734-008-9175-8

Grudin, J. (2008). A moving target: the evolution of HCI. In A. Sears & J. A. Jacko (Eds.), *The human-computer interaction handbook: fundamentals, evolving technologies and emerging application* (2nd ed.). NY: Taylor and Francis Group.

HEFCE. (2005). *HEFCE Strategy for E-Learning*. Higher Education Funding Council for England.

Ho, M. R., Smyth, T. N., Kam, M., & Dearden, A. (2009). Human-Computer Interaction for Development: The Past, Present, and Future. *Information Technologies & International Development*, *5*(4), 1–18.

Jonassen, D. H. (2005). Tools for representing problems and the knowledge required to solve them. In S. O. Tergan & T. Keller (Eds.), *Knowledge visualization and information visualization: Searching for synergies, LCNS (Vol. 3246, pp. 82-94)*. Berlin: Springer-Verlag. doi:10.1007/11510154_5

Jones, S. (2007). Online Discourse: Encourage active student participation in large classes. In E. McKay (Ed.), *Enhancing learning through Human-computer interaction*. Hershey: Idea Group Reference. doi:10.4018/978-1-59904-328-9.ch005

Kehrwald, B. (2008). Understanding social presence in text-based online learning environments. *Distance Education*, *29*(1), 89–106. doi:10.1080/01587910802004860

Kirschner, P. A., Sweller, J., & Clark, R. E. (2006). Why minimal guidance during instruction does not work: An analysis of the failure of constructivist, discovery, problem-based, experiential, and inquiry-based teaching. *Educational Psychologist*, *41*(2), 75–86. doi:10.1207/s15326985ep4102_1

Könings, K. D., Brand-Gruwel, S., & Merriënboer, J. J. G. (2010). An approach to participatory instructional design in secondary education: An exploratory study. *Educational Research*, *52*(1), 45–95. doi:10.1080/00131881003588204

Lauwers, T. (2010). Aligning capabilities of interactive educational tools to learner goals. [Unpublished Thesis 3470163]. Carnegie Mellon University, United States -- Pennsylvania.

Limniou, M., & Smith, M. (2010). Teachers' and students' perspectives on teaching and learning through virtual learning environments. *European Journal of Engineering Education*, *35*(6), 645–653. doi:10.1080/03043797.2010.505279

Marcus, A. (2008). Global/intercultural user interface design. In A. Sears & J. A. Jacko (Eds.), *The human-computer interaction handbook: fundamentals, evolving technologies and emerging applications* (2nd ed.). NY: Taylor and Francis.

McKay, E. (2008). *The human-dimensions of human-computer interaction: Balancing the HCI Equation*. Amsterdam: IOS Press.

McKay, E., & Martin, J. (2007). Multi-disciplinary collaboration to unravel expert knowledge: Designing for effective human-computer interaction. In M. J. Keppel (Ed.), *Instructional Design: Case studies in communities of practice*. Hershey, PA: Information Science Publishing. doi:10.4018/978-1-59904-322-7.ch016

Meister, D. (1989). *Conceptual aspects of human factors*. Baltimore: Johns Hopkins University Press.

Merrill, M. D. (2002). First principles of instruction. *Educational Technology Research and Development*, *50*(3), 49–59. doi:10.1007/BF02505024

Merrill, M. D., Barclay, M., & Van Schaak, A. (2008). Prescriptive principles for instructional design. In J. M. Spector, M. D. Merrill, J. V. Merriënboer, & M. P. Driscoll (Eds.), *Handbook of research on educational communications and technology* (pp. 173–186). NY: Lawrence Erlbaum Associates.

Miles, K. S. (2010). Reconceptualizing Analysis and Invention in a Post-Techne Classroom: A Comparative Study of Technical Communication Students. *Technical Communication Quarterly*, *19*(1), 47–68. doi:10.1080/10572250903373056

KEY TERMS AND DEFINITIONS

Case Study: A case study is an implementation of a research method involving an up-close, in-depth, and detailed examination of a subject of study (the case), as well as its related contextual conditions. Although no single definition of the case study exists, case-study research has long had a prominent place in many disciplines and professions, ranging from psychology, anthropology, sociology, and political science to education, clinical science, social work, and administrative science.

Free Online Offerings: This term refers to online courses offered by most of the schools around the world. These classes are typically offered as part of an Open Course Ware (OCW) project. Materials can be accessed at any time and the coursework is self-directed, though no academic credit is awarded for course completion.

Learner Engagement: Also known as Student Engagement, this term refers to the degree of attention, curiosity, interest, optimism, and passion that students show when they are learning or being taught, which extends to the level of motivation they have to learn and progress in their education. Generally speaking, This concept is predicated on the belief that learning improves when students are inquisitive, interested, or inspired, and that learning tends to suffer when students are bored, dispassionate, disaffected, or otherwise disengaged. Stronger student engagement or improved student engagement are common instructional objectives expressed by educators.

Massive Open Online Courses (MOOCS): MOOCs are online courses aimed at unlimited participation and open access by web. In addition to traditional course materials such as filmed lectures, readings, and problem sets, many MOOCs provide interactive user forums to support community interactions between students, professors, and teaching assistants (TAs). MOOCs are a recent and widely researched development in distance education [1] which was first introduced in 2008 and emerged as a popular mode of learning in 2012.

Online Community-Based Practices: Also known as a Virtual Community of Practice (VCoP), is a Community of Practice (CoP) that is developed on, and is maintained using the Internet. To qualify as an OCoP, the characteristics of a Community in Practice (CoP) as described by Lave and Wenger must be met. To this end, an OCoP must include active members who are practitioners or experts, in the specific domain of interest. Members must participate in a process of collective learning within their domain. Additionally, social structures must be created within the community to assist in knowledge creation and sharing. Knowledge must be shared and meaning negotiated within an appropriate context. Community members must learn through both instruction-based learning and group discourse. Finally, multiple dimensions must facilitate the long-term management of support as well as enable immediate synchronous interactions.

Student Motivation: Some authors define this concept as "A student's willingness, need, desire, and compulsion to participate in, and be successful in, the learning process." Nevertheless, there are many perceptions and approaches to be able to have a single definition.

Chapter 7
Using Design Patterns to Incorporate Usability in Notifications from MOOCs

Ricardo Mendoza-González
Instituto Tecnológico de Aguascalientes, Mexico

ABSTRACT

Feedback provided by interactive systems is crucial to ensure a good user experience. In this vein, notifications represent the most common kind of feedback from interactive systems, such as MOOCs. In this scenario, notifications from system to users require a special look from designers since three basic types of interaction/communication converge in MOOCs: User-User; User-Platform (content); User-group. Every kind of interaction may require a specific mode of notifications, nevertheless it is possible to extract the basic types of notifications from MOOCs and then specify them into a pattern-based structure which could be easily incorporated into the systems life cycle. This strategy may contribute both to facilitate designers to create well designed notifications for MOOCs and to enhance user experience through its final application.

INTRODUCTION

Currently Massive Open Online Courses (MOOCs) have had a tremendous impact on education and its popularity increases day by day. Millions of users around the world use MOOCs through courses management platforms such as edX, Coursera, Udacity, and many more (Gutierrez-Rojas, et al. 2014; Riel & Lawless, 2014). This massive availability of contents, tools, and many kinds of learning resources, demands timely effective notifications (feedback from the course) in different levels such as content-user; user-user; course staff-user, among others, disclosing and distributing information about new content available; remainders of specific deadlines; third-parties involved; new activities uploaded; comments from students or instructors; and even the list of student joined to the course (Riel & Lawless, 2014; Kay et al., 2013; Knox et al., 2013).

DOI: 10.4018/978-1-4666-9743-0.ch007

In order to provide distribution of notifications or remainders many course management platforms implements e-mail services and SMS instant messages to mobile devices (Kay et al., 2013). This information is complemented by messages from the platform to users showed during the course by means of dialogue boxes; pup-ups; plain text; figures; graphs; stats; among other graphic elements (Agrawal, Kumar, & Agrawal, 2015). Independent to the form of notifications it is important that this feedback goes in-line with the coherent learning sequence of the MOOC; learning materials; assessments; and other activities available to ensure an adequate learning (Kay et al. 2013).

Said notifications are required to help students and other stakeholders keeping track of deadlines and whole set of course activities. Interactive distribution of this kind of information is common and relatively "easy" in face to face courses; nevertheless it becomes a complex task in MOOCs because there are thousands of students enrolled in a specific course and they are in different locations and / or countries.

As mentioned before, notifications are strongly related to the kind of communication (content-user; user-user; course staff-user, among others). In this vein, MOOCs provide several scenarios and tools when feedback and notifications from the system are required, such as forums where registered students in MOOCs courses are able to post comments and ask questions in this scenario feedback from facilitators is also required but the large number of students makes really difficult to provide this kind of feedback in a timely manner (Shatnawi, Gaber, & Cocea, 2014).

Independently of the scenario, students enrolled to MOOCs courses demand feedback that responds questions such as: What it means: good performance? What is my own performance? What it means the difference between current performance and the good one? And, what can I do to close these gaps? Timely feedback represents a crucial factor here and delays may compromise the advances in learning by the students (Yair, 2014). Related to previous aspects, Price et al (2014) emphasize seven principles to consider in order providing good feedback for students enrolled to MOOCs courses. Broadly speaking, these set of principles are addressed to promote incorporate of clear definitions of those levels of performance in order to complement detailed information about the specific student's performance. Both should be conveyed to students in a proper manner, this means that information should encourage certain reflections in the student on her / his personal learning performance.

As mentioned above, it is very important that feedback related to any communication form valid for MOOCs should be well designed. In this way a good design brings people joy since a well-designed technology helps them to complete complex tasks, long activities, or even those daily little things that care people about (Klemmer, Hartmann, & Takayama, 2006). In order to achieve well designed technologies it is necessary to implement a User Centered Design process (UCD) complemented with Human-Computer Interaction techniques. Before continuing it is important to define these two concepts; User Centered Design emerged from Human Computer Interaction (HCI) is a methodology commonly used, but not limited, for software development and it is oriented to help designers and developers to create technology that meet the needs of the users (Lowdermilk, 2013). On the other hand, HCI focuses in provide tools, strategies, and theories to effectively perform the design, implementation, and evaluation of user interfaces (particularly for those computers related) (Dix et al., 2004). Additionally, well designed technology is oriented to provide good user experiences (UX). According to Lowdermilk (2013), UX is a term used to summarize the entire experience of a (software) product, not only focusing on functionality but also strongly considering how delightful a technology is to use.

Joining together previous paragraphs, it is possible to visualize the importance of providing well designed notifications to MOOCs students, considering important factors such as adequacy to the MOOCs content and momentum, deepness, clarity, and individuality. The impact of these aspects increases when MOOCs provide feedback on assessments and assignments because notifications from MOOCs should convey information that really helps students to improve their learning.

There is no doubt that notifications plays a crucial role on how MOOCs provides feedback to students and that well designed notifications could encourage a good user experience, which at the same time, relates to one of the bigger gaps on MOOCs, the massive desertion of students.

BACKGROUND

Bearing in mind general aspects contextualized above, there are several proposals that discuss the problem and provide alternatives oriented to tackle those related issues from different perspectives and approaches. Following, some of the most significant works are summarized highlighting their main porpoise.

- **Encouraging Forum Participation in Online Courses with Collectivist, Individualist, and Neutral Motivational Framings:** This research reported an interesting study that revealed the importance of the time when encouragement emails should be sent to students enrolled in online courses (e.g. MOOCs). Authors found that neglecting this aspect could lead to negative (contrary) effects. They also observed that framing of communications such as individual "Student benefit from participation"; collectivist "Everyone benefits from participations"; and neutral "Forum general-participations" provoked a similar behavior on learners. Authors' findings suggested that neutral encouragements for participations achieve better results while it was convenient dosage those non-neutral reminders. (Kizilcec, Schneider, Cohen, & McFarland, 2014)
- **ASQ: Interactive Web Presentations for Hybrid MOOCs:** Authors of this research created a tool called ASQ, which is addressed to help teachers to gather real-time feedback from students while delivering their lectures. ASQ is an HTML5 presentations how-based application, which includes sets of questions into slides oriented to promote and enhance bi-directional communication between the teacher and a large audience. Bi-directional questions are combined with specific timely notifications and feedback from the tool to take advantage from idle time to ask for and providing feedback. (Triglianos, & Pautasso, 2013)
- **How Students Learn Using MOOCs: An Eye-Tracking Insight:** This research work reported findings from an eye-tracking based study on MOOCs. Authors used stimuli-based notifications to foster student's focus on specific areas of the user interface. Findings helped to identify a relation between stimuli-based gaze variables and indicators for performance and learning strategies. This study was reported as the basis for a long term analysis of gaze variable data to define students' profiles considering performance and learning strategy. Authors consider a concept called Area of Interest (AOI), which is said to be missed by a participant who does not look at a particular AOI at all during the period that AOI was presented on the stimulus. It could be translated to complete ignoring some parts of the slides. This information could be used to give feedback to students about what they missed in the lecture and also about students' re-reading behavior. (Sharma, Jerman, & Dillenburg, 2014)
- **A Platform that integrates quizzes into Video:** Authors proposed a platform which suggest integrating a set of several lightweight quizzes through a MOOC lectures, highlighting the beneficial effects embedded to this strategy which are supported by pedagogical background. The set of

quizzes are complemented by videos and a searchable multimedia encyclopedia whose individual lessons could be incorporated to other websites. The project is oriented to achieve - in the short time – support for real-time production of quizzes, and also open the platform to crowdsourcing in order to encourage enhancements on the implementation of quizzes strategies in MOOCs. (Woll, Buschbeck, Steffens, Berrang, & Loviscach, 2014)

- **Structure and Messaging Techniques for Online Peer Learning Systems that Increase Stickiness:** Authors emphasize the role of software to encourage scaffolding of peer interactions focusing on contextual data to complement wide data in order to offer feedback that foster intuitions from students on feedback provided. Authors concludes interesting aspects related to said situation stating that when peer systems and curricula are well integrated, the social context is illuminated and teachers' and systems designers' intuitions for scaffolding are guided by software, students do adopt these systems. (Kotturi, et al., 2015)
- **Automatic Content Related Feedback for MOOCs Based on Course Domain Ontology:** Authors provide a strategy for automatic feedback providing based on content-knowledge from posts on MOOCs forums. This strategy uses course domain ontology and provides students with timely informative automatic feedback. Additionally, this approach provides facilitators with information about students' posts such as frequent topics students ask about. Authors concluded that domain ontology complemented with Neuro-Linguistic Programming (NLP) can scaffold teaching and learning processes in MOOCs being domain ontologies an effective representation of course context knowledge. (Shatnawi, Gaber, & Cocea, 2014)
- **A Study on the K_MOOC Platform Standardization Measures:** In this research was presented an interesting study oriented to analyze those specific features that a MOOC platform should cover in order to provide an adequate ecology for online learning. For this particular case, said features were reinforced considering the current status and research trends in MOOCs adapted to the specific Korean social and cultural context into a particular platform called K-MOOC. After their application, the findings obtained from this research was structured into a set of standardization measures which were then expanded to support user-centered teaching and learning commonly used in general courses. The components of the proposed platform include teaching and learning management systems, teaching and learning contents management system, teaching and learning contents authoring system, smart device support system, integrated search system, user management system, operation and management system, and learning outcomes management system. (Kim, 2015)

MAIN FOCUS OF THE CHAPTER

Issues, Controversies, Problems

As mentioned before, interest in MOOCs grows every day around the world joining scientific and academic communities in a common cause "Improve current MOOCs to exploit them in benefit of learning people". Experts from diverse areas putting together their ideas and propose valuable strategies such as approaches, frameworks, standards, interactions, educational models, methods and methodologies, among others all of them oriented to said goal.

Analyzed research works were not the exception, authors of these researches provided interesting scenarios of applications and MOOCs' platforms which are currently in operation. All of them summarized particular aspects from their findings some of them from the technological internal structure of MOOCs platforms, other from the vantage point of content and educational strategies to follow but all of them converge in the importance of consider users into the process of creating MOOCs and MOOCs' platforms. From this specific vantage point derive several opportunities for enhancements in current MOOCs platforms and services.

There is no doubt that interactions and environments offered by available MOOCs are into this set of improvements to do. In this vein, it is necessary to increase the researches from the Human-Computer Interaction and User eXperience vantage point. Considering that changes in the environment may change behaviors, it is crucial to analyze, more in depth, those issues related to interactions between users / learners – platform, platform – teacher, between users / learners – teachers.

Obviously this is not a "piece of cherry pay", it require a lot of hard work in research and analysis including studies focused on user experience oriented to identify behaviors and reactions from users to specific interactions. Then, those findings should be structured into strategies such as models, approaches, methods, and methodologies that guide developers to achieve adequate MOOCs environments that encourage effective massive on-line learning.

A good starting point could be to analyze the communication between users and MOOCs platform, specifically the notifications provided by the system to the users in order to inform them about several aspects including both course related information (e.g. content, activities, news, assessments, resources available, other students enrolled, among others) and system information (e.g. internal errors, success or failure in information uploads, among others).

There are several researches that aboard the feedback problem in MOOCs from the perspective of massive communication teacher - students and vice versa. This is one of the most critical pain-points in MOOCs and it relates with other serious aspect "The massive desertion in massive on-line learning". Nevertheless, a step before this communication level, it is important to ensure an adequate design and structure of the notifications provided from the MOOCs platforms to the users. Whether the notifications are well designed could improve the user experience with current automatic feedback generators and simulate most "human" interactions offering students individual feedback and suggestions of learning improvements most personalized. Additionally, the users could perceive more control over the system since it will keep them correctly informed about the status of the activities with, on, and even under the platform, e.g. security notifications when personal or confidential information is managed.

SOLUTIONS AND RECOMMENDATIONS

Aspects described in previous sections demand attention from diverse areas, in this case the solutions and recommendations provided here are oriented to contribute from the interactions design particularly from the perspective of notifications' design. According to the paragraphs at issues controversies and problems, notifications from MOOCs' platforms to users represent a good starting point to contribute mitigating the problem. In this way, a good strategy could be establish a set of design patterns oriented to provide designers and developers the basics to achieve well designed notifications.

In order to conform this approach first, a user centered design strategy should be structured which could be the applied to gather feedback from target users (e.g. students enrolled in a MOOC) about their user experience with the platform specifically with notifications provided by the platform through the lectures, assessments, among other class activities. This information will lead the content of the patterns which will be then structured to facilitate its comprehension and application. A good alternative is to use patterns structure. A pattern is widely known (in general terms) as a proven solution to a specific problem in a certain environment (Buschmann, et, al., 1999), according to this definition it is possible to take the user feedback in its abstract form and extract and order the knowledge hidden into it by means of a patterns fashion structure.

Following previous general path here was proposed a set of design patterns oriented to reinforce current notification available in MOOCs platforms and to suggest / provide other that are not available yet but that could contribute to offer a better user eXperience. This strategy rises from the idea that the feedback of any interactive system should include elements that facilitate operation and use of the available system features including interactions, resources, content, and communications, among other services. The proposed patterns were structured into a non-exhaustive classification which is divided in three principal levels considering the basic aspects to handle a user interface of an interactive system:

- **Informative Feedback**: This level includes those design patterns useful to guide developers and designers to convey and present users information about: content features available, the correct way to use these features, and internal status of the system through particular activities (e.g. work for assessment upload). This level also includes suggestions for designing notifications related the request of complementary information about specific resource or activity available during a particular lecture. This level integrates three sub-levels, system outlook that includes design suggestions about internal and content related tasks, features and services available for a particular MOOC (or even for a particular lecture); additional feedback that includes guides to design both general interactive notifications and for particular or specific situations; and auditive feedback which concentrate those guidelines to design complementary notifications to highlight important situations that require immediate attention. It is important to mention that in this case a complementary feedback was selected to reinforce visual notifications offering a multimodal interface based in auditive feedback.
- **Interaction Feedback**: This level brings together those interactive notifications that could be useful to encourage a comfortable and fluent navigation and operation of principal features and services manipulation. This level includes design patterns with suggestions to provide feedback addressed to facilitate enabling or disabling specific features, complemented by interactive notifications to present suggestions of actions to follow when some problem (from both platform internal or related to content, services, resources, or activities) is detected. The interaction level integrates three sub-levels that include guidance to design notifications about services available (abled or disabled), navigation through the available services in a particular lecture, and dialogues including both informative dialogues, and suggestive dialogues.
- **Interactive Feedback**: This level collects those design patterns oriented to facilitate the specification, design, and implementations of interactive notifications oriented to convey information related to internal activities and actions are taken when interactive elements of the interface,

services, features, or content are handled or activated by means of the mouse, keyboard, stylus, or gestures such as touch, swipe, pinch, among others (if a touch screen is available). This level is sub-divided into sublevels accuracy and contextual which treat, respectively, those interactive notifications for indicate localization and limits of specific areas, resources, or features available; and to provide quick descriptions of user interface components.

Table 1 present the description of some of the design patterns for notifications proposed. This represents a fragment of the entire collection conformed by twenty six design patterns. In this case, one pater from each sub-level was selected. Chosen patterns are structured under the well-known format provided by Professor Erik Gamma, which includes a common design problem to mitigate, the context of the design problem, a motivational situation for the use of a specific pattern, and a suggested solution provided (Gamma et al., 1994).

Proposed design patterns offered simple solutions easy but powerful and reliable, easy to be implemented by designers and developers. Additionally are supported by traditional statements from human computer interaction such as consistency in interfaces design and simple feedback conveyed from system to users, basics to avoid bad designs (Nielsen, 1999).

FUTURE RESEARCH DIRECTIONS

This research is intended to provide a starting point for other contributions in order to improve the user eXperience in MOOCs. Particularly, to consolidate and reinforce this proposal some important aspects are visualized as future venues to explore, being one of the most immediate the materialization of the suggested set of patterns through several prototypes using rapid prototyping techniques. Said stage of this project is currently underway. Prototypes will be the axis of a longitudinal study oriented to obtain feedback from real MOOCs' users. Information gathered will be used not only to improve prototypes but also to refine the solutions offered by the current set of patterns and the reinforcement of it by incorporating new patterns and even levels to the classification.

There is no doubt that MOOCs topic has a tremendous impact and a wide spectrum for research opportunities and designing notifications is one of the most important by its implications to other ones.

On the other hand mobile, aspects should be considered too since several researches emphasize the importance and positive impact to explore possibilities in mobile for MOOCs. By example, (Raza, 2014) states that mobile learning is a potential cost alternative to expensive training programs. In this vein mobile notifications are also a way to explore, having the opportunity to analyze gestural interfaces commonly applied in mobile devices. Additionally, performing studies to find discrepancies or similitudes among behaviors and reactions from users when interact with specific notifications in web MOOCs against their mobile version. According to this idea, (Covadonga & Iniesto, 2015) suggest to provide users mobile options oriented to facilitate accessibility to learning resources, better communicating tools, or even personalized user interfaces taking advantage from the virtues of mobile social technologies available improving accessibility from both, content and user preferences.

Explore more alternatives for multimodal interfaces for MOOCs; this topic is currently in vogue by example, (Ezen-Can, et al. 2015) which authors highlight the importance of supporting learning with rich natural language dialogue focusing on adaptive learning environments with natural language input, improved by leveraging multimodal cues to understand learners better. Authors investigate the positive

Table 1. A fragment of the set of design patterns for notifications for MOOCs

Informative Feedback	
Pattern's Name	**Description**
Tasks information	Problem: How to provide users useful information about the status of features and resources available during their use? Context: It is important to inform users about those situations related to usage of specific elements of the user interface, resources, and features available in order to encourage an environment of control over the system. Motivation: Providing users with a controlled environment could increase confidence in the system. Suggested Solution: To incorporate to the MOOCs platforms slide banners with announcements about important things happening when some feature, service, or resource is in use.
Adds of Information	Problem: How to provide users of sufficient information about usage of a particular service, resource, feature, or interaction available through the time of a lecture or during the whole course? Context: Sometimes additional or complementary information is necessary to clarify particularities of use or vantages and limitations of specific services, features, resources, or interactions available. Motivation: When users are well informed about the virtues of a particular service, feature, resource, or interaction available in a MOOCs platform, it could be most profitable for users increasing possibilities for learning. Solution: Offer users possibilities and alternatives to get additional information about a particular service, feature, resource, or interaction available in a MOOCs platform by integrating links or automatic messages, contacts for questions via mail, among others.
Multimodal Information	Problem: How to highlight important or urgent aspects avoiding being too much interruptive? Context: Sometimes there are some situations that may require to be treated urgently, such as security issues, e.g. accounts access-attempts. Motivation: If users are well informed about some threats such as identity thief they will trend to trust in the system. Suggested Solution: Inform users about those threats detected during a lecture or course even when users are off-line. A good alternative is to incorporate multimodal notifications to highlight a potentially serious situation. A common multimodal solution is to reinforce visual notifications with auditive notifications.
Interaction Feedback	
Pattern's Name	**Description**
Status of services	Problem: How to proper inform users about those specific features, services, resources, and interactions available for a specific lecture or for the entire MOOC? Context: Users need to be informed about those specific features, services, resources, and interactions available in order to achieve complete learning experience. Motivation: When users know what specific features, services, resources, and interactions are available they may select the most adequate tool or strategy to increase learning according to their personal or particular needs and capabilities. Suggested Solution: Integrate a panel that shows those specific features, services, resources, and interactions available highlighting those that are active for a specific lecture. Integrate a description of the lecture from the beginning including a list and brief description of those tools available for the particular lecture.
Navigation Information	Problem: How to encourage fluent navigation though the features, services, resources, and interactions available? Context: Fluent navigation reduces the cognitive load in users allowing them to get focus on the content of the lecture. Motivation: If MOOCs platforms provide users with fluent and comfortable navigation, they instantly trend to perceive MOOCs easy to use and this may contribute to increase the user interest in offered content. Suggested Solution: Integrate consistency in user interfaces designs and to provide users with interaction with no more than three levels in depth (usability cost).
Information Boxes	Problem: How to provide more control to users over the MOOC platform in a particular lecture or during the entire course? Context: Users may require of certain flexibility in how content, features, services, resources, and interactions available are conveyed from MOOCs platforms. Motivation: Whether users are allowed to make some fine adaptations in how information or tools are conveyed they could create a semi-custom environment which at the same time could enhance the user eXperience and learning. Suggested Solution: To incorporate dialogue boxes that allow users to change some specific features available in order to create an environment that contribute to cover their particular learning needs.
Interactive Feedback	
Pattern's Name	**Description**
Mark Off Information	Problem: How to inform users about the area limits of particular features, services, resources, and interactions available? Context: Sometimes users need to be aware of where ends a specific control, feature, interaction, service, or other resource. Motivation: When users are conscious of area limits they have more control over the infractions available and contributes to more comfortable navigation and usage. Suggested Solution: to integrate changes in the shape of the mouse cursor that get activate when limits of particular features, services, resources, ore interactions were exceeded.
Quick Context	Problem: How to provide users briefs about the usage or basic features of a particular services, resources, and interactions available? Context: Sometimes users require a quick look into features or usage way for particular features, services, resources, and interactions available. Motivation: Providing users with quick contextual information about particular features, services, resources, and interactions available could contribute to better use of them through the course or a specific lecture deriving in a better use and learning experience. Suggested Solution: Integrate tip tags in specific interface an interactive components could provide a concise context about usage and purpose.

impact of utilize posture and gesture features in learning models. Other alternative is described at (Yadav et al., 2015) where authors show the advantages to integrate non-linear navigation in educational videos using features derived from a combination of audio and visual content of a video. They propose a system that provides multiple dimensions for quickly navigating to a given point of interest in a video including customized dynamic time-aware word-cloud, video pages, a 2-D timeline, among others resources.

All of mentioned alternatives suggested to explore as future researches are suitable with the main purpose of this chapter "improve the user eXperience by means of well designed environments", starting from the notifications offered to the users from the system. All the analyzed scenarios require of well designed notifications which should offer, at the same time, a diversity of interactions and consider the best place in canvas to be conveyed to the user, this could be interpreted like a chez game when player try to find the best strategy to win. In this case the price is a good design of ecology for MOOCs' students, which could be achieved by a correct strategy of development and design.

Another interesting road to explore in these venues is the assessment and providing feedback to students from students. This idea consist in encourage participation of advanced students in peer reviewing and providing feedback to other students. This strategy had been previously explored by (Piech, et al., 2013; Huang, et al., 2013) and authors concluded that represents a viable strategy that could impact positively in MOOCs from both obtaining / giving personalized peer feedback, and maintaining the massiveness of MOOCs. This last topic is closely related to the different ways that student engage with learning through MOOCs, as stated in (Conole, 2013).

CONCLUSION

Massive Open Online Courses (MOOCs) represent a revolution for higher education and learning in general and more and more people are interested on them. Currently many improvements for MOOCs including design suggestions, big data management, security aspects, among others are available, even some of them had been applied and multiple variants of MOOCs have emerge such as the Selectively Open Online Courses (SOOCs) which, essentially, adds an entrance requirement to mitigate the diversity problem that comes integrated to massiveness in MOOCs, in other words SOOCs allow everyone to apply but access is restricted to a smaller number of students in the range of hundreds and not of ten thousands (Hall, 2014; Raza, 2014). Even SOOCs have a variant, the Selective Private Online Courses (SPOCs) which are closed or private to a particular set of students, e.g. The SPOC "The Architectural Imaginary" from HarvardX which initially was available just for the Design School incoming students, after a time the course will be open to a wide audience (Fox, 2013; Daniel, Vázquez-Cano, & Gisbert, 2015).

Ideas like SOOCs and SPOCs are interesting and may have good results in tackling one of the principal problems in MOOCs, the management and providing of individual feedback, this because of the reduction of enrolled students. However, at the same time this alternative reduce the principal virtue of MOOCs their massiveness.

Certainly, current MOOCs platforms and MOOCs content provided needs a lot of work to make them more adequate to offer a better learning experience for users. But the suggested improvements need to be addressed to preserve massiveness and openness. Perhaps, the key is to change the idea that MOOCs could be the substitute of "on-campus education" and perceive MOOCs as a complement for students enrolled in on-campus programs (like a textbook), but also like a complete on-line course that provide learning for people around the world, free and with good quality contents without the intention of substitute Universities or other learning institutes. In this vein several studies such as (Khalil, & Ebner, 2013; Hernández - Rizzardini, et al., 2013; Du, 2014; Zheng, et al., 2015) emphasize the importance of online tools in creating efficiencies in both teaching and learning performance in students. Actually, some Universities use MOOCs as a tool for students recruitments (Choudaha, Chang, & Kono, 2013; Karsenti, 2013).

Having this vantage point, it could be easy to create solutions, improvements, or reinforcements for current MOOCs leading to better results which could derive in useful environments for learning opened to thousands of students with diverse backgrounds.

In this way, this chapter is intended to contribute to improve MOOCs according to the current trends e.g. maintaining environments that encourages interactive and dynamic learning experiences, incorporating challenging activities such as short assessments after each lecture, integrate illustrative videos and / or video games to complement learning lectures, integrate options to show or offer specific pricing or rewards for students. These topics are undoubtedly the principal motivations for this proposal.

In order to help closing gaps in making MOOCs more interactive and dynamic, in this chapter was suggested a strategy with guidance for designers and developers to integrate better communications from the system to the users. The proposal was structured as a set of patterns to design notifications from MOOCs platform to the students. These notifications could be perceived to foster communications from MOOC platform – users; Staff (including Faculty) – Users; and Content – Users.

To conform this proposal were analyzed several alternatives which goes from timely feedback providing to students via e-mail, to gathering real-time feedback from students while faculty delivering their lectures. Other researches reviewed provided interested findings from an eye-tracking based study on MOOCs, helping to identify relations between stimuli-based gaze variables and indicators for performance and learning strategies. Similarly, were reviewed several strategies which suggested integrating a set of several lightweight quizzes through a MOOC lectures, highlighting the beneficial effects embedded to this strategy which are supported by pedagogical background, in this way several authors emphasized the role of software to encourage scaffolding of peer interactions focusing on contextual data to complement wide data in order to offer feedback that foster intuitions from students on feedback provided. Other authors provide a strategy for automatic feedback providing based on content-knowledge from posts on MOOCs forums.

Even though previous efforts analyzed for this chapter are good ideas and intentions are correctly addressed, such as the feedback generators, all of them fail in concentrate the idea for the alternative solution in a user centered design strategy where user leads the following path during the design project. User should be included since early stages of the process implementing human computer interaction methods and tools to gather feedback which could be applied in a controlled manner contributing to create evolutionary designs. Thus, the proposed patterns are intended to improve notifications design for MOOCs platforms easy to be incorporated into a user centered design strategy. A good set of well-designed notifications could represent a good alternative to starting improvements in the environments provided by MOOCs platforms for users. These improvements will derive into most interactive content which could foster a most individual attention and feedback for users.

As a final comment, it is important to bear in mind that although most of the alternatives and approaches, strategies, tools, methods, models, and methodologies for better MOOCs design and development currently available in literature go towards total automation there always be gaps that could be filled only with the intervention of human experts in a particular topic or subject whose propose new activities, do updates to the content, suggest new quizzes forms, among other activities.

REFERENCES

Agrawal, P., Kumar, A., & Agrawal, A. (2015). Massive Open Online Courses: EdX.org, Coursera.com and NPTEL, A Comparative Study Based on Usage Statistics and Features with Special Reference to India. *Proceedings of the 10th International CALIBER,* Shimla, Himachal Pradesh, India (pp. 390-403). INFLIBNET.

Buschmann, F., Maunier, R., Rohnert, H., Sommerlad, P., & Stal, M. (1999). *A System of Patterns. Pattern-Oriented Software Architecture*. Siemens Ag, Germany: Wiley.

Choudaha, R., Chang, L., & Kono, Y. (2013). International Student Mobility Trends 2013: Towards Responsive Recruitment Strategies. *World Education News & Reviews, 26*(2)

Claros, I., Cobos, R., Guerra, E., De Lara, J., Pescador, A., & Sánchez-Cuadrado, J. (2013). Integrating open services for building educational environments. *Proceedings of the Global Engineering Education Conference,* Berlin, Germany (1147-1156). IEEE. doi:10.1109/EduCon.2013.6530253

Conole, G. (2013). MOOCs as disruptive technologies: strategies for enhancing the learner experience and quality of MOOCs *Revista de Educación a Distancia*, 39.

Covadonga, R., & Iniesto, F. (2015). Holistic vision for creating accessible services based on MOOCs. *Proceedings of the Open Education Global Conference*, Banff Calgary, Alberta, Canada, Open Education Consortium.

Daniel, J., Vázquez-Cano, E., & Gisbert, M. (2015). The Future of MOOCs: Adaptive Learning or Business Model? *Universities and Knowledge Society Journal*, *12*(1), 64–74. doi:10.7238/rusc.v12i1.2475

Dix, A., Finlay, J., Aboud, G. D., & Beale, R. (2004). *Human – Computer Interaction* (3rd ed.). Essex, England: Pearson / Prentice Hall.

Du, Y. (2014). Massive Open Online Course: The Implication to iSchool Education. Proceedings of iConference, Berlin, Germany (884–888).

Ezen-Can, A., Grafsgaard, J. F., Lester, J. C., & Boyer, K. E. (2015). Classifying student dialogue acts with multimodal learning analytics *Proceedings of the Fifth International Conference on Learning Analytics And Knowledge*, Poughkeepsie, NY, USA (280-289). ACM Press. doi:10.1145/2723576.2723588

Fox, A. (2013). From MOOCs to SPOCs. *Communications of the ACM*, *56*(12), 38–40. doi:10.1145/2535918

Gamma, E., Helm, R., Johnson, R., & Vlissides, R. (1994). *Design Patterns: Elements of Reusable Object-Oriented Software*. United States: Addison-Wesley Professional Computing.

Gutierrez-Rojas, I., Alario-Hoyos, C., Pérez-Sanagustin, M., Leony, D., & Delgado-Kloos, C. (2014). Scaffolding Self-learning in MOOCs. Proceedings of European MOOCs Stakeholders Summit Lausanne, Switzerland (pp. 43-49).

Hall, O., Jr. (2014). Future Trends in MOOCs and SOOCs in Management Education. *Proceedings of Society for Information Technology & Teacher Education International Conference* Chesapeake, VA, (pp. 192). Association for the Advancement of Computing in Education (AACE).

Hernández - Rizzardini., R., Gütl, C., Chang, V, & Morales, M. (2013). MOOC in Latin America: Implementation and Lessons Learned. *Proceedings of the 2nd International Workshop on Learning Technology for Education in Cloud*, Kaohsiung, Taiwan (pp. 147-158). Springer.

Huang, J., Piech, C., Nguyen, A., & Guibas, L. (2013). Syntactic and Functional Variability of a Million Code Submissions in a Machine Learning MOOC. *Proceedings of the Workshop on Massive Open Online Courses,* Memphis, Tennessee, USA, LCNS (pp. 25-32), , Springer Verlag.

Karsenti, T. (2013). What the research says. *International Journal of Technologies in Higher Education, 10*(2), 23–37.

Kay, J., Reinmann, P., Diebold, E., & Kummerfeld, B. (2013). MOOCs: So Many Learners, So Much Potential…. *IEEE Intelligent Systems, 28*(3), 2–9. doi:10.1109/MIS.2013.66

Khalil, H., & Ebner, M. (2013). How satisfied are you with your MOOC? - A Research Study on Interaction in Huge Online Courses. *Proceedings of World Conference on Educational Media and Technology,* Victoria, Canada (pp. 830-839). Association for the Advancement of Computing in Education (AACE).

Kim, JI. (2015). A Study on the K_MOOC Platform Standardization Measures. *International Journal of Software Engineering and its Applications, 9*(1), 221-236.

Kizilcec, R. F., Schneider, E., Cohen, G. L., & McFarland, D. A. (2014). Encouraging Forum Participation in Online Courses with Collectivist, Individualist, and Neutral Motivational Framings. In Proceedings of European MOOCs Stakeholders Summit, Lausanne, Switzerland (pp. 80-87).

Klemmer, S., Hartmann, B., & Takayama, L. (2006). How bodies matter: five themes for interaction design. In *Proceedings of the 6th conference on Designing Interactive systems* (pp. 140-149), University Park, PA, USA, ACM Press. doi:10.1145/1142405.1142429

Knox, J., Ross, J., Sinclair, C., Macload, H., & Bayne, S. (2013). MOOC Feedback: Pleasing All the People? In S. D. Krause & C. Lowe (Eds.). Invasion of the MOOCs: The Promise and Perils of Massive Open Online Courses (98-104), San Francisco, CA: Parlor Press

Kotturi, Y., Kulkarni, C., Berstein, M. S., & Klemmer, S. (2015) Structure and Messaging Techniques for Online Peer Learning Systems that Increase Stickiness. *Proceedings of L@S*, Vancouver, Canada (pp. 31-38). ACM Press. doi:10.1145/2724660.2724676

Lowdermilk, T. (2013). *User Centered Design: A Developer's Guide to Building User – Friendly Applications. Sebastopol.* CA: O'Reilly.

Martin-Monje, E., Bárcena, E., & Read, T. (2014). *Peer-to-peer interaction and linguistic feedback in foreign language MOOCs. Revista Profesorado, 18(1).* Universitat de Oberta de Catalunya.

Neubaum, G., Wichmann, A., Eimler, S., & Krämer, N. (2014). Investigating Incentives for Students to Provide Peer Feedback in a Semi – Open Online Course: An Experimental Study. *Proceedings of International Symposium on Open Collaboration*. Berlin, Germany, ACM press. doi:10.1145/2641580.2641604

Nielsen, J. (1999). *Designing Web Usability*. United State, New Riders.

Piech, C., Huang, J., Chen, Z., Do, C., Ng, A., & Koller, D. (2013). Tuned Models of Peer Assessment in MOOCs. *Proceedings of The 6th International Conference on Educational Data Mining*, Memphis, Tennessee, United States.

Price, M., Handley, K., Millar, J., & O'Donovan, B. (2010). Feedback: All the effort, but what is the effect? *Assessment & Evaluation in Higher Education*, *35*(3), 277–289. doi:10.1080/02602930903541007

Raza, M. (2014). MobiSOOCs for In-Service Teacher Education: Design Considerations for Developing Countries. *Proceedings of the e-Skills for Knowledge Production and Innovation Conference*, Cape Town, South Africa (pp. 371-381).

Riel, A., & Lawless, K. A. (2014). Massive Open Online Courses (MOOCs) and the Technologies That Support Learning with Them. In M. Khosrow-Pour (Ed.), *Encyclopedia of Information Science and Technology* (3rd ed., pp. 7529–7535). Hershey, PA: IGI Global Publishing.

Sharma, K., Jerman, P., & Dillenburg, P. (2014). How Students Learn Using MOOCs: An Eye-Tracking Insight. In Proceedings of European MOOCs Stakeholders Summit Lausanne, Switzerland (pp. 80-87).

Shatnawi, S., Gaber, M., & Cocea, M. (2014). Automatic Content Related Feedback for MOOCs Based on Course Domain Ontology. *Proceedings of the Intelligent Data Engineering and Automated Learning*, Wroclaw, Poland, Springer International Publishing (pp. 27-35). doi:10.1007/978-3-319-10840-7_4

Triglianos, V., & Pautasso, C. (2013). ASQ: Interactive Web Presentations for Hybrid MOOCs. *Proceedings of the WWW Conference* Rio de Janeiro, Brazil (pp. 209-210). ACM Press.

Whitelock, D., Gilbert, L., & Wills, G. (2013). Feedback Generators: Providing Feedback in MOOCs. *Proceedings of the Computer Applications and Quantitative Methods in Archaeology,* Western, Australia (pp. 1-6). CAA Publishing.

Woll, R., Buschbeck, S., Steffens, T., Berrang, P., & Loviscach, J. (2014). A Platform that Integrates Quizzes into video. Proceedings of European MOOCs Stakeholders Summit, Lausanne, Switzerland (pp. 80-87).

Yadav, K., Shrivastava, K., Prasad, M. P., Arsikere, H., Patil, S., Kumar, R., & Deshmukh, O. (2015). Content-driven Multi-modal Techniques for Non-linear Video Navigation. *Proceedings of the 20th International Conference on Intelligent User Interfaces*, Atlanta, GA, United States (pp. 333-344). ACM Press. doi:10.1145/2678025.2701408

Yair, Y. (2014). Did You Let a Robot Check My Homework? *ACM Inroads*, *5*(2), 33–34. doi:10.1145/2614512.2614522

Zheng, S., Rosson, M. B., Shih, P. C., & Carroll, J. M. (2015). Understanding Student Motivation, Behaviors and Perceptions in MOOCs. *Proceedings of the 18th ACM Conference on Computer Supported Cooperative Work & Social Computing*, Vancouver, Canada (pp. 1882-1895) ACM Press. doi:10.1145/2675133.2675217

ADDITIONAL READING

Burrow, L. (2013). What can MOOCs do for you?: Local Implications of a Global Phenomenon. *Proceedings of Society for Information Technology & Teacher Education International Conference* (pp. 280-282). Chesapeake, VA: Association for the Advancement of Computing in Education (AACE).

Chen, Y. (2014). Investigating MOOCs through blog mining. *The International Review of Research in Open and Distributed Learning*, *15*(2).

Chen, Y., & He, W. (2013). Security risks and protection in online learning: A survey. *The International Review of Research in Open and Distributed Learning*, *14*(5).

Dimitriadou, C., Palaiologou, N., & Nari, E. (2014). E-Learning Training Courses on Multicultural Education: An Example from Greece. In V. Zuzevičiūtė, E. Butrimė, D. Vitkutė-Adžgauskienė, V. Vladimirovich Fomin, & K. Kikis-Papadakis (Eds.), *E-Learning as a Socio-Cultural System: A Multidimensional Analysis* (pp. 102–116). Hershey, PA: Information Science Reference. doi:10.4018/978-1-4666-6154-7.ch006

Greene, J. (2014). Introductory Study Using MOOCs for Homeless Education. *Proceedings of World Conference on E-Learning in Corporate, Government, Healthcare, and Higher Education* 2014 (pp. 724-728). Chesapeake, VA: Association for the Advancement of Computing in Education (AACE).

Jones, S. E. (2014). The emergence of the digital humanities. *Reviews in History*, *1634*, 1–5.

Kilgore, W., & Lowenthal, P. R. (2015). The Human Element MOOC. In R. Wright (Ed.), *Student-Teacher Interaction in Online Learning Environments* (pp. 373–391). Hershey, PA: Information Science Reference.

Manjikian, M. (2013). Why We Fear MOOCs. *The Chronicle of Higher Education*, *4*(5).

Miguel, J., Caballe, S., & Prieto, J. (2013) Providing Information Security to MOOC: Towards Effective Student Authentication. *Proceedings of The 5th International Conference Intelligent Networking and Collaborative Systems,* Xi'an, China, (pp. 289-292). IEEE Press. doi:10.1109/INCoS.2013.52

Ronkowitz, K., & Ronkowitz, L. C. (2015). MOOCs: Evolution and Revolution. In E. McKay & J. Lenarcic (Eds.), *Macro-Level Learning through Massive Open Online Courses (MOOCs): Strategies and Predictions for the Future* (pp. 183–211). Hershey, PA: Information Science Reference. doi:10.4018/978-1-4666-8324-2.ch011

Thrun, S. (2013). MOOCs: The Future Is Here. *The Journal of Nursing Education*, *52*(1), 3–4. doi:10.3928/01484834-20121227-10 PMID:23293938

Tømte, C., Fevolden, A., & Olsen, D. S. (2014). To MOOC or not to MOOC?: A Case Study of Norway. In V. Zuzevičiūtė, E. Butrimė, D. Vitkutė-Adžgauskienė, V. Vladimirovich Fomin, & K. Kikis-Papadakis (Eds.), *E-Learning as a Socio-Cultural System: A Multidimensional Analysis* (pp. 210–223). Hershey, PA: Information Science Reference. doi:10.4018/978-1-4666-6154-7.ch012

Tu, C. H., & Sujo-Montes, L. E. (2015). MOOCs. In R. Papa (Ed.), *Media Rich Instruction* (pp. 287–304). New York: Springer International Publishing.

Valentin, C. (2015). MOOCs Global Digital Divide: Reality or Myth? In F. Nafukho & B. Irby (Eds.), *Handbook of Research on Innovative Technology Integration in Higher Education* (pp. 376–397). Hershey, PA: Information Science Reference. doi:10.4018/978-1-4666-8170-5.ch019

Wu, Y. (2014). MOOC and the Opportunities, Challenges and Responses of Universities. *Journal of Guizhou Minzu University (Philosophy and Social Science), 5.*

Wu, Z., Ou, Y., & Liu, Y. (2011). A Taxonomy of Network and Computer Attacks Based on Responses. Proceedings of the *Information Technology, Computer Engineering and Management Sciences International Conference* (pp. 26-29). doi:10.1109/ICM.2011.363

KEY TERMS AND DEFINITIONS

Auditive Feedback: Also known as sonification or auralization is the use of auditive adutive alerts to convey something to users. It is commonly used in security notifications and combined with visual notifications because these marriage permits a very efficient sensorial correlation in humans.

Cognitive Load: It refers to the mental effort used to complete a task or activity using a device or tool.

Interface Feedback: Is all the communications provided from the system to the users through the user interfaces, the most common Interface Feedback are notifications.

Multimodal Interfaces: A multimodal interface could be generated combining two or more feedback forms in one interface.

Usability: Ease of use, efficiency, and learnability of a technology (software or hardware) which derives in helping users to complete a task (satisfaction of use).

User Centered Design: Process to create technology (not restricted to software) based in incorporate users into each stage of the design process by obtaining and implementing feedback to refine design ideas.

User eXperience: It involves a combination of several aspects from emotional to cognitive when a person uses a device or a tool to complete a task.

Section 3

Inclusive MOOCs:

Exploring Some Alternatives to Design Inclusive MOOCs for Diverse Users

Chapter 8
Design, Implementation and Evaluation of MOOCs to Improve Inclusion of Diverse Learners

Sandra Sanchez-Gordon
National Polytechnic School of Ecuador, Ecuador

Sergio Luján-Mora
University of Alicante, Spain

ABSTRACT

This chapter presents accessibility requirements that need to be considered in the design, implementation and evaluation of Massive Open Online Courses (MOOCs) to ensure they are inclusive. Accessibility requirements take in account particular needs, preferences, skills and situations of diverse learners, e.g. people with disabilities, elderly people and foreign students. The accessibility needs have to be considered in the design and implementation of MOOCs' interfaces, contents and learning/assessment activities. Due to its open and massive nature, with an adequate implementation, MOOCs can overcome inclusion barriers for the benefit of potential learners worldwide, both able and disabled. For evaluation, there are accessibility evaluation tools that identify accessibility problems in the content, semantic and structural elements of a website that can be used to evaluate the level of accessibility of MOOCs. Additional expert-based and user-based evaluations are always recommended in order to achieve valid results.

INTRODUCTION

Humankind is diverse. Hence, there is also great diversity among learners, especially in the context of Massive Open Online Courses (MOOCs). This diversity imposes accessibility needs associated to students with different types of disabilities, elderly students with combined disabilities, and foreign students with cognitive issues due to lack of proficiency in the second language.

DOI: 10.4018/978-1-4666-9743-0.ch008

Persons with Disabilities

According to the World Report on Disability made by the World Health Organization (2011), more than one billion people live with some form of disability. This is around 15 per cent of the world's population. This fact makes this community the world's largest minority.

The World Report on Disability is a guide to implement the United Nations' Convention on the Rights of Persons with Disabilities (CRPD). The CRPD entered into force in 2008 after decades of work by the United Nations to change attitudes towards viewing persons with disabilities as capable of claiming their rights as well as being active members of society. The CRPD simply guarantees that the same rights recognized in the Universal Declaration of Human Rights of 1948 are respected for persons with disabilities.

The CRPD stresses that persons with disabilities should be able to live independently and participate fully in all aspects of life. To this end, signatories should take appropriate measures to ensure that persons with disabilities have access to the physical environment, to transportation, to information and communications technology, and to other facilities and services open or provided to the public.

Of particular importance in the context of this chapter is Article 24 of the CRPD. This article recognizes the right to education for persons with disabilities. Signatories must make sure that persons with disabilities are able to get access not only to general education but also to tertiary education, vocational training, adult education and lifelong learning without discrimination and on an equal basis with others (United Nations, 2008).

As of April 2015, 154 countries or regional integration organizations have signed and ratified the CRPD, Kazakhstan being the latest one so far (United Nations, 2015). When a country signs and ratifies a convention, it becomes a legal promise and it often leads the government to adapt and change its own laws to support the goals of the ratified convention.

Nevertheless, Morales (2007) reports that in Spain only 3.6% of the population with disabilities completes higher education while the correspondent percentage for general population is 20%. Besides, 84% of Spain college students with disabilities state that they face several barriers through their studies.

In the same line, Molina (2007) presents the following data from Colombia: only 2.3% of the population with disabilities has some level of higher education (technical, technological or professional), 1% completes their higher education and 0.1% obtains graduate degrees.

That is, higher education penetration among population with disabilities has a long way to go before reaching similar levels than general population. Part of the problem is that higher education institutions might not have had accessibility in mind when getting facilities and equipment.

The adaptations of facilities and equipment to make a college campus accessible might be costly. A study made in the European Higher Education Area (EHEA) about standards and indicators for disability (Diez et al., 2011), describes 31 indicators such as: ensure students with disabilities have priority accessible rooms in residential accommodations or rooms near buildings where classes are taught; ensure computer labs are accessible to students with disabilities (e.g. appropriate sits or space for wheelchairs, height adjustable desks, alternative keyboards); ensure that classrooms and labs consider the needs of students with disabilities (e.g. physical access, adequate sound and light conditions); ensure that the aisles are wide enough to allow a person with a physical disability or a wheelchair user to get around them; ensure that alarms and security devices are available in both sight and hearing formats; ensure that campus maps and signs are available in Braille and long print.

There are also attitudinal and communication barriers with teachers, fellow students and administrative personal in educational institutions. People often do not known how to interact and communicate with persons with disabilities, thus prefer to avoid contact. Finally, adaptations in policies, procedures, curricula, learning and assessment activities must be put in place in order to accommodate students with disabilities.

In this context, online learning -and more specifically MOOCs- are a great opportunity for persons with disabilities than would not be able to engage in learning otherwise. Moreover, in a MOOC environment the situation of a person with disabilities may go unnoticed; hence the person can be treated truly equally by their teachers and peers. Best of all, currently the design and implementation of inclusive MOOCs is pedagogically, technically and financially feasible.

Elder People

Another human group that deserves special attention is the elderly population. Velasco (2010) explains that humanity is assisting in the past four decades to an unprecedented fact in its history: the aging of the population; consisting in the presence of an increasing number of elderly, especially in Europe, where birth rates and life expectancy have operated in reverse order in the last years. This fact raises cultural changes, economic burdens and social demands.

Worldwide life expectancy has increased from 50 years in 1900 to 66 years today. By 2050, general life expectancy might increase to 76 years. In Japan and Spain, life expectancy is already 82 years old. The general increase of life expectancy due to better health care and environment conditions is provoking an increase in the fraction of the elderly population. Currently, one in ten people is 60+ years old (600 million people). Moreover, the world's older population is expected to exceed one billion by 2020. By 2030, 13% of the population (i.e. one in eight people) will be 65+ years old, of an estimated total of 8.321 billion people. That is, 1.165 billion of people will be 65+ years old. In United States, older adults (65+ years old) already are the largest population group according to the latest census report (Werner, 2011).

Waldmeir (2014) reports that by 2050, China could have nearly 500 million people aged over 60, more than the total population of USA. Local governments across China are investing in elderly education as one way to achieve healthy old people. At Shanghai University of the Elderly the average students' age is 65 years old. There are five universities for elder people in Shanghai that serve more than five million students.

Various authors have stated that e-learning is an opportunity to help older people to become integrated with the rest of society (Tsai et al., 2014; Githens, 2007; Notess & Lorenzen-Huber, 2007). In this context, MOOCs bring great opportunities to enhance the quality of life of older people by enabling lifelong learning and inclusion in learning communities, which in turn favors cognitive stimulation, a sense of belonging, and social engagement.

However, MOOCs can present some barriers that could hamper full participation by elderly students due to diminish capacities related to natural aging such as vision decline, hearing loss, decremented motor skills and cognition issues (Sanchez-Gordon & Luján-Mora, 2013).

Foreign Students

Regarding the languages in which MOOCs are offered, Shah (2014) presents the following data from the MOOC aggregator Class Central: 80% of MOOCs are offered in English, followed by 8.5% of courses offered in Spanish, of a total offer of 13 different languages.

Similarly, a quick review made in April 2015 of the leading MOOC platform Coursera shows that from a total of 1,117 courses, 794 are offered in English (71%), Chinese is the second language with 126 courses (11.3%) and Spanish is the third language with 49 courses (4.4%). These data may seem discouraging in terms of language diversity, but actually it shows a positive trend, since a year before, from a total of 585 courses hosted on Coursera, 515 of them were offered in English, corresponding to 90% of the offered courses back then.

Students taken a course offered in a language different from their own might face difficulties due to their level of proficiency in the course language, e.g., non-native speakers read at slower speed, which leads to information overload and cognitive problems. This causes them to take longer to perform certain learning/assessment activities as well. Non-native speakers also experience stress related to workload and visibility of their written responses in essays, forums and textual chats. For these reasons, the language barrier discourages many potential users to participate in MOOCs (Sanchez-Gordon & Luján-Mora, 2014a).

Chapter Objectives

The accessibility needs of diverse learners must be taken in account in the design, implementation and evaluation of MOOC interfaces, contents and learning/assessment activities. This chapter focuses on learners with disabilities, elderly learners and foreign learners in the context of MOOCs.

The main objectives of this chapter are:

- Identify MOOCs' potential users accessibility needs.
- Specify accessibility requirements for non-disabled learners, learners with disabilities, elderly learners and foreign learners.
- Explain how to design and implement accessible MOOCs.
- Explain how to evaluate the level of accessibility of MOOCs.

BACKGROUND

Massive Open Online Courses

MOOCs can be simply defined as:

Online courses with no formal entry requirement, no participation limits, and free of charge. (Gaebel, 2013)

Oxford dictionary defines MOOC as:

A course of study made available over the Internet without charge to a very large number of people. (Parr, 2013)

With a brief history of seven years, MOOC is relatively a new phenomenon and its definition is still evolving. The term was coined in 2008 by Dave Cormier and Bryan Alexander to refer to the course "Connectivism and Connective Knowledge" organized by George Siemens and Stephen Downes of University of Manitoba, with 2,300 online students. The first MOOC to get really massive was "Introduction to Artificial Intelligence", offered in 2011 and organized by Sebastian Thrun of Stanford University and Peter Norving of Google. It got a registration of 160,000 students. In 2012, "Circuits and Electronics", organized by Anant Agarwal of the Massachusetts Institute of Technology, registered 120,000 students (Daniel, 2012; Adams, Yin, Vargas, & Mullen, 2014).

Since then, the concept has evolved in such a way that to date every letter of the acronym has several interpretations (Sanchez-Gordon & Lujan-Mora, 2014b):

- The term MASSIVE implies that a MOOC should support access to a very large number of users and have the capacity to scale in the number of users in several orders of magnitude, for example, going from 1,000 to 100,000 students, without significantly affecting its functioning and quality.
- The term OPEN has several meanings. First, it means open enrollment, i.e. the course should be open to all users with no prerequisites nor previous studies. Second, open also comes from the concept of Open Educational Resources. In this sense, open means that the course is based on "open content" and the content generated by the course should also be published with an open license, so it could be reused by others. In addition, open also means that access to the content and learning/assessment activities of the course should be free. Also, open is often interpreted as not using just a closed platform but the entire cloud, i.e. social networks, multimedia repositories, web portals, blogs, wikis. Finally, open can also mean that the platform hosting the MOOCs is under open source licenses, so code adaptation and improvement of the platform is possible and all changes should be also shared.
- The term ONLINE implies that the course is delivered via Internet. That is, instructors and students interact and communicate, as well as access to content and learning/assessment activities on the Internet. But the character of online goes beyond the fact that communication is mediated by a computer network: when a user enrolls in a MOOC, they are not only a student of the course, but also a user of a software system designed to provide a service to their satisfaction.
- Finally, the term COURSE implies that there is learning objectives, learning outcomes, content and educational activities. In general, a course is a space in which an instructor leads a group of students in learning about a specific topic. A traditional course takes place in spaces such as classrooms or laboratories, in a specific period and uses educational resources. A course is not necessarily part of an official curriculum towards a professional degree or certification. A course can also be taken by personal interest and growth in the context of lifelong learning, as might be the case of elderly students.

The first MOOCs did not use specific platforms. For instance, the MOOC "Connectivism and Connective Knowledge" was based on various blog aggregators. However, currently MOOCs are hosted in specific platforms. In principle, any educational institution can become a MOOC provider if they develop their own platform or use a local instance of an open platform, such as edX.

To date, the main MOOC platform providers are: Coursera, edX and Udacity (USA); MiriadaX and Unimooc (Spain); FutureLearn (United Kingdom); Open2Study (Australia); Iversity (Germany). These providers and others offer hundreds of MOOCs in several knowledge areas to potential learners, with almost 17 million of users registered worldwide, distributed as following (Shah, 2014):

- Coursera: 10.5 million
- edX: 3.0 million
- Udacity: 1.5 million
- MiriadaX: 1.0 million
- FutureLearn: 800,000
- Others: 200,000
- **Total:** 17.0 million

Human-Computer Interaction

Preece et al. (1994), in their classic book, states that the term human-computer interaction (HCI) was adopted in mid-1980s as a mean to acknowledge the need of a field of study dedicated to the communication between human and computers. They propose important challenges: keep abreast of changes in technology and ensure designs offer good HCI, and explain that that goal of HCI is produce usable, safe and functional systems. Usability is a key concept in HCI that is concerned with designing and implementing digital products in such a way that are easy to use and easy to learn.

Horton & Sloan (2014) explains that when usability is envisioned in terms of a large and diverse population, including persons with disabilities, it becomes accessibility.

Accessibility

The International Organization for Standardization (ISO) defines accessibility as:

The usability of a product, service, environment or facility by people with the widest range of capabilities. (ISO, 2012)

The inventor of the World Wide Web and director of the World Wide Web Consortium (W3C), Tim Berners-Lee, states:

Accessibility is the art of ensuring that, to as large an extent as possible, facilities (such as, for example, web access) are available to people whether or not they have disabilities of one sort or another. (W3C, 1999)

The W3C created the Web Accessibility Initiative (WAI) with the aim of studying the problems of accessibility in the web, develop guidelines and provide resources. The WAI is recognized as an international authority on web accessibility. W3C recognizes that accessibility depends on several components working together. WAI has developed three sets of guidelines (WAI, 2014):

- **Content:** WCAG - Web Content Accessibility Guidelines.
- **Authorship:** ATAG - Authoring Tool Accessibility Guidelines.
- **User tools:** UAAG - User Agent Accessibility Guidelines.

The WCAG defines how to make web content accessible to disabled persons. These guidelines include website conformance requirements and define three levels of conformance: A, AA and AAA. WCAG establishes four principles that give the foundation for web content accessibility:

- **Perceivable**: the information and components of the user interface should be presented to users so they can perceive them.
- **Operable**: the components of the user interface and navigation must be operable.
- **Understandable**: the information and manipulation of the user interface must be understandable by the users.
- **Robust**: content must be robust enough to be reliably interpreted by a wide variety of user agents, including assistive technology software or devices.

These principles are known by the acronym POUR. This chapter uses the POUR principles to categorize accessibility needs of potential MOOC users.

The W3C created the ATAG to address the software people use to create websites. The ATAG defines how web development tools should help website developers produce content that is accessible and conforms to the WCAG. The ATAG compliant tools provide web developers with a means to produce accessible websites, prompt the developer for accessibility related information and provide ways to verify the content is accessible. The tools themselves should also be accessible to disabled persons.

The UAAG explains what is required for the accessible design of user agents. User agents are web browsers, media players and assistive technology software that disabled persons use to interact with computers.

WCAG, ATAG and UAAG work together to make the web accessible. Smith (2012) gives the following example to illustrate the combination of the three sets of guidelines: for alternative text on images, the WCAG would require images be accompanied by descriptive text, the ATAG would require that the web design software verify that images on the website contain alternate text, and the UAAG would require the browser to display the alternate text in a manner that works with screen reading software.

Current versions of the three set of guidelines are: WCAG 2.0 released in 2008, ATAG 2.0 released in 2015 and UAAG 1.0 released in 2002. In addition, WCAG 2.0 was approved as the standard ISO/IEC 40500 in 2012. UAAG 2.0 is currently in draft stage.

DESIGN, IMPLEMENTATION, AND EVALUATION OF ACCESSIBLE MOOCS

Issues, Controversies, Problems

In 2013, the president of edX Anant Agarwal stated:

MOOCs are transforming education in both quality and scale. MOOCs make education borderless, gender-blind, race-blind, class-blind and bank account-blind (...) MOOCs are democratizing education. (Agarwal, 2013)

In 2012, the co-founder of Coursera Daphne Koller said in a TED Talk:

If we could offer a top quality education to everyone around the world for free, what would that do? Three things. First it would establish education as a fundamental human right, where anyone around the world with the ability and the motivation could get the skills that they need to make a better life for themselves, their families and their communities. Second, it would enable lifelong learning. It's a shame that for so many people, learning stops when we finish high school or when we finish college. By having this amazing content be available, we would be able to learn something new every time we wanted, whether it's just to expand our minds or it's to change our lives. And finally, this would enable a wave of innovation, because amazing talent can be found anywhere. (Koller, 2013)

Nevertheless, Palin (2014) presents data that shows that most current MOOCs beneficiaries live in developed countries and have university studies. For instance, on Coursera, 28% of users are from United States.

Perna et al. (2013) made a study on sixteen courses of University of Pennsylvania in Coursera that concluded that most students come from United States, with a few students from Central and South America; and very few students from Africa.

Liyanagunawardena, Williams & Adams (2013) compiled data confirming that the majority of MOOC students come from United States and Europe with limited participation from the rest of America, Asia and even less from Africa. The difference is overwhelming, especially because most of the world's population is concentrated in those continents.

Guo & Reinecke (2014) presents learning analytics of four MOOCs on the platform edX, where the top-five list of countries with the most certificate-earning students were: United States (22%), India (17%), Spain (11%), Russian Federation (8%) and United Kingdom (6%).

On the other hand, Martinez-Cruz (2014) reports an interesting success case where students from El Salvador, motivated by a teacher, enrolled on 2012 to the second version of "Circuits and Electronics" and got a 27.6% of certificate attainment for this country, compared to the global percentage of 5.8% from 97 different countries.

Despite of this last experience, for now, MOOCs are elitist.

Bohnsack & Puhl (2014) conducted a study that determined that none of the current MOOC platforms is fully accessible: most lack of correct HTML syntax (e.g., language definition, heading structure and labels in input fields) and accessible design (e.g., clean interface, keyboard navigation, links to skip to main content). These authors concluded that accessibility was not in focus when these platforms were built.

Al-Mouh et al. (2014) conducted an experiment that included a heuristic evaluation of ten Coursera MOOCs with respect to WCAG 2.0. All the evaluated MOOCs failed to comply with A, AA and AAA accessibility levels.

Calle-Jimenez et al. (2014) described some of the challenges that exist to make accessible MOOCs on Geographical Information Systems (GIS). These kinds of MOOCs, by nature, have inherent problems of accessibility.

Aboshady et al. (2015) presents the following results regarding the awareness and use of MOOCs among medical undergraduates in Egypt as a developing country: one-fifth of Egyptian medical undergraduates have heard about MOOCs but only 6.5% actively enrolled in courses. Students who actively participated showed a positive attitude towards the experience, but better time-management skills and faster Internet connection speeds are required.

Finally, in February 2015, the National Association of Deaf filed federal lawsuits against Harvard and M.I.T. (Lewin, 2015), saying both universities violated antidiscrimination laws by failing to provide closed captioning in their online lectures, courses, podcasts and other educational materials, including MOOCs provided through edX.

So for now, MOOCs are not accessible enough.

Hence, the promise of democratizing education and giving access to education to everyone is yet to be fulfilled. Therefore, it is necessary to analyze the problem and propose solutions to improve inclusion of diverse learners, both able and disabled, in MOOCs.

SOLUTIONS AND RECOMMENDATIONS

There are several strategies to improve the level of accessibility of MOOCs.

One option is to avoid certain types of features, content and learning/assessment activities that are not readily accessible to diverse learners, e.g., people with disabilities, elderly students and foreign students. However, this is not a good solution because it leads to a general reduction of features offered to MOOC learners in general. Besides, it generates the idea that in order to make a MOOC accessible, it is necessary to reduce its functionality. That may induce some users to perceive accessibility as a negative thing.

A second option is to develop a generic version of the MOOC and several alternative versions for different categories of disabilities. This path is not suitable, because the development, maintenance and support of multiple versions are expensive and in most cases not possible. Also, this does not solve the problem of segregation.

A better strategy is to apply universal design to define MOOC features, content, and learning/assessment activities. Universal design "is the design of products and environments to be usable by all people, to the greatest extent possible, without the need for adaptation or specialized design" (Mace et al., 1996). Next sections identify MOOCs users' accessibility needs, specify MOOCs' accessibility requirements, and explain how to design, implement and evaluate accessible MOOCs

Diverse Learners Accessibility Needs

For identifying MOOCs potential users' accessibility needs, this section considers people with the widest range of capabilities, including people with permanent, temporary or progressive disabilities:

- A permanent disability might be congenital (i.e. person born blind) or acquired (i.e. person that become blind due to an accident).
- A temporary disability starts and ends in some point of a person's life. Examples of temporary disabilities are: people recovering after surgery (i.e. eye, ear, throat), with trauma injuries (i.e. broken bones in upper limbs), and circumstantial situations such as parents with their baby in arms, foreign students, or students in a silent library.
- A progressive disability appears and develops over time. Examples of progressive disabilities are: vision, hearing, motor, cognitive, and psychosocial progressive loss due to natural aging, as is the case of elderly students. Progressive disabilities might develop combined.

Accessibility needs of potential MOOC users can be organized according to the four POUR principles proposed by the WCAG: perceivable, operable, understandable and robust.

Accessibility Needs to Perceive

The main senses considered in the perceivable category are vision and hearing.

People with full use of their vision are able to read text, view images, understand the visual meaning of colors, and in general they can use their eyes to make sense of information that is presented to them (WebAIM, 2015).

On the other hand, MOOC users with visual disabilities cannot properly access visual information or use the mouse, and they need to mainly rely on audio information. There are three main types of users with visual disabilities:

- Blind people that uses text-to-speech software, also known as screen readers, and optionally audio descriptions (Christensen, 2001).
- Users with low vision that use magnifiers and screen readers (Prougestaporn, 2010).
- Users with color-blindness that need alternatives to color conveyed-information.

The web enables several kinds of audio interactions among people that can hear, such as engage in voice chats, watch videos, hear music, listen web radio broadcasts and podcast (WebAIM, 2015).

MOOC users with hearing disabilities cannot properly access to audio information, such as speech, music or sounds. For them, it is important to make auditory content available in alternative format. There are three main types of users with hearing disabilities:

- People with mild, moderate or severe hearing loss that uses captions and transcripts. Hearing loss generally affects to elderly people.
- People with post-lingual deafness (after the acquisition of language) that lip-read and also use captions and transcripts.
- People with pre-lingual deafness (deafness impaired the ability to acquire a spoken language) that uses captions and transcripts and optionally videos in sign language.
- People with deaf-blindness. In this case, touch is the main form of communication. These users use text-to-Braille devices.

Although touch, smell and taste are not significant on the web, they might be necessary to perform learning or assessment activities outside the MOOC platform. For instance, a video lecture can instruct the student to perform an experiment at home where they have to taste different kind of foods to classify them by type of flavor, and then perform statistics calculations with the data obtained. If a student has some kind of taste disability, they won't be able to perform this activity. Hence, alternative activities must be designed.

Accessibility Needs to Operate

Users generally rely on the use of mouse and standard keyboard to input information and navigate through and interact with web content.

Nevertheless, MOOCs users with motor disabilities in upper limbs have inability or difficulty using mouse and keyboard. Moreover, users with visual disabilities have also difficulties using mouse.

Hence, the user interface components and navigation must be operable not only with mouse and standard keyboard, but also with assistive technology devices and software, e.g., voice recognition software, mouth stick, head wand, single-switch access, sip and puff switch, track-ball mouse, adaptive keyboard, on-screen keyboards (Burgstahler, 2002; WebAIM, 2015).

Additionally, it is important to consider that these users require extra time to input information and also to navigate and interact with the MOOC.

Accessibility Needs to Understand

Any user might potentially experience problems understanding web content or how to operate a web interface. The frequency and level of difficulty of such problems increase if the user has some cognitive, psychosocial or speech disability.

In general terms, a user with a cognitive disability has more difficulties with one or more types of mental tasks than the average user. Cognitive disabilities include difficulties with memory, problem-solving, attention, reading, linguistic/verbal comprehension, math comprehension, and visual comprehension (Pouncey, 2010; WebAIM, 2015).

A common cognitive disability is dyslexia (10% of the global population has it). Dyslexia is a neurological condition that impairs a person's ability to read, recognize words, spell correctly and decode written information (Kalyvioti & Mikropoulos, 2013).

The disabilities arising from mental health conditions are called psychosocial disabilities. Conditions leading to psychosocial disabilities include depression, psychosis, epilepsy, post-traumatic stress disorder and dementia. Depression can cause the affected person to suffer greatly and function poorly at work, at school and in their family. Dementia is a syndrome in which there is deterioration in memory, thinking, behavior and the ability to perform everyday activities. Dementia generally affects to elderly people.

Speech disabilities includes: lack of speech, slurred, slowed, hoarse, stuttered or rapid speech. In these cases, the person's articulation, voice quality, or fluency patterns impair listeners' ability to understand the intent of the speaker. At present, users input information mostly using mouse and keyboard. However, it is very likely that different forms of voice activated user computer interfaces become more popular in the near future, especially in circumstances in which the use of mouse and keyboard is not the best option (for example, when there is also a motor impairment). Users with speech disabilities uses communication devices that produce either synthetic or digital speech output based on their textual input (Hasselbring & Williams, 2000). Additionally, users with speech disabilities might have difficulties performing learning/assessment activities involving oral communication.

There is also needs associated to users level of proficiency of the course language. This circumstance might affect the understanding of platform functionality, course content and learning/assessment activities. Language proficiency issues affects users taking MOOCs in a language different to their native one; including users born deaf whose native language is sign language (Holcomb & Kreeft, 1992). In addition, MOOC contents and activities might be culturally bound, hence they need to be reviewed to make sure they don't conflict with cultural and religion backgrounds of foreign users. This applies also for people born deaf who belong to a culture proper of their community.

In addition, users with low levels of digital literacy, or literacy in general, may find difficult to perform MOOC tasks such as navigate course contents, post in forums, or perform assessment activities. Digital literacy levels of users from developing countries tend to be low. For instance, Sri Lanka has a computer literacy rate of 20.3%, even though literacy rate is 91% (Satharasinghe, 2004). Users with low levels of digital literacy may find difficult to perform MOOC platform general tasks, e.g., sign up, sign in, sign out, update their profile; as well as course tasks such as enroll, navigate course contents, post in forums, or perform assessment activities. Social network skills are part of digital literacy and are necessary to understand and successfully participate in MOOCs (McAuly et al., 2010).

Besides blind users, screen readers also help users with low levels of literacy or cognitive disabilities. Screen readers are an example of how the same assistive technology can help users with different accessibility needs (Perez-Gonzales et al., 2014).

Accessibility Needs to Robust Access

Users should be allowed to choose their own technologies to access web content. If a web content requires a particular software or hardware technology, e.g., certain browser, media player, plug-in or assistive technology, it may exclude some types of users who either don't want to use that technology or can't use it.

Robust access is also related to having adequate access to technological resources, e.g., electricity supply, affordable and quality internet, updated computer devices.

In countries of sub-Saharan Africa, 36% of the population does not have regular access to electricity. In Burundi, 97% of the population lives without electricity, and those who have access to electricity only get it on certain days of the week (Legros et al., 2009).

Only around one-third of the total world population has regular access to Internet. Whereas in most European countries (Norway, Sweden, Denmark, Finland, United Kingdom, Germany, Belgium, France), Japan, Canada and United States, the number of Internet users is 80% or above; in countries such as Burundi, Ethiopia, Guinea, Myanmar, Niger, Sierra Leona, Somalia, and Timor-Leste is less than 2% (World Bank, 2014). Internet connection speed in many developing countries is not sufficient to download large files or watching videos in an acceptable way.

Also, users in developing countries might have difficulties to have adequate access to affordable and updated computers, laptops, tablets or smart phones (Post, 2006).

MOOC's Accessibility Requirements

In the previous section, accessibility needs of potential MOOC users have been identified. This section presents the corresponding MOOC accessibility requirements and their related disabilities. It is important to note that in general the compliance of these accessibility requirements favors not only users having the related disabilities but non-disabled users as well.

Accessibility Requirements to Perceive

These are requirements mainly oriented to solve the needs of users with difficulties to perceive, such as blind users (B), users with low vision (V), users with hearing loss or post-lingual deafness (H), users with pre-lingual deafness (D), and users with deaf-blindness (DB). Users with cognitive disabilities (CG) including dyslexia (DX) and users with low levels of foreign language proficiency (L) might also beneficiate from the compliance of these requirements. Table 1 lists the specification of accessibility requirements to perceive.

Table 1. Accessibility requirements to perceive

Code	Accessibility Requirement	Related Disabilities
P1	Provide explanatory alternative text for non-textual elements such us, images, sensitive areas of image maps, audio content and speech content.	B, DB, V, DX
P2	Provide informative titles for links.	B, DB, CG, DX
P3	Use labels for form fields.	B, DB
P4	Make sure tables are comprehensible when read sequentially.	B, DB, CG
P5	Do not use nested tables.	B, DB, CG
P6	Provide mechanisms to stop and resume animations and other moving content.	CG
P7	Provide textual narratives for images and audio descriptions for videos.	B, DB, CG
P8	Include explanatory hidden text content for screen readers.	B, DB
P9	Support text and images resizing up to 200% at least.	V, CG, DX
P10	Provide adequate ratio contrast between foreground and background colors of at least 4:5:1.	V
P11	Do not use color as the only mechanism to convey information.	B, DB, V, CG
P12	Provide captioning to video content.	L, H, D, CG
P13	Make sure content in documents, presentations and files in pdf format comply with accessible rules.	B, V, H, D, DB, CG, DX
P14	Provide alternative video content in sign language.	D
P15	Provide textual transcripts of audio content.	H, D, CG
P16	Simplify textual content.	D, DB, CG, DX

Accessibility Requirements to Operate

These are requirements oriented to solve the needs of users with motor disabilities (M), visual disabilities: blind (B) and low vision (V), and hearing disabilities: pre-lingual deafness (D) and deaf-blindness (DB). These requirements also benefits users with cognitive disabilitics (CG) including dyslexia (DX), users with low levels of digital literacy or literacy in general (DL) and users with low levels of foreign language proficiency (L). Table 2 lists the specification of accessibility requirements to operate.

Accessibility Requirements to Understand

These are requirements oriented to solve the needs of users with cognitive disabilities (CG) including dyslexia (DX), psychosocial disabilities (P), speech disabilities (S), low levels of foreign language

Table 2. Accessibility requirements to operate

Code	Accessibility Requirement	Related Disabilities
01	Make sure all the functionality is fully operable by keyboard.	M, B, V, DB
02	Provide proper spatial distribution of the elements of the web pages.	M, CG, DX
03	Design and implement web pages to be error-tolerant.	M, B, V, DB, CG, DL
04	Provide mechanisms for skipping over long lists of links.	M, B, DB, CG, DX
05	Provide mechanisms for skipping over long content.	M, B, DB, CG, DX
06	Make sure learning/assessment activities do not have time limits or provide extra time.	M, B, V, D, DB, CG, DX, P, L, DL

proficiency (L), cultural/religion background (CU), and low levels of digital literacy (DL). In addition, blind users (B), low vision users (V), hear loss and post-lingual deaf users (H), pre-lingual deaf users (D), and blind-deaf users (BD) might also beneficiate of the compliance of these requirements. Table 3 lists the specification of accessibility requirements to understand.

Table 3. Accessibility requirements to understand

Code	Accessibility Requirement	Related Disabilities
U1	Make sure relevant data is included in graphs.	CG, P, V
U2	Use consistent structure for web pages.	CG, P, DL, B, D, DB,
U3	Make sure content have only short, simple, clear paragraphs focused on a single idea at a time.	CG, P, DX, L, DL, B, D, DB
U4	Make sure content is logically and consistently organized.	CG, P, DX, L, DL, B, D, DB
U5	Provide a glossary for complicated, unusual, technical vocabulary.	CG, P, DX, L, CU, DL, D, BD
U6	Avoid content with non-literal text, such as sarcasm, satire, parody, allegory, metaphor, slang, and colloquialisms.	CG, P, L, CU, D, BD
U7	Provide conceptual explanations of mathematical expressions.	CG
U8	Use correct spelling and grammar.	CG, DX, L, D, BD
U9	Use consistent navigation mechanisms, including links to home page and previous page, a navigation bar and a website map.	CG, P, B, DB, D, DL
U10	Provide options to disable multimedia elements and automatic refreshing of content.	CG, P, B, DB
U11	Use adequate text font and text size.	DX, V
U12	Use adequate line spacing and line length.	DX, V
U13	Make sure text is left-aligned.	DX, V
U14	Use white space adequately.	DX, V
U15	Include a search option.	CG, P, L, DL, D
U16	Provide appropriate error messages and feedback.	CG, P, L, DL, D, DB
U17	Use appropriate examples and study cases.	CG, P, L, CU, D, BD
U18	Provide positive feedback to learning/assessment activities.	CG, P, CU
U19	Use appropriate vocabulary in video lectures.	CG, P, L, CU, D, BD
U20	Provide option to start, stop and resume relaxing music.	P
U21	Provide option to switch to relaxing colors.	P
U22	Provide alternative mechanism using written communication to voice chats or video conferences that require user's synchronic participation using vocal communication.	CG, P, S, L, H, D, BD
U23	Provide alternative mechanism using written communication to assignments that imply creation of audio content using vocal communication.	S, L, D, BD
U24	Provide alternative mechanisms to learning/assessment activities, such as texting chats and forums that require user's participation via written statements.	L, DL
U25	Provide alternative mechanism to assignments, such as essays and academic papers that involves users' creation of text content.	L, DL
U26	Select content, examples and learning/assessment activities that are not strange or offensive to users with diverse cultural backgrounds.	P, CU, D, DB
U27	Provide mechanisms to curate post in forums.	CG, L

Accessibility Requirements for Robust Access

These are requirements oriented to solve the needs of users with limited access to: base software (SW), electricity (E), affordable and quality internet (I), and updated computer devices (HW); which are usual limitations in developing countries. Table 4 lists the specification of accessibility requirements for robust access.

Accessibility Requirements Model

The integration of the POUR accessibility requirements sets up the accessibility requirements specification model for MOOCs. Figure 1 presents a partial view of the associated UML Use Case Model. The actor Learner can specialize in Blind, Low Vision, Dyslexia, and so on. The actor Learner performs the use case MOOC Platform Tasks including the use case Manage Profile, which has a use case extension Manage Accessibility Preferences. When the actor Learner performs the use case Navigate MOOC content, the appropriate use case extensions are executed. The alternative accessible interfaces are created by the actor Platform Developer. The alternative accessible content formats are created by the actor Content Author.

Design and Implementation of Accessible MOOCs

Although currently there are accessibility options in most operating systems, special-purpose applications and assistive technologies for several disabilities, many of them require the user to explicitly invoke them. Also, the potential negative psychological effects caused by the introduction of an assistive technology that change how a user interacts with a computer may lead to the user rejection of that assistive technology or computer use altogether (Stephanidis et al., 2001; Sloan et al., 2010).

As an alternative, this chapter proposes satisfying the MOOC users accessibility needs with an approach based in user profiling and the use of questionnaires that combines explicit user-invoked adaptations with automatic adaptive content presentation.

Table 4. Accessibility requirements for robust access

Code	Accessibility Requirement	Related Disabilities
R1	Ensure content or learning/assessment activities do not requires a particular software technology.	SW
R2	Ensure there is no data loss in case of power failure.	E
R3	Make sure content can be downloaded, so users can work offline.	I
R4	Provide a mechanism to synch back offline work.	I
R5	Avoid heavy content in the web pages.	I, HW
R6	Provide mechanisms to allow views of videos with different levels of quality.	I, HW
R7	Provide an option to enable loading only text content in the web pages.	I, HW
R8	Make sure learning/assessment activities do not require downloading or uploading big volumes of data.	I, HW
R9	Ensure maximum compatibility with outdated hardware or software.	SW, HW
R10	Ensure maximum compatibility with future hardware or software.	SW, HW

Figure 1. UML use case model – partial view
Source: Authors, 2015

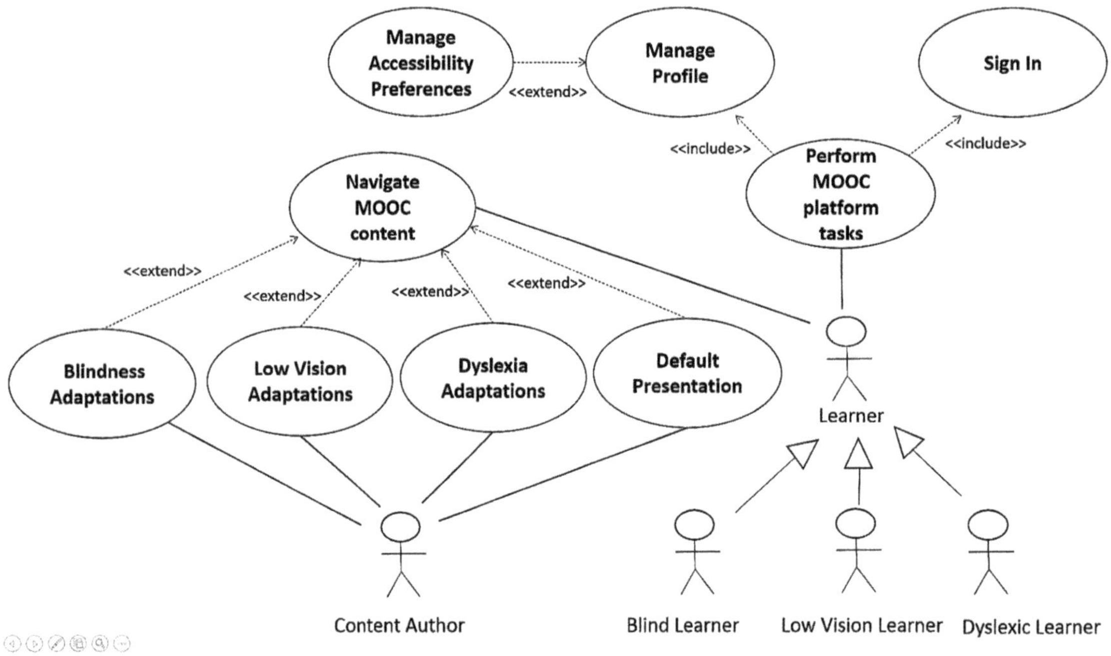

Adaptive content presentation involves personalizing the contents delivered to the user to enhance their accessibility (Stephanidis, 1998). To successfully achieve this, it is necessary an accurate detection of the particular user accessibility needs through user profiling and a mechanism that allows transparent selection and presentation of the appropriate adaptations according to the registered needs (Sloan et al., 2010).

On one hand, the design allows authors to configure parameters and define features so the MOOC can adapt to diverse potential learners. On the other hand, the design allows MOOC users to manage their accessibility user profile by selecting a combination of accessibility issues that best suit their current life situation and optionally taking quick questionnaires to define specific accessibility preferences (e.g., text size, color contrast, line spacing). The use of an accessibility user profile represents an improvement compared with current approaches used in websites and web applications, where the user must manually select specific technical adaptations. Nevertheless, the Accessibility Preferences user interface has an "Advanced Options" feature that provides more savvy users with freedom to select specific adaptations if desired. Figure 2 shows a user interface prototype to select accessibility preferences.

The user does not need to know what adaptations should be applied to the MOOC to make it more accessible for them. User needs to know only their reality and keep it updated in their profile. From that, the adaptive content presentation engine automatically applies all the necessary adaptations.

The architecture of the adaptive content presentation extension is composed of three layers, as illustrated in Figure 3. The Presentation Layer receives the course content in the appropriate format from the Logic Layer, where the adaptive engine resides. To select the appropriate content format, the adaptive engine scans the user profile and applies the necessary adaption rules to the course contents. The Persistence Layer contains three databases for storing user profiles, adaptation rules and course contents.

Figure 2. User interface prototype to select accessibility preferences
Source: Authors, 2015

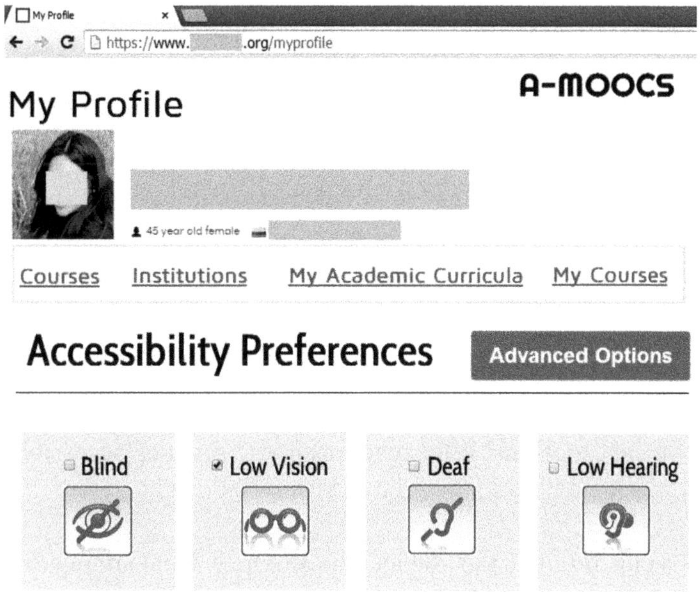

Figure 3. Three-layer architecture
Source: Authors, 2015

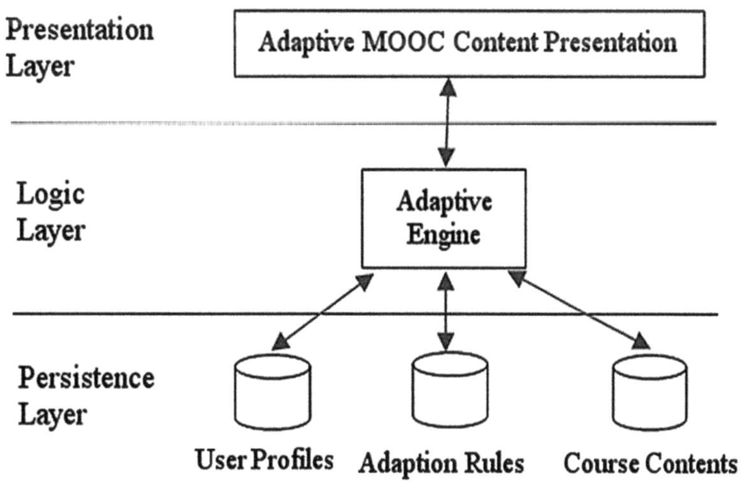

The course contents' database must contain several alternative formats for the same content, as illustrated in Figure 4. The user must be able to access any of the available alternative formats for any course content if desired.

Figure 4. Example of alternative formats for same course content
Source: Authors, 2015

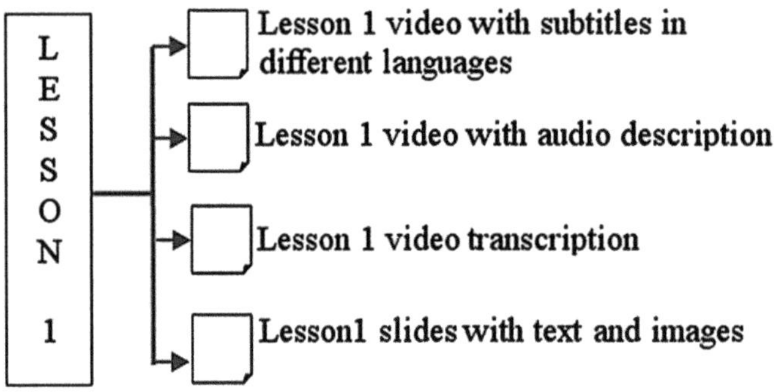

To populate the course contents' database with several alternative formats for the same content, authors use ATAG compliant tools that offer functionality to produce accessible content. These tools provide wizards and forms to guide authors through actions such as:

When a multimedia object is inserted, the title and the alternative text are requested.
When a video is inserted, different tracks of captions can be defined.
The structure of the web page can be organized with different levels of headings.
When a graph is inserted, it is possible to create an accompanying data table using the values used to create the graph.

Accessibility checking is an integrated function that helps make authors aware of web content accessibility problems during the authoring process, so they can be immediately addressed.

As an example of the adaption ruleset, Box 1 shows an extract of the adaption ruleset sequence to be executed if the user accessibility preferences profile indicates dyslexia. This adaption ruleset sequence is based on the research on dyslexia developed by De Santana et al. (2012).

Box 1.

```
FOR UserPreference[i] {
        #adaption ruleset sequence for dyslexia
        IF UserPreference[i] EQUALS dyslexia
        THEN
        {
            #U11 Text font without serif
            TextFont = p {font-family: Verdana, Arial, Calibri, Sans-serif} AND
            #U11 Text size minimum 12
            TextSize=12 AND
            #U12 Line spacing of minimum 1.5
            LineSpacing=1.5 AND
            #U12 Line length of maximum 80
            LineLength = 80 AND
            #U13 Text without justification
            TextJustification=Unjustified AND
            #More rules here
            ...
        }
} NEXT i
```

Figure 5 shows the implementation of a default presentation of a typical lesson of a MOOC course that includes text content and a graph. In this default presentation, there are some accessibility issues, such as small text size, justified text, poor color contrast, meaning conveyed only by color, graph without data.

Figure 6 shows the implementation of the same lesson adapted to a low vision user profile. The requirements applied in this use case scenario are:

P10: Text has a contrast ratio of at least 4.5:1.
P11: Button and graph includes border pattern.
U1: Graph includes data.
U9: Better text font and bigger text size.

In the next scenario for user with both low vision and dyslexia, the additional requirements applied are:

U11: Sans serif text font and bigger text size.
U12: Bigger line spacing, smaller line length.
U13: Text left-aligned.
U14: Better use of white space.

These adaptations improve legibility, readability, and reduce visual stress caused by dense paragraphs, as illustrated in Figure 7.

Figure 5. Accessibility implementation: Default presentation
Source: Authors, 2015

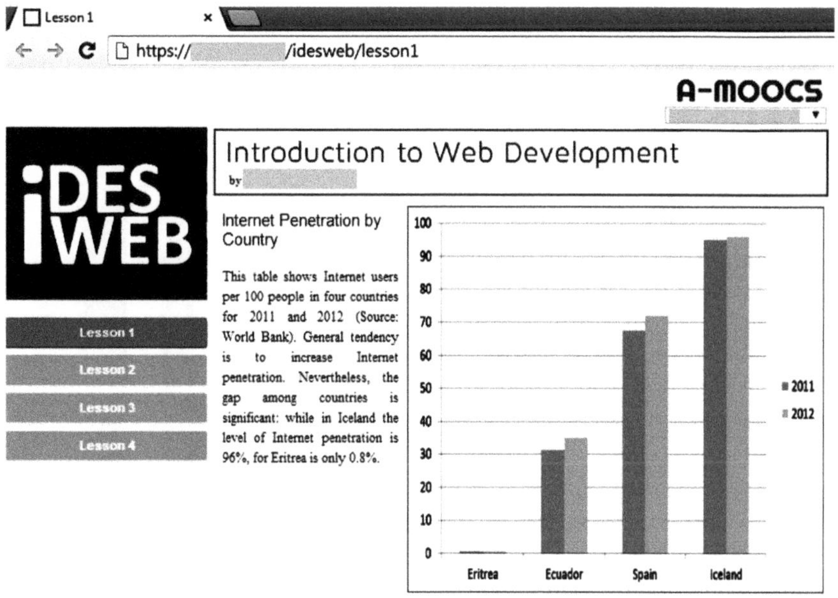

Figure 6. Accessibility implementation: Low vision adaptation
Source: Authors, 2015

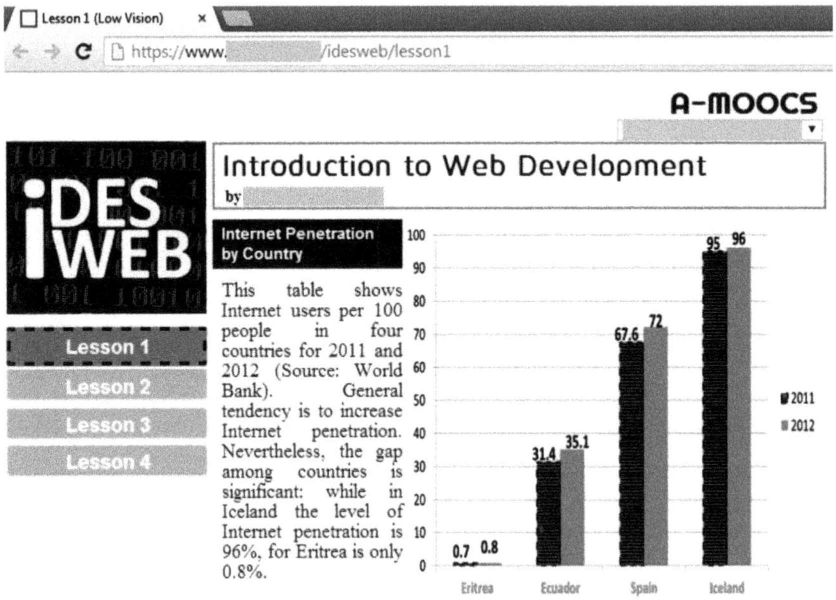

Figure 7. Accessibility implementation: Low vision and dyslexia adaptation
Source: Authors, 2015

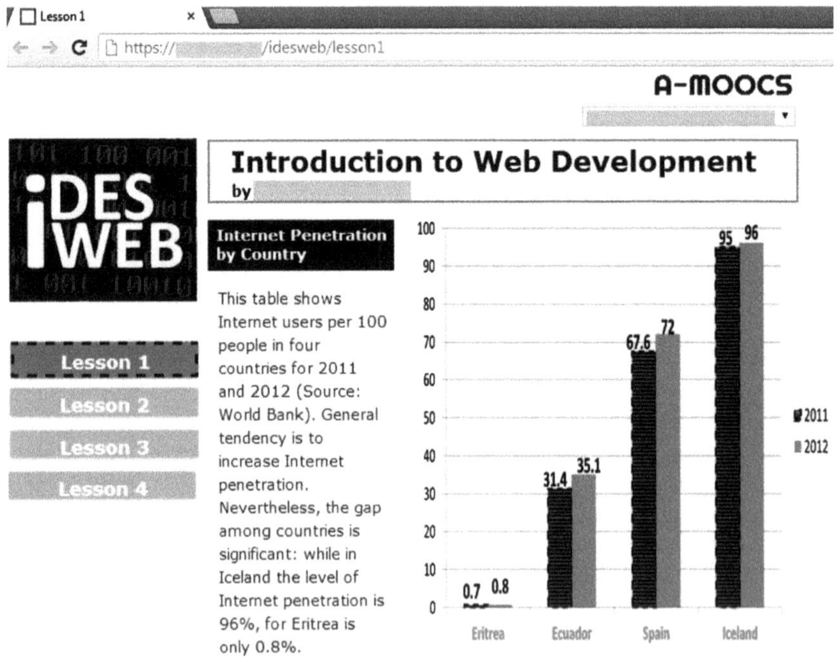

Finally, the adaption for a blind person is shown in Figure 8. A table with the data that generated the graphic has been added. The requirements applied in this use case scenario are:

P1: Graph has alternative text.
P4: Table is structured in a way that can be read by a screen reader.
O5: There is an option to skip to main content.

In order to make the table accessible to screen readers, the correct HTML tags must be used to define the table structure (Calle-Jimenez et al., 2014).

Accessibility Evaluation of MOOCs

In July 2014, WCAG released the Website Accessibility Conformance Evaluation Methodology WCAG-EM 1.0. The WCAG-EM describes a procedure to evaluate existing websites to determine their level of accessibility. The procedure is composed of five sequential steps: define the evaluation scope, explore the target website, select a representative sample, audit the selected sample, and report the findings. Besides, the WCAG-EM also includes considerations to guide evaluators through the evaluation process. This chapter proposes the adoption of WCAG-EM to use it during the design and implementation stages of MOOCs including automated, expert-based and user-based accessibility evaluations.

Figure 8. Accessibility implementation: Blindness adaptation
Source: Authors, 2015

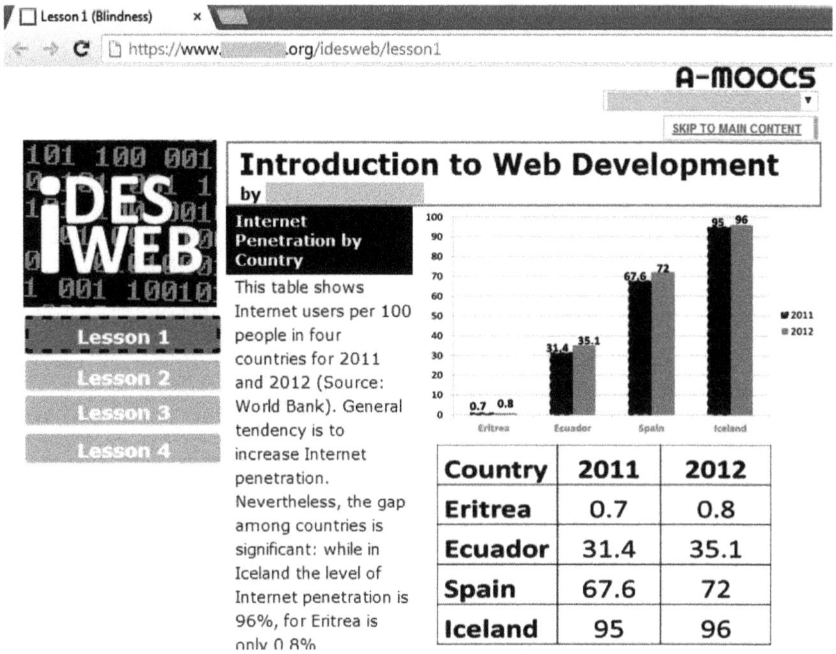

While most accessibility checks are not fully automatable, automated tools can significantly assist evaluators during the accessibility evaluation process and contribute to more effective evaluation. Accessibility evaluation tools are software applications or online services that help determine if a website meets accessibility requirements. There are several open web accessibility tools available, e.g., WAVE, AChecker, TAW, Total Validator, eXaminator and Accessibility Audit of Chrome Developer Tools.

The accessibility evaluation tools not necessarily produce reliable results since not all the accessibility problems can be automatically detected. Besides, a tool can produce fail positives that need to be discarded by expert-based and user-based evaluation. These tools are best exploited when used by experts on the subject of accessibility. When developers don't have expertise in accessibility, they tend to rely on the tool results only.

Accessibility evaluation tools are a useful resource to identify accessibility problems but they cannot solve them. Developers have to solve them by making changes on the web content to improve accessibility based on the automated evaluations results, but also on the evaluation results obtained with the help of accessibility experts and potential users with different types of disabilities. It is recommended to involve potential learners with aging-related disabilities and foreign language learners. These users may help to identify additional accessibility barriers that are not easily discovered by expert-based evaluation alone.

FUTURE RESEARCH DIRECTIONS

Continuing research is essential for improving inclusion of diverse learners in MOOCs. As Howard A. Rosenblum, CEO of the National Association of the Deaf stated, "Online content represents the next frontier for learning and lifelong education" (NAD, 2015).

For future work, next step is to formally validate the specified accessibility requirements. This validation will ensure that the accessibility requirements specification model is complete, correct, consistent, clear, unambiguous, and truly reflects MOOC potential users' needs.

Also, future work includes developing extensions for authoring tools that allow MOOCs creators to design and implement courses with improved accessibility.

CONCLUSION

Software solutions and educational content must adapt to users, not the other way around. This is the best cost-effective way to design a solution, especially in scenarios where large numbers of diverse users are expected to access and use a product, as is the case in MOOCs.

That is why this chapter proposed a specification of accessibility requirements for MOOCs based on the accessibility needs of potential users; and the design, implementation and evaluation of MOOCs using this specification.

More important, with this approach the particular situation of a person with disabilities may go unnoticed for both instructors and peer students, so the person with disabilities can be treated truly equally, hence assuring real inclusiveness.

REFERENCES

Aboshady, O., Radwan, A., Eltaweel, A., Azzam, A, & Aboelnaga, A. (2015). Perception and use of massive open online courses among medical students in a developing country: multicentre cross-sectional study. *BMJ open*. Retrieved from http://bmjopen.bmj.com/content/5/1/e006804.short

Adams, C., Yin, Y., Vargas, L., & Mullen, C. (2014). Snapshots from the Lived World of Massive Open Online Courses (MOOCs): A phenomenological study of learning large. *Proceedings of the 9th International Conference on Networked Learning*.

Agarwal, A. (2013). Online universities: It's time for teachers to join the revolution. *The Guardian*. Retrieved from http://www.theguardian.com/education/2013/jun/15/university-education-online-mooc

Al-Mouh, N., Al-Khalifa, A., & Al-Khalifa, H. (2014) A First Look into MOOCs Accessibility. *Proceedings of the 15th International Conference on Computers Helping People with Special Needs ICCHP* (pp. 145-152). Springer. doi:10.1007/978-3-319-08596-8_22

Bohnsack, M., & Puhl, S. (2014). Accessibility of MOOCs. *Proceedings of the 15th International Conference on Computers Helping People with Special Needs ICCHP. Springer International Publishing,* 141-144. doi:10.1007/978-3-319-08596-8_21

Burgstahler, S. (2002). Real connections: Making distance learning accessible to everyone. Retrieved from https://www3.cac.washington.edu/doit/Brochures/PDF/distance.learn.pdf

Calle-Jimenez, T., Sanchez-Gordon, S., & Luján-Mora, S. (2014) Web Accessibility Evaluation of Massive Open Online Courses on Geographical Information Systems. *IEEE Global Engineering Education Conference EDUCON* (pp. 680-686). doi:10.1109/EDUCON.2014.6826167

Christensen, S. (2001). How We Work to Make the Web SPEAK. *Computers in Libraries, 21*(9), 30–34.

Daniel, J. (2012). Making sense of MOOCs: Musings in a maze of myth, paradox and possibility. *Journal of Interactive Media in Education, 2013*(3).

De Santana, V. F., De Oliveira, R., Almeida, L. D. A., & Baranauskas, M. C. C. (2012). Web accessibility and people with dyslexia: a survey on techniques and guidelines. *Proceedings of the International Cross-Disciplinary Conference on Web Accessibility*. doi:10.1145/2207016.2207047

Diez, E., Alonso, A., Verdugo, M.A., Campo, M., Sancho, I., & Sánchez, S. (2011). European Higher Education Area: standards and indicators of good practices for the attention of college students with disabilities. Retrieved from http://sid.usal.es/libros/discapacidad/26032/8-1/espacio-europeo-de-educacion-superior.aspx

Gaebel, M. (2013). MOOCs: Massive Open Online Courses. European University Association Occasional Papers. Retrieved from http://www.eua.be/Libraries/Publication/EUA_Occasional_papers_MOOCs.sflb.ashx

Githens, R. (2007). Older Adults and E-learning: Opportunities and Barriers. *The Quarterly Review of Distance Education, 8*(4), 329–338.

Guo, P., & Reinecke, K. (2014). Demographic differences in how students navigate through MOOCs. *Proceedings of the first ACM Conference on Learning @ Scale* (pp. 21-30). doi:10.1145/2556325.2566247

Hasselbring, T., & Williams, C. (2000). Use of computer technology to help students with special needs. *The Future of Children, 10*(2), 102–122. doi:10.2307/1602691 PMID:11255702

Holcomb, T., & Kreeft, J. (1992). ESL Literacy for a Linguistic Minority: The Deaf Experience. Retrieved from http://www.cal.org/caela/esl_resources/digests/ESLlit.html

Horton, S., & Sloan, D. (2014). Accessibility in Practice: A Process-Driven Approach to Accessibility. In Inclusive Designing (pp. 105-115). Springer International Publishing. doi:10.1007/978-3-319-05095-9_10

ISO. (2012). ISO 9241-171 Ergonomics of human-system interaction – Guidance on software accessibility.

Kalyvioti, K., & Mikropoulos, T. (2013). A Virtual Reality Test for the Identification of Memory Strengths of Dyslexic Students in Higher Education. *J. UCS, 19*(18), 2698–2721.

Koller, D. (2012). What we're learning from online education. *TED Talk*. Retrieved from http://www.ted.com/talks/daphne_koller_what_we_re_learning_from_online_education/

Legros, G., Havet, I., Bruce, N., & Bonjour, S. (2009). *The energy access situation in developing countries*. United Nations Development Programme and World Health Organization.

Lewin, T. (2015). Harvard and MIT are sued over lack of closed captions. *The New York Times*. Retrieved from http://www.nytimes.com/2015/02/13/education/harvard-and-mit-sued-over-failing-to-caption-online-courses.html

Liyanagunawardena, T., Williams, S., & Adams, A. (2013). The impact and reach of MOOCs: A developing countries' perspective. *eLearning Papers*, 33.

Mace, R. L., Hardie, G. J., & Place, J. P. (1996). *Accessible Environments: Toward Universal Design*. The Center for Universal Design, North Carolina State University.

Martinez-Cruz, C. (2014). An experience using a Massive Open Online Course at the University of El Salvador. *Proceedings of the 5th International Conference on Quality and Accessibility of Virtual Learning CAFVIR* (pp. 536-538).

McAuly, A., Bonnie, S., Siemens, G., & Cormier, D. (2010). The MOOC Model for Digital Practice, Knowledge Synthesis Grants on the Digital Economy, *University of Prince Edward Island*. Retrieved from http://www.elearnspace.org/Articles/MOOC_Final.pdf

Molina, R. (2010). Higher education for disabled students. *The R Journal, 34*(70), 95–115.

Morales, A. (2007). White Paper on University and Disability. *Royal Board on Disability*.

Mordini, E., Wright, D., Wadhwa, K., De Hert, P., Mantovani, E., Thestrup, J., & Vater, I. (2009). Senior citizens and the ethics of e-inclusion. *Ethics and Information Technology, 11*(3), 203–220. doi:10.1007/s10676-009-9189-7

National Association of the Deaf. (2015). NAD Sues Harvard and MIT for Discrimination in Public Online Content. Retrieved from http://nad.org/news/2015/2/nad-sues-harvard-and-mit-discrimination-public-online-content

Notess, M., & Lorenzen-Huber, L. (2007). Online learning for seniors: barriers and opportunities. *eLearn*, 2007(5). Retrieved from http://doi.acm.org/10.1145/1266885.1266893

Palin, A. (2014). Moocs: Young students from developing countries are still in the minority. *Financial Times - Online learning*. Retrieved from http://www.ft.com/cms/s/2/8a81f66e-9979-11e3-b3a2-00144feab7de.html#axzz3T66iShyI

Parr, C. (2013). MOOC makes Oxford online dictionary. *Times Higher Education*. Retrieved from http://www.timeshighereducation.co.uk/news/mooc-makes-oxford-online-dictionary/2006838.article

Perez-Gonzalez, D., Soto-Acosta, P., & Popa, S. (2014). A Virtual Campus for E-learning Inclusion: The Case of SVC-G9. *J. UCS*, *20*(2), 240–253.

Perna, L., Ruby, A., Boruch, R., Wang, N., Scull, J., Evans, Ch., & Ahmad, S. (2013). The Life Cycle of a Million MOOC Users. Retrieved from http://www.gse.upenn.edu/pdf/ahead/perna_ruby_boruch_moocs_dec2013.pdf

POST. (2006). ICT in Developing Countries. Parliamentary Office of Science and Technology Postnote, 261.

Pouncey, I. (2010). Web accessibility for cognitive disabilities and learning difficulties. Retrieved from http://dev.opera.com/articles/view/cognitive-disability-learning-difficulty/

Preece, J., Rogers, Y., Sharp, H., Benyon, D., Holland, S., & Carey, T. (1994). *Human-computer interaction*. Addison-Wesley Longman Ltd.

Prougestaporn, P. (2010). Development of a web accessibility model for visually-impaired students on Elearning websites. *International Conference on Educational and Network Technology ICENT* (pp. 20-24). doi:10.1109/ICENT.2010.5532117

Sanchez-Gordon, S., & Luján-Mora, S. (2013b). Web accessibility of MOOCs for elderly students. *Proceedings of the 12th International Conference on Information Technology Based Higher Education and Training ITHET* (pp. 1-6). doi:10.1109/ITHET.2013.6671024

Sanchez-Gordon, S., & Luján-Mora, S. (2014a). Web Accessibility Requirements for Massive Open Online Courses. *Proceedings of the 5th International Conference on Quality and Accessibility of Virtual Learning CAFVIR* (pp. 530-5350.

Sanchez-Gordon, S., & Luján-Mora, S. (2014b). MOOCs Gone Wild. *Proceedings of the IEEE 8th International Technology, Education and Development Conference INTED* (pp. 1449-1458).

Satharasinghe, A. (2004). Computer Literacy of Sri Lanka. Retrieved from http://www.statistics.gov.lk/CLS/index.htm

Shah, W. (2014). MOOCs in 2014: Breaking Down the Numbers. *edSurge*. Retrieved from https://www.edsurge.com/n/2014-12-26-moocs-in-2014-breaking-down-the-numbers/

Sloan, D., Atkinson, M., Machin, C., & Li, K. (2010). The potential of adaptive interfaces as an accessibility aid for older web users. *Proceedings of the International Cross Disciplinary Conference on Web Accessibility*. doi:10.1145/1805986.1806033

Smith, M. (2012). Application of the ADA to Websites: Congress Should Rely on the Standards Created by the World Wide Consortium. Retrieved from http://works.bepress.com/marad_smith/1

Stephanidis, C. (2001). Adaptive techniques for universal access. *User Modeling and User-Adapted Interaction*, *11*(1-2), 159–179. doi:10.1023/A:1011144232235

Stephanidis, C., ... (1998). Adaptable and adaptive user interfaces for disabled users in the AVANTI project. Intelligence in Services and Networks: Technology for Ubiquitous Telecom Services, 153-166.

Tsai, H., Shillair, R., & Cotten, S. (2014). Social Support and 'Playing Around': An Examination of How Older Adults Acquire Digital Literacy with Tablet Computers. *Proceeding of the 42nd Research Conference on Communication, Information and Internet Policy*.

United Nations. (2008). *Convention on the Rights of Persons with Disabilities and Optional Protocol*. Retrieved from http://www.un.org/disabilities/documents/convention/convoptprot-e.pdf

United Nations. (2015). *United Nations ENABLE Rights and Dignity of Persons with Disabilities*. Retrieved from http://www.un.org/disabilities/

W3C. (1999). Weaving the Web Berners Lee. Retrieved from http://www.w3.org/People/Berners-Lee/Weaving/glossary.html

W3C. (2014). Website Accessibility Conformance Evaluation Methodology (WCAG-EM) 1.0. Retrieved from http://www.w3.org/TR/WCAG-EM/

Velasco, R. (2011). *Health and Longevity I: Aging*. CODEU, 14-16.

WAI. (2014). WAI: Web Accessibility Initiative. Retrieved from http://www.w3.org/WAI/

Waldmeir, P. (2014). China's elderly flock back to university. *Financial Times*. Retrieved from http://www.ft.com/cms/s/0/aa918952-7ac8-11e4-8646-00144feabdc0.html#axzz3RrTJjcZW

WebAIM. (2015). Constructing a POUR website. Retrieved from http://webaim.org/articles/pour/perceivable

World Bank. (2014). World Development Indicators: Internet users. 2013. Retrieved from http://data.worldbank.org/indicator/IT.NET.USER.P2

World Health Organization. (2011). *Word Report on Disability*. Retrieved from http://www.who.int/disabilities/world_report/2011/en/

ADDITIONAL READING

Bates, A. W. (2015). Teaching in a Digital Agechnology, e-learning and distance education. Routledge. 999

Horton, S., & Quesenbery, W. (2014). *A web for everyone: designing accessible user experiences*. Rosenfeld Media.

Langdon, P., Clarkson, P. J., & Robinson, P. (2008). *Designing inclusive futures*. Springer Science & Business Media. doi:10.1007/978-1-84800-211-1

Pomerol, J. C., Epelboin, Y., & Thoury, C. (2015). *MOOCs: Design, Use and Business Models*. John Wiley & Sons. doi:10.1002/9781119081364

KEY TERMS AND DEFINITIONS

Accessibility: Extend to which a person can use an object, reach a place or obtain a service.

ATAG: A set of guidelines to maximize the accessibility of authoring tools used to produce web content.

Disability: A condition that limits a person's activities or participation in a permanent or temporal fashion.

Diversity: The awareness and acceptance that there are differences among human beings that ought to be embraced in a positive way.

HCI: A discipline related to the communication between humans and computers, its design, implementation and evaluation.

MOOC: A type of online course that can accept massive number of students without pre-requisites.

UAAG: A set of guidelines to maximize the accessibility of user agents, such as browsers and video players.

WAI: An initiative of the World Wide Web Consortium to promote the accessibility of the Web.

WCAG: A set of guidelines to maximize the accessibility of web content.

Web Accessibility: The grade in which web content is accessible to diverse users.

Chapter 9
Addressing Accessibility of MOOCs for Blind Users
Hearing Aid for Screen Orientation

Teresita de Jesús Álvarez Robles
Universidad Veracruzana, México

Alma Rosa García Gaona
Universidad Veracruzana, México

Alfredo Mendoza González
Universidad Juárez Autónoma de Tabasco, México

Francisco Alvarez Rodríguez
Universidad Autónoma de Aguascalientes, México

ABSTRACT

The concept of universal access to information society stands for the guaranteed access for all people in the world to internet services, online learning including. Blind users have been benefited by accessible tools such as screen readers, auditory interfaces, etc., nevertheless this kind of external software would not be required if the blind user's requirements were taking into account since the design process. This chapter presents a set of guidelines for designing hearing messages that help blind students to navigate in a MOOC's interface.

INTRODUCTION

The advantages of e-learning have been widely documented in literature. Nowadays more and more institutions have extended their programs to distance and online education, changing the tradition way things in education were doing. MOOCs have enhanced e-learning by giving the opportunity to students to have official certificates, high-qualified instructors in renowned institution. Nevertheless, the pedagogic protocols have to be transformed away from the traditional in-classroom perspective.

Universal Access to Information Society is a whole philosophy that encourages efforts to assure equal access to digital services such as internet, e-learning, cloud services and mobile technology to all people in the world. Equal access has a wide meaning, including ease of use and delightful user experience, goals that only can be achieved when the technology includes all users' requirements and goals in its design. On this point, blind users' needs of computer based technology has limited satisfied.

DOI: 10.4018/978-1-4666-9743-0.ch009

Accessibility tools like screen readers generally requires third party software; implying that users, besides learning the way the main software works, also have to learn to use this accessibility tool (and expend additional money to purchase it).

This situation in MOOCs' field makes the student required a double learning effort: learn the academic content (the main objective of the course) and learn how the user interface (menus, tools, and all interactive elements) works with this third party software. Accessibility in MOOCs must include ways to attend blind people's requirements, with tools that do not require additional cognitive load.

This chapter is focused in presenting a interface navigation tool that facilitates the interaction of blind users with all the element of a graphical user interface of an online course, converting the mouse in a cane.

BACKGROUND

E-Learning Introduction

The concept of e-learning is defined to many ways, from the perspective of conception and development as a learning tool; the e-learning systems have a pedagogical and technological duality. The first because in these systems must not be containers of digital information, but it must be transmitted according to models and pedagogical patterns defined to meet the challenges of these new context. Technology, because the whole process of teaching and learning is based on applications software, mainly developed in web environments, this is known as training platforms.

The e-learning, in its broadest sense may comprise any educational activity using electronic means to carry out all or part of the training process.

There are definitions that open the spectrum of e-learning in any process related to education and technology, such as the definition of the American Society of Training and Development: "term that covers a wide range of applications and processes, such as web-based learning, computer-based, virtual classrooms and digital collaboration learning, including delivery of content via Internet, intranet / extranet, audio and video recordings, satellite transmissions, interactive TV, CD-ROM and more." (Alwi & Fan, 2010).

E-learning, as Marc Rosenberg defined in (Rosenberg, 2001), is the use of Internet technologies to deliver a range of solutions that enhance knowledge and performance. The author also pointed three key criteria for e-learning:

1. It is based on networking: making it able to be instantly updated, stored, retrieved, distributed and shared.
2. It is delivered to the end user through the use of computers using Internet technology.
3. It is focused on broadest view of learning: learning that breaks traditional methods and techniques

Paul Henry indicates that a comprehensive e-learning solution involves three key elements: the technology (platforms, virtual campus, etc.), the content (quality and mentions structuring thereof are taken as capital elements for the success of e-training initiative) and the services (actions of teachers, management elements, communication elements, elements of evaluation, etc.). By varying the weight of these three components, are obtained different models of e-learning.

In practice, to carry out a training program based on e-learning, is made use of platforms or software systems that enable communication and interaction between teachers, students and contents.

A recent popular trend in e-learning is MOOCs or Massive Online Open Courses: MOOCs are a continuation of the trend in innovation, experimentation and the use of technology initiated by distance and online learning, to provide learning opportunities for large numbers of learners (Siemens, 2013).

Research work presented in (Burgos et al., 2013) indicates that MOOCs are a means of facilitating the efficient creation, distribution and use of knowledge and information for learning by taking advantage of freely available online resources such as Open Educational Resources (OER), and that they can be used to support social networking and other forms of "connectivity" among the participants.

Any well-designed e-learning platform must apply the next characteristics (Bruzzi, et al., 2012):

1. Personalization (considering a student's knowledge level, objectives, time and pace)
2. Learning by doing (through practical activities, simulations, virtual laboratory, etc.)
3. Active participation and collaboration with other students in the Virtual Learning Environment (sharing resources with other students, teachers, tutors or mentors).
4. The use of different sensory channels, ideal for understanding their effects on learning and delivering educational content.

Education for Blind People

The purpose of providing an additional curriculum for children with Visual Impaired (VI) is to enable the child to develop independence. Fully sighted children learn much through observation and imitation. Children with severe or profound VI require sustained teaching to learn many of the skills that fully sighted children learn with little input

Education for people with VI begins with some areas that are considered important and are closely related to the Orientation and Mobility (O&M), such as (Villalobos, 2012):

- **Physical Education:** In this regard, to develop physical skills necessary for mobility and displacement are necessary.
- **Activities of Daily Living (ADLs):** This area has a close relationship, as in O&M there is a projection of the subject in the social environment and ADLs techniques that allow the subject to deal appropriately with their means they work perform different daily task.
- **Early Stimulation:** In the case of dealing with a congenital blind or blind child at an early age is important for the sensory-perceptual towards this development work, favor the interpretation of the signals from the environment and the need for a sensory integration correct representation of space.
- **Psychology:** In the case of adults, the contact with the therapist is very necessary, because this is the area where the subject begins to work the disability.

Talking about education of blind and visual impaired people, schools limits all their capacities mainly because the lack of accessibility in the design of their furniture, buildings, classrooms, chairs, walking ways, etc. This barely favorable environment makes very difficult the learning process.

The ignorance about abilities, capacities and limitations of blind students only reflects in fail attempts in academic activities. Generally, the blind student represents a source of stress to instructors, since he/she do not know how to communicate with him/her. This fact makes instructor to believe that the student is the one that cannot communicate, the one that cannot complete the activities, and the one that cannot learn. At this point instructor reduces the work load, the activities number, and the cognitive demand; to the blind student education does not really represent a challenge more than a boring activity.

In (Kinash & Paszuk, 2007) there are seven considerations that teachers and instructors must attend when deal with blind students:

1. **Look at the Person First, and the Disability Second:** Blind students, like all others, have feelings, expectations, capacities, abilities, and limitations. Teachers must ensure a great environment to diminish al barriers.
2. **Blind Learners Deserve Expectations:** Just like all other students, blind students need challenges to test their abilities; have desire for success and must know how to get up when falls.
3. **Make Connections:** The learning process for a blind student must involve every person that can contribute: parents, specialists, teachers, etc.
4. **Review the Blind Student's "Eye Report":** Eye report is a medical document that informs about the visual capacity of the patient and includes (Willings, 2015):
   a. Visual acuity with and without glasses.
   b. The prescription being worn.
   c. The etiology (Cause of a disease or abnormal condition.)
   d. The diagnosis.
   e. The prognosis (The prospect of recovery from disease.)

When teachers analyze it, eye report may help to define a strategy to attend the student limitations.

5. **Braille Means Literacy:** For enhance the blind student abilities and opportunities, they must to learn to read and learn Braille as soon as possible, through formal instruction of qualified teachers.
6. **Planned Redundancy of Information:** To make accessible the information in class, teachers must plan how to provide the same information in multiple channels. This way, not only blind students will be benefited.
7. **Organization is Critical:** Multiple accessible class activities and materials represents a lot of work for teachers, so that they must plan and organize everything before class rather than at the time of presentation.

There is not a specific way to design and present a class to blind students, but there are several key elements that teachers must include in their work. Accessible education for blind students must have nine characteristics (Kinash & Paszuk, 2007):

1. Braille literacy.
2. Know and apply the expanded core curriculum.
3. Access to textbooks in advance of course.

4. Convenience of digital formats.
5. Relationships bridging (and fading of adult supports).
6. Teaching responsibility of classroom teacher with supports.
7. Universal design (include disabled persons up-front).
8. Attitude is paramount.

In order to develop additional skills and reinforce the current, (Davis, 2003) propose a set of extra-class activities for visual impaired (VI) students, but some of them fit for blind students:

- To enhance mobility.
    - Asking the child to fetch or return the register.
    - Asking the child to take messages to other teachers in other parts of the building.
    - Making the child a room monitor, e.g. light monitor.
    - Giving time before school for the child to use a walking machine.
- To enhance tactile awareness
    - Providing as many real objects as possible in class for illustrative purposes. These can be touched by the child with VI but can also enliven the lesson for the other children.
- To reinforce life skills:
    - Making sure that at lunchtime the child eats alongside peers, with or without a support assistant.
    - Making sure that the child plays outside at the same time as peers.
    - Establishing a lunchtime Braille club available for all children to join.
    - Organizing visits to civil associations, accessible enterprises, inclusive schools, etc

MAIN FOCUS OF THE CHAPTER

Issues, Controversies, Problems

E-Learning for Blind Students

General rules of accessibility should benefit all users no matter knowledge, health or disability. Coombs and Banks' (2000) proposed 16 tips for teachers when start working in online learning:

1. It's about people and not technology. Teachers must avoid to lean in technology wanting to show off their knowledge and potential, losing the fact that technology is only the way to share information effectively to the learner.
2. Do not replicate the classroom. Teachers must find a way to create a virtual presence in the course. Having control, authority and support. This way students will behave correctly in a controlled environment feeling comfortable and protected.
3. Be interactive. Promote interactivity between students but do not forget to also be the most interactive member of the course.

4. Keep it simple. All information in the course must be transmitted as clear as possible, since when students misunderstand something, they expend valuable time by trying to resolve what the teacher wants to say.
5. Modularize. In order to have more focused students, it will be better to break the content into small units.
6. Beware of techies. Teachers must be aware of trying to convert students into experts of the software or platform where the course stands. They have to focus in the course's content and only acquire the basic technical skills that allow them to take advantage of technology.
7. Remember e-mail. A powerful tool to maintain individual and group communication is the e-mail. Teachers must remember this when try to reinforce instructions, solutions and solving problems.
8. Design for universal access. All materials in the course must meet a wide variety of learning styles including off course the needs of students with disabilities.
9. Understand the problems of students with disabilities.
10. Be a virtual host.
11. Be accessible.
12. Make it a team project.
13. Provide redundant communication modes.
14. Have a system to deal with special problems.
15. Understand adaptive technologies.
16. Set Boundaries.

It is clear that all ideas about enhancing accessibility implemented in the course design will benefit students with disabilities including those with blindness, but is important to satisfy the particular needs of them by defining particular design rules.

A very important part of an online course is its interface. It is a whole world the issue of interface design, full of standards, process, frameworks, etc. Nevertheless, there are easy understandable and basic rules focused in particular characteristics of users or trying to enhance a particular characteristic of the interface. For example, (Kinash & Paszuk, 2007) propose 10 golden rules for programmers to enhance interface's accessibility.

1. Images and animation. Use the alt attribute to describe the function of all visuals.
2. Image maps. Use client-side MAP and text for hotspots.
3. Multimedia. Provide captioning and transcripts of audio, descriptions of video and accessible versions in case inaccessible formats are used.
4. Hypertext links. Use text that makes sense when read out of context. For instance, do not use "click here."
5. Graphs and Charts. Summarize or use the longest attribute.
6. Page organization. Use headings, lists, and consistent structure. Use Cascading Style Sheets (CSS) for layout and style where possible.
7. Frames. Label with the title or name attribute.
8. Scripts, applets, and plug-ins. Provide alternative content in case active features are inaccessible or unsupported.
9. Tables. Make line-by-line reading sensible. Summarize. Avoid using tables for column layout.
10. Validate. Check your work

SOLUTIONS AND RECOMMENDATION

Designing Software for Blind Users

In the design of users' interfaces for the blind, (Bruzzi, et al., 2012) propose three initial elements:

1. Making accessible and usable interfaces for blind students: this feature will also facilitate and simplify the interaction of other users.
2. Increasing the accessibility of awareness information on other collaborators: every user (especially the blind) want to know who is collaborating, what, when and where she/he is doing something, and desire to be updated on her/his and others' status.
3. Providing educational content in different sensorial channels: interaction and integration between blind students and students without disabilities will develop perception of less exploited internal sensorial representations in everyone

As mentioned in (Bruzzi, et al., 2012) interaction based on screen readers may be difficult and frustrating for blind people because:

1. Content serialization produces an overload of vocal information in sequence.
2. A blind user has no overall perception of the whole interface.
3. The screen reader announces information mixing content and structure (related to description of interactive elements).
4. The screen reader can announce information in the wrong order, depending on theHTML code (for instance a table's content is generally organized in columns but it isread by rows).

In (Bruzzi, et al., 2012), authors analyze five disadvantages of screen readers:

1. Many interactive elements cannot be detected by a screen reader nor be accessed via keyboard (since they are not standard (X)HTML elements and their labels are announced by the screen reader as simple text), making some tasks impossible to complete.
2. Blind users have difficulty orienting themselves during interaction, listening to the interface contents sequentially, with no possibility of quickly moving from one part of the interface to another or using main editing functions (such as creating or accessing a document) or the document list.
3. Lack of a summary attribute for table used as layout purposes for the list of documents in the Main page does not quickly provide useful information on its content, and this requires and extra effort for blind users who have to read all cells sequentially to understand the content of the table (see area 5 of Figure 2).
4. The editor is not practically accessible. The main menu (file, edit, view, insert, format, etc.) and the style formatting toolbar (font type or size, etc.) are inaccessible because they cannot be reached via keyboard, while bold, italic or underlined functions can only be used through keyboard shortcuts (CTRL+b, CTRL+i, etc).
5. Some dialogue windows are not accessible at all and messages notifying the presence of other users are not announced by the screen reader, against the awareness principle

In (Perisa, et al., 2011), an approach to usability guidelines for interfaces designed to blind and visually impaired users, proposes that any interface must provide:

- The exact position of the elements in the screen
- Simple design
- The option of changing font size
- The option of changing background color
- Correct description of images
- Adequate language support for letters
- In case of video files, voice and text support must be included
- Web frames with designated names
- Standard web forms
- Text cannot be in image form
- If web page uses visual verification (CAPTCHA), alternative auditory verification must be available

Designing Screen Orientation Trough Hearing Aid

One of the first skills that blind people acquire, commonly by instruction in a formal program, is orientation and mobility. They learn to:

- Sensory development: Obtain information about the environment through sound, smell, touch and perception.
- Spatial concepts: Realize that there are objects around, even if they cannot be touch or heard, and notice the relation between them.
- Search skills: To locate things and places efficiently.
- Independence in movement.
- Self-protection: Skills to maintain face in unknown places

In a previous empirical study, authors made a mobile application that help blind users in the orientation of key elements in an indoor environment. By using markers (QR codes printed in floor) read by the phone's cam, users receive information about their location, clues to a previously defined destination, or characteristics of the object (e. g. stair with 12 steps, 10 inch potted cactus, 20 feet long bridge, etc.). This is a pilot test that is still in progress, but the idea was to provide certain useful information through hearing aid to blind people about the objects in around them

All markers were detected by the phone's camera (which was always enabled), every time a marker was detected a sound was played, then the user choose to hear the information of the marker or to skip it (Figure 1).

Sound Markers were classified in three categories; each of them makes a particular sound in detection.

1. Indicators. Indicator markers help users by informing about directions: corners, long corridors (to keep same direction), crossroads, turns, etc.

Figure 1. Blind user interacting wiyh a marker.

2. Descriptors. These markers provide information about relevant objects and places: stairs, elevators, ramps, doors, trees, chairs, etc.
3. Helping. This is a special category for those markers designed to provide extra help for the user: emergency phones, alarms, evacuation routes, shelters, etc

This idea was taken by authors and mapped to help in the orientation and mobility through a user interface: specifically through the elements of a MOOC's interface.

Navigation with Sound Markers

Each interactive element (button, menu, icon, etc.) of the interface will have a marker; even elements as borders, rulers, organizers, divisions, etc. This way, markers will be grouped in the next categories:

1. Layout: These markers inform about elements of the interface that conformed the structural design layout.
2. Interactive: These markers provide information about all elements that require direct interaction with the users to trigger some action.
3. Help: These markers provide common user help

Markers will trigger different sounds for each category, and in the learnability process it will be accompanied by vocal feedback about the category (Figure 2). Over time users will relate the sound with the action and this feedback will turn unnecessary. All interfaces must be as configurable as possible, in order to adapt the user knowledge of the interface. This way, users will recognize all categories by sound (Figure 3), and for blind users this process is very quick.

Users will have the option between hear the information of the marker by keeping the pointer in the position where the sound were played, or to skip it by leaving from there (Figure 4).

Markers will play the information if the user does not move the mouse after the initial warning sound, designers must leave a time for tolerance that may be the duration of the sound or the whole area of the element. Also they must define the area of the element where it is possible to trigger the sound; it can be a point at the center (Figure 5a) or a specific area (Figure 5b).

Figure 2. When mouse stands over an element triggers sound and vocal feedback.

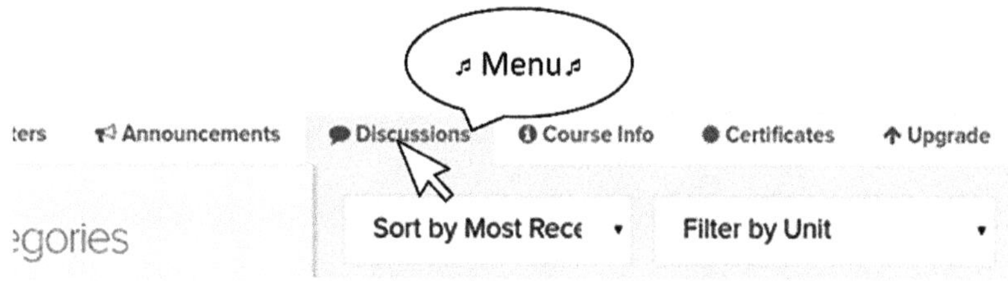

Figure 3. For already-familiarized users, when mouse stands over an element triggers only sound.

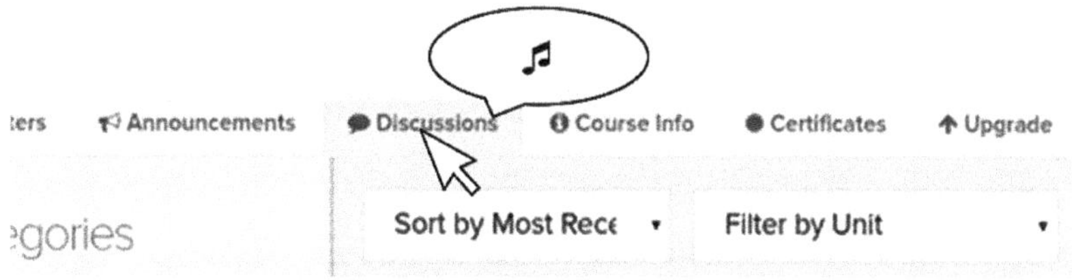

Figure 4. Marker triggers sound about the information of the element

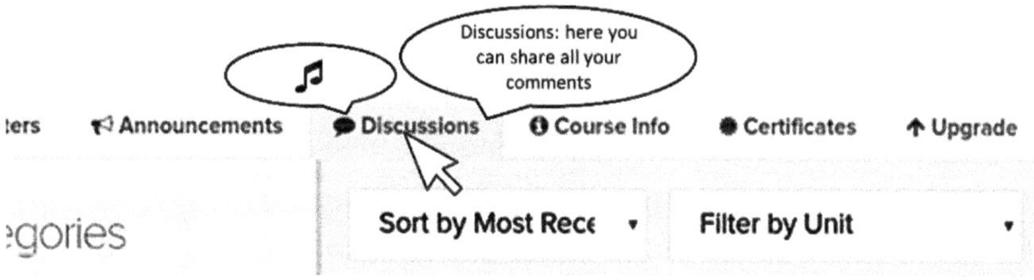

Figure 5. Area of action

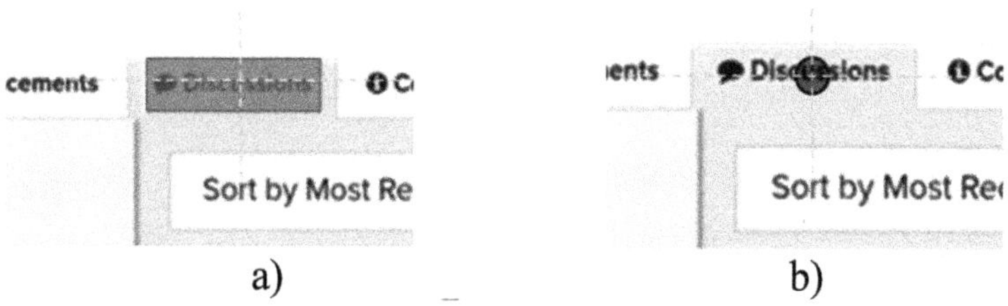

Layout Markers

Since there is not a single general layout format for MOOCs' interfaces, these markers orient about the user's position in the screen, indicating things like corners, dividers, windows, etc. For instance, Figure 6 shows a screen layout style where markers a, b, and c, indicate:

Figure 6. Screen layout with four markers

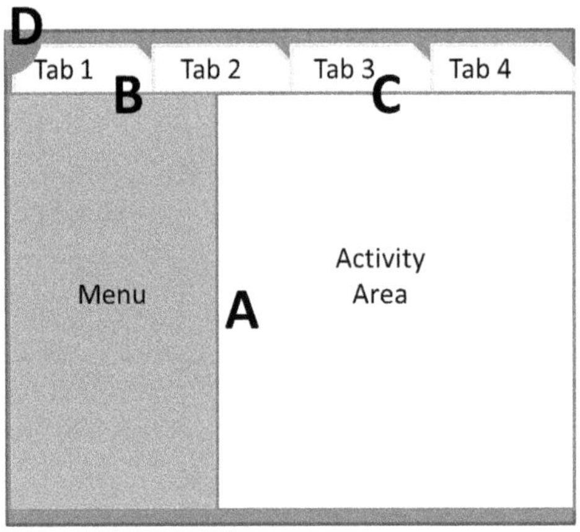

1. The divisor between the Menu and the activity area.
2. The division between the menu and tabs.
3. The top left corner of the window

E-Learning Interactive Markers

Interactive markers provide specific information about an interactive element such as hyperlink, menu bar, button, icon, etc. This particular information includes:

- The identifiers of the element (name, tag, class, etc.)
- The action that triggers
- The way to interact with it.

Figure 7 shows the message that markers play (after the identifier sound is played) when users interact with a) button, b) Hyperlink.

Figure 7. Examples of two interactive markers

Help Markers

Sometimes users lose the track of the spatial organization interface's elements, when it happens, users may use help parkers by activating some specific key (like ESC or F1) or by finding them in a specific area at the screen (like in the upper right corner). Minimize, maximize and close buttons were arranged in this category since they always have the same location (upper right in windows systems and upper left in IOS systems) and they can be used as escape way. For instance, in Figure 8, the user press ESC key, it triggers a marker that indicates how to close the interface. Help markers, unlike others, have additional information in order to assist, for example by indicating what action did just do, what should be done, what kind of sound should be listened, and what action to expect.

Additional Considerations

General rules of accessibility should benefit all users no matter knowledge, health or disability. Coombs and Banks'

There are several characteristics that hearing aid must include.

About general interface design

1. About general interface design
    a. Frequent users must be able to skip additional information.
    b. Interface must be error friendly especially with beginners.
    c. Additional feedback when errors happen.
2. About audible messages
    a. An audible marker is composed of one or more sequential audible messages.
    b. An audible massage provides specific information in the clearest way as possible.
    c. At more messages in a sequence, more specific is the information provided by each one.

Figure 8. Example of a help marker

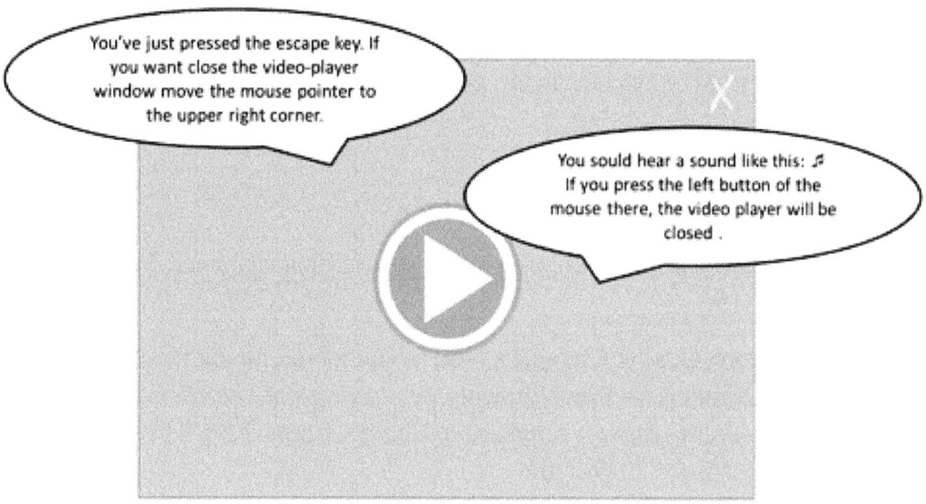

FUTURE RESEARCH DIRECTIONS

This chapter presents an initial research of interface orientation guided through audible markers. There are many opportunity research points in this issue: usability of interfaces, user's learning enhances, markers guidelines, markers learnability, markers usability, metrics for markers and audible messages, etc. Also, a very interesting line of this research is how an interface can be usable for beginner, intermediate and expert users, since they may process information at different levels and understand audible messages at very different speed.

CONCLUSION

Despite all progress in technology accessibility and inclusivity, designers, developers and researchers still have much work to do. Fortunately, there is not a single restricted way to do it, and therefore, there is not unworthy effort. Authors of this chapter were compromised with blind users by exploring alternative ways to enhance accessibility of online-courses' interfaces. It is very difficult to visual-guided designers (and researchers) to achieve this goal, especially with visual-based interfaces, but it is not compared with the difficulty that blind users have when dealing with regular interfaces.

Audible markers are now a very powerful tool to provide extra information about the environment to blind people; authors introduce this idea to interface design. This way, users move a pointing device (such as mouse) through the interface and markers inform him/her about the elements that are in its way. User chooses the amount of audible information that receives by holding or moving the pointing device. Initially, only a simple sound (such as "ding") is triggered, if user does not move the pointer, additional messages are played, until full information is provided or until user move the pointer.

Markers where divided in three categories according with the information that is provided: layout markers, inform about elements of the interface that conformed the structural design layout, interactive markers, which provide information about all elements that require direct interaction with the users to trigger some action, and finally, help markers, which provide common user help.

Additional markers may be also useful, such as markers that inform about the location in the screen, not in pixels or coordinates, but as spatial orientation like above, center, right, upper right; or like cardinal directions: north, south; and even by using clock orientation (known by blind people that had receive such training) 12 o'clock, 6 o'clock, etc. The advantage with markers is mainly its interaction. Users may hear as many as they need or avoid as many as they want.

REFERENCES

Alwi, N., & Fan, I. (2010). E-learning and information security management. *International Journal of Digital Society*, *1*(2), 148–156.

Arnim, D., Piuzzi, B. S., Nam, C. S., & Chung, D. (2007), Guidelines for the Development and Improvement of Universal Access Systems for Blind Students. *Proceedings of The 4th International Conference on Universal Access in Human-Computer Interaction,* Beijing, China, LNCS (Vol. 4554, pp. 603-612). Springer. doi:10.1007/978-3-540-73279-2_67

Burgos Aguilar, J. V., Cox, G., Czerniewicz, L., D'Antoni, S., Diallo, B., Downes, S., . . . Lane, A. (Eds.), (2013). Perspectives on Open and Distance Learning: Open Educational Resources: Innovation, Research and Practice, Athabasca, Alberta, Canada. Commonwealth of Learning.

Buzzi, M. C., Buzzi, M., Leporini, B., & Mori, G. (2012). Designing E-Learning Collaborative Tools for Blind People. In E. Pontes, A. Silva, A. Guelfi & S.T. Kofuji (Eds.), E-Learning - Long-Distance and Lifelong Perspectives, Rijeka, Croatia. InTech Open Access.

Davis, P. (2003). *Including Children with Visual Impairment in Mainstream Schools: A Practical Guide*. London, England: David Fulton Publishers.

Kinash, S., & Paszuk, A. (2007). *Accessible Education for Blind Learners: Kindergarten Through Post-secondary*. Charlotte, North Carolina, USA. Information Age Publishing.

Rosenberg, M. (2001). *E-Learning: Strategies for Delivering Knowledge in the Digital Age*. New York, NY, United States: McGraw-Hill.

Siemens, G. (2014). *The Future of MOOCs*. Retrieved from http://www.educause.edu/blogs/gbayne/george-siemens-future-moocs-0

Villalobos, L. (2012). *Orientación y movilidad. Notes from the Course "Orientación y Movilidad"*. Universidad Popular de Veracruz.

Willings, C. (2015). *Interpreting the Eye Report*, Retrieved April 01, 2015, from: http://www.teachingvisuallyimpaired.com

ADDITIONAL READING

Bonk, C., Lee, M. M., Reeves, T., & Reynolds, T. (2014). MOOCs and Open Education around the World: Recapping the Past Year, Mapping the Road Ahead. *Proceedings of World Conference on E-Learning in Corporate, Government, Healthcare, and Higher Education 2014* (pp. 238-241). Chesapeake, VA: Association for the Advancement of Computing in Education (AACE)

Kilgore, W., & Lowenthal, P. R. (2015). The Human Element MOOC. In R. Wright (Ed.), *Student-Teacher Interaction in Online Learning Environments* (pp. 373–391). Hershey, PA: Information Science Reference.

LeClair, J., & Ferrer, T. (2014). A case for MOOCs, In *Proceedings of the ASEE Gulf-Southwest Conference* (1 - 8) New Orleans, Louisiana, United States, American Society for Engineering Education.

Thrun, S. (2013). MOOCs: The Future Is Here. [PubMed]. *The Journal of Nursing Education*, *52*(1), 3.

Valentin, C. (2015). MOOCs Global Digital Divide: Reality or Myth? In F. Nafukho & B. Irby (Eds.), *Handbook of Research on Innovative Technology Integration in Higher Education* (pp. 376–397). Hershey, PA: Information Science Reference.

KEY TERMS AND DEFINITIONS

Accessibility: Accessibility refers to the design of products, devices, services, or environments for people with disabilities. The concept of accessible design ensures both "direct access" and "indirect access" meaning compatibility with a person's assistive technology (for example, computer screen readers). Accessibility can be viewed as the "ability to access" and benefit from some system or entity.

Blindness: According to the National Institutes of Health (NIH), blindness is a lack of vision. It may also refer to a loss of vision that cannot be corrected with glasses or contact lenses.

Braille: According to the Oxford Dictionary, braille is a form of written language for blind people, in which characters are represented by patterns of raised dots that are felt with the fingertips.

Disability: Is the consequence of an impairment that may be physical, cognitive, mental, sensory, emotional, developmental, or some combination of these. A disability may be present from birth, or occur during a person's lifetime.

Screen Reader: Is a software application that attempts to identify and interpret what is being displayed on the screen. This interpretation is then re-presented to the user with text-to-speech, sound icons, or a Braille output device. Screen readers are a form of assistive technology (AT) potentially useful to people who are blind, visually impaired, illiterate or learning disabled, often in combination with other AT, such as screen magnifiers.

Techies: According to the Oxford Dictionary, is a person who is expert in or enthusiastic about technology, especially computing.

Visual Impaired: Is when a person has sight loss that cannot be fully corrected using glasses or contact lenses.

Chapter 10
Enabling MOOCs' Usage to Mild and Moderate Intellectual Disabled Users:
An Approach to Enhance Mobile Interfaces

Alfredo Mendoza González
Universidad Juarez Autónoma de Tabasco, México

Francisco Alvarez Rodríguez
Universidad Autónoma de Aguascalientes, México

ABSTRACT

The intention of Massive Open Online Courses (MOOCs) is to extend online learning worldwide and to the most users as possible. Nowadays MOOCs have been used not only by undergraduate and hig-school students, but also by the elderly and the children. MOOCs have the potential to change the education in a better way to all people, including off course, the cognitive disabled people. From basic mathematics to specialized technical courses, MOOCs may enhance the opportunity to have better educational programs for cognitive disabled users, nevertheless, there are many things to do, about accessibility to guarantee a delightful user experience. This chapter introduces a new perspective to design inclusive MOOCs' interfaces.

INTRODUCTION

Computers usage has been wide extended to almost all people in the world; this has been abled due to better usability. User Centered Design Process (UCDP) has improved this usability making products easier to use. Nevertheless, there are some users for whom this improvement has not been completely reached, especially in recent fields as MOOCs.

Not only because MOOCs started with college courses, will means that always be this way. Nowadays students of basic education can find a variety of courses about math skills, lecture and language skills, and many other interesting and useful subjects. MOOCs' flexibility make possible to design any kind

DOI: 10.4018/978-1-4666-9743-0.ch010

of courses, technical courses made by companies about a standardized process or about how to use an specific mechanical tool. Although there are cases of college students with mild intellectual disability that has the potential to take a common MOOC, moderate disabled students may take MOOCs to reinforce their educational instruction in school or job. One important aspect of online learning related with intellectual disabled students is about the personalization of rhythms of studying, that goes according to student abilities (Buzzi et al., 2012) .

Making clear the potential of MOOCs to benefit special education, it is necessary to design more inclusive and accessible interfaces.

There are some specific characteristics of users with disability that makes especially necessary the implementation of universal design in all the elements of the software interfaces, the most important is the variety of abilities and limitations found in a user population, even in the most heterogeneous.

Of all approaches for designing software present in literature, when the population of users involves or is totally formed by disabled people, there are more than a few that can help to build more usable products for them. When defining this kind of software, the designer should consider two main points of accessibility: First the accessibility in how the tasks of the system are going to help the user to reach the functional objective (as construct a text document, to watch a video, to check e-mail, etc.), and second, how should be designed the graphical/communicative elements of the systems in order to facilitate the interaction with the user (zoom tools, speech tools, screen readers, etc.), this last point is where the chapter focuses.

All these have led concepts of universal software, accessible software, design for all, universal usability, among others; which although the differences in foundations, all of them propose usable software to the most diverse users as possible. Universal Design provides the general guidelines that improve the usability to reach the most variety of users as possible. Through a Universal Design (UD) process, every design decisions are taken considering the needs of all target users, finding creative design proposals that are usable enough to all possible users.

By including the Universal focus in a User Centered Design Process, there is a better opportunity to find all users' needs that can be computationally satisfied according to their characteristics, extending the usability independently of the users' expertise.

In this chapter, a tool, based on screen overlays also called transparencies, to enhance mobile interfaces for MOOCs is presented

Describe the general perspective of the chapter. End by specifically stating the objectives of the chapter.

BACKGROUND

The disability condition would affect the performance of a user only when the interface (and the entire computational environment) is designed without taking in consideration the users' needs.

The nature of MOOCs makes them vulnerable to the previous fact, since the variety of users (in capabilities and limitations) that may be interested in some curse, and that all those users may present some difficulties or limitations during the course and it is impossible for designers to attach all possible users.

The Potential of MOOCs

It is difficult to visualize the image of a Down syndrome young girl having enrollment in an online course with other thousands of similar companions. Does she have the skills to understand the content? Does the academic content of special education can be integrated in MOOCs? Are there enough students with similar condition to full fill a MOOC? Do MOOCs benefit in any way these students?

Not only for Down syndrome, but for all intellectual disabled people, technology has brought extraordinary tools that help in academic, job and daily life. Desktop computers, tablet computers, smartphones and others have become essential in their lives.

In general, people with intellectual disability learn and process information slower than their pairs and have more difficult in the understanding of abstract concepts (CDDH, 2014). In order to answer the first question, it is necessary to know about intellectual disability. There are four levels of intellectual disability: Mild, moderate, severe, and profound. As it was mentioned before, this chapter focuses the potential of MOOCs to be used by people living in the first two levels doe to they have in one side, the potential to develop social, academic and job skills; and to the other, they have the potential to develop a wide range of abilities as computer's users.

Besides some difficulties in the process, people with mild intellectual disability can learn to read and write; with the proper help, they develop skills in transportation, housework, cash management, etc.; also they may be competitive in jobs that do not require conceptual skills (DSM-V, 2014). With the proper capacitation, mild intellectual disabled people have no trouble to reach a good level in the use of computers and Internet services.

Furthermore, moderate intellectual disabled people need help to develop and apply any social, academic and job skill; adults may develop reading, writing and math skills in elemental level, after a long and continuous period of capacitation; in the job living, they may assume roles that require no conceptual and limited communicative skills, but they will need help all companions, supervisors and other people to reach the job responsibilities (DSM-5, 2014).

Next, some examples of scientific work about computer users with intellectual disability, in both academic and job situations are shown

- Hu, R., (2013) analyzes the use of computers and internet services by down syndrome people.
- Kumin, L., et al. (2012) presents how Down Syndrome people achieve several job tasks by using mobile devices.
- In Wu, M., et al. (2007) authors presents how a mobile app called *OrientingTool helps* people with anterograde amnesia.
- Al Faraj, K., et al., (2009) shows how people with Alzheimer can be benefit with *BigKey*, a mobile app designed to make the keys of virtual keyboard easier to acquire.

Online learning for special education is very limited. Besides PresenceLearning (presencelearning.com) there is no other provider of courses (or therapy) based in online services. Also, the literature reported cases are limited to educational blogs. Megan Mead, Project Manager and Math Contributor of Getting Smart (gettingsmart.com), wrote several interesting articles about how e-learning may benefit special education students. In general Mead comments about e-learning and e-therapy advantages:

- Avoid distance
- Flexible scheduling
- Easy sharing information between parents, specialists and teachers
- Avoid unfamiliar place and context

The next list point out the direct benefits that MOOCs can bring to mild and moderate intellectual disabled people:

- Support for the academic content viewed in classroom.
- As complement of certain development or therapy over a specific skill.
- As a way to enhance specific competences.
- As complement of job training.
- As a way to guarantee job permanence.

Universal Design

Roald Mace in (Connell et al., 1997) coined the concept, Universality, to describe products and environments usable and aesthetic to the greatest extent possible by everyone, regardless of their age, ability, or status in life. Nowadays, the universality should be taken as a motivation, since its notional foundations, to design products, services and environments: functional, usable, aesthetic and delightful to everyone.

Several concepts and approaches have surged in order to reach universality. Since some of them now are taken as synonymous (Person et al., 2014), it is important to know the thin line that differences them. In table 1 are presented all of these concepts, the work where each of them was formally defined for the very first time, their premise and finally the knowledge area from which emerged.

The first attempt to provide universal services was the enactment of the United States Communications Act of 1934, where quality communication services for all were required: "For the purpose of regulating interstate and foreign commerce in communication by wire and radio so as to make available, so far as possible, to all the people of the United States, without discrimination on the basis of race, color, religion, national origin, or sex, a rapid, efficient, Nation-wide, and world-wide wire and radio communication service with adequate facilities at reasonable charges"

Over 1960's, motivated by the willing of offering job and educational opportunities for the increasing number of wounded Vietnam War's veterans, the US President's Committee on Employment of the Handicapped and others worked on making accessible buildings, by defining the "Barrier Free" standards as the ANSI A117 "Making Buildings Accessible and Usable by the Physically Handicapped" (Person et al., 2014). This was the first formal effort to provide a friendlier environment for those with disabilities.

Authors of this research have considered that the next paragraph may help in understanding the approaches of Universality: A software product that is usable for the most extend variety of users, regardless their characteristics, environment and objectives, (i. e. with universal Usability), is considered as Universally Designed. And it can be achieve by following an abstraction of the Inclusive Design process, in order to define User Interfaces designed for all. Only through Universal Software, the Universal Access to technologic products and services can be reach.

It implies that a software designer should visualize the universal Design as an objective that can be reach by including to the design process the principles, rules, guides, etc., that considers successfully applicable, from all the Universal approaches. There are seven general Universal Design Principles (Connel et al., 1997):

1. **Equitable Use:** The system should provide identical use for all when possible, equivalent when not.
2. **Flexibility in Use:** The system should support a wide range of user abilities and preferences in both, methods of use and appearance.
3. **Simple and Intuitive Use:** Regardless the user's experience, skills, knowledge, or current concentration level, the system should be understandable and ease of use.
4. **Perceptible Information:** The system should communicate effectively to the user, regardless sensory abilities or ambient conditions.
5. **Tolerance Error:** The system should minimize adverse consequences of accidental user's mistakes.
6. **Low Physical Effort:** A minimum of fatigue should be required for a efficient and comfortable use.
7. **Size ad Space:** Regardless the user's body size, posture or mobility, the system should provide the necessary and appropriate size and space to complete the tasks.

In the search of its universality, a product design may require the use of specialized tools in order to have a more accessible product. Accessible Design dictates that every accessible product must:

1. Provide the necessary assistive tools to the user (volume controls, zoom controls, speech tools, etc.), or
2. Be compatible with the assistive tools of the user (headphones, haptic devices, augmentative devices, etc.)

Universal Usability, as Horton and Leventhal say in (Hortn & Leventhal, 2008) requires Universal Access, Usability and Universal Design. They remark,

... User Centered Design contributes to Universal Access and Usability, but the key to Universal Usability is a Universal Design Methodology (Hortn & Leventhal, 2008)

Formally, a Software product that is universally usable requires three key elements at least (Hortn & Leventhal, 2008):

- **Universal Access**: Elements of the user interfaces must be accessible.
- **Usability**: The user interfaces must be functional and delightful.
- **Universal Design**: The capacity of the software to be accessible and usable for everyone, must be integrated in the design.

The approach User Interfaces for All is another specification for software design of the Universal Design and Universal Access seeking to minimize the need for posteriori adaptations and deliver products that can be used by the widest possible e-user population (Stephanidis, 2001). Stephanidis also mentions that "User Interfaces for All is an attempt to apply, exemplify, and specify the principles of Universal Access and Design for All in the context of HCI)". The author also express that the key ingredient of User Interfaces for All is the capability to encapsulate alternative interactive behaviors.

Again, if the designer wants to define a user interface for all, the approach provides the characteristics that should be reached, some good practices and even some evaluations that must be done, but, the whole design process could be completed by adding best practices, rules, guides, etc., of other approaches.

Making a universal software means that the software will be useful and usable for disabled people, since it no matter what abilities, skills or capacities have. By following the general principles of Universality, it is possible to define elements of the software product that reach universality; nevertheless, this will depend of the variety of the population.

The variety in skills, needs and capacities of the user population will affect directly how hard will be for designers to reach the universality in their products. Definitely, at some point, applying the universal approach turns to be infeasible, since the objective of usability for all is impossible to reach due to this variability. Designers could minimize this infeasibility by:

- Reducing the range of users in order to create a more homogenous population.
- Applying more specific approaches in the design process that specifically dictates how to manage a varied population of users.

Disability

Disability is the inability to accommodate to the world as it is currently designed (Vanderheiden, 1995).

Generally speaking, humans are limited in their capacity to process information; this has important implications for design (Dix et al, 2010). Evidently, knowing the user needs will help to reach the level of usability required by the user, in other words, when designer can translate user capacities, abilities and limitations to the design process, the system has a clear opportunity to be as expected by the user (Dix et al, 2010). The functional activity of a person (user) will be restricted by 4 factors (WHO, 2001):

1. Health conditions
2. Contextual factors
3. Body structure and functions

These factors are part of the International Classification of Functioning, Disability and Health (ICF) and take both biological and social aspects that affect every individual, this approach is called *biopsychological model* (Figure 1).

Furthermore, there are 5 interaction limitations that, at some level, affect the Body structure and functions (Vanderheiden, 2012):

1. Vision impairments
2. Hearing impairments
3. Speaking impairments
4. Motor impairments
5. Learning impairments

Figure 1. Biopsychological Model

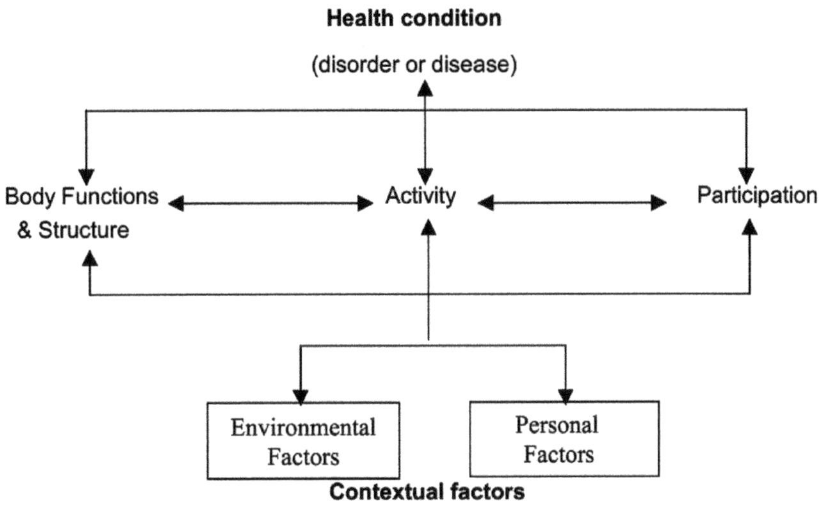

So what is the difference between the disabled user and the functional user? There is apparently no difference, since all users may be considered, at some level, disabled. But, in analyzing and attending the users' needs, the main difference will be the level of affection in the 5 interaction limitations, and in the 4 factors of restriction.

MAIN FOCUS OF THE CHAPTER

More Accessible Inclusive MOOCs

Mobile touch screen devices have become the most popular way to access internet services; MOOCs' interface designers most consider this fact; also, for some users, the first approach to this technology may be through the MOOC, so that the interface must provide help to the general interaction with the device.

An empirical study over a population of intellectual disabled users, at its first stage (not completed yet), shows that users have troubles to understand the basic gestural interaction, having problems not only with some gestures but even with the concept of touching the screen (rubbing the surface of the device): instructors must explicitly indicate to touch and rub the device's surface to interact with it. This happened in a population of mild-moderate intellectual disabled users that has the potential to develop job skills.

The next paragraphs explain a useful tool for enhance the accessibility of MOOCs interfaces by explaining explicitly the way to manipulate with their elements of interaction.

A Tool for Accessibility

When update or a considerable modification is applied over a web site, designers have developed ways to facilitate users the transition from the old version to the new one. The most popular among designers is the transparency.

Figure 2. Example of Transparency (Courtesy of ComunicAide for iPad)

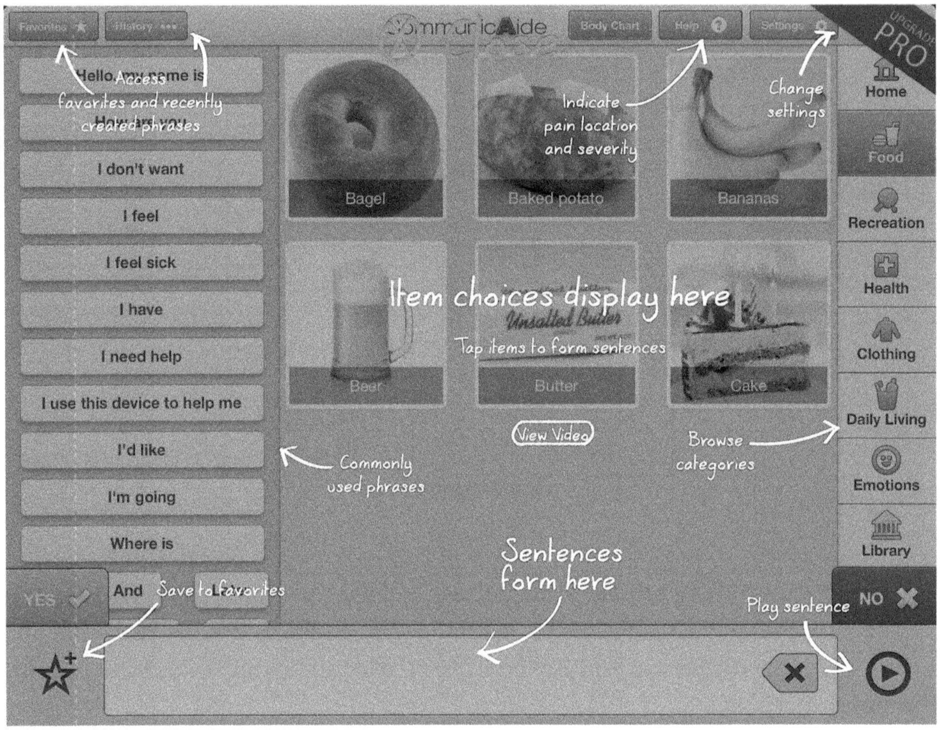

Transparencies explain the way the elements of the interface should be used. In a MOOC's interface could be dozens of elements that the user may interact with. They usually are shown in the home page and they should be removed once the interaction starts. The next figure shows an example of how the user is informed of the used of new elements through a transparency (figure 2).

Never the less, it is complicated to new users to difference the static elements of the interactive ones. When an intellectual-disabled user encounters for the very first time with a MOOC's interface, it will be a challenge to know what things can be done on it.

Unfortunately, there some characteristics in transparencies that makes them difficult to understand by intellectual-disabled user.

- Greater number of elements to explain, great cognitive load.
- Text based.
- Greater number of elements to explain, smaller the size of the text and figures.
- Limited explanation.

Actually, there are some gold rules to user's help that can be added to the transparency. When the interface pretends to teach anything about it to the user (any way of user's help) it must be done with specifics characteristics (Neil, 2014):

1. Use less text
2. No frontloading

3. Make it rewarding
4. Reinforce learning through use
5. Listen to your users

Number one is ok. Since the reading comprehension of the user could be limited, the fewer text, the best. There is no way to apply number two, because the user must know since the beginning at least how to use the tool. Numbers three and four should compromise the weight of the tool, and the objective of build an assistive tool is to facilitate the user's interaction, not to make it worst by adding loading time. Finally, number five will be very difficult to exploit since the intellectual-disabled users have difficulties to express they thoughts.

This gives the idea that even the best ideas for neuro-typical users, may not be applied with such success with intellectual-disabled users.

SOLUTIONS AND RECOMMENDATIONS

Transparencies for Cognitive Disabled Users

The help assistive tool here presented is based on a set of transparencies, one for each interactive element in the interface indicating the user how to interact with them individually. The main characteristics are listed below:

- Simple, understandable phrases
- Expositive simple images
- Explicit interaction
- Explicit activation/deactivation
- Current-state feedback

By default the tool would be disabled and the first transparency is about how to enable/disable the tool. When the user enables the tool, the system shows the way the tool works through a transparency.

At this time, all the interactive elements have an extra icon to indicate that there is a transparency witch explains how to interact with it.

The next paragraphs of this section will be used to explain the possible transparencies for the most common interactive elements used in MOOCs.

There is no rule for the general layout of transparencies, but here, the conventions used by most designers are followed, where transparency imitate the function of a blackboard with a white marker. All guidelines shown next, are recommendations that may lead to many different transparency designs but all of them usable for intellectual-disabled users.

Basic Interface Interactions

There are some interactions that might be intuitive by default to all users, but designers must be very careful when deal with intellectual-disabled users and assume this kind of facts. In a previously made study over a population of DS users, some of them have some troubles with the basic interaction with the mobile device, possibly in the first entrance of the home page or as screen saver in a communal device.

Touching the Screen

There are some interactions that might be intuitive by default to all users, but designers must be very careful when deal with intellectual-disabled users and assume this kind of facts. In a previously made study over a population (Figure 3).

Scrolling

Generally, mobile interfaces of web browsers show the scroll bars (vertical and horizontal) only until users make the action. A way the interface may explicitly exhibit to user that he/she can move the visualized zone is presented in figure 4.

Zooming In/Out

A test over the most commonly used mobile gestures over a population of intellectual-disabled users, shows that the pinch and spread gestures are the most complicated to develop by them; so that, the presentation of this action should be very understandable. The next figure shows a transparency that indicates the user how to use the pinch and spread gestures to zoom out and zoom in the current page in the web site (Figure 5).

Text-Based Links

Experienced users may almost recognize text-based links in a web-site. A generic format of these interactive elements is underlined blue-colored text. Actually, for novice users is very simple to identify

Figure 3. Help for touching action (background image courtesy of edx.org)

Figure 4. Help for scrolling (background image courtesy of edx.org)

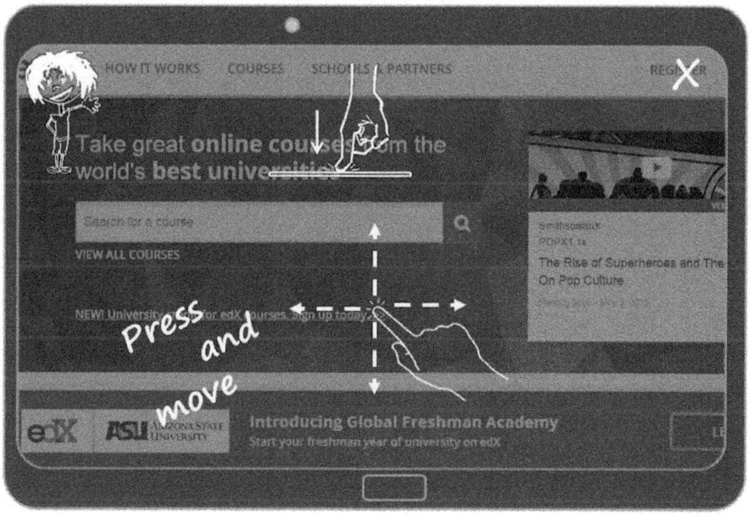

Figure 5. Help for zoom out/in (background image courtesy of ndss.org)

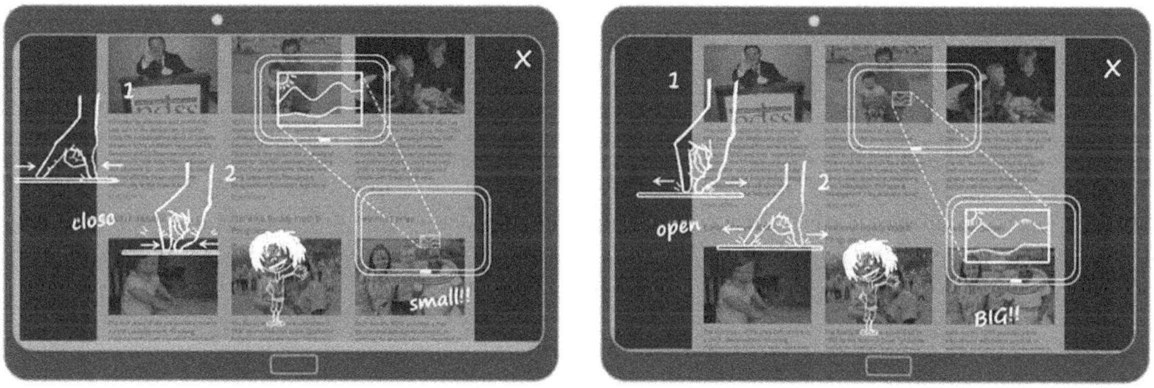

them with the pointer. But, for mobile interfaces that do not use any pointing device, it represents quite a challenge to novice users to identify witch part of text results to be a link (figure 6).

Image-Based Links

A little more difficult is to any user to find out which image or picture in the interface has link to another page on it. Figure 7 shows a transparency that indicates user what to expect when touching an image.

Slider

Designers use sliders to present different content, pages or options to user in a more interactive way. In mobile touching interface, users use touch-and-drag gesture to interact with it, figure 8 shows visual help to explain it.

Figure 6. Help for text-based links (background image courtesy of ndss.org)

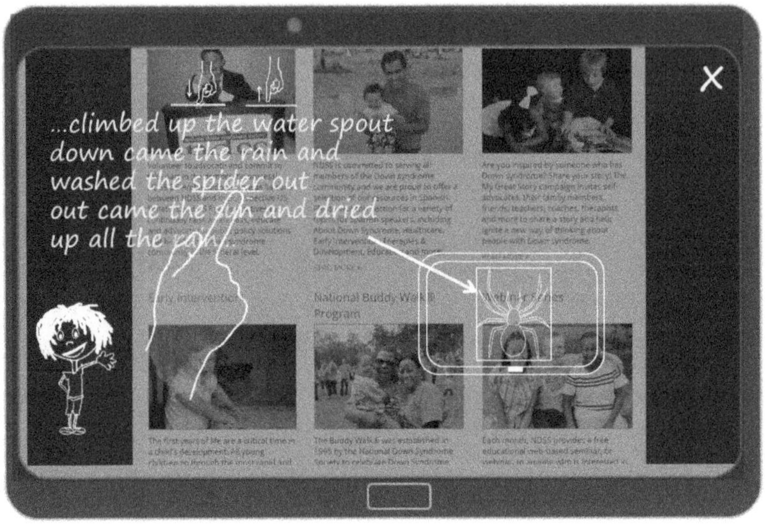

Figure 7. Help for image-based link

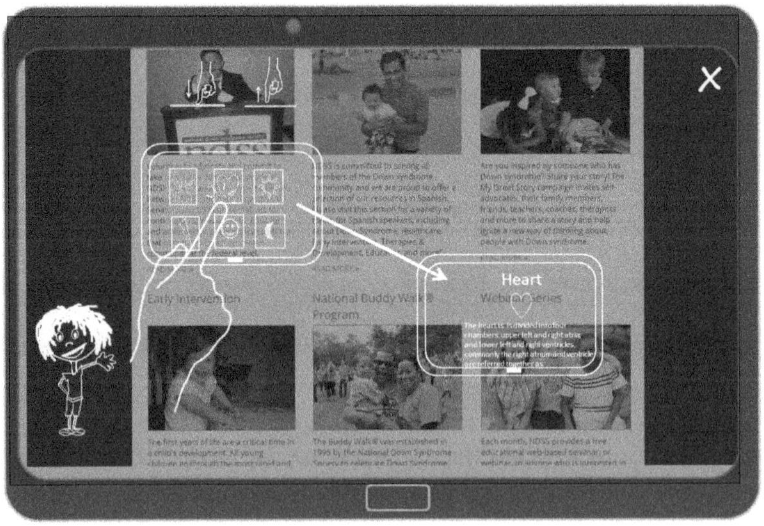

A test over the most commonly used mobile gestures over a population of intellectual-disabled users, shows that the pinch and spread gestures are the most complicated to develop by them; so that, the presentation of this action should be very understandable. The next figure shows a transparency that indicates the user how to use the pinch and spread gestures to zoom out and zoom in the current page in the web site.

Figure 8. Help for Slider

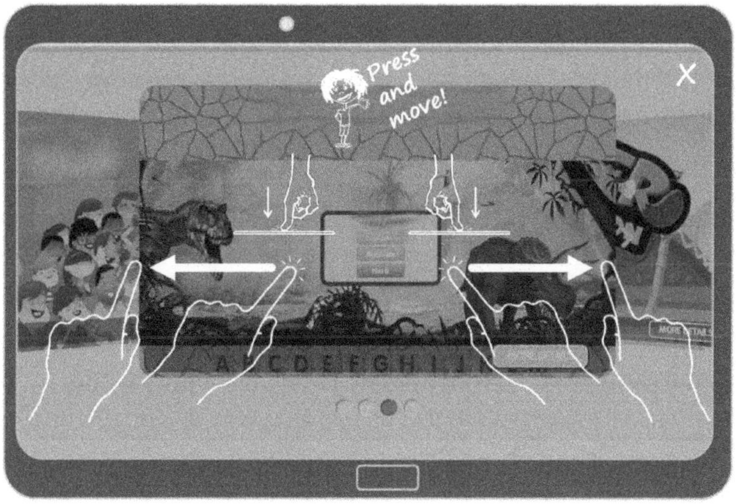

Drop-Down List

The trouble with drop-down list is that requires three gestures to interact with it: first, user have to touch the button to display all elements in the list, depending on the number of elements, if all elements do not fit in the screen, user must hold and drag the list from top to bottom to scroll it. Finally, user selects and element. Figure 9 shows a way to indicate this process to users.

Figure 9. Help for drop-down list

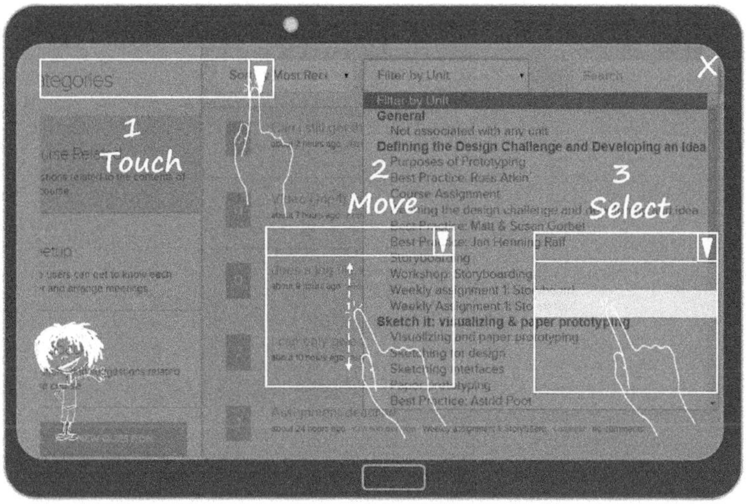

Menu List

Menu list presents all options arranged vertically. In order to inform the user about his/her progress, all elements are presented all the time, and the current one selected is some way labeled. An independent scroll for the menu and for the current screen is the better way to facilitate navigation, so that, user must know that dragging the menu from top to bottom to scroll it (figure 10).

Tabs

Tabs are used to present different screens in a single window. By selecting one of the tabs, user can change of current screen. Al the other elements in the window will not change (menus, tool bars, etc.). Figure 11 shows how the user can be informed about the interaction with tabs.

Video Player

Generally, videos posted in MOOCS are configured to watch them inside the interface, in this way, besides all the tools that user can use in the player, only has to touch the play button to start playback (figure 12).

FUTURE RESEARCH DIRECTIONS

Designers must find a way to enable/disable the transparencies in the MOOC interface in order to respect the preferences of users. Nevertheless the tool must be there to help those that may need it and some of them could not be skilled to find out how to enable it.

The easiest way to do it is to leave the disabling process far away of novice users but accessible to those who had reach this skill, for example explaining it in the FAQ section.

Figure 10. Help for Menu list

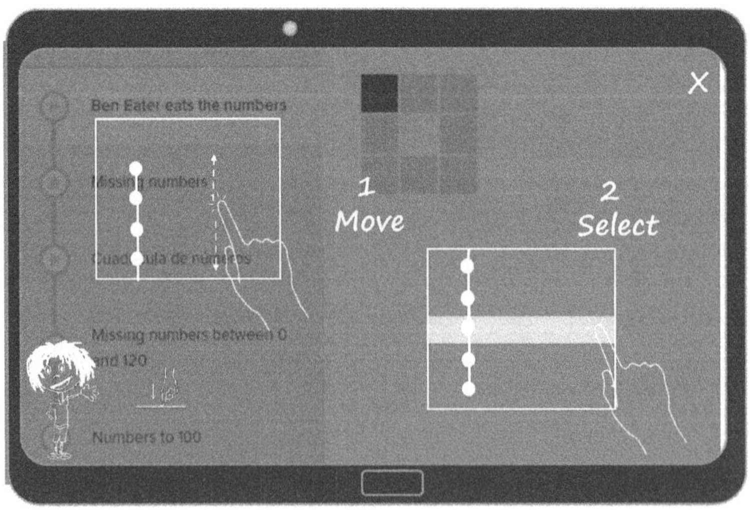

Figure 11. Help for Tabs

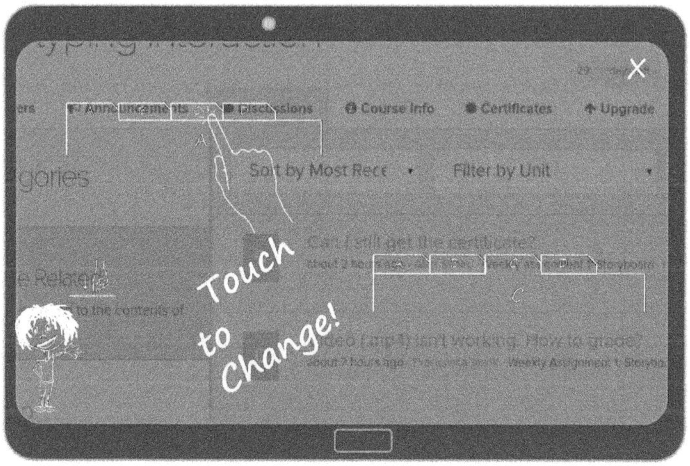

Figure 12. Help for video player

Besides some users will need all the possible help at every moment, some intellectual disabled users may reach some level of computational skills where extra help could turn exhaust, but configurable user preference could be far to understand yet. Two ways to assist users are presented next.

A Digital Companion

The purpose to include in every transparency a funny character is to make a bound with the user. If the character is always presented in the MOOC, by interacting with it, it can present the option to display or hide the transparencies. The key is that this companion must remind the user its availability to help, but avoiding being annoying.

Help Icons

Another easy way to present transparencies is by adding extra icons to the interface. Figure 13 presents a MOOC interface where help icons were added to all of its interactive elements. The extra icon chosen was a question mark.

The very first transparency must show the user how to interact with these help icons (figure 14).

Figure 13. Example of help icons

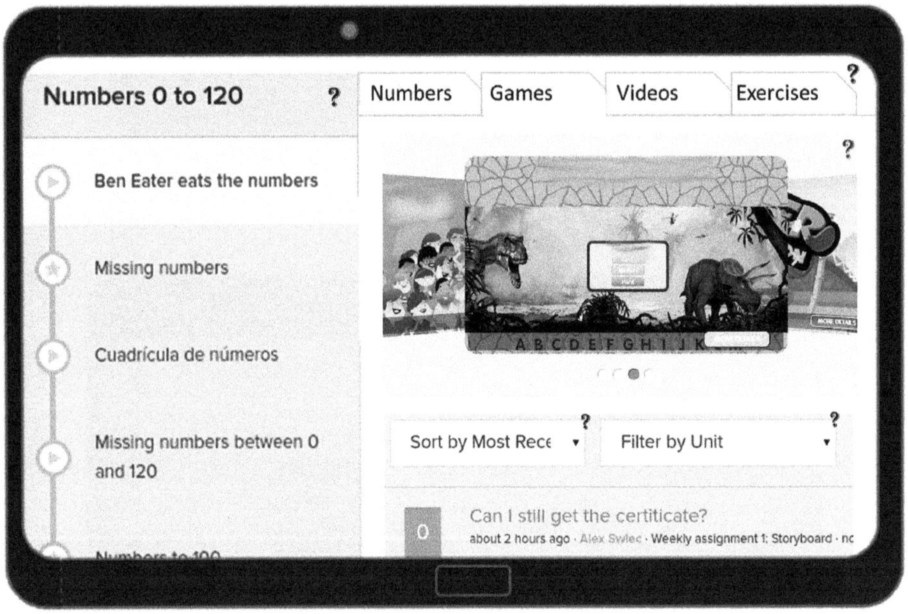

Figure 14. First transparency

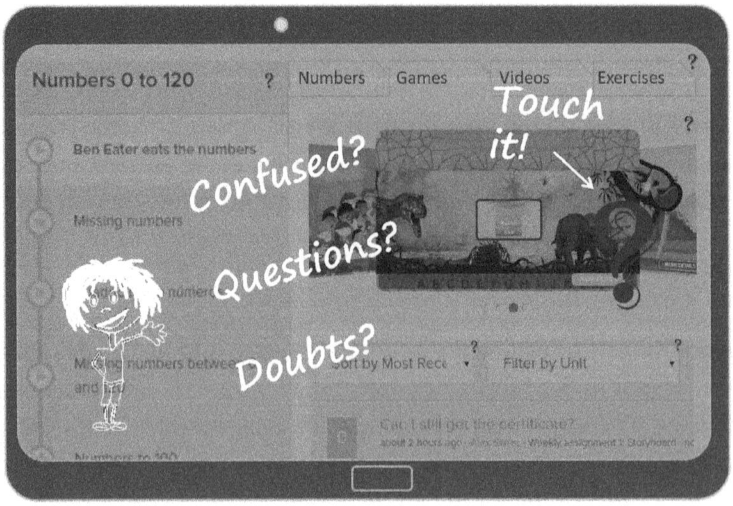

CONCLUSION

Accessibility in the Information Society has brought a revolutionary thought where not only experts and trained users should have a great experience using technology, but everybody.

Internet services as e-learning have also provide access to education to people that in other condition would never have it, diminishing barriers as distance and time.

MOOCs have revolutionized the way e-learning have been going, providing new opportunities to all students over the world. The potential of MOOCs can be extended, with the proper changes and adjustments, to the intellectual disabled students. It has begun with a couple of web sites were people with this disability can have their suitable and personalized therapy. With MOOCs, students might have not only therapy but academic enhancement and even job capacitation; resulting in a better quality of life.

In this chapter an example of how designers can make a little more accessible MOOCs' interfaces have been presented. This aid is based on screens overlay where some considerations of users with intellectual disabilities were integrated to its design. Nevertheless, it is too much wide the rank of abilities, capacities and limitation of all people with intellectual disabilities, to clearly define only one user profile. Thus, designers must define rules wide enough to improve usability to the more variety of users as possible.

There is too much work to be done, in order to enhance the communication between MOOCs interfaces and cognitive disabled users, but this chapter presents an effort to firstly, recognize that there is a group of users with special needs that might be benefited with them, and secondly that these needs can be satisfied in design without affecting the typical user.

REFERENCES

Al Faraj, K., Mojahid, M., & Vigouroux, N. (2009). BigKey: A Virtual Keyboard for Mobile Devices. *Proceedings Of The 13th International Conference, HCI International*, San Diego, CA, USA, LNCS (Vol. 5612, pp. 3-10). Springer. doi:10.1007/978-3-642-02580-8_1

APA. (2014). *Diagnostic and Statistical Manual of mental disorders (DSM) 5*. Arlington, VA: American Psychological Association.

Buzzi, M. C., Buzzi, M., Leporini, B., & Mori, G. (2012). Designing E-Learning Collaborative Tools for Blind People. In E. Pontes (Ed.), *E-Learning - Long-Distance and Lifelong Perspectives* (pp. 125–144). Rijeka, Croatia: InTech.

CDDH. (2014). *The Center for Developmental Disability Health Victoria Fact Sheet*. Retrieved from http://www.cddh.monash.org/assets/documents/working-with-people-with-intellectual-disabilities-in-health-care.pdf

Connell, B., Jones, M., Mace, R., Mueller, J., Mullick, A., Ostroff, E., & Sanford, J. (1997). *The Center for Universal Design- North Carolina State University*. Retrieved from http://www.ncsu.edu/ncsu/design/cud/

Dix, A., Finlay, J., Abowd, G., & Beale, R. (2004). *Human-Computer Interaction* (3rd ed.). London, England: Pearson Prentice Hall.

Horton, S., & Leventhal, L. (2008). Universal Usability. In S. Harper, & Y. Yesilada (Eds.), Web Accessibility: A Foundation for Research (pp. 346-355). Berlin, Germany: Springer-Verlag.

Hu, R., Feng, J., Lazar, J., & Kumin, L. (2013). Investigating input technologies for children and young adults with Down syndrome. *Universal Access in the Information Society*, *12*(1), 89–104. doi:10.1007/s10209-011-0267-3

Kumin, L., Lazar, J., Feng, J., Wentz, B., & Ekedebe, N. (2012). Usability Evaluation of Workplace-Related Tasks on a Multi-Touch Tablet Computer by Adults with Down Syndrome. *Journal of Usability Studies*, *7*(4), 118–142.

Neil, T. (2014). *Mobile Design Pattern Gallery: UI Patterns for Smartphone Apps* (2nd ed.). Sebastopol, CA: O'Reilly Media.

Stephanidis, C. (2001). User Interfaces for All: New perspectives into Human-Computer Interaction. In C. Stephanidis (Ed.), *User Interfaces for All - Concepts, Methods, and Tools* (pp. 3–17). Mahwah, NJ: Lawrence Erlbaum Associates.

Vanderheiden, G. (n. d.). *Application Software Design Guidelines: Increasing the Accessibility of Application Software to People with Disabilities and Older Users*. Retrieved from http://trace.wisc.edu/docs/software_guidelines/software.htm

WHO. (2001). *International classification of functioning, disability and health: ICF, World Health Organization*. Retrieved from http://www.who.int/classifications/icf/en/

Wu, M., Baecker, R., & Richards, B. (2007). Designing Cognitive Help for and with People Who Have Anterograde Amnesia. In J. Lazar (Ed.), *Universal Usability*. Hoboken, NJ: John Wiley and Sons.

ADDITIONAL READING

Conole, G. (2013). MOOCs as disruptive technologies: strategies for enhancing the learner experience and quality of MOOCs, *Revista de Educación a Distancia*, 39.

Fox, A. (2013). From MOOCs to SPOCs. *Communications of the ACM*, *56*(12), 38–40. doi:10.1145/2535918

Hall, O., Jr. (2014). Future Trends in MOOCs and SOOCs in Management Education. *Proceedings of Society for Information Technology & Teacher Education International Conference* (p. 192). Chesapeake, VA, Association for the Advancement of Computing in Education (AACE).

Kay, J., Reinmann, P., Diebold, E., & Kummerfeld, B. (2013). MOOCs: So Many Learners, So Much Potential.... *IEEE Intelligent Systems*, *28*(3), 2–9. doi:10.1109/MIS.2013.66

Martin, F. G. (2012). Will massive open online courses change how we teach? *Communications of the ACM*, *55*(8), 26–28. doi:10.1145/2240236.2240246

Neil, T. (2012). *Mobile Design Patterns Gallery: UI Patterns for iOS, Android, and more*. Sebastopol, CA: O'Reilly Media.

Saffer, D. (2009). *Designing Gestural Interfaces: Touchscreens and Interactive devices*. Sebastopol, CA: O'Reilly Media.

Sánchez-Vera, M.-M., León-Urrutia, M., & Davis, H.Sánchez-Vera. (2015). Challenges in the creation, development and implementation of MOOCs: Web Science course at the University of Southampton. *Comunicar*, *22*(44), 37–43. doi:10.3916/C44-2015-04

Wulf, J., Blohm, I., Leimeister, J. M., & Brenner, W. (2014). Massive Open Online Courses. *Business & Information Systems Engineering*, *6*(2), 111–114. doi:10.1007/s12599-014-0313-9

KEY TERMS AND DEFINITIONS

Accessible Design: The accessible design ensures unassisted and assisted-device compatibility to technology.

Alzheimer Disease: An irreversible, progressive brain disease that slowly destroys memory and thinking skills, and eventually even the ability to carry out the simplest tasks.

Anterograde Amnesia: A selective memory deficit, resulting from brain injury, in which the individual is severely impaired in learning new information.

Disability: Disability is the consequence of an impairment that may be physical, cognitive, mental, sensory, emotional, developmental, or some combination of these. A disability may be present from birth, or occur during a person's lifetime.

Down Syndrome: A chromosomal condition that is associated with intellectual disability, a characteristic facial appearance, and weak muscle tone (hypotonia) in infancy. All affected individuals experience cognitive delays, but the intellectual disability is usually mild to moderate.

Family-Centricity: The belief that family is central to well being and that family members and family issues take precedence over other aspects of life.

Interactive Element: An interactive element (in a user interface) is every component that implies any interaction with the user.

Usability: Usability means making products and systems easier to use, and matching them more closely to user needs and requirements.

User Interface: Everything designed into an information device with which a human being may interact -- including display screen, keyboard, mouse, light pen, the appearance of a desktop, illuminated characters, help messages, and how an application program or a Web site invites interaction and responds to it.

Section 4

Evaluation Strategies for MOOCs:

Describing Some Proposals for Students Evaluation in MOOCs

Chapter 11
Automatic Item Generation for Elementary Logic Quizzes via Markov Logic Networks

Davor Lauc
University of Zagreb, Croatia

Nina Grgić Hlača
University of Zagreb, Croatia

Sandro Skansi
Infigo IS, Croatia

ABSTRACT

The aim of this chapter is to present an exam preparation system designed to generate exams for propositional logic. The main challenge was to determine a filter to single out relevant problems. An expert assessment was used to generate initial learning data for Markov Logic Network and then the result was analyzed in terms of evaluation conducted on students. The results point out that there is no significant difference (p-value of 0.2708) between problems prepared by a human examiner and problems generated.

INTRODUCTION

Preparing quality exam questions and practice problems for courses at university level can be a time consuming task. This process becomes increasingly difficult if one wishes to prepare many different problems, to assure that every student has an original exam and an immense source of different practice problems.

The evolution of computational technologies has inspired many to try to resolve this problem by creating databases of practice problems (Frosini, Lazzerini, & Marcelloni, 1998). For these databases to be of practical use, they must contain a sufficient number of practice problems: although this number is not large by database standards, it is too large to be created manually. For that reason some have taken it a step further, relying on a database of templates of problems and generating a pool of original ones

DOI: 10.4018/978-1-4666-9743-0.ch011

with the help of template variables, such as (Deane & Sheehan, 2003), (Liu, Wang, Gao, & Huang, 2005) and many others. This is not a viable path to take for generating large enough number of problems for most logical and advanced mathematical courses. Wolfram Alpha recognized the need for developing a program which could automatically generate problems in the field of mathematics and developed their recently launched Wolfram Problem Generator.

For courses in elementary physics and elementary mathematics, the main part of creating such a database is the preparation of templates, while the selection of template variables is almost trivial. On the other hand, in courses in logic and advanced mathematics, the difficult part is finding adequate values of template variables. Only small number of the possible values are valid items. In this article, a valid item is a template variable that forms a formally correct problem (e.g. in the context of propositional logic, if the exam problem is to check whether a given formula is a tautology, only well-formed formulas are considered valid items).

Moreover, only a fraction of valid items in elementary logic would be selected as interesting, hereby defined as "applicable to the real-world testing". The most of computer generated valid items are either too trivial, in the sense that they are too easy or even when complex enough, they are too repetitive and doesn't teach student anything of interest. Valid items that are too difficult are also not applicable to real-world testing, especially if the difficulty of problem is due to a large number of mechanical, repetitive steps required to solve the problem. For that reasons, the authors have stipulated that the desired properties of exam questions and practice problems should not only be adequate difficulty but also, somehow subjective property of "interesting question".

The first step to preparing problems in propositional logic was to decide which formulas of propositional logic are appropriate for use in practice problems. Although it is easy to automatically generate all well-formed formulas (wffs) of propositional logic, it is not easy to automatically generate wffs of propositional logic that meet the previously stated requirements. A program that could automatically generate such propositional formulas would be a useful tool for exam authors, authors of online courses, and students, as a source of practice exercises.

This article describes an attempt to create such a program, an efficient problem generator for symbolic logic. After writing a simple program which generates well-formed formulas of propositional logic, it was obvious that only a few of the generated formulas (valid items) are suitable for use as exam questions. The next step was to generate a dataset of well-formed formulas and use it as training data to build a classifier using machine learning techniques. To enable learning from both positive and negative examples, the authors have created a dataset of formulas classified in two classes, interesting formulas (positive examples) and not interesting formulas (negative examples). Although, we could have approached this problem as a regression, marking every case with a value in the interval, the authors concluded this would make the training data more subjective.

A set of features of wffs was defined and analyzed. Using standard statistical methods, among many possible features for machine learning, the most significant features for classifying wffs as being interesting or not interesting were selected. The final classifier was developed within one of the probabilistic logic frameworks — Markov logic networks. Combining a basic program for generating wffs with the help of formal grammars and the classifier, we developed a problem generator, which was used for a few introductory logic courses. The evaluation of this model is presented in the last section.

BACKGROUND

Dataset

Using modern computers and standard formal language algorithms one can easily generate a large quantity of valid items. From the problems generated only a few would be considered adequately difficult and chosen as exam problems by an examiner, i.e. only few of them would be considered interesting. This is the most demanding part of developing an automatic problem generator for symbolic logic.

In order to achieve this functionality, the authors have developed a binary classification algorithm, which classifies the elements of a given set of formulas (valid items) in one of two classes — the class of interesting wffs or the class of wffs which are not interesting. Since it is not a problem to generate a large number of wffs, the main goal was not to create an algorithm with high sensitivity (i.e. one that will classify as many interesting wffs as possible), but to create one with as high as possible specificity (i.e. one that assures that most of the wffs classified as interesting are indeed interesting).

An essential part of developing an efficient classification algorithm is defining a relevant set of features and training data. The concept of interesting wffs is inherently subjective. The experts interviewed by the authors have failed to reach a definite consensus on the formal definition of the concept. Although there was a clear agreement on the negative (uninteresting) cases, there was no absolute agreement on the positive ones, which prompted us to choose the dataset (a set of wffs) was labelled by single expert. From the group of experts' datasets, we selected the largest one, which will provide the largest number of training data. The reason for not taking all datasets is avoiding heterogeneity. Another reason for selecting this dataset is that one was manually classified twice with high autocorrelation. Although the selected dataset was sufficient for the scope of this paper it is susceptible to future improvements.

Set of Features

In order to ensure that a classification algorithm works optimally, it is important to choose an adequate set of features. An adequate set of features should be discriminating and adjusted to the type of data that is being classified. The authors recognized which features are discriminating and cover all the essential syntactic and semantic properties of wffs of propositional logic, and therefore seem as an adequate choice of features for the process of machine learning.

The chosen features and their brief informal descriptions are listed in the following paragraph:

- **Balanced:** The value is computed based on the symmetricity of the syntactic tree of a given wff, using the formula $1.0 - \frac{abs\left(l-d\right)}{\left(l+d\right)}$ where l and d are the numbers of leaves in the left and the right side of syntactic tree obtained by parsing the *wff*. Intuition is that very unbalanced formulas are not interesting.
- **Ratio of Connectives:** The value is computed as the ratio of the number of unique connectives, and the total number of connectives in a given *wff*. Intuition behind this feature is that formulas in which only one type of logical connective occurs are rarely interesting.

- **Uniformity of Connectives:** The value is computed using the standard Pearson's χ-squared test of discrete uniform distribution of the frequency of connectives in a *wff*. Motivation for this feature is similar to the previous one.
- **Ratio of Propositional Variables:** The value is computed as the ratio of the number of unique propositional variables, and the total number of propositional variables in a given *wff*. Idea behind this feature is that the number of distinct variables contributes to "interestingness" of a formula.
- **Uniformity of Propositional Variables:** The value is computed using the χ -squared test of discrete uniform distribution of the frequency of propositional variables in a *wff*, similarly to the previous one.
- **Semantic:** A value is assigned based on the *wff's* truth functional status, as a tautology, contingency or contradiction. Generally in many contexts tautologies and contradictions are the interesting formulas.
- **Length:** The value is computed as the total number of connectives and propositional variables in a given *wff*. Idea is that very short and very long formulas are mostly uninteresting.
- **Similar to Paradigmatically Interesting:** The value is computed using Levenshtein distance of the given wff to any wff from the created database of *wffs* of propositional logic used in the most of textbooks. Minimal value of all calculated similarities is used. Intuition is that formulas with close string metrics to famous, well-known formulas are interesting.
- **Similar to a Tautology:** The value is computed as minimal Levenshtein distance of the given *wff* to any tautology. Idea behind the feature is that tautologies are interesting but rare and formulas "looking like a tautology" could be interesting either as example of an error or in other contexts.

The listed features are designed only for classifying a *wff* as interesting or not interesting. Several other features were defined for further classification into formulas interesting for specific types of problems in symbolic logic, i.e. interesting for reduction ad absurdum, interesting for semantic trees, interesting for natural deduction, etc. These features are not covered in this article because their implementation is planned in the next phase of development of the problem generator, alongside with the improvement of the training data and customization for first order logic.

Methods

There are numerous ways to build binary classifier using the abovementioned features. However, one relatively new promising approach is through using probabilistic logic and statistical relational learning (Popescul & Lyle, 2003), (Domingos & Richardson, Markov Logic: A Unifying Framework for Statistical Relational Learning, 2007), (Domingos & Lowd, Markov logic: An interface layer for artificial intelligence, 2009).

Probabilistic logic can be viewed as a generalization of classical first-order logic. In our context, the classical first-order rule would be, for example, $\forall x \left(tautology\left(x\right) \rightarrow interesting\left(x\right)\right)$ codifying the rule that tautologies are interesting formulas. However, such rules do not allow exceptions. It is not the case that all tautologies are interesting. There is hardly any empirical law in education, which allows such hard interpretationIn probabilistic logic it is possible to attach probability to such rules and soften them, allowing exceptions and regularities that are not law-like. For example, in the dataset there is approximately 0.46 probability of the above rule.

Probabilistic logics have been successfully used in many areas (Domingos & Lowd, Markov logic: An interface layer for artificial intelligence, 2009), (De Raedt, Kimmig, & Toivonen, ProbLog: A Probabilistic Prolog and Its Application in Link Discovery, 2007). Their biggest advantage in this context is that they enable not only learning of probabilistic models from designed dataset, but can be relatively easily combined with other theoretical laws and regularities or "background knowledge constraints". Additionally, such models can be easy modified for context specific purposes, when it is important to manually favor or forbid questions with some characteristics.

Another advantage of using probabilistic logics, albeit a more subjective one, is that models in probabilistic logic are "semantically transparent", at least compared with the state-of-the-art machine learning models such as Support Vector Machines and Neural Networks. Although interaction of the many rules in probabilistic logic can be complicated, and resulting probability distribution not easily readable from the model, there is at least some sense of the regularities and rules that contribute not only to the predictive power but to the explanatory and descriptive power of the model as well.

There are varieties of approaches to probabilistic logic (Getoor & Taskar, 2007), (De Raedt, Logical and relational learning, 2008), but for the model it seems that the most appropriate are Markov Logic Networks (Domingos & Richardson, Markov Logic: A Unifying Framework for Statistical Relational Learning, 2007).

SOLUTION AND RECOMENDATIONS

Markov Logic Networks

In our research we use the Markov logic networks (MLN) extensively. A Markov Logic Network is the application of a Markov Network to first order logic (over finite domains), and can be thought of as a different way to generate a graphical probabilistic model. In general terms, the MLN proceeds from first isolating the task at hand and afterwards selecting a feature. The main difference between Markov Networks and Markov Logic Networks then follows: in MLNs, the graphical model is generated from weighted first order formulas.

More formally speaking, a Markov Logic Network L is a set of pairs $\left(F_i, w_i\right)$ (Domingos & Lowd, Markov logic: An interface layer for artificial intelligence, 2009, p. 113), where F_i is a first order formula, and w_i is a real number, which serves as its weight. When a set of constants is added $C = \left\{c_1, c_2, \ldots, c_c\right\}$ a Markov network $M_{i,c}$ is obtained such that $M_{i,c}$ contains one binary node for each possible grounding of each predicate appearing in *L*. The value of this node is 1 if the ground atom is true, and 0 otherwise. Also, $M_{i,c}$ contains one feature for each possible grounding of each formula $F_i \in L$. The value of this feature is 1 if the ground atom is true, and 0 otherwise. The weight of this feature is w_i associated with F_i. When a different set of constants is selected, the result will be a different Markov Network, but there will be certain regularities in all networks dependent on the formulas at hand.

Three main tasks of MLNs are representation, inference and learning. Representation is done through weighted formulas of first order predicate logic. Inference via MLN is done once the graph structure and parameters are known, and the goal is to determine marginal distributions. In this paper we will focus on the third task, learning. Generally speaking, learning in MLNs uses training data and features are equated to ground formulas, and then learns parameters or graph structure. The MLN weights can be learned from one or more datasets, containing positive and negative examples of relevant properties (Domingos & Lowd, Markov logic: An interface layer for artificial intelligence, 2009, p. 122). Additional clauses (structure) for MLN are usually learned by applying some Inductive Logic Programming techniques, using an evaluation function based on pseudo-likelihood (Kok & Domingos, 2005), (Domingos & Lowd, Markov logic: An interface layer for artificial intelligence, 2009, p. 124).

When those techniques were applied to the training dataset, the 136 clauses with non-zero probability were learned. A few examples of the learned clauses with the highest weight (probability indicator – in square brackets) are:

$$[4,95344]\, interesting(a1) \leftarrow (balanced(a1,1) \wedge uniform\_con(a1,0) \wedge simtaut(a1,2) \wedge short(a1,0))$$

Meaning that a well-balanced formula with non-uniform distribution of propositional connectives that is very similar to tautology and is not short is interesting with a very high probability.

$$[4,67213]\, interesting(a1) \leftarrow (balanced(a1,0) \wedge uniform\_pv(a1,1) \wedge semantic(a1,T) \wedge short(a1,0))$$

Meaning that a unbalanced formula with uniform distribution of propositional variables that is tautology and is not short is very probable to be interesting. On the other hand, example of formulas with negative weight (low probability) is:

$$[-3,8268]\, interesting(a1) \\ \leftarrow (balanced(a1,0) \wedge uniform\_pv(a1,1) \wedge uniform\_con(a1,1) \wedge semantic(a1,0) \wedge simtaut(a1,0))$$

Codifying the fact that unbalanced formulas with an uniform distribution of connectives and propositional variables that are neither tautologies nor contradictions nor similar to tautology are very unlikely to be interesting.

Evaluation

While labelling the automatically generated formulas, it became evident that out of the space of all possible automatically generated elementary logic questions, only a small subset of it is applicable to the real-world testing. However, the model of the concept of "applicable to the real-world testing" question developed in this research cannot be easily empirically evaluated. Short survey and interviews conducted with experts teaching logic at various level of education (higher education institutions and high schools) and various educational fields (philosophy, mathematics, computer science), demonstrate great variance among and within those groups. Concept of "applicable to the real-world testing" seems to be highly context dependent and inherently subjective.

However, what can be empirically evaluated is the related issue whether there is significant difference among validity (i.e. distribution of correct answers) of questions generated by the model developed in this research and questions prepared by a human examiner. On-line testing was conducted on 97 students of an introductory course of logic at university level. Subjects were randomly assigned to questions from the pool generated by the model and the pool designed manually. Altogether 2,450 questions were answered, with the following distribution (see Table 1).

Applying two-sample test for equality of proportions with continuity correction, measuring proportion of correct answers in both groups, results in of and p-value of 0.2708. The relatively large p-value suggests that we cannot reject the null hypothesis. The evidence on this test does not suggest any significant difference in validity between questions automatically generated by the model and ones manually designed by human experts.

CONCLUSION AND FURTHER RESEARCH

The evolution of computational technologies had a great impact on the development of modern education. These technologies are used to facilitate tasks which would otherwise be very time consuming or even impossible. One of the previously tedious tasks which can now be solved almost automatically is the preparation of exam questions and practice problems with the help of automated problem generators.

An automated problem generator for elementary logic problems could be useful for many different disciplines, and would be a valuable asset for courses in mathematics, philosophy, computer science and many others. It can be used for the preparation of exams, homework or as a source of practice problems for students. Using a generator for these purposes allows the examiner to generate original problems for every student learning session and ensures that anyone who wants to master elementary logic has an inexhaustible source of practice problems.

A problem generator should be able to generate problems that are original, adequately difficult and interesting enough for examiners to choose. In this paper we presented one such generator and its development.

The automated problem generator for elementary logic consists of two separate programs - the generator and the classifier. The generator automatically generates well formed formulas of propositional logic based on the formal grammars. The binary classifier classifies the generated formulas in one of two classes - the class of interesting formulas, which are suitable for use as exam questions and practice problems, and not interesting formulas, which are not suitable for these purposes. It was developed through Markov logic networks (a probabilistic logic) and statistical relational learning. This approach enables learning of probabilistic models from labeled datasets, as well as integrating background knowledge and specific constraints for different usage scenarios.

Table 1. Distribution of correct and incorrect answers

	Incorrect	Correct
Generated	580	633
Manually	620	617

The evaluation of the model was conducted through empirical evaluation of the validity of questions and has not shown a great difference between the validity of manually written problems and the automatically generated ones.

The presented preliminary results are promising and the automated problem generator for propositional logic is being used in it current state of development. However, further research is needed to automate more aspects of logic examination, including more types of problems and other systems of logic. The manually labeled dataset will be extended with more cases and new context specific features, for propositional logic and also other logics covered in higher education curriculum, as predicate logic. This task is far more challenging due to computational complexity and undecidability of predicate logic. The completion of this system will be a significant breakthrough in e-learning of symbolic logic and related academic fields.

REFERENCES

De Raedt, L. (2008). *Logical and relational learning*. Berlin: Springer. doi:10.1007/978-3-540-68856-3

De Raedt, L., Kimmig, A., & Toivonen, H. (2007). ProbLog: A Probabilistic Prolog and Its Application in Link Discovery. *Proceedings of the 20th international joint conference on Artifical intelligence*, Hyderabad, India (pp. 2468-2473). Morgan Kaufmann Publishers.

Deane, P., & Sheehan, K. (2003). *Automatic item generation via frame semantics: Natural language generation of math word problems (Unpublished work)*. Princeton, NJ: Educational Testing Service.

Domingos, P., & Lowd, D. (2009). Markov logic: An interface layer for artificial intelligence. In R. Brachman, W. Cohen, & P. Stone (Eds.), *Synthesis Lectures on Artificial Intelligence and Machine Learning* (pp. 1–155). Los Angeles, CA: Morgan & Claypool Publishers. doi:10.2200/S00206ED1V01Y200907AIM007

Domingos, P., & Richardson, M. (2007). Markov Logic: A Unifying Framework for Statistical Relational Learning. *Proceedings of the Workshop on Statistical Relational Learning and its Connections to Other Fields*, Banff, Canada.

Frosini, G., Lazzerini, B., & Marcelloni, F. (1998). Performing automatic exams. Computers & Education, p. 281-300. *Computers & Education*, *31*(3), 281–300. doi:10.1016/S0360-1315(98)00042-6

Getoor, L., & Taskar, B. (2007). *Introduction to statistical relational learning*. Cambridge Massachusetts, MA: MIT press.

Kok, S., & Domingos, P. (2005). Learning the structure of Markov logic networks. *Proceedings of the 22nd international conference on Machine learning*, Bonn, Germany (pp. 441-448). ACM Press. doi:10.1145/1102351.1102407

Liu, C.-L., Wang, C.-H., Gao, Z.-M., & Huang, S.-M. (2005). Applications of lexical information for algorithmically composing multiple-choice cloze items. *Proceedings of the second workshop on Building Educational Applications Using NLP*, Ann Arbor, MI (pp. 1-8). ACM Press. doi:10.3115/1609829.1609830

Popescul, A., & Lyle, H. (2003). Statistical Relational Learning for Link Prediction. *Proceedings of the 2nd Workshop on Learning Statistical Models from Relational Data* Amherst, MA (pp. 109-115). UMass Press.

ADDITIONAL READING

Agrawal, P. (2013). *Group No. 5-Peer Evaluation System For Moocs.* (Unpublished Report). Retrieved from http://www.it.iitb.ac.in/frg/brainstorming/sites/default/files/Priya.Agrawal_Week_04_Report_01.pdf

Bousquet, O., Boucheron, S., & Lugosi, G. (2004). Introduction to statistical learning theory. In O. Bousquet, U. von Luxburg, & G. Rätsch (Eds.), *Advanced Lectures on Machine Learning* (pp. 169–207). Berlin, Germany: Springer Link. doi:10.1007/978-3-540-28650-9_8

Cheng, Y. (2009). Computerized adaptive testing for cognitive diagnosis. *Proceedings of the GMAC Conference on Computerized Adaptive Testing*, Mineapolis, MN.

Konstan, J. A., Walker, J. D., Christopher Brooks, D., Brown, K., & Ekstrand, M. (2014). Teaching recommender systems at large scale: evaluation and lessons learned from a hybrid MOOC. In *Proceedings of the first ACM conference on Learning @ scale conference*, Edinburgh, UK (pp. 61-70). ACM Press. doi:10.1145/2556325.2566244

Lai, H., Alves, C., & Gierl, M. J. (2009). Using Automatic Item Generation to Address Item Demands for CAT. *Proceedings of the GMAC Conference on Computerized Adaptive Testing,* Mineapolis, MN.

Padilla Rodríguez, B. C., Bird, T., & Conole, G. (2015). Evaluation of Massive Open Online Courses (MOOCs): A Case Study. In Proceedings of Global Learn (pp. 527-535). Berlin, Germany, Association for the Advancement of Computing in Education (AACE).

Perris, K. (2015). *Massive Open Online Course (MOOC) on MOOCs: Course Evaluation.* Retrieved from http://oasis.col.org/handle/11599/568

Pundak, D., Sabag, N., & Trotskovsky, E. (2014). Accreditation of Moocs, *European Journal of Open. Distance and E-Learning.*, *17*(2), 117–129.

Rao, C. J., & Dong, J. H. (2014). Study on Evaluation Index System and Methods of Vendor Selection, *Advanced. Materials Research*, 989–994, 5140–5143.

Yousef, F. A. M., Amine Chatti, M., Schroeder, U., & Wosnitza, M. (2015). A usability evaluation of a blended MOOC environment: An experimental case study. *International Review of Research in Open and Distributed Learning*, *16*(2).

Yu, C. (2015). Challenges and Changes of MOOC to Traditional Classroom Teaching Mode. *Canadian Social Science*, *11*(1), 135–139.

KEY TERMS AND DEFINITIONS

Automatic Item Generation: AIG involves creating test items in an automated manner under a pre-defined structure known as an item model. There are numerous approaches for generating items using a computer, but they generally require the availability of an item model.

Markov Logic Networks: A Markov logic network, a.k.a MLN, is a probabilistic logic which applies the ideas of a Markov network to first-order logic, enabling uncertain inference. Markov logic networks generalize first-order logic, in the sense that, in a certain limit, all unsatisfiable statements have a probability of zero, and all tautologies have probability one.

Online Education: Online education is defined as the creation and proliferation of the personal computer, the globalization of ideas and other human acts, and the use of technology in exchanging ideas and providing access to more people. Audio, video, computer, and networking technologies are often combined to create a multifaceted instructional delivery system.

ProbLog: ProbLog is a tool that allows you to intuitively build programs that do not only encode complex interactions between a large sets of heterogenous components but also the inherent uncertainties that are present in real-life situations. The engine tackles several tasks such as computing the marginals given evidence and learning from (partial) interpretations. ProbLog is a suite of efficient algorithms for various inference tasks. It is based on a conversion of the program and the queries and evidence to a weighted Boolean formula. This allows us to reduce the inference tasks to well-studied tasks such as weighted model counting, which can be solved using state-of-the-art methods known from the graphical model and knowledge compilation literature.

Statistical Learning: The main goal of statistical learning is to provide a framework for studying the problem of inference, that is of gaining knowledge, making predictions, making decisions or constructing models from a set of data.

Chapter 12
An Elastic Platform for Large-scale Assessment of Software Assignments for MOOCs (EPLASAM)

Michael Walker
Vanderbilt University, USA

Douglas C. Schmidt
Vanderbilt University, USA

Jules White
Vanderbilt University, USA

ABSTRACT

To address this efficiency and the resulting inherent scalability problems of Learning at Scale, this chapter propose a platform called SPLAShED: Software Platform for Large-Scale Assessment of Software-Development for Education-at-a-Distance, that uses Linux containers to provide OS-level virtualization. This gives each desired service the equivalent of a Virtual Private Server (VPS) that creates a temporary private userspace on the server. Each VPS provides a separate working environment for each desired application, but does not incur the overhead of traditional virtualization techniques. Our SPLAShED platform applies recent advances in Linux container deployment automation, resources isolation, portability, and usability. These advances enable the SPLAShED platform to serve both as. This chapter explores assignments as a case study: an Android based software design assignment. This case study shows how the SPLAShED platform will able to accommodate and facilitate advanced Software Development courses with features and abilities currently not available.

INTRODUCTION

A Massive Open Online Course (MOOC) is a web-based class environment aimed at open large-scale global participation via the Web (EdX, 2015). In contrast to traditional forms of face-to-face (F2F) education, MOOCs enable flexible learning styles, where learners can pick and choose which classes they take, as well as when and where they do their work. Conventional methods and tools used in F2F

DOI: 10.4018/978-1-4666-9743-0.ch012

education, however, are not ideal for use at scale in MOOCs. F2F methods and tools are particularly poorly suited to software-intensive MOOCs where the majority of the assessments focus on design and programming assignments. The following challenges must therefore be addressed by learning management platforms used for these types of MOOCs.

1. **Supporting the Scale of MOOCs**: The number of learners in MOOCs is typically orders of magnitude greater than even the largest F2F courses (i.e., tens of thousands vs. hundreds). The tools and techniques for F2F courses are therefore not sufficient to handle the number of learners and/or assignments to assess. In particular, learning management platforms for software design and programming assignments require new tools/techniques to work effectively at the scale of MOOCs.
2. **Alleviating Limitations of Distance:** The distance between teaching staff and learners also increases significantly in MOOCs as compared to F2F classes, which introduces challenges that traditional F2F courses need not address. For example, it is infeasible for the teaching staff to meet with learners in software-intensive MOOCs to provide them with meaningful feedback on their assignments. Therefore, learning management platforms for these types of MOOCs must alleviate the challenges that distance can cause with respect to personalizing the learning experience.
3. **Providing Security for the Learning Management Platform and its Users:** Security concerns arise when software submitted by learners is automatically compiled and tested. In particular, server-side compilation/execution and peer-review of code by other learners must be handled carefully to avoid security exploits, due either to malicious or accidental harm to the platform due to software bugs in learner solutions. The learning management platform for software-intensive MOOCs therefore requires a secure environment in which assignment submissions can be tested in isolation without harming the evaluation system or other learner submissions.
4. **Minimizing the Heterogeneity of System and Network Environments:** Software-intensive MOOCs that focus on concurrent and distributed applications requires multiple instances of software running in their own-networked environments. The architecture of these environments (e.g., the target architecture, such as mobile devices, embedded, or cloud services, etc.) may be heterogeneous and thus not identical to the assessment platform (e.g., x86 vs. ARM processors). The learning management platform should therefore support customizable target hardware architectures and dynamic virtual network topologies.
5. **Reducing Operational Overhead:** Various operational issues must be addressed by learning management platforms for software-intensive MOOCs, including information technology (IT) infrastructure tasks, such as logging and auditing of system execution and stability, load balancing, and data loss prevention strategies. Other operational issues relate to (1) transferring learner submissions from the front-end MOOC hosting server(s) to the learning manage platform and returning result(s) back to the front-end servers and (2) handling robust and secure peer-evaluation of learner submissions.

BACKGROUND

To address the challenges listed in previous section, we are developing EPLASAM, which is both a learning management platform and method aimed at supporting the needs of learners and teaching staff in software-intensive MOOCs. EPLASAM is based on our experiences teaching the Mobile Cloud

Computing with Android (MoCCA) MOOC course sequence, which is the first trans-institutional Specialization offered on the Coursera platform (Coursera, 2015). Over 400,000 learners have taken the MOOCs in the MoCCA Specialization over the past several years.

EPLASAM provides several contributions to R&D on learning management platform support for software-intensive MOOCs:

- It employs a model-based method of creating assignments, which addresses the challenges of (A) Supporting the scale of MOOC courses and (B) Alleviating limitations of distance listed above via various capabilities, such as (1) personalized assignment creation for different learner cohorts to minimize the impact of plagiarism and enable controlled experiments on different teaching methods, (2) testing-at-scale to evaluate learner submissions for correct-ness in an automated manner, and (3) meaningful evaluation and feedback to personalize learner experiences.
- It provides a scalable, secure, and customizable learning management platform for compiling, testing, executing, and assessing software-intensive assignments, which addresses the challenges of (C) Providing security for the learning management platform and its users, (D) Minimizing the heterogeneity of system and network architectures, and (E) Reducing operational overhead listed list above via various capabilities, such as (1) securely testing submitted code to ensure a robust process of compiling, executing, and assessing learner assignments, (2) standardizing the development and runtime environments to eliminate potential discrepancies in learner configurations, and (3) supporting assignments that require customizable hardware and network configurations.

Together, these contributions enable EPLASAM to enhance the delivery of meaningful feedback to learners, while simultaneously decreasing workload of the teaching staff in software-intensive MOOCs.

Related Work

Previous work exists on the creation (Menage, 2007) and benchmark testing (Soltesz, Pötzl, Fiuczynski, Bavier, & Peterson, 2007) of generic Linux-based containers, shows that Linux containers are a more lightweight means of virtualization compared to traditional hypervisors. Similarly, related work uses containers as a means to provide isolation and a lightweight replacement to hypervisors in specific use cases. For example, High Performance Computing (HPC), reproducible network experiments, and peer-to-peer testing environments focus on different aspects of Linux containers that they leverage. Xavier et al. (Xavier et al., 2013) show that in the domain of HPC that containers provide an excellent lightweight hypervisor replacement, but at the time the solutions available were immature and unable to provide effective isolation. Handigol et al. (Handigol, Heller, Jeyakumar, Lantz, & McKeown, 2012) discuss the creation of reproducible network experiments via container-based emulation, which is intended to spur other researchers to publish runnable versions of their experiments. They leverage the ability to package, distribute, and run containers. Bardac et al. (Bardac, Deaconescu, & Florea, 2010) show how peer-to-peer testing environments can be developed using Linux containers. The focus on EPLASAM in this paper is on the scalability and limitations of networked applications in a container-based testing environment.

Both the papers from Bardac et al. and Handigol et al. use Linux containers to provide reproducible network-based application testing. However, the focus in each paper differs slightly. In particular, Bardac et al. are concerned with repeatability, whereas Handigol et al. are concerned with the scalability of network-based applications, particularly peer-to-peer applications.

On the other hand, With the advent of MOOCs, the interest in automatically generating assignments at scale has grown. Automating Exercise Generation (Sadigh, Seshia, & Gupta, 2012) describes using a template-based generator together with mutation and satisfiability solving to automatically generate assignment problems, valid solutions, and grading of submitted solutions. The problems they target are a subset of problems from an embedded systems class textbook, which they found had problems that did not fit well into their platform.

In addition to automatic assignment generation, related work has focused on creating Domain Specific Languages (DSL) for code generation of mobile and cloud-based applications. PhoneApps (Mannadiar & Vangheluwe, 2010) is a custom DSL built to help simplify the creation of standalone mobile applications using Statecharts with modular components at different levels of abstraction. Manjunatha et al. design an approach for creating MobiCloud (Manjunatha, Ranabahu, Sheth, & Thirunarayan, 2010), which is a DSL for creating Cloud Mobile Hybrid applications via an agnostic Model-View-Controller (MVC) code generation pattern, treating both the cloud and mobile portions of an application as single entity. MobiCloud supports multiple target mobile device and cloud hosting platforms but requires a custom code generator that accepts the custom ModiCloud-DSL model as input, for each target platform. The MVC pattern is also used by Buck et al. the Objektgraph IDE (Buck, Diethelm, & Sheneman, 2013), which uses a graphical UML editor to generate Java applications, and anticipates Android and Google Web Toolkit support.

In addition to automated generation of assignments and mobile applications, related work has focused on generating meaningful feedback to MOOC learners on their programming assignments. Singh et al. describe a technique for automated feedback generation of introductory programming assignments (Singh, Gulwani, & Solar-Lezama, 2013). Their technique requires a correct reference implementation and a set of rules in a custom error model language (EML) that define errors (and corresponding corrections) that learners are likely to produce. These EML rules are used to define a space of candidate programs that will be generated from the learner submission and then searched for the minimal number of corrections required to transform the submission to match the reference program.

Carbunescu et al. present their results and experiences from using a framework they designed for auto-grading of parallel code for the 2013 and 2014 XSEDE Parallel Computing Course (Carbunescu et al., 2014). Their platform used a C program to verify the output results and a Python script to manage file handling, job processing, and final grade calculations. Grades are based upon runtime performance for a variety of input sizes for each of three assignments in the course to evaluate both strong and weak potential scalability. They present the concessions and modifications they made when designing each assignment's implementation, such as how verification of non-deterministic simulations can be hard to validate

This related work shows the extent to which trial and error can be applied to create tests with meaningful feedback.

MAIN FOCUS OF THE CHAPTER

Emerging Trends and Challenges

In this section we provide more detailed coverage of key challenges and design concerns confronting learners and teaching staff in software-intensive MOOCs. In order to clarify as design concerns the context we classify the challenges of scale, distance, security, heterogeneity, and operational overhead facing learners and teaching staff in software-intensive MOOCs. See Figure 1. In addition, these challenges are described broadly in the following sub-subsections.

Supporting the Scale of MOOCs

The number of learners in MOOCs is orders of magnitude greater than even the largest F2F courses. Conventional tools and techniques devised for F2F courses are therefore often not adequate to handle differences in scale. For example, traditional F2F education has a much lower ratio of teaching staff to learners, so it is often feasible (and desirable) for the staff to individually assess each assignment of—and even individually meet with—every learner throughout the course. In contrast, it is infeasible for the teaching staff to individually assess each assignment in a MOOC with tens or hundreds of thousands of learners distributed around the world.

A particularly vexing challenge faced by software-intensive MOOCs involves scalable assessing assignment submissions from learners. Some types of courses lend themselves to questions (such as short answer, multiple choice, or fill-in-the-blank questions) that can be assessed automatically and scalable with high precision. These types of questions are often relevant in certain engineering and mathematics courses, where learners are tested on the proper application of formulas or algorithms via a range of randomized input values for questions asked of each learner. Likewise, short answer problems can be evaluated via regular expression checking for keywords and multiple choice, matching, and fill-in-the-blank questions whose pass¬/fail states can be checked automatically.

Conversely, the assessment of software-intensive solutions—especially solutions to design-oriented software assignments—is hard to automate via conventional learning platforms available for MOOCs. In particular, since software-intensive assignments do not conform to the assessment categories outlined earlier they face challenges that other types of assignments do not when applied in MOOCs. We there-

Figure 1. Taxonomy of Challenges and Design Concerns for Software-Intensive MOOCs

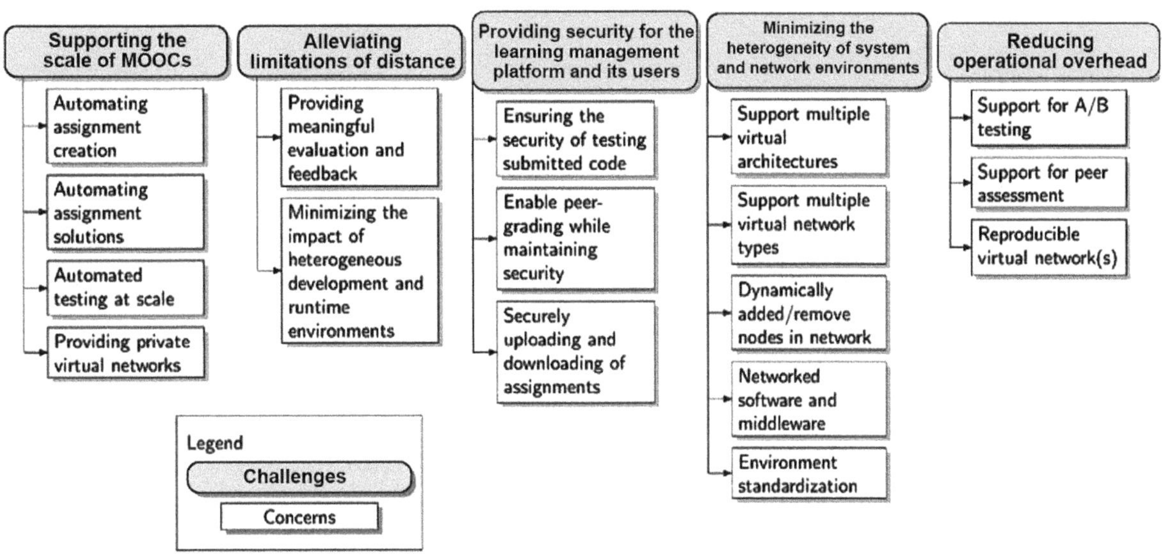

fore identified three goals associated with creating assignments for software assignments: (1) creating assignments in a scalable manner, (2) facilitating meaningful feedback to the learners, and (3) deterring cheating. As shown in Figure 2, it is hard to achieve all of these goals simultaneously.

The following are design concerns that must be resolved to address the challenge of scale in software-intensive MOOCs:

- **Automating Assignment Creation:** Software-intensive assignments in F2F classes often have similar correct implementations, so it is hard to create assignments that both help deter cheating and are reusable for subsequent courses. This challenge becomes even more pronounced in a software-intensive MOOC, where the subject matter has a limited number of correct solutions, such as deadlock-free concurrency or robust distribution. An efficient means of creating assignments that deters cheating among learners is therefore needed for these types of MOOCs. For example, generating different variants of an assignment for each cohort of learners in a MOOC offering helps deter "cut-and-paste" plagiarism from assignments given in previous MOOC offerings. Automating the assignment creation process is essential to free the teaching staff from having to continuously and manually updates learner assignments, which is not scalable without devoting substantial human resources.
- **Automating the Generation of Assignment Solutions:** Creating unique assignment variations for learner cohorts helps deter plagiarism, but without the corresponding assignment solutions it is infeasible to automatically assess assignments at scale. Certain considerations therefore must be taken into account when generating assignments, such as storing the associated solutions to each learner cohort's unique assignments, as well as ensuring that all created assignments have valid solutions that can be assessed automatically.
- **Automating Testing at Scale:** Each assignment submitted by learners should be assessed individually, ideally in a private workspace that does not affect other learner submissions. Moreover, assessing the quality of software designs in a MOOC environment is hard since the appropriate

Figure 2. Assignment Creation Goals

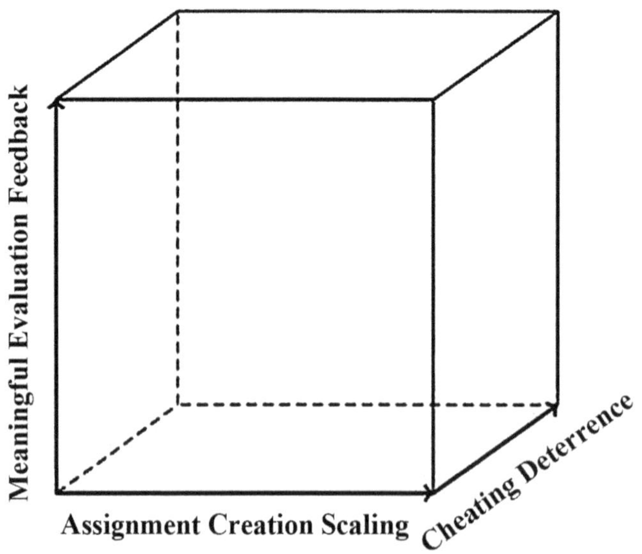

choices of component design and implementations often involve subjective criteria, such as "understandability" and "extensibility," which are hard to automate. Software-intensive solutions can also be hard to analyze automatically if learners have improperly implemented portion(s) of a known design or have chosen to apply a poor design.

- **Providing Private Virtual Networks:** Assignments containing network communication create additional challenges for a scalable learning management platform attempting to host and automatically assess MOOC assignments. Firstly, the platform must support not only a private workspace for each component, but also a virtual network between workspaces. Handling this networking infrastructure at scale requires complex resource management to satisfy quality-of-service.

Alleviating Limitations of Distance

The increased distance between teaching staff and learners also increases significantly when transitioning from F2F courses to MOOCs, which introduces challenges that traditional F2F courses often need not address. For example, it is infeasible for the teaching staff to meet personally with all learners in a MOOC. The following are design concerns that must be resolved to address the challenge of distance in software-intensive MOOCs.

- **Providing Meaningful Evaluation and Feedback:** The need to create meaningful feedback for learners has always existed, but with F2F courses it has been possible to individualize the feedback, often creating it on-demand when questioned by a learner. This level of personalized feedback is not possible in MOOCs due to the inability to meet and assist every learner. Moreover, it is hard to provide learners with feedback on their work in an informative manner that is neither so overly-constrained that learners lack sufficient information to gain insight from further analysis or so extensive that learners can derive the correct answer(s) without having to conduct deeper analysis on their own, on the other hand. While these issues occur in traditional F2F courses, they are exacerbated in MOOCs due to the increased scale and distance between learners and teaching staff, which motivates the need for meaningful automated evaluation and feedback.
- **Minimizing the Impact of Heterogeneous Development and Runtime Environments:** Software development and design courses, even F2F ones, face challenges with software development tool standardization and compatibility. Traditionally these challenges have been surmountable due to the relative small number of learners in a course. Moreover, each learner receives personalized assistance from teaching staff, who can help install the necessary software and/or help learners debug obscure configuration problems. Software development in MOOCs, however, is complicated due to the heterogeneous learning configuration space and subtle interactions between different variants of operating systems, middleware, software development kits (SDKs), programming language compilers, software library versions, etc.

Providing Security for the Learning Management Platform and Its Users

Security concerns arise when testing untrusted software logic submitted by learners. For example, submissions should be considered untrusted at all points to prevent malicious or faulty logic from harming the evaluation system or interfering with other learner's. The following are design concerns that must be resolved to address the challenge of security in software-intensive MOOCs:

- **Ensuring Security While Testing Untrusted Learner-Submitted Code:** For programming assignments that require both compilation and execution of untrusted (and possibly malicious) code, steps must be taken to prevent learner-submitted code from interfering with the automated testing system as a whole and/or with other learner submissions.
- **Enable Peer-Grading While Maintaining Security:** To support peer-grading as a learning tool, mechanisms are needed to prevent peer assessors (both human and machine) from exposing their own personal system to potential security threats.
- **Securely Uploading and Downloading of Assignments:** Secure authentication is needed to protect the integrity and privacy of learners by encrypting transmission of all assignments to and from the learner, the learning management platform, and any other MOOC servers (such as forums, grade book, etc.). Moreover, the learning management platform should be integrated with the compilation build environment and associated analysis tools to select only the desired files for assessment.

Minimizing the Heterogeneity of System and Network Environments

Software-intensive MOOCs that focuses on concurrent and distributed applications require multiple instances of software running in their own networked private environments. The private environments and system architectures (e.g., ARM, x86, AVR/Arduino) may be heterogeneous and thus not identical to the assessment platform (e.g., x86_64). In this case, the learning management platform must support efficient and scalable execution of emulators.

Even if the architecture is the same for both development and assessment platforms, the need for networked separate environments still exists. Complicating the matter, user-definable network topologies will be required. Custom network designs not only require customizable topologies, but also must be repeatable with customizable background network traffic and QoS settings. In addition, the communication infrastructure should support dynamic configurations that can simulate either changing network or physical conditions. These features are needed to develop and test network-based code that can adapt to changing network conditions.

The following are design concerns that must be resolved to address the challenge of heterogeneity in software-intensive MOOCs:

- **Support Multiple Virtual Architectures:** To enable adaptability in the learning management platform, multiple architectures should be supported. A wide variety of architectures are in use today and with the advent of the Internet of Things (IoT), the need to support an even wider range of heterogeneous architectures will increase.
- **Support Multiple Virtual Network Types:** The ability to configure and adapt to the communication infrastructure is also required. While the processing of the learners' assignments is typically handled in a cloud environment, it may be necessary to simulate network connections of different types, such as 100mbps Ethernet, 10gbps Ethernet, 802.11N wireless, and Near Field Communication (NFC).
- **Dynamically Add/Remove Nodes in Network:** The learning management platform will need to create and remove nodes dynamically to simulate real world events, such as devices moving away from each other, going offline/online, and new resources being added to the network.

- **Networked Software and Middleware:** Development and analysis of networked software especially concurrent and distributed middleware—requires scalable environments for experimental evaluation. These environments should be able to isolate a group of private virtual networks together and provide realistic communication between each virtual network based on targeted channel capabilities, such as wire line or wireless channels. A Learning management platform therefore requires the ability to create repeatable virtual networks between unique workspaces that have learner submitted code executing. These virtual networks must also ensure end-to-end QoS requirements (e.g., for latency and bandwidth) and have the ability to handle configurable network traffic and topologies.
- **Environment Standardization:** If the development environment (which consists of compilers, operating systems, and associated programming and testing tools) is not defined in a standard manner, various compilation and compatibility issues can arise, which are hard for the teaching staff to assist individuals with at scale. Even minor differences between development environments can yield significant differences in the generated results that increase the amount of effort required by the (often limited) MOOC teaching staff. The learning management platform should therefore standardize these potential incompatibilities to lessen the burden on the teaching staff while the MOOC is live.

Reducing Operational Overhead

Numerous operational challenges arise when developing a learning management platform for software-intensive MOOCs, including traditional information technology (IT) tasks, such as logging and auditing of system execution and stability, load balancing, and data loss prevention strategies. There are other desired features that conventional learning management platforms either do not support or do not support in the domain of software-intensive MOOCs, including private virtual networks and secure peer review. The following are design concerns that must be resolved to address the challenge of logistics in software-intensive MOOCs:

- **Support for A/B Testing:** Validation of teaching methods, practices, and hypothesis can be supported via a platform that generates assignments for MOOC learners. Two-sample hypothesis testing (often known as A/B Testing) allows statistical analysis of hypothesis with two variants. A similar approach, called split testing, can be applied with more than two variants. To reduce teaching staff overhead during the MOOC, the learning management platform should be able to configure certain criteria for partitioning learners, learner assignments, peer-reviewers, and other possible criteria into either two or more groupings automatically.
- **Support for Peer Assessment:** Peer assessment helps reduce the overhead of teaching staff grading at scale, as well as improving learner abilities to, read, judge, and improve each other's' code. The learning management platform must therefore automatically facilitate various aspects of peer assessment, such as peer review (e.g., grading others' code by applying a rubric) and peer evaluation (e.g., having peers compile, execute, and evaluate each other's assignments).
- **Reproducible Virtual Network Configuration(s):** Certain types of software design and programming assignments (e.g., peer-to-peer file sharing, network discovery protocols) require vari-

ous types of network topologies, bandwidth, QoS settings, and background traffic. If any of these conditions change the results may vary. The learning management platform must therefore reproducibly create the same virtual network so that individual learner submissions can be tested under the consistent conditions.

SOLUTIONS AND RECOMMENDATIONS

The Structure and Functionality of EPLASAM

EPLASAM consists of several interchangeable hierarchies and parts, each providing a specific portion of its overall capabilities. Linux containers provide individualized, secure, and potentially customized runtime environments for code compilation, testing, and evaluation. EPLASAM handles the distribution of Linux containers to different hosts. It also uses interchangeable command-line build-tools to run each step of the compilation, testing, and evaluation. Finally, it provides generators that automatically produce assignments that are customized for learner cohorts. The remainder of this section describes each of these capabilities and outlines how they address the challenges presented in subsection "*Emerging trends and challenges*", highlighting aspects such as:

- How EPLASAM addresses the design concerns associated with the scale challenge via the use of assignment randomization and assessment, Linux containers, and a container distribution manager.
- How EPLASAM addresses the design concerns associated with the distance challenge via the use of automating and standardizing tooling used for building, testing, and assessing programming assignments.
- How EPLASAM addresses the design concerns associated with the security challenge via the use of Linux containers, a distribution manager to securely automate container processing, and secure submission of assignments via the compilation tooling.
- How EPLASAM addresses the design concerns associated with the heterogeneity challenge via Linux containers that can run isolated emulators to provide support for additional architectures, a distribution manager to handle all communication-related issues (such as virtual private networks), and Linux containers and compilation tooling providing environment standardization.
- How EPLASAM addresses the design concerns associated with the logistics challenge via the use of Linux containers, a distribution manager, and compilation tooling to provide an automated system with low operational overhead.

Linux Containers

The technology for general purpose OS-Level Virtualization for Linux has existed as open-source software since 2005 with OpenVZ. OS-Level virtualization is a technique where virtual private instances of the same OS as the server are provided to virtualized application(s) running on the host server. This approach offers many advantages over other virtualization technologies, such as hypervisors and full VM emulations. In particular, it enables Virtual Private Server (VPS) instances, each of which runs its own copy of an OS and enables users to install almost any software that runs on that OS.

A VPS differs from a hypervisor or fully emulated virtual machine technologies in several ways that make them attractive for use in EPLASAM. Figure 3 shows how EPLASAM employs OS-level virtualization to provide a VPS to each learner application submission. We manage each VPS via a central workload distribution manager and Docker, which automates the deployment of applications by providing an additional layer of abstraction and automation of OS-level virtualization on Linux (Docker, 2014).

Two key ways in which a VPS differs from the other virtualization options are the startup time and resource overhead of each instance. For example, the time for a VPS instance to start is significantly shorter than for an entire OS to boot, as is the case for hypervisor and full virtual machine emulation technologies. In particular, the base OS in a VPS has already been instantiated, so only the portions required for the VPS to instantiate must be started. Moreover, the resource overhead of VPS is significantly lower than a full virtual machine emulation instance.

VPS does have several drawbacks, however. For example, the host machine's kernel must support OS-Level virtualization at the OS kernel level. Likewise, the OS type on the host machine must be the same OS type on the virtualized instance.

Until recently, distribution of OS-level virtualization, also called "software containers," was not easily automated and therefore required a high degree of skill and knowledge to configure properly. The broad adoption of Docker, however, enables automated deployment of application(s) in these containers in networked configurations, thereby simplifying ease of use and reducing deployment time.

A key improvement to Linux container technology provided by Docker is the creation and use of a central server hosting images (which is called a Registry) and the build scripts required to create those images called DockerFiles. We apply Docker in a partially closed-source environment, i.e., where answers to assignments are kept secret, which leverages its ability to host a private Registry.

Figure 3. Diagram of Docker Container Deployment and Management

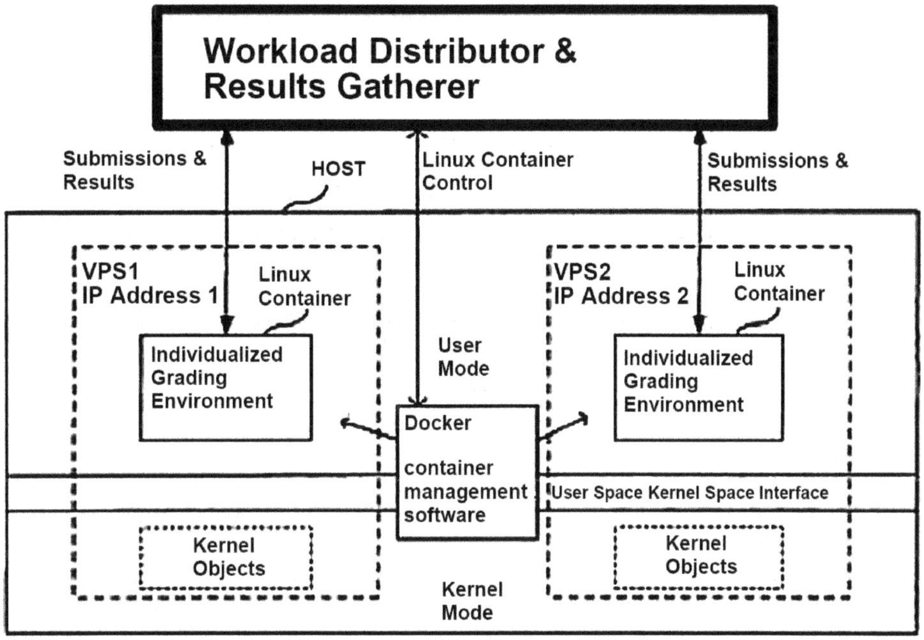

The central workload distribution manager mentioned above stores the deployment strategies EPLASAM uses to create the rules for container deployment and virtual network configuration. Existing tools, such as Shipyard (Shipyard, 2014), handle the low-level migration, monitoring, and management of Docker servers and Docker images. Shipyard can easily be controlled via a public API, thereby enabling the use of EPLASAM's custom Domain-Specific Modeling Language (DSL) tools provided by the Distribution Manager to manage physical servers, container deployment and execution, handling of assignment files, and setting up of virtual networks.

The abilities that Docker containers give the EPLASAM platform help address concerns presented in subsection "*Emerging trends and challenges*". Specifically, it gives the ability to provide private networks of virtual machines at scale. The VPS design provides separation of each student's virtual environment. Containers help to standardize student submission environments, supports multiple virtual networks and architectures via emulators. They also provide support for reproducible virtual networks by providing easily reproducible environments.

Distribution Manager

The design of EPLASAM requires a means to automate the distribution of containers to the required hosts, as well as the distribution of submitted assignments to these servers for processing. Figure 3 shows how Docker is used along with a Workload Distributor to distribute the processing of assignments. Currently EPLASAM can use multiple server host machines and multiple Docker VPS per host, though the distribution of assignment workloads must be deter-mined manually. Automating this distribution is an area we are looking at for future work.

We observed two general approaches in Docker management: (1) either have the deployment management system itself manage container deployment strategies or (2) allow users to manually deploy containers where they choose. In our initial experiments we opted for manually deploying containers and have used Shipyard since it offers the most feature from amongst the myriad of software solutions comprising the Docker software ecosystem. In particular, Shipyard has an HTTP/REST-based API—unlike many alternatives, such as Kubernetes (Kubernetes, 2015) —that allows finer control of which server(s) specific container(s) are executed. This capability helps EPLASAM configure the virtual private networks used to connect containers.

Shipyard works via an installed controller on each host machine that is configured with Docker. It requires configuring a single central Shipyard instance to manage all the hosts that Shipyard is responsible for. It then connects to a private repository of DockerFiles describing each container image, after which point management of all VPSs and containers can begin.

EPLASAM's custom Domain Specific Language (DSL) and tool-chain handle the management of the physical servers, container deployment and execution, handling of assignment files, and setting up of virtual networks. This custom DSL interacts with different levels of the platform, multiple custom applications, and other DSLs. For clarity, we call the top-level DSL that interacts with the other layers/DSLs within the platform the "Platform-DSL" and call the DSLs for assignments the "Assignment-DSLs." The Platform-DSL is designed to allow hierarchical composition of multiple assignment-DSL model instances, thereby allowing EPLASAM to handle simultaneous assessment of multiple different assignments and adjust to handle complex interactions between different assignments. For example, one adjustment involves distributing network-bound and a CPU-bound processes across the available hardware to minimize interference. The Assignment-DSL likewise needs to support multiple container definitions, expected container runtime requirements and profiles, assignment variations, and virtual network requirements. EPLASAM is designed via a multi-layered approach, where each component has well-defined interaction with the overall platform, to facilitate adoption since it is easier to add new/modify features or components.

Existing distribution managers, such as Shipyard, provide the EPLASAM platform the ability to address concerns related to automate assignment grading at scale. It also facilitates the secure transfer of assignment submissions between different servers in the process of grading. A Distribution Manager addresses the concerns of dynamically adding/removing network nodes and supporting multiple virtual network types. Additionally, it also addresses the concern of reproducible virtual networks.

Compilation Tooling

EPLASAM does not require any specific project build tool or integrated development environment (IDE). Since Linux containers are only executable via the command line, the use of an automated build tool is an integral part of the overall framework we have developed. The grading of programmatic questions is decomposed into two phases: compilation and testing. Both phases may have sub-phases that will depend upon the problem and code being evaluated, though EPLASAM just focuses on these two phases for now (the specifics of sub-phases will be addressed by both the choice of build-tools chosen and the desired evaluation techniques chosen by the staff of a course).

Although EPLASAM is build-tool agnostic, support for each tool¬/tool-chain must be integrated into the platform. This requirement enables the proper handling of both the specific starting commands and reading of results from the compilation and testing framework execution. We adopted Gradle as the default build tool for EPLASAM. Other build automation tools, such as Maven, Ant, and Make, were considered, but Gradle was selected since it is the build system utilized in the material our MOOCs are covering. The specific build system chosen will depend upon the programming language being tested, its conventions, and the personal choice of the MOOC staff.

Currently, EPLASAM contains manual script implementations to launch and evaluate compilation results, unit testing, and integration testing results. Future work will expand these abilities to operate via a plugin system that enables the use of other tool¬/tool-chains, such as Gradle, Make, and Ant. Future work will also provide an automated and secure method for assignment transfer via the chosen tool/tool-chains to/from the learner and EPLASAM.

Automated build tools help to address specific issues described in subsection "*Emerging trends and challenges*". Automating build tools helps to provide meaningful evaluation and feedback, even at a distance, and reducing the impact heterogeneous development and runtime environments. Automated build tools also help to address the concern of providing security for testing submitted code. They also help to address the concern of environment standardization. And finally, the use of automated build tools also helps to reduce the overall operational overhead concern.

Programming Assignment Assessment

Assessing programming assignments yields additional challenges not faced by commonly asked question types, such as multiple choice or true/false questions. In particular, how can the teaching staff craft a validation method for an assignment that is both effective and provides learners with meaningful feedback. If a suite of unit tests for an assignment returns a number of passed tests, but has no feedback as to what or even why a test was not passed, then it will fail the 'Alleviating Limitations of distance' challenge shown in Figure 2.

To address this issue, EPLASAM employs advanced built tools, such as Gradle, to automate the entire process of compiling, unit testing, and integration testing. Gradle currently supports C, C++, and Java and is on the road map to become the official build script for Android. We therefore chose it as our standard automation script. Since EPLASAM is designed in a modular manner, however, if Gradle does not support the programming language the teaching staff intends to use for a course or assignment it is relatively straightforward to integrate the desired command line build system in its place. This modularity adds flexibility to EPLASAM to support languages and features beyond the scope of a single build system. It also provides the ability to use additional testing frameworks, such as Junit or SureLogic that best fits a specific assignment type.

The use of custom code-analysis tools in addition to testing frameworks is supported with both Gradle and Maven, but we also plan to support individualized command line executions to support for custom evaluation and grading techniques. This customizability will further enhance EPLASAM's flexibility by allowing the application of more advanced analysis tools and techniques.

In our experience teaching MOOCs, we found it helpful to withhold some tests from learners, thereby providing a multi-tiered grading process. The teaching staff is responsible for selecting which tests, if any, to keep from learners. This capability enables the teaching staff to create their own grading criteria and methodologies or to create a series of questions/assignments that reveal more of the tests to learners over time to help refine and improve their understanding of the material.

The design of EPLASAM helps to bridge gaps such as assignment and solution automation. Automated assignment and solution creation contribute to address the concern of providing meaningful evaluation feedback.

Assignment Randomization

Assignment creation techniques aimed at preventing cheating and facilitating the potential reuse of assignments in a MOOC environment face challenges that traditional educational situations do not. In particular, the geographic distance between the teaching staff and learners makes it harder to detect certain types of cheating. Some problem types (such as short answer, multiple choice, and fill-in-the-blank) have exactly one correct answer or answer combination. These problems can be pre-created and a random subset can be given to each learner to help address the needs of cheating prevention and facilitate question reuse. Essays or short answer-based questions can use statistical analysis methods to detect (and thereby prevent) cheating. The 'correct' answers to these types of problems need not be determined exactly. Instead, keywords/order input can be entered into a regular expression parser to check validity/uniqueness.

Software-based assignments are often have structurally similar solutions, depending on the assignment specification. Thus, if a single correct solution leaks to the learner community, the question cannot be reliably reused in future offerings due to the likelihood that learners will find this solution online and apply it without having to do the work themselves. Therefore, to address the issues that software-based questions have with respect to similarity of assignment solutions between learner cohorts—and to help prevent reuse of solutions between offerings—EPLASAM applies a model-based approach to individualized assignment generation.

Our initial work for this approach has yielded a generator that takes a model as input and outputs the full source code and all files required to compile a data-centric Create, Read, Update, & Delete (CRUD) based Android application. This generator is given the desired model file as input and uses custom template groups to define the output files. It is possible to turn individual templates from within a group on or off, giving the teaching staff the ability to choose what code they wish to generate. This feature allows the creation of variants of assignments, which can be used for either subsequent assignments or for creating different versions for A/B Testing.

The input model for the custom code generator is an XML file describing the data-centric view of the information to store in the desired application, along with some metadata. Figure 4 shows the application specific section of a sample model. This model describes the application, its underlying database table, and the fields to store in the table. All components of the model have a 'name' value used for variable name and string construction for use in different locations within the application. These locations range from the underlying database to the user interface. Field values have a 'type' that describes the type of data to store. The default value of a field is configurable via the 'default_val' property. The base data types supported currently are those of the Java primitive types, with the addition of String and byte[], which are referred to as STRING and BLOB, respectively. Future work will expand these options to include more complex data types, such as images, audio, and video.

Figure 4. Sample Application Definition Model

```
<application name="example app">
  <content-provider
          name="provider example">
    <table name="table 1">
      <field type="TEXT"
            name="field 1"
            default_val="" />
      <field type="LONG"
            name="field 2"
            default_val="-1" />
      <field type="CHAR"
            name="field 3" />
      <field type="BLOB"
            name="field 4" />
      <field type="SHORT"
            name="field 5" />
      <field type="INTEGER"
            name="field 6" />
      <field type="FLOAT"
            name="field 7" />
      <field type="DOUBLE"
            name="field 8" />
      <field type="BOOL"
            name="field 9" />
    </table>
  </content-provider>
</application>
```

EPLASAM's focus on Android for the initial code to generate with our custom DSL code-generator tool stems from the component-based architecture of the Android platform, which allows us to remove portions of code from the list of templates to generate. This feature, in turn, helps narrow the code that is given learners at any one time to test them on the material being covered. It also allows the use of the same code to teach multiple concepts, thereby allowing the teaching staff to create exercises that reinforce each other.

Assignment randomization helps to address the concerns of automated assignment & assessment creation. Particularly, it helps to allow the reuse of created assignments in subsequent offerings of the same course.

FUTURE RESEARCH DIRECTIONS

The analysis of available alternatives provided a good perspective of virtues from EPLASAM bearing in mind three particular areas:

1. The use of Linux containers for virtualization.
2. Generation of assignments, and
3. Automated generation of grading and meaningful feedback for programming assignments.

These areas are relevant since developing a platform for automated grading of software-intensive assignments in a MOOC environment requires effective resource management at the cloud infrastructure-level, as well as the ability to scale both assignment creation and evaluation with the addition of (potentially many) new learners.

Even if EPLASAM provides good support to listed areas, this context requires several improvements to our proposal. By example it is necessary to emphasize aspects, such as lightweight, isolation, and ease of distribution. Additionally it is necessary to reinforce features to create custom containers and share them in a manner that's more straightforward than possible in prior work.

EPLASAM can build a standard DSL interface that simplifies swapping of future generator components. This interface provides flexibility to the overall platform and simplifies adoption allowing the use of custom code generation tools. However it is important to clearly distinct EPLASAM virtues against similar services such as MobiCloud and Objektgraph, which use the MVC pattern with templates to generate targets.

The goal of this project is to provide an environment for flexibility creating and evaluating new techniques and approaches, in this way there are several adjustments to perform in the future.

CONCLUSION

This chapter summarized the motivations, challenges, and solutions related to EPLASAM, which is a platform for software-intensive MOOC assignment creation and grading. We discussed the EPLASAM design goals and the related challenges associated with creating meaningful software programming assignments that deter cheating. We show how the overall platform is split into two major portions: (1) the server portion, which acts as the infrastructure, and (2) the tools portion, which facilitates teaching staff creating new assignments that are automatically generated and assessed at scale. We then explain how EPLASAM accomplishes its design goals and explain why various technical choices were made. Finally, we compared EPLASAM with related work to show how our approach builds upon and extends previous work to leverage our experiences teaching software-intensive MOOCs.

Three main categories of future work stem from our work on EPLASAM:

- **Enhanced Platform Analysis and Development:** We are currently integrating EPLASAM into our Mobile Cloud Computing with Android (MoCCA) Specialization. Measurements and analysis of its performance and scalability will be conducted to evaluate its effectiveness. We anticipate that additional software capabilities will be needed to create the DSL(s) and related tools required to manage the platform logistics of container management and deployment, particularly in a heterogeneous hosting scenario where the platform utilizes multiple cloud services, such as Amazon EC2, Microsoft Azure, DigitalOcean, RackSpace, etc.
- **Applying the Platform in Learning-at-Scale Environments and Analyzing its Impact on Learners:** Using EPLASAM our MoCCA Specialization will provide an opportunity for research into the science of education on software-intensive design and programming topics. For example, the ability to assess A/B group learners at the scale of tens to hundreds of thousands of learners will enable us to refine our current teaching and testing techniques and explore new ones. With tighter coupling between the testing framework and other course material, it will be possible to test things such as which order of introducing topics leads to better overall results. It will also be possible to explore variations in both the number and difficulty of programming assignments and determining which combinations provide the best overall result. Future work will be possible on the analysis of learner learning results based on the quality and quantity of meaningful feedback they receive from the build system, e.g., using the assignment submissions to adapt and enhance auto-grading tools. Improvements in accuracy, quality feedback, runtime efficiency, and breadth of testing coverage are metrics by which differing approaches can be evaluated to identify effective methods.
- **Using the Platform for Research on Advanced Middleware and Networked Applications:** Future work in the area of middleware development and analysis will be enabled by EPLASAM. The platform, with its dynamic virtual networking and repeatable experiments, will assist in addressing the challenges Chaqfeh et al. concerning Internet-of-Things enabled middleware (Chaqfeh & Mohamed, 2012). The ability to simulate both variable networking conditions and resource constraints allows better development and analysis into specialized network-based middleware. Two important industries that are ever increasing are video games (Correa, 2013), which has been larger than Hollywood for more than a decade (Yi, 2004), and consumer mobile devices. Both these domains have specialized requirements that EPLASAM can assist with in terms of middleware development and analysis, such as strict timing constraints or minimum levels of robustness that EPLASAM can simulate. In addition, both video games and mobile devices are popular topics that can serve as a basis for future MOOCs that teach additional core computer science principles, methods, and tools.

REFERENCES

Bardac, M., Deaconescu, R., & Florea, A. M. (2010). Scaling peer-to-peer testing using linux con-tainers. *Proceedings of the 9th Roedunet International Conference,* Sibiu, Romania, (pp. 287–292). IEEE Press.

Buck, D., Diethelm, I., & Sheneman, S. (2013). Objektgraph: why code when mvc applications can be generated with uml-based diagrams? *Proceedings of the 2013 Companion Publication for Conference on Systems, Programming, & Applications: Software for Humanity*, Indianapolis, IN, (pp. 25–26). ACM Press. doi:10.1145/2508075.2514576

Carbunescu, R., Devarakonda, A., Demmel, J., Gordon, S., Alameda, J., & Mehringer, S. (2014). Architecting an autograder for parallel code. *Proceedings of the 2014 Annual Conference on Extreme Science and Engineering Discovery Environment,* Atlanta, GA, (pp. 68:1–68:8). ACM Press.

Chaqfeh, M. A., & Mohamed, N. (2012). Challenges in middleware solutions for the internet of things. *Proceedings of the International Conference on Collaboration Technologies and Systems,* Denver, CO, (pp. 21–26). IEEE Press. doi:10.1109/CTS.2012.6261022

Correa, C. (2013). *Why Video Games are More Addictive and Bigger than Movies Will Ever Be*. Retrieved October 20, 2014, from: ttp://www.forbes.com/sites/christophercorrea/2013/04/11/why-video-games-are-addic¬tive-and-bigger-than-movies-will-ever-be/.

Coursera -. *Free Online Courses From Top Universities*. (n. d.). Retrieved from https://www.coursera.org/specialization/mobilecloudcomputing2/36

Docker Inc. (2013) *Doker official site*. (n. d.). Retrieved from http://docker.com

edX, (2013). *How It Works*. Retrieved from https://www.edx.org/how-it-works

Google. (2013). *Kubernetes by Google*. Retrieved from http://kubernetes.io/

Handigol, N., Heller, B., Jeyakumar, V., Lantz, B., & McKeown, N. (2012). Reproducible network experiments using container-based emulation. *Proceedings of The 8th International Conference on Emerging Networking Experiments and Technologies,* Nice, France, (pp. 253–264). ACM Press. doi:10.1145/2413176.2413206

Manjunatha, A., Ranabahu, A., Sheth, A., & Thirunarayan, K. (2010). Power of clouds in your pocket: An efficient approach for cloud mobile hybrid application development. *Proceedings of The Second International Conference on Cloud Computing Technology and Science* (Indianapolis, IN, pp. 496–503). IEEE Press. doi:10.1109/CloudCom.2010.78

Mannadiar, R., & Vangheluwe, H. (2010). Modular synthesis of mobile device applications from domain-specific models. *Proceedings of The 7th International Workshop on Model-Based Methodologies for Pervasive and Embedded Software*, Antwerp, Belgium, (pp.21–28). IEEE/ACM Press. doi:10.1145/1865875.1865879

Menage, P. B. (2007). Adding generic process containers to the Linux kernel. *Proceedings of the Linux Symposium*, Ottawa, Canada (Vol. 2, pp. 45–57). Kernel.org.

Sadigh, D., Seshia, S. A., & Gupta, M. (2012). Automating Exercise Generation: A Step towards Meeting the MOOC Challenge for Embedded Systems. *Proceedings of The Workshop on Embedded and Cyber-Physical Systems Education*, Tampere, Finland, (p. 2). ACM Press.

Shipyard. (2014). *Shipyard*, Retrieved from http://shipyard-project.com/

Singh, R., Gulwani, S., & Solar-Lezama, A. (2013). Automated feedback generation for introductory programming assignments. *Proceedings of the 34th ACM SigPlan Conference on Program-Ming Language Design and Implementation,* New York, NY (pp. 15–26). ACM Press. doi:10.1145/2491956.2462195

Soltesz, S., Pötzl, H., Fiuczynski, M. E., Bavier, A., & Peterson, L. (2007). Container-Based Operating System Virtualization: A Scalable, High-Performance Alternative to Hypervisors. *Operating Systems Review*, *41*(3), 275–287. doi:10.1145/1272998.1273025

Xavier, M. G., Neves, M. V., Rossi, F. D., Ferreto, T. C., Lange, T., & De Rose, C. A. (2013). Performance Evaluation of Container-Based Virtualization for High Performance Computing Environments. *Proceedings of the 21st EUROMICRO International Conference on Parallel, Distributed and Network-based Processing*, Belfast, Northern Ireland (pp.233–240). IEEE Press. doi:10.1109/PDP.2013.41

Yi, M. (2004). *They Got Game / Stacks of New Releases for Hungry Video Game Enthusiasts Mean It's Boom Time for an Industry Now Even Bigger than Hollywood.* Retrieved from http://www.sfgate.com/news/article/THEY-GOT-GAME-Stacks-of-new-releases-for-hungry-2663371.php

ADDITIONAL READING

Bass, S. A. (2014). Simple Solutions to Complex Problems—MOOCs as a Panacea? *The Journal of General Education*, *63*(4), 256–268. doi:10.1353/jge.2014.0023

Burrow, L. (2013). What can MOOCs do for you?: Local Implications of a Global Phenomenon. In *Proceedings of Society for Information Technology & Teacher Education International Conference* (pp. 280-282). Chesapeake, VA: Association for the Advancement of Computing in Education (AACE).

Chen, Y. (2014). Investigating MOOCs through blog mining. *The International Review of Research in Open and Distributed Learning*, *15*(2).

Davidson, C. N. (2014). Why Higher Education Demands a Paradigm Shift. *Public Culture*, *26*(1), 3–11. doi:10.1215/08992363-2346313

Flynn, J. (2013). MOOCS: Disruptive innovation and the future of higher education. *Christian Education Journal*, *10*(1), 149–162.

Greene, J. (2014). Introductory Study Using MOOCs for Homeless Education. *Proceedings of World Conference on E-Learning in Corporate, Government, Healthcare, and Higher Education* (pp. 724-728). Chesapeake, VA: Association for the Advancement of Computing in Education (AACE).

Jones, S. E. (2014). The emergence of the digital humanities. *Reviews in History*, *1634*, 1–5.

Kilgore, W., & Lowenthal, P. R. (2015). The Human Element MOOC. In R. Wright (Ed.), *Student-Teacher Interaction in Online Learning Environments* (pp. 373–391). Hershey, PA: Information Science Reference.

Thrun, S. (2013). MOOCs: The Future Is Here. *The Journal of Nursing Education*, *52*(1), 3–4. doi:10.3928/01484834-20121227-10 PMID:23293938

Wu, Y. (2014). MOOC and the Opportunities, Challenges and Responses of Universities, *Journal of Guizhou Minzu University (Philosophy and Social Science)*, 5.

KEY TERMS AND DEFINITIONS

Large Scale Assessment: According to The Montana Office of Public Instruction "Large-scale assessment means tests are administered to large numbers of students, such as those in a district or state".

Learning-at-Scale: According to the description from the prestigious ACM conference L@S, this term "refers to new approaches for students to learn and for teachers to teach, when engaging large numbers of students, either in a face-to-face setting or remotely, whether synchronous or asynchronous, with the requirement that the techniques involve large numbers of students (where "large" is preferably thousands of students, but can also apply to hundreds in in-person settings)".

Linux Containers: Linux Containers (A.K.A. LXC) is an operating-system-level virtualization environment for running multiple isolated Linux systems, called containers, on a single Linux control host.

Middleware: Computer software that provides services to software applications beyond those available from the operating system. It can be described as "software glue". Middleware makes it easier for software developers to perform communication and input/output, so they can focus on the specific purpose of their application. Middleware is the software that connects software components or enterprise applications. Middleware is the software layer that lies between the operating system and the applications on each side of a distributed computer network. Typically, it supports complex, distributed business software applications. Middleware includes Web servers, application servers, content management systems, and similar tools that support application development and delivery. It is especially integral to information technology based on Extensible Markup Language (XML), Simple Object Access Protocol (SOAP), Web services, SOA, Web 2.0 infrastructure, and Light weight directory access protocol (LDAP).

Section 5

Future Trends and Applications:
Analyzing Some Future Venues to Enhance Interaction and Applications of MOOCs

Chapter 13
The Role of Virtual Worlds for Enhancing Student-Student Interaction in MOOCs

Rosa Reis
Instituto Superior de Engenharia do Porto, Portugal

Paula Escudeiro
Instituto Superior de Engenharia do Porto, Portugal

ABSTRACT

This theoretical chapter attempts to clarify interaction role in Massive Open Online Courses (MOOCS) and increased emphasis on utilization the virtual worlds, as tools to a constructive process where the learner should be actively involved. An overview of the core concepts of the MOOCs and Virtual Worlds is provided and an explanation of how these environments can be used for helping in creation more authentic learning activities. The chapter presents an interaction model based on collaboration, so as to elucidate the major design differences. In conclusion, we want explore the changing role of formal learning in an era open education, where the Massive Open Online Courses can allow access, in many cases completely free of cost to the learner.

INTRODUCTION

MOOCS have intrinsic characteristics: to community feeling, peer-to-peer interactions and collaboration. These features lead to a large heterogeneity of participants that are often unmanageable and may cause high dropout rates of the courses.

One of the current challenges of the MOOCs is to reduce dropout rates by providing customized strategies and resources for the different profiles of participants (Nunez et al, 2014). The integration of external social tools in the training model of the MOOCS arises as an opportunity to perform that customization. The incorporation of virtual worlds may provide greater interaction between the students, increase collaborative process and give support to people with difficulties.

DOI: 10.4018/978-1-4666-9743-0.ch013

We believe if the MOOC course is developed in a rigid manner, the students can give up before the course starts. We believe that must exist activities, which facilitate collaborative learning, in other words, should be allowed students to learn while are associated with more experienced participants of the learning community. This is one of the key factors for the MOOC success.

Based on these points, this chapter begins with a brief history of MOOCs and sets them in the wider context of the evolution of educational technology and open/distance learning. It then describes the MOOC phenomenon, their advantages and their limitations; and also, describes the main concepts associated to Virtual Worlds. The next section discusses the role of interaction in engaging and supporting both learners and teachers in MOOCs. It then is discussed how Virtual Worlds can contribute to greater involvement of the participants in the teaching/learning process of MOOCS and presents a interaction model, a first step toward a theory in which the two main forms learning - collaborative and autonomous (independent) - are presented, with a brief discussion of the advantages and disadvantages of each. The chapter ends with a synthesis of the most relevant points of the work. It is drawn the findings with particular reference to the fulfillment of the proposed objectives.

BACKGROUND

MOOCs Overview

The development of the Internet and the Information and Communication Technology has enabled the creation of contents, expanding the learning through distance courses, most recently the MOOCs.

The MOOCs (Massive Open Online Courses - Open Courses Online Massive) are open courses developed by universities. Given its free nature, they have a large number of student's subscribers, which are geographically dispersed and not affiliated with the education institution.

The MOOCs appeared in 2008 to describe a particular model of online course developed by George Siemens and Stephen Downes.

This concept has evolved through time. According Vizoso (2013) there are two streams of courses: the cMOOC and xMOOC. The cMOOC uses a participatory and collaborative methodology. These courses coming of the first initiatives of George Siemens are based on the principle of connectivism. In cMOOCs, the participants can have a feeling of disorientation; participation is timely, students are discouraged throughout the course and the participant need to have digital competence. The second current, ie the xMOOC have a more traditional view of knowledge and learning being "the student a duplicator and not a content generator". In xMOOCs the interaction between the participants is weak: the course is focused on the teacher, the content and the assessment is traditional (MORGADO & SILVA, 2013). In summary, cMOOCs focus on the creation and generation of new knowledge, while xMOOCs aim to duplicate the knowledge to other students, whose education is based on traditional and is more likely to motivate discussions on innovation in higher education (Gaebel, 2013). However, both have the characteristics, systematized in Figure 1.

MOOCs Advantages and Limitations

MOOC is a new paradigm of education that came up with numerous opportunities both for students as well as teacher. Studies have cited several advantages and some limitation of which we emphasize:

Figure 1. Main features of MOOCs (http://www.wamda.com/)

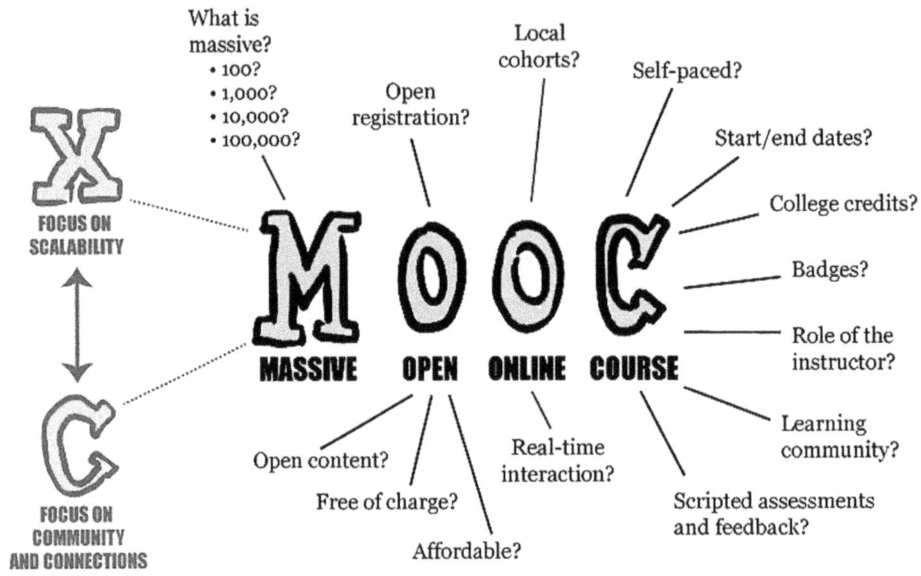

- **Sharing Ideas and Knowledge:** The MOOCs are based on the connectivist learning theory, or connectivism. This theory stimulates the production and sharing of knowledge. This sharing is achieved through of learning, which is seen as a network-forming process (Martin, 2013)
- **Enhances Active Learning:** Studies shows that participants learn more through active learning. The active learning includes a wide range of activities that share the common element of —— involving students in doing things and thinking about the things they are doing (Bonwell & Eison 1991). These activities can be created and used to engage participants in (a) thinking critically or creatively, (b) speaking with a partner, in a small group, or with the entire class, (c) expressing ideas through writing, (d) exploring personal attitudes and values, (e) giving and receiving feedback, and (f) reflecting upon the learning process (Eison, 2010). In this context, the MOOCs are structured by - short lectures alternating with assignments and quizzes. Some participants can need longer to assimilate the content of the lecture, and prefer to listen to it again before doing the assignment. The Peer-to-peer contact facilitated by MOOC can also trigger effective active learning.
- **Provide the Autonomy and Collaboration of Participants:** The core of MOOCs is collaboration: Addition to providing open resources to support the study, the participants can share and become co-authors of other resources and activities that are posted on blogs, discussion forums, etc. This allows, the moocs are built with the active involvement of students who organize themselves according to their objectives, common interests and their prior knowledge.
- **It Improves a Cross:** cultural relationship - which leads to collaboration between institution educators and learners locally and internationally.
- However, as a new educational modality, there are still limitations and controversies regarding the benefits. To Velásquez (2013), the lack of certification and lack of commitment of the students to the course are some of these limitations.

- The correction of activities usually made peer assessment (peer) make the fragile reviews (PLAYA, 2013). Peer evaluation sometimes leads to discouragement among students, which lead them to dropout from the course. According to Acosta (2013), this is motivated by curiosity and lack of knowledge to follow the course. So, to make it possible learning in massive courses is necessary to design the course in order to contemplate the diversity of people who follow the courses.

Virtual Worlds

Richard Bartle (2004) in the mid 70 defines virtual world as an environment whose inhabitants regard as being self-contained. This leads us to the concept of world, but not as the world becomes virtual. Raph Koster (2004) defines this concept as a persistent space, which may be experienced by several participants at the same time and being represented by avatars. With this definition we can easily observe some features of virtual worlds: persistence and multi-user. However, does not specify the technology required for the virtual world. In 2004, Edward Castronova introduced the technology element when describes the virtual worlds as places worked by computers, which are designed to accommodate a large number of people" (Castronova, 2004).

If we blend the elements and put emphasis on people, we obtain a more precise definition of virtual worlds:

A virtual world is a simulated persistent space based on the interaction by computer, inhabited by several users, who are represented by iconic images called avatars, who can communicate with each other's and the world in a synchronized way. (Reis,2010)

This definition allows us to demonstrate that a virtual world is more than a simple virtual environment. The term "virtual world" usually brings us to mind a space similar to the real world where we can live, with details and action of gravity, the surface topography of the different ways to move the objects, passage of time and finally, the possibility of active communication between the various objects created by the users. This world must not be interrupted; however it should continue to exist if the user is not connected. The persistence means that the participant is a member of a dynamic community and so, they communicate and interact with each other and with the environment. The participants have the feeling of sharing time, should be able to see the behavior of each other and, for communication between users. This view is the basis for an actual virtual world that should allow, some kind of communication occurs between the participants. Such as the interactivity tends to be dynamic, the communication is in real time. Moreover, the sense of presence, which is related to the individual and collective, allows when we got in a shared space, each participant becomes a "virtual person", known as avatars, i.e., is a digital representation (graphic or text) in the virtual world:

- **Shared Space:** The world allows many users to participate at once. All the users have the feeling of being in the same place, room, land. The shared space is a common location where interactions may be occurring. The place can be real or fictional, and this space must have the same characteristics for all participants.
- **Immersion and Interactivity:** The idea of virtual world allows the users in the interaction with the environment, to alter, develop, build or submit contents. The user must feel immersed in the

environment and fully engaged with the activities being undertaken. This is normally achieved through representation of the user and environment in world.

- **Persistence:** The world's existence continues regardless of whether individual users are logged in. The persistence of de world leads us to the immediacy feedback and synchronous use of the actions that take place in the world.
- **Immediacy:** An immediate virtual world allows real-time interaction between the user and the world. Interaction between users is also real time. It is a definitional quality of virtual worlds.
- **Socialization:** The world allows and encourages the formation of in-world social groups or communities.

These characteristics have contributed to represent in virtual world the different categories of information by means of three-dimensional objects, and thus, it is possible to develop a world similar to the real life.

MAIN FOCUS OF THE CHAPTER

Issues, Controversies, Problems

Types of Interaction

The virtual worlds when applied in education, can allow to students and teachers, represented by avatars, a full interaction with the system and vice-versa. This interaction can occur through problem solving, graphical analysis, simulation, and active participation in own environment. Enable students to solve real-world problems and share knowledge (collaboration). Collaboration among learners is modelled as "socially distributed cognition" (Dillenbourg, 1992).

The interaction should be natural, efficient and appropriate for users. Bowman [2] proposed that any interaction within the virtual worlds must be represented in three perspectives: (1) Avatars-Avatars. (2) Avatar-Object; (3) Objects-Objects.

In first perspective, the users represented by avatars communicate with each other. The interaction is a process of human communication. This can be understood as "the process of social interaction carried out by means of symbols or any other messaging system" (Martinez, 2008). Can occur between an avatar and another, between an avatar and a group of avatars or between a group of avatars and another group of avatars.

The second and third perspectives are related. Interaction is achieved by the selection and manipulation of virtual objects. The result of this interaction comes from the actions and activities conducted by users in space and in locations available in the environment.

Interaction in MOOCs

Nowadays, education leads us to some concepts that are own a society called society of knowledge or society of information, where individuals through the use of information technology can access, replace digital information, communicate and relate with others. Thus, when we refer to education, regardless of the approach, we talk about the interaction. The interaction is intrinsically connected to the teaching/learning process, due to new learning theories, which have arisen because of modern society. They establish that learning takes place through the interactions of students using a computer or through the Internet. Simple information receivers, the students want to interact with content, talking, participating and intervening, through the mediation of computer or other technological tools. The school must facilitate interactivity, for us to have students able to intervene significantly in various situations. In this scenario, we understand that interactivity is facilitated by new technologies. However, understanding how students interact with MOOCs is a crucial issue because it affects how we evaluate their efficacy and how we design future online courses.

With Web 2.0, teachers have different ways to interact with students and handle content in different ways. This concept relates the connection and adaptation of knowledge collaboratively on the network. Siemens argues that knowledge is distributed across the network; the act of learning is to develop new forms, in different networks and in various connections that we have and that tend to create new standards (Siemens, 2008). Thus, learning is predominantly participatory, active, interactive, social, adapted to the requirements of students, encouraging communication between students and teachers. They are persons responsible for the creation of learning communities and as Garrison and Anderson says: "Teachers and students interact with the aim of strengthening, build and validate understanding, and develop skills that will lead to continuing training in the future" (Garrison & Anderson, 2005).

Chou et al. (2010) developed a list of five types of interaction that can take place in a MOOC, namely:

- **Student-Student:** Students can interact with other learners by using CMS-based digital channels
- **Student–Content:** Learners can access multimedia-learning contents in a CMS
- **Student–Teacher:** Students can interact with instructors by using digital channels provided by a CMS
- **Student–Interface:** Students can access desired information with a user-friendly interface
- **Student–Himself:** Students can monitor their learning progress by reflection facilitated by CMS functions

However, to ensure that the interaction is effective is necessary that students are involved cognitively. The involvement depends on the type of learner, because not all learners will interact and participating in the MOOC in the same way and their path through the course may vary. Studies, as Goldwasser (2011) have demonstrated this issue and he categorize learner engagement into the following types:

- **Active:** Assigned to learners who show explicit signs of engagement by posting on the discussion forums, submitting quizzes and assessments. These signs require an active involvement from the learner.
- **Passive:** Assigned to learners who show more implicit signs of engagement by viewing, subscribing or voting on posts/comments on discussion forums and views lectures. These users typically do not make an active effort to participate.
- **Disengaged:** Learners that show signs of being disengaged from the course, either by posting text that indicate their disengagement or show a significant decrease in posting, viewing, voting, and assessment submitting activity.

It is for the second and third learner profile that we consider that teachers must play a vital role in student engagement. They must adapt their teaching strategies accordingly to learning styles of students.

Understanding the responsibilities of students, facilitators, and institution administrators is essential to ensuring the enhancement of student engagement in MOOCs now and in the future (Chen et al, 2003).

SOLUTIONS AND RECOMMENDATIONS

How Virtual Worlds can Contribute to a Greater Involvement of the Participants in the Teaching/Learning Process of MOOCs

With the internet services increasing popularity together with their high potential to reach a large number of users, a new generation of applications has emerged on the Web: three dimensional (3D) multi-user interactive applications. These applications are characterized by sharing a 3D environment synthesized by the computer for multiple users. These applications, called virtual worlds, are placed in the context of Virtual Real, that is, Virtual Reality (VR), "computer-simulated environment, whether that environment is a simulation of the real world or an imaginary world", (Al-Saedi & Ibrahim, 2014). According to Tiffin and Rajasingham (2003), VR provides some kind of immersion that involves the user in a fantasy only made possible by 3D digital technology. These worlds allow the creation of spaces through the metaphorical associated with a set of services available for users. With the virtual worlds we can extend the education process, using not only the physical spaces but also the virtual. The flow of interactions is retained either graphically by means of the world itself, or in the form of movement evidencing the avatar's actions. In this context, the virtual worlds aim to contribute to their increasing use in the teaching/learning process, stimulating knowledge acquisition, including the development of learner's autonomy and collaborative learning. From the literature review, MOOCs and virtual worlds are two types of applications that can, according to our view, be used together in a teaching/learning process, because:

- **Virtual Worlds and MOOCs are Similar:** (M) Massive - virtual worlds can hold many avatars; (O) Open - virtual worlds are open on global scale; (O) Online - virtual worlds allow online communication; (C) course – in a virtual world the courses take place in synchronous and asynchronous manners;
- **Virtual Worlds Facilitate Face-to-Face Communication:** One of the characteristics of virtual worlds is the Presence - the sense of being in the immediate vicinity of others. In other words, Presence is about the feeling of "being there." Presence is the characteristic that differentiates virtual worlds from other online technologies. We have learned through our experience designing and working within virtual spaces that the role of presence serves as precursor to interactivity - among people and between people and information.
- **Virtual Worlds Increase the Collaborative Work:** Virtual Worlds have been used to simulate the real world and facilitate social interactions. Collaborative virtual worlds provide an experience set within a technological space with several benefits for educational contexts (Chittaro & Ranon, 2007). Cited by (Abedin, 2013): They allow students to create customized avatars and virtual objects to actively collaborate with other avatars, to join communities, and gain a sense of being present in an environment (Warburton, 2009). These virtual worlds possess a number of common characteristics (Warburton, 2009): (i) Persistence of the in-world environment, (ii) Simultaneous

multiple users participation, (iii) Use of an avatar for a 3D personable representation of the self, (iv) Interactions between avatars and objects in a 3-D environment, (v) Real time interactions, (vi) Similarities to the real world such as movement and physics.

In order to understand implications of virtual 3D worlds on the teaching and learning process; and to assess opportunities and challenges of incorporating virtual worlds into MOOCs units, in attempt to overcome some of MOOCs' limitations, we decided to develop a design model to MOOCs, where we emphasize the interaction. The interest in this study arose because the Computer Science Department of ISEP has a Master degree in Graphics Systems and Multimedia. Multimedia Systems (SIMU) is one of the course units in this master degree, within which students have been developing curricular work about MOOCs.

Our design philosophy is based on the learners and on their learning experience. We want to give learners a significant opportunity to explore an efficient and effective environment that allows them to build a more dynamic learning experience. Learning is a constructive process where the learner should be actively involved. As research indicates, learner engagement is a key factor in the effective transfer of learning. Simply put, engaged learners learn more.

The proposed solution that stems from our design philosophy starts with the identification of a structure course, which is based on two main characteristics:

- **Contextualization of Concepts:** Done through explanations for facts and ideas provided in the context of a practical and real framework, which in turn facilitates organization of knowledge for retrieval and application. The MOOC should be based on knowledge-transferable-to-skill-at-workplace.
- **Define a Learning Space:** To determine the learning strategies and types of tasks that are appropriate to the environment purposes. The tasks that enable students to achieve the learning objectives should be idealized in order that the performance results are consistent with the knowledge acquired. The environment must be student-centric. Learners must collaborate and exchange ideas from different fields to make an integrated whole.
- **Course Content:** The content selected must comprise instructional screens interspersed, containing information, resorting to different types of media such as text, videos, etc. Each module must have some knowledge checks.
- **Definition of Learning Activities:** We must define activities according to subject matter. We recommend creating activities that promote the interaction between the learners. These activities can be games, quizzes, simulations and small case studies, for motivate the reflexive and critical analysis.
- **Collaboration (Interaction Model):** Here, we must including Instructor-Led Collaborative Exercises in the form of Discussions and Further Challenges. These exercises must be resolved in virtual worlds. To facilitate the collaboration we suggest designing an interaction model. Our model is designed to visualize the interactions that the system contains, because if we see "an interaction between a student (avatar) or students (avatars) and one environment (optionally including content resources, tools, instruments, systems computer services, real-world events and objects) to be held in response to a task intended to be learning something - Learning Activity - the interaction model becomes crucial.

Table 1. The table of action

Participants	
Social Groups	**System**
• Choose activities • Request changes • Analyze and reflect suggestions • Communicate with other members • Give suggestions • Build a partial solution • Build the final solution • Final solution Socialize • Build function • Sends Resolution • Participate in forums • Constructs interface • Asks for suggestions	• Provides activities • Identify a member of social group • Provides alternate content (moodle, Google) • Registers suggestions • Send mail to the other social groups • Displays chat • Notice on the monitoring activity • Sends alert guardian • Notes members who participated in the activity • Discussion of the solution to the problem Actions presented

The interaction model aims to capture all interaction of the system. It consist of several diagrams, namely.

- **Table of Action:** The table of action aims to identify all participants of the system and their actions within the system. This table action is similar to the methodology used X-Tec. and requires the creation of a matrix, where the tasks are characterized (actions) of the various stakeholders in the environment (see Table 1). Its construction involves obtaining the structured description of the ideas for development to occur in a rigorous way and with quality (Escudeiro, 2007).
- **Collaboration Diagram:** This diagram is based on the methodology of Menchaca (2005), which involves the creation of social groups. Social groups are working groups, consisting of a set of students, who will perform some tasks in the environment to be built. For example, suppose that our environment will support the teaching of PL-SQL. The social groups that can be created are (see Figure 2): Social group I (BD) - responsible for creating the database of a given problem; Social group II (Programming) - responsible for programming functions; Social group III (Interface) - responsible for the design of the interface.

So, one possible structure and flow that integrates virtual worlds in the design of a MOOC could be represented as shown in Figure 2.

After identifying the social groups and with the table action, we will do a short description of the functions (Table 2), restrictions and services that each group offers to another social group the table. See Figure 3.

FUTURE RESEARCH DIRECTIONS

In this vein, as part of the learning strategy, MOOCs must include the tools that improve the socialization and cooperation. They are fundamental to improve both the learning process as the quality, quantity and variety of resources. Learning communities must have at least some technological resources to grow and endure.

Figure 2. Suggested structure and flow virtual worlds and MOOCs Integration

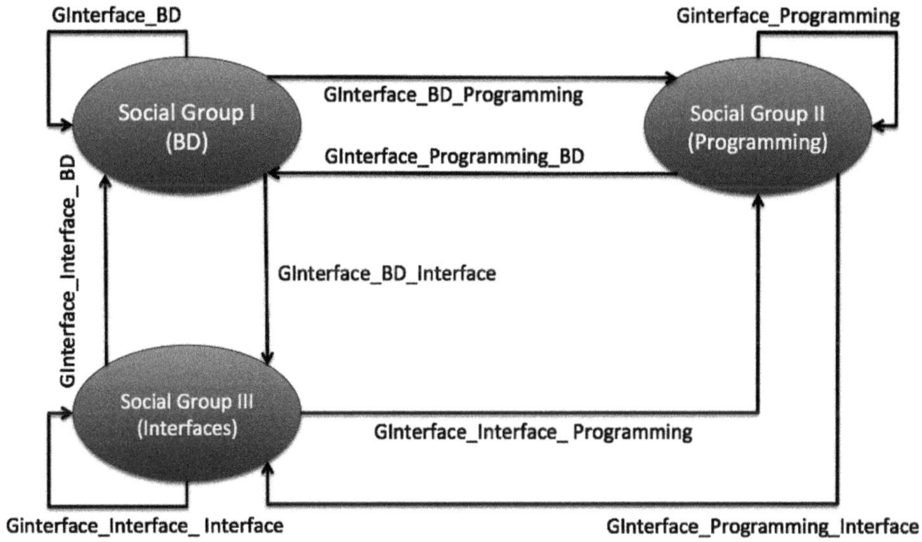

Table 2. The functions, services and restrictions of social groups

	Social Group I	Social Group II	Social Group III
Functions	Build partial solution	Build partial solution	Build partial solution
	Communicate with members	Communicate with members	Communicate with members
	Ask suggestion		
	Give suggestion	Give suggestion	Give suggestion
	Analyze suggestions	Analyze suggestions	Analyze suggestions
	Build the solution		
		Building Functions	
Services		[if you build the database then we can design the functions	
			[if you have any information from the social group BD and Programming] then design of interface
Restrictions	Submit the solution to the database		

Figure 3. The social groups

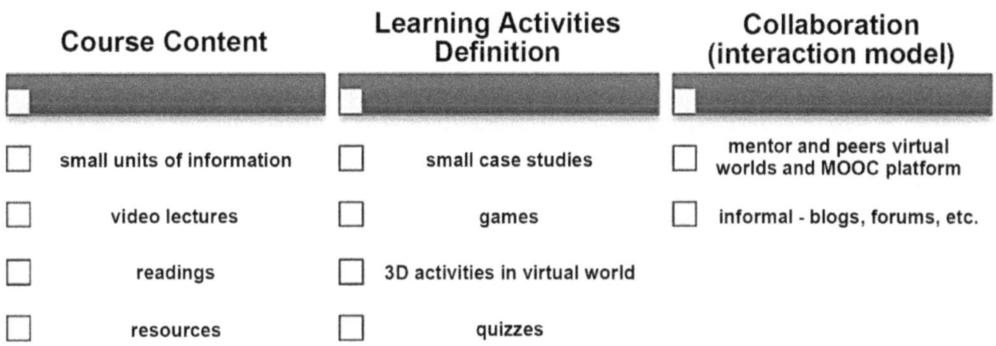

CONCLUSION

To overcome distances and to give opportunity to individuals have access to Education, sometimes we resort to tools like forums, blogs and LMS, when we can use others environments that enhance the engagement and satisfaction of learners.

The systems, like virtual worlds are being used in education because they have particular characteristics, allowing learners have the feeling of place and presence of other individuals, facilitate communication beyond chat, voice, and automatic synchronization of documents to the supporting the community of learning.

However, if we are to develop Massive Open Online Courses that can reduce the number of drop out students and involve more teachers in the teaching / learning process, we must integrate the virtual worlds. Was in this sense, that if wrote the chapter, to demonstrate and explain our ideas of how virtual worlds can contribute for a greater involvement of participants in the teaching/learning process of MOOCs, giving emphasis on the interaction of students-tutor-students. We agree with (de Figueiredo & Afonso, 2006), when he states, "we must create a space to stimulate the imagination because "who participates without dreaming hardly will be creative."

For this to be achieved there needs to be a high quality of learning resources available and learner must be capable of highly skilled time management. In sum, the ability to manage the cost and the time for learning is becoming extremely critical to formal students and lifelong learners in this emergent world of network enhanced learning.

REFERENCES

Abedin, B., Daneshgar, F., & D'Ambra, J. (2013). Do non-task interactions matter? The relationship between non-task sociability of computer supported collaborative learning and learning outcomes. *British Journal of Educational Technology*, *43*(3), 385–397. doi:10.1111/j.1467-8535.2011.01181.x

Acosta, E. S. MOOC (2013). Resultados reales. Retrieved from http://revistaeducacionvirtual.com/mooc-resultados-reales/

Al-Saedi, I. (2014). Implementation of Terrain Height Detection and Collision Check Systems in a 3-Dimensional Environment. *American Journal of Intelligent Systems*, *4*(4), 148–153.

Bartle, R. (2004). *Designing Virtual Worlds*. Indianapolis, IN: New Riders Publishing. Bowman.

Bonwell, C., & Eison, J. (1991). *Active Learning: Creating Excitement in the Classroom AEHE-ERIC Higher Education Report No. 1*. Washington, D.C.: Jossey-Bass.

Castronova, E. (2004). *Synthetic Worlds*. Chicago, IL: The University of Chicago Press.

Chen, X. D., Barnett, R., & Stephens, C. (2013, September). Fad or Future: The Advantages and Challenges of Massive Open Online Courses. *Paper Presented at the Research-to Practice Conference in Adult and Higher Education*, St. Charles Missouri.

Chittaro, L., & Ranon, R. (2007). Special issue on Web3D technologies in learning, education and training. *Computer & Education, 49*(1), 3–18. doi:10.1016/j.compedu.2005.06.002

de Figueiredo, A. D., & Afonso, A. P. (2006). *Managing Learning in Virtual Settings: The Role of Context*. Hershey, PA: IGI Global. doi:10.4018/978-1-59140-488-0

Doug, A. (2001). An Introduction to 3-D User Interface Design. *Presence (Cambridge, Mass.)*, *10*(1), 96–108. doi:10.1162/105474601750182342

Escudeiro, P. (2007). X-Tec Model and QEF Model: A case study. *Proceedings of World Conference on E-Learning in Corporate, Government, Healthcare, and Higher Education*, Quebec City, Canada (pp. 258-265).

Gaebel, M. (2013). MOOCs: Massive Open Online courses. European University Association. Retrieved from http://www.eua.be/news/13-02-25/Massive_Open_Online_Courses_MOOCs_EUA_to_look_at_development_of_MOOCs_and_trends_in_innovative_learning.aspx

Garrison, D. R., & Anderson, T. (2005). *El e-learning en el siglo xxi: Investigación y práctica*. Barcelona: Octaedro.

Goldwasser, D., & Roth, D. (2011). Learning from natural instructions. *Procedings of the International Joint Conference on Artificial Intelligence* IJCAI, Beijing, China. doi:10.1007/s10994-013-5407-y

Koster, R. (2004). *Raph Koster's writings on game design*. Retrieved on January 20, 2015 from: http://www.legendmud.org/raph/gaming/index.html

Martin, F. (2013). Will Massive Open Online Courses change how we teach?: Sharing recent experiences with an online course. *Communications of the ACM*, *55*(8), 26–28. doi:10.1145/2240236.2240246

Menchaca, R., & Ballares, B., Quintero & Carreto,C. (2005). Software Engineering, HCI Techniques and Java Technologies Joined to Develop Web-Based 3D Collaborative Virtual Environments. *Proceedings of the Latin American conference on Human-computer interaction*, Cuernavaca, México, (pp. 40-51). ACM Press doi:10.1145/1111360.1111365

Morgado, L., Spilker, M., & Silva, P. (2013). Novos Ambientes de Aprendizagem PLE, MOOC, Mobile Learning. *Proceedings of the 2nd Encontro de Bibliotecas do Ensino Superior*, Aveiro, Portugal.

Núñez, M. M., Oriol, G., & Ángel, B. (2014). Social community in MOOCs: practical implications and outcomes. *Proceedings of the Second International Conference on Technological Ecosystems for Enhancing Multiculturality*. Salamanca, Spain. ACM Press.

Pierre Dillenbourg, P., & Self, J. (1992). A computational approach to socially distributed cognition. *European Journal of Psychology of Education*, *7*(4), 252–373.

Playa, J. (2013) *Los cursos on line y gratuitos obligan a las universidades a replantear su modelo*. Retrieved from http://www.lavanguardia.com/vida/20130205/54366352711/ cursos-on-line-gratuitos-universidades-replantear-modelo.html

Reis, R., Escudeiro, P., & Escudeiro, N. (2010) Comparing Social Virtual Worlds for Educational Purposes. *Proceedings of the 10th IEEE International Conference on Advanced Learning Technologies*, Sousse, Tunisia (186-190). IEEE Press. doi:10.1109/ICALT.2010.57

Siemens, G. (2008). *Learning and knowing in networks: changing roles for educators and designers*. Retrieved from: http://itforum.coe.uga.edu/Paper105/Siemens.pdf

Tiffin, J., & Rajasingham, L. (2003). *The Global Virtual University*. London, New York, Canada: Routledge. doi:10.4324/9780203464670

Velásquez, T. MOOCS (2013). *Un mundo gratuito de conocimientos a um clic de distancia*. Retrieved from http://nochesdemedia.com/2013/01/27/moocs-un-mundo-gratuito-de-conocimientos-a-un-clic-de-distancia/

Vizoso, M. (2013). ¿Serán los COMA (MOOC), el futuro del e-learning y el punto de inflexión del sistema educativo actual? Retrieved from http://scopeo.usal.es/seran-los-coma-mooc-el-futuro-del-e-learning-y-el-punto-de-inflexion-del-sistema-educativo-actual/

Warbuton, S. (2009). Out of control-Managing our digital reputations. Retrieved from: http://www.slideshare.net/stevenw/out-of-managing-our-digital-reputations

ADDITIONAL READING

Fasihuddin, H. A., Skinner, G. D., & Athauda, R. I. (2013). Boosting the Opportunities of Open Learning (MOOCs) through Learning Theories. *Journal on Computing*, 3(3), 112-117.

Flynn, J. (2013). MOOCS: Disruptive innovation and the future of higher education. *Christian Education Journal*, *10*(1), 149–162.

Graf, S., & Kinshuk, K. (2007). Providing Adaptive Courses in Learning Management Systems with Respect to Learning Styles. *World Conference on E-Learning in Corporate, Government, Healthcare, and Higher Education*

Yuan, L., & Powell, S. (2013). MOOCs and Open Education: Implications for Higher Education. *CETIS JISC*, 2013

Zemsky, R. (2014). With a MOOC MOOC here and a MOOC MOOC there, here a MOOC, there a MOOC, everywhere a MOOC MOOC. *The Journal of General Education*, *63*(4), 237–243. doi:10.1353/jge.2014.0029

KEY TERMS AND DEFINITIONS

Active Learning: It is a model of instruction that focus the responsibility of learning on learners.

Collaboration: The action of working with someone to produce something.

Connectivism: It is the application of network principles to define both knowledge and the process of learning. Knowledge is defined as a particular pattern of relationships and learning is defined as the creation of new connections and patterns as well as the ability to maneuver around existing networks/patterns.

Design: It is the creation of a plan or convention for the construction of an object or a system.

MOOC: A massive open online course (MOOC) is a free Web-based distance learning program that is designed for the participation of large numbers of geographically dispersed students.

Social Networks: A social network represents relationships and flows between people, groups, organizations, animals, computers or other information/knowledge processing entities.

Virtual Team: It is a group of individuals who work across time, space and organizational boundaries with links strengthened by webs of communication technology.

Chapter 14
Towards a Gamification Design Process for Building Engaging MOOCs

Aikaterini Kalogeraki
Open University of Cyprus, Cyprus

ABSTRACT

MOOCs offer a model of massive, free and personalized education and they are consider by many educators and researchers as a potential alternative to global education and providing massive open lifelong learning, indispensable in the "Information Society" we live in today. Nevertheless research conducted have observed a large dropout rate among MOOCs, mainly because courses are massively open and centered around learners with different ages, experiences, skills and motivations. The author believes that it is vital to introduce Gamification elements in order to commitment the learners for completing the courses, with willingness and pleasure. In this chapter will be presented the theoretical background of Gamification elements that can be combined with the principles of UX, guidelines for the design interface of MOOCs and their involvement of learning theories and game-based theory. It will also include a design proposal for the interface of MOOCs that will engaged UX with elements of Gamification.

INTRODUCTION

Even though MOOCs are a descendant of distance education, they differ in regard to the scope of services that they offer. Since the acronym indicates that the aim is a Massive Open Online Courses give everybody the opportunity to learn at any time of their lives, from anywhere on the planet. More specifically, the Canadian teacher Dave Cormier describes MOOCs as a new kind of education and defines it as a lesson with a start and end date, which is open to all, with no barriers to entry, without cost and without educational criteria. (Morrison, 2014)

Offering a model of massively, free and personalized education, as well as, use of organized web based collaborative tools is what makes them unique, in combination with the requirements of the "Information Society" we live in today. (Bruce et al., 2014) The main characteristics of MOOCs are therefore

DOI: 10.4018/978-1-4666-9743-0.ch014

based on the idea by means of which we provide free education from renowned teachers and prestigious universities with a simple connection to the network, seen by many educators and researchers a potential alternative to global education that will provide massive open lifelong learning. This is evident when look at the number of enrolled learners in Coursera, of which 61.5 percent originates from outside the United States. (Lane & Kinser, 2012)

Nevertheless research conducted have observed a large dropout rate among MOOCs, around 90% (Reece, 2013). The problem arises mainly because the courses are massively open and centred around learners along different ages, experiences, skills and motivations. (Grünewald et al., 2013)

In the field of digital marketing to rapidly gained and traction consumers (Zichermann & Linder, 2010), as well as in various workplaces to create engaging workplaces (Reeves & Read, 2013) or facilitate mass-collaboration (McGonigal, 2011) have created numerous "gamified" applications. This design approach integrates successfully Gamification techniques using video game elements in non-game services and applications (rather than full-fledged games), giving to the operation system a service layer of reward and reputation systems with points, badges, levels and leader boards to improve user experience and user engagement services.

Consequently the author believes that it is vital to introduce Gamification elements in MOOCs, in order to commitment the learners for completing the courses, with willingness and pleasure. In this chapter will develop the theoretical background of Gamification elements that can be combined with the principles of UX, guidelines for the design interface of MOOCs and their involvement of theories of learning and game-based theory. It will also include a design proposal for the interface of MOOCs that will engaged UX with elements of Gamification. The design guidelines and the framework are supported by several studies and are based on literate review that combines elements of Gamification to generate an interactive gamify educational interface.

BACKGROUND

UCD and UX Reduced Cognitive Load

MOOCs are based on active participation of hundreds learners, who will communicate with the software and will interact with the computer through an interface. If learners have previous related experiences and perceptions, they will be able to orient themselves in the environment of MOOCs and will know how to navigate and attend by choosing the most appropriate way.

This is called User Experience-UX and usually people use the expression in this case "user friendly". Essentially they referred that the user has prior experience to use easily a device, a functional etc. (Buley, 2013) For example users-learners, often click on buttons or links without looking at their content, but perceived by their shape, their color, their position, what is going to appear on screen. (Johnson, 2010)

The UX of learners who attend courses in MOOCs is difficult to predict, due to targeted at mass population who are of different ages, experiences, skills and motivations. (Grünewald et al., 2013) As a result, it has reduced the quality of MOOCs, because within the definition of quality of electronic distance education, include the quality of instructional design which encompasses the quality of the educational interface. It is interesting the view of researchers for the first MOOCs who had high-quality content, but observed high dropout rates, confusion, disappointment and failure of learners and they accuse for that the low design quality of the interfaces. (Conole, 2014; Legon, 2014)

More specifically, some of the main reasons that have been highlighted in several studies are the following:

1. The level of commitment is very low, especially when there is no personal support and feedback, although it can occur in any e-learning environment, open or closed. (Reece, 2014).
2. The lack of digital literacy is an obstacle, especially amongst older learners. (Reece, 2014).
3. The lack of standards or cognitive conditions for monitoring a course, creates a strange mix of learners with connoisseurs and those who lack the basic knowledge and skills, causing them frustration by the level of the course. (Legon, 2014; Reece, 2014).
4. The architectural design of the information meaning the design of interfaces, graphics and learning objects are unsuitable for this kind of learning and do not achieve the visual and audio communication that is expected. (Colman, 2013).
5. The online educational material which provided by new technologies, is not alone learning instrument, but must be combined with a proper educational environment. (Colman, 2013).
6. The amount of information that contains a MOOC, can be very disorientating for learners who have the urge to read the entire contents, all comments and posts. George Siemens highlights that in the design must be intentionally defined what the important concepts to be followed are and how to form subnets and subsystems, to help understanding as a solution to abundance of information. (McAuley, Stewart, Siemens, & Cormier, 2010).
7. Lack of strong collaboration and communication instruments, as we are accustomed to internet interfaces. (Jennings, 2013; Koper & Tattersall, 2005).
8. Individual instruction is not provided which is essential component in any kind of successful instruction. As a result thousands of learners all over the world attend a course, with approximately same course, same content from the same teacher. (Management Services, I & J, Reece, 2014).
9. Lack of continuous formative assessment and replacement with review by peers, which deprives the contact and interaction between teacher and learner. (Legon, 2014).
10. The instructional and the architectural design mainly based on functional rules, which satisfy the needs of teachers and administrators and exclude the needs of learners. Mainly they are focused on creating sequences of activities and the integration quick evaluation quiz, rules and various learning resources (attached PDF files - learning materials, videos etc.). Combining these with the physical absence of the teacher, makes a virtual classroom look like as a typical adult class where the teacher comes, make lecture, gives some photocopied pages and the course ends. (Reece, 2013).
11. While the instruction follow a modern pedagogical method, in fact the method is not transferred at the e-learning environment. (Conole, 2014).

Following principals of User-Centered Design Strategies-UCD and UX, they aims to reduce the extraneous cognitive load of the interface, so that learners do not have to think of how to use the educational environment, but to perceive intuitively the use of an object to help them focus on learning and not so much on the operation. (Dorian, 2013) This design approach will also help to interpret the screen in the same way regardless of whether they are an experienced computer users or not. It is important because MOOCs target the mass population and it is impossible to know in advance their knowledge and experience. (Johnson, 2010).

To follow a UCD framework required interdisciplinary working group which shall consist of teachers, IT engineers until designers who will combine pedagogical, sociological and educational theories with computer knowledge and visual communication in order to create an interactive learning interface. (Ring, 1993) Minimalism is the key to everything is designed to create an interface as efficient as possible which will (Dorian, 2013; Forni, 2012).

- Enhance communication between interface and learner.
- Enhance the understanding of what objects are, how they work and why.
- Enhance the learning experience.
- Increase the percentage of learners to remember learning content for a longer time.

These are supported by several studies, which demonstrate that the affected aesthetic feelings of the learner, the interaction with the system may eventually have an impact on how the learners will respond to the learning process. Specific there is a research which refers that if two interfaces with same function, which are considered as the most attractive to the users, are also considered user-friendly. (Dorian, 2013)

Gamification as a Design Strategy

Researchers are trying to find ways to integrate elements in the interfaces to Human-Computer Interaction (HCI) based always on UCD and UX (Malone, 1980; Malone, 1982). In the last two years it took wide publicity the use of gamification elements in numerous gamified marketing applications and workplaces while timidly used in educational environments. In recent research the findings mentioned that users have a positive attitude, increased motivation and enjoy the gamified applications. (Farzan & Brusilovsky, 2011)

Although the term Gamification was invented in 2002, gained popularity and defined as a particular concept after 2010. Gamification is the application of game dynamics and mechanics into non-gaming environments to increase engagement (Deterding, Dixon, Khaled, & Nacke, 2011; Domínguez et al., 2013; Downes-Le Guin, Baker, Mechling, & Ruylea, 2012; Kapp, 2012). Nevertheless, until now the definition is described differently by many researchers (Kapp, 2012) arguing that it needs to be extended. (Farzan & Brusilovsky, 2011) Therefore, for a better understanding of the term Gamification needed the combination of terms in order to deduct non-essential elements and analyze their common points. All definitions mentioned the following meanings which in practice be considered techniques of Gamification and if they properly used in e-learning, should raise motivation to complete the course, with willingness and pleasure from the learner. (Kapp, 2012).

1. **Game-Based:** Gamification is based on the game, so it follows the basic concepts of the game. The aim is to create a system in which learners will involve on an abstract challenge target by rules, interaction and feedback that will lead to a measurable effect and cause an emotional reaction.
2. **Mechanics of a Game:** Includes levels of success, medals, trophies, rewards, scores, and time constraints. These elements alone are not sufficient to convert a lackluster experience in an exciting game, but it is vital elements that are used in Gamification process.
3. **Aesthetics:** If the interfaces and the graphics are not properly designed in an aesthetically pleasing environment, will not gain the gaze of the learner and will affect the willingness to accept the Gamification.

4. **Thinking Game:** Maybe it is the most important element of the Gamification. The basic idea is to integrate in an activity the elements of competition, cooperation, exploration and storytelling. Learners are competing with each other, while offering encouragement in a collaborative environment.
5. **Engagement:** An explicit objective of the process Gamification, is to gain the attention of the learner in order to participate in the process and commit to its completion.
6. **Motivation:** It is a process that will activate the teachers and provide direction, purpose and meaning to their behavior and their actions. In order to be effective, the motives should not be too difficult or too simple.
7. **Problem Solving:** The collaborative nature of the game can help solve problems which requiring the participation of a group. At the same time the competitive nature of games usually encourage the learners to do their best to achieve the aim of victory.
8. **Promotion of Learning:** The Gamification can be used to promote learning, because many of its elements are based on educational psychology and techniques that instructional designers have already used. Objects such as activities, presentations, corrective feedback and encouraging cooperation are the basis of the instructional design and the difference with the introduction of Gamification is that now presented in a pleasant gaming environment that motivates and trains them.

From the brief analysis realize that Gamification builds on the user experience as a player. (Farzan & Brusilovsky, 2011) To be effective, must satisfy their expectations and build on the previous experiences consider the "four personality" of players as follows and include their goals (Bartle, 2004):

1. **Achievers:** Interested to complete in a short time and climb to the game hierarchy.
2. **Explorers:** Interested to penetrate deep into the game to discover new areas whether they will get grade and are proud of their knowledge.
3. **Socializers:** Interested to expand their social network and be proud for their friendships.
4. **Killers:** Want to act to other players even without their consent and want to prove that they are superior.

The design of interfaces might be complicated, but can be controlled design with a Gameful User Experience by purposefully incorporating game design elements by imbuing the service with affordances for that purpose. The majority of the researchers methods follow a common procedure with small modifications of the following elements (Deterding, 2014; Domínguez et al., 2013; Farzan & Brusilovsky, 2011):

1. Identify the system's objectives.
2. Identify the desired behavior of end users and quantification to measurable the objectives of the system.
3. Identify the user's profile.
4. Selection and determination design of patterns that will be followed when designing the gamified environment.
5. Structure a sequence by objectives (missions, challenges, levels), which is increasing difficulty, in an environment that will be traveling with rules, opponents and colleagues, direct feedback, desired behaviors and rewards.

Frameworks and methods that follow the gamified environments are presented in the Table 1 and are based on game and learning theories. Aim is learners to feel during learning process what is termed enjoyment and fun. Also with the introduction of elements of Gamification, the MOOCs are further supported by various game theories in cognitive learning, the emotional and the social aspect. In the cognitive domain with the system requirements and the work, the learner is involved in a cyclic process of tasks, which they are trying to accomplish in order to go to the next level. Therefore they acquire positive or negative feelings depending on the success of the work, they overcome the difficulties and receive rewards. In their interaction they undertake various roles which are influenced by the social aspect of MOOC and they receive recognition from peers. (Domínguez et al., 2013).

After all, engaged the introduction of Gamification techniques will enhance the interfaces as observed in commercial platforms, facing serious problems in respect to MOOCs. (Ong, 2013) In particular the literature seems to emphasize that theories of learning games involving pedagogical theories, but also the mechanics of the game, provide more benefits for learners such as (Domínguez et al., 2013; Öztürk, 2013):

1. Independent learners and their responsibilities in the process of learning, acquiring new ways to study through the collection of medals, gifts etc. (Öztürk, 2013).
2. Discovery of different disciplines involving cooperation (Öztürk, 2013).
3. Positive self-esteem and recognition capabilities (Öztürk, 2013).
4. Feels immediate gratification after the execution of an activity and distraction (if not careful, you will not learn) (Kapp, 2012).
5. Learning in a fun way, increasing the willingness to learn (Nolan & McBride, 2013).
6. Daily involvement with MOOCs because it will contribute to the cumulative performance of the learner (De Freitas & De Freitas, 2013).
7. Training in different problem solving techniques, which will lead to the greatest benefit so as to quickly progress to the next level (Kapp, 2012).
8. Adaptive work rate which is commensurate with the abilities of the learners so that they do not feel pressure and anxiety (Kapp, 2012).
9. Reduce gaps in learners with continuous feedback (Laszlo, Rowland, Johnston, & Taylor, 2012).
10. Simple communication language for learner because the interface will present the information using visualization and icons (Laszlo et al., 2012).
11. Developing skills that are metacognitive in the field such as critical thinking, self, empathy etc. (Kapp, 2012).

Furthermore it is worth mentioning the opinion of the researcher Lee JJ & Hammer J. which argues that: "A well designed Gamification system can help the learner to undertake essential fruitful role in learning. By developing a new playful identity and rewarding it appropriately, can help him to think differently about his abilities in school and what the school might mean for him." (Öztürk, 2013).

Learning Theories at Industrial Design of Interfaces

The learning theories although in the beginning it seems not to affect the way that has been designed a learning technology, in fact as explained in UCD, UX and Gamification, they provide explanations of

Table 1. Frameworks and learning game-based theories which involved with Gamification (Kapp, 2012)

Frameworks/Theories	Gamification
Social Learning Theory (Robert Bandura, 1970)	People learn by observing and imitating desired behaviors. This theory achieved using of avatars, wherein transferring an appropriate behavioral model, while learners observe repeatedly in a safe environment to enable assimilated.
Cognitive Apprenticeship	The environment should be authentic and provide to the learners feedback and guidance about the activities. This theory achieved by modeling the real world, using authentic context through the activities and social interaction. Also each task should be based on skills and attitudes which learned in a previous level and the system make corrections by giving constantly advices and comments.
Flow	The system continuously adapts to the interest of the learners to keep a steady state. It should constantly adapt proper level of challenge that is neither too easy nor too difficult and concentrate the learners in their aims.
Operant Conditioning (Skinner 1930)	Provide appropriate rewards, prizes etc. with variable timing to enhance a behavior and maintain the interest of the learners.
ARCS Theory of Motivation (John Keller, industrial design-e-learning)	The ARCs model is represented by four factors: Attention, Relevance, Confidence and Satisfaction Namely aim is to gain the attention of the learners, providing relevant information and targeting the right level of challenge so they confident that they will succeed, satisfaction and make them produce intrinsic and extrinsic motivation.
Distribute Practice	While playing with time, providing repetitions of the content with distance during MOOCs, enhanced the long term memory and recall of content. This theory achieved by repeating a similar activity randomly at different times.
Theory of Intrinsically Motivating Instructions (Thomas Malone, 1980)	Three essential elements incite a game: • **Challenge** by using variable level of difficulty, multiple objectives, levels, hidden information, and randomness. Also there must be personal meaning, and provide information on progress and enhance self-esteem. • **Fantasy** by creating educational environment that causes conceivable images of things that do not exist in the senses or in reality. So learners will implement the new knowledge on the old, will create vivid images that will improve long-term memory and will feel emotional satisfaction. • **Curiosity** with complexity, exciting environment (light, sound, or other sensory stimuli), surprise (incomplete, hidden or inconsistent knowledge structures) and feedback.
Intrinsic Motivation (Mark Lepper – Principals for Instructional Design)	Four essential principals: • **Control** the activities by learners about the time and how their conduct, and avoid unnecessary rewards. • **Challenge** to activities by intermediate level of difficulty, uncertain achievement timely feedback, multiple targets or multiple levels and by constantly being challenged as they progress. • **Curiosity** (such as Intrinsically Motivating Instructions). • **Contextualization** presentation of the activity as simulation or with fantasy.
The Taxonomy of Intrinsic Motivations for Learning (Lepper – Malone)	Include internal motivations such challenge, curiosity, control, imagination, and external motivations such as cooperation, competition and recognition.
Self-Determination Theory (SDT)	Provides learners a sense of autonomy and competence and felling connected with the other learners. This theory achieved by direct connection, but even then, there is no cooperation between them and they feel that they control their actions.
Scaffolding (Lev Vygotsky Zone of proximal development)	In the beginning a great deal of guidance is provided in order for the problems to be solved which increases as the experience of the learners is reduced manage to solve them on their own. The use of levels according to their skills and displaying corresponding information on the screen, will provide an adaptive learning.
Episodic Memory	Episodic memory calls information that is stored in long term memory of the learners and is related to their experiences associated by a particular place or time. The aim is to provoke emotions of the learners and to encode richer classes in their memory. This theory achieved by using visual indicators and providing figures, so quickly they recall information that otherwise would not have remembered.

how the learners learn and why make specific choices. Therefore the purpose of the analysis is to select the best or most appropriate learning theories and include them in the design of the interfaces in order to provide effective learning. (Dorian, 2013).

Although MOOCs are a new way of teaching and using new tools of instruction, are based on 25 years' experience at e-learning. Characteristic of MOOCs as well as e-learning, is the continuing evolution as the time goes by combining new technologies with existing pedagogical methods Each theory is based on the previous ones and all together hold an important position in a completed instructional design which aims at learning. (Daniel, 2012) Educational environments of MOOCs are based mainly in combination of three pedagogical models (Table 3). (Anderson & Dron, 2011)

The early educational projects in distance online learning were created by Gagne 1965 and Keller & Sherman and were based on cognitive behavioral theory. This theory studies the parts of the human brain that are used for learning and thinking, the behavior of learners and their reaction to a stimulus. It is used in the design of educational materials following guidance, structured, linear path and using various instruments and materials which stimulates the brain with different ways and maximize the efficiency. (Anderson & Dron, 2011) The teleconference, direct or indirect communication, multimedia, practice and drilled systems (tutorials), is one of the most successful instruments that are used in e-learning. Cognitive behavioral theory is connected with the introduction of Gamification techniques and proposes to set clear objectives and rewards to the educational environments like Bravo, Congratulations etc. in order to motivate and engage learners in the learning process. (Dorian, 2013) These instruments are essential for e-learning in order to reduce some of the problems that it has, as the physical absence of the teacher, the almost complete lack of socialization and to achieve interaction, personalization and transmit the style and the personality of the teacher and the learners. (Anderson & Dron, 2011)

The next pedagogical model is Social Constructivism which has its roots in the great pedagogues and researchers as Piaget Vygotsky, Bruner and Dewey. This theory supports that knowledge is growing according to the social and cultural background of the learners and the creation of new knowledge integrated with preexisting knowledge in the minds of learners. (Anderson & Dron, 2011). At constructivism educational environments proposes collaborative tools such as wikis, chat rooms, forum, building communities that will help the group conversation and knowledge construction and 3-D virtual worlds that allow learners to participate in virtual experiences and investigations, collect various data and suggest solutions (Dorian, 2013).

Finally a modern pedagogical method Connectivist was established in 2007 by Canadian authors of MOOCs, George Siemens and Stephen Downes. (Anderson & Dron, 2011) The theory although presented as separate pedagogy, actually encompasses the other pedagogical methods and based on theorists of the past such as Bandura, Bruner, Vygotsky and the specific context of networked technologies which Pask developed in 1975. (Baggaley, 2013) It launched by the abundance of information in modern society where the aim of learning is not to learn a specific content, but to learn how to learn. They argues that learning builds an information network of contacts and resources applicable to real problems. (Anderson & Dron, 2011) Knowledge is not only internally in the neural network of the brain of a person but also at the outside of Web 2.0 environment (Siemens, 2006) where each learner is a node connected to other nodes for example inputs, tools, other learners, etc. (Clarà & Barberà, 2013) The connections between people, objects and educational content that is available on the World Wide Web is more important in learning from prior knowledge of learner. So it must be structured an accessible open learning environment, with links where members participate according to their actual learning needs, self-trained and filter information according to their interests so with continuous feedback to the network will be provided effective learning. (Siemens, 2005) This view is also supported by Vygotsky on the assumption that knowledge has social nature and is constructed through the process of cooperation, interaction and communication between learners. (De Waard et al., 2011) Therefore to provide knowledge the MOOCs, must necessarily provide online activities such as user comments, wikis, blogs, twitter, Voicethreads, and multimedia webcasts, which will provide dialogue and exchange of experiences through social networks to turn the learning outcomes into permanent knowledge. Learning is not a linear process but a continuous repetition which linking new knowledge with prior, influenced each of the ideas of other learners, while at the end interpreted and evaluated by the same learner, who produces collaborative new content for future use by others. (De Waard et al., 2011)

Additives in educational instructor due to their critical mass must include the theory of Howard Gardner (Gardner, 1985) of multiple types of intelligence (Table 4) to enhance the adaptability of the educational environment and to suit each learner. Knewton and Kuntz, based on theory of Gardner and the study of Pearson about how technology is incorporated in the instruction, they believe that MOOCs must proceed to a greater extend automated adaptability by use of machine learning. (Meisel, 2012) Ideally it will be the system could provide for learners needs and for better understanding a different course or adapts the view of material, according to every learner choices, answers, even with the slowdown of the mouse or the acceleration of video. This will allow different learners to learn with the most appropriate for them way. Besides, some people learn best by reading the text, others watching a video, others playing a game, and others participating in dialogue. Also video lecture can fit now to the learner, but in next lesson a written exercise could be more relevant.

The theory of multiple intelligence types corroborated by the surveys have been conducted on the learning styles, to adapt or diversification teaching to cover the needs of most learners. A learning style can be defined as the application, within a learning situation, of an individual's typical mode of problem solving, thinking, perceiving and remembering. (Cassidy, 2004) Mainly focused on learners' interactions between peers, teachers, and generally of learning and consists of six figures (Riechmann & Grasha, 1974) which have some commons with personality of players:

- **Avoidant:** Not excited about learning, usually not involved, is indifferent and prefer tests with Promote points and not enthusiastic teachers.
- **Collaborative:** Prefer teaching through discussion, participation in group work and feel they learn best by exchanging ideas and contribution of different talents.
- **Competitive:** The aim is to better performance relating to the others, they want rewards and led in the discussions.
- **Dependent:** Lack of curiosity in learning focus to the necessary information and depend on the support and guidance of the teacher and learners that is why is necessary instructions, notes, clear deadlines etc.
- **Independent:** Prefer to work on their own even though they hear the ideas of others and want to follow their own learning rhythm.
- **Participant:** Prefer lectures through discussion and want to take part in most of the activities which the analyze and synthesize information and take responsibility for processing.

From all the above information, theories, disadvantages and advantages that already been researched, the author support the idea that many problems of MOOCs which are about engagement of learners can overcome. The introduction of Gamification technics in the design of the interface, can help so that the content, an evaluation standards, the feedback, the personalized teaching and the general instructional design to be effective, quality and successful gamify educational interface.

MAIN FOCUS OF THE CHAPTER

Issues, Controversies, Problems

The review of the related literature proved that the visual display of an interface is not a secondary and an optional component in educational design of MOOCs. Too many criticisms mentioned in the previous section that they have their roots in the visualization of the interface and at interactivity.

These problems start from the fact that most of the existing MOOCs have not been based on HCD because it is usually not possible to invest financially or time for their design. It also does not take account the modern learning theories, the instructional design models and does not innovative techniques such Gamification in order to satisfy learners giving a sense of pleasure, thus ensuring more success and higher efficiency in the cognitive domain. This problem increases if added that Prensky characterized this generation as "Digital Natives" which do not want passive participation in learning with lectures and exams, but interactive content. (Domínguez et al., 2013) The generations of the 1970s and 80s grew up playing video games and saw the whole evolution from the Game Boy in 3DS, from PlayStation in PlayStation 4, from the Nintendo in Wii U and social Facebook games and they argue that video games have taught useful skills. (Kapp, 2012) At the same time they have easy access to internet information and devices such as smart phones and iPad most have innovative design.

As mentioned above, in the majority of current MOOCs, even though offering high instructional design, studies mentioned lack of visual design, of interactive content and of Gamification elements with few exceptions such as the Khan Academy, Codecademy and some Universities of Michigan. (Hamari, Koivisto, & Sarsa, 2014) This comes to a contradiction with any form of learning. Even in traditional instruction the teacher every time depending of learning population, trying to stimulate learners with beautiful books, pleasant pictures and words, while leads, entertains and keeps active and energetic the class with questions, feedback, by tying them together in order to operate all the elements in a beautiful classroom. Moreover the teacher to distract motivate the learners, rewards their efforts for completion of an activity or behavioral change and create a virtual competitive multiplayer game.

Therefore the author argues as many researchers that although MOOCs are considered a revolution in education, there is a high degree of skepticism about their capacity to provide effective learning to the masses. Researchers continue with more detailed surveys, discuss and are informed through user experiences to solve problems of learners and to obtain as most complete the objectives of MOOCs.

Thus the author concludes that is essential and necessary for the design of the interface of the MOOCs to create a model in order to resolve criticism who they have received because of non-adaptability of courses depending on the background knowledge of the learner and the lack of direct contact with the learners. The interface design should follow HCD and principles of design according to the UX and also including Gamification techniques which will increase motivations and the interest of learners in order to become engaged into it and complete the courses. At the same time the learning theories will support the design by introducing instruments that will enhancing dialogue and collaborative, so each learner follow his own learning process. Simultaneously the MOOCs and e-learning will gain for the most part pretty innovative graphic design, like the world of communication and information that come in daily contact (TV, print, advertising, websites, iPad, etc.). (Forni, 2012).

SOLUTIONS AND RECOMMENDATIONS

The interfaces of MOOCs order to be efficient and attractive needed more than a text and some random graphics. The aim is to create an improved and efficient interface, where all learners will have access to learning content, having the best display, with interactivity and easy manipulation, to enhance learning and to achieve behavioral change by reducing monitoring abandonment rates MOOCs.

Therefore in this section the author separates the design of interfaces of MOOCs into stages and propose guidelines principles of design focused on the needs of learners, while engaged UX with elements of Gamification based mainly on Connectivist theory and game-based theories. In addition to the end of each stage indicative presents a design proposal for interfaces of MOOCs. The guidelines principles do not aim to design a fancy interface, with visual effects, but a "quiet environment" that will allow learner to absorb in the learning process and do not be distracted. Generally learners should not be burdened with extraneous information and the interface should transfer the content quickly, clearly, with fun, and enjoyably.

1st Stage: Principles of Design Based on Attributes of MOOCs Learners

Before designing the interfaces of MOOCs investigation is required to providers and learners of MOOCs in order to identify features that learners may have and could affect their behavior and their targets. With the elements that will be collected should be:

- Design a usage scenario for personas of MOOC, analogical to the needs of the public, priorities and attitudes (Conole, 2014).
- Create a list of measurable design principles according to the preferences and the frustrations of the learners, which must be fulfilled by the design for interfaces of MOOCs.

The design proposal presented here is the result of a research (Table 2) and have been created Personas that they would like the educational environment, be more attractive, more organized, more visualized, to provide more tools and possibility of adaptability (Kalogeraki, 2014)

2nd Stage: Collection of Elements and Tools from Familiar Interface

In this stage in order to create a user friendly and efficient interface it is required:

- Checking of the existing interfaces and choose elements and tools already known to learners in order to recognize them and use easily.

Table 2. Catalog of principles design based to persons. (Kalogeraki, 2014)

Frustrations		
Confusion	repeated navigation on the home page to find links or learning objects that interest	
	various ways of communication which are: • away from video • unorganized by topic	
	• large number of participating learners • unable to find cooperation groups with common objectives	
Disappointment and stress	• lack of skills or knowledge • digital literacy • lack of specifications or cognitive preconditions	
	• complex flow and structure of MOOCs • disorientating amount of information	
	time limitations	
	evaluation	
Preferences		
Educational environment	• friendly • comfortable	• fun • playful
	visible organization progress of other learners	

The design proposal is enriched by composing elements and instruments from the educational environments Lams and Moodle, the social network Facebook, of video games Angry birds, Mario, Farmville, League of Legends, from operating systems apple, windows and by communication instruments Skype and Yahoo.

3rd Stage: Design Approach of Interfaces

Learners at MOOCs always start their course from home page and they continue to the main interesting pages. For this reason it is proposed in this stage in order to create a user friendly and efficient interface it is required:

- Use of an alternative way design approach of interfaces which mixed the top-down approach with the bottom-up. In the top-down approach the learners starts contact with the interface from the home screen and slowly they get further deepen into others, while bottom-up approach starts from key destinations or learners transition points and connects them with those preceding or following. (Buley, 2013; Dorian, 2013).
- Create abstract sketches of interfaces which will include work flow and the subject. In this way, simple sketches acquire technical specifications in order to create a bridge for the next stage which is design interfaces on the computer. In particular respecting the principles of design must focus on to:
    - What is the starting point, what ensues and how to reach to final?
    - What are the elements that should be displayed on a screen?
    - What is the appropriate hierarchy of data and information?
    - What should be located?

- What details must appear?
- What navigation must be available to help learners move from one page to another?
- How to change the behavior of a button giving interactivity?

4th Stage: Design Interfaces of MOOCs

Following the catalog of principles design and the information collected in the previous stages, can begin the design of the interfaces to the computer. The design aims to be as tense as possible and must contain all the necessary tools and learning objects that require the learners to attend the MOOC while engaged them with Gamification technics. So in this stage are presented a framework with the design guidelines and the design proposal which accompanying them with functions, expectations for learning and the feeling that will be transferred to the learners.

Design Guideline 1: Organizing Information

The interfaces of MOOCs consist of six main elements that must have a clear distinction in order to organize the information and be easy to use interface which are:

1. Tools to adapt experience of the interface
2. Learning content
3. Learning tools
4. Instructions
5. Feedback
6. Communication and social networks

Following the UX principles in the design, the interface of MOOCs should be coded to these areas following consistency on style and in the design structure as follows:

1. Code each area either by position or by color or by any chassis frame.
2. Place the learning objects, activities, feedback, tools etc. in a hierarchically order, at easily visible point separated from content to provide direct use.
3. Put the important information such as content learning in the central middle area of screen that catches first the learners attention so they will communicate with the main concept.
4. Keep in interfaces same layout, colors, sizes, fonts, titles, navigation so that even a learner left the main screen, to feel that it remains in the same environment and keeps focusing (Forni, 2012
5. Embower learners to hide elements and information in order to relieve their eye and focus better
6. Give permanent access to learners on tools and menu so they used them whenever they want and without requiring leaving the page which they attend
7. Provide interaction with various control points and numerous ways of handling a condition like scroll bars drop-down menu in order to reduce the cognitive demands from the interface and the learner has effective learning.

The design proposal was based on an example of coding areas in the educational interface (Oppermann, 2002) and author propose the following coding and organization of information (Figure 1).

Figure 1. Coding areas of MOOCs in the design proposal

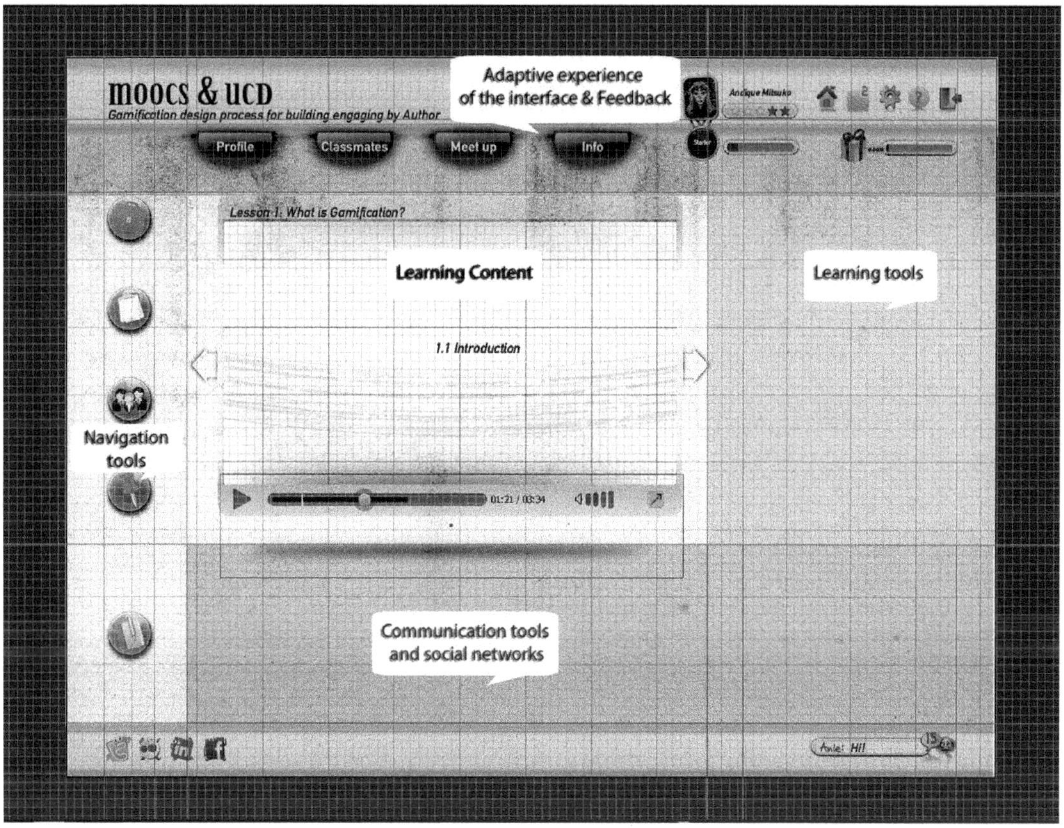

Top Area: Tools for Adaptive Experience of the Interface and Feedback

As usual World Wide Web site, on the upper left area should refer the name of the provider, of the teacher who has created the course and the title of it. At right side display essential tools to adapt experience of the interface with interactive visualized information and gamification as: profile with the learner as avatar, completion counters, e-mail, settings, homepage, help, sign in-out and permanent menu just below".

Middle Area: Learning Content, Materials, and Tools

The middle largest area contain the learning objects of MOOC while right and left appear the interactive tools Course, Note, Forum, Sticker, Homework and additional learning objects and materials.

Bottom Area: Communication Tools and Social Networks Learning Content, Materials, and Tools

In the bottom area there are available to learners social networks chat for direct communication and forum with comments for indirect communication.

Design Guideline 2: Readability Information

Knowing from surveys that one of the most unreadable places for reading a text, is a computer screen. So it is necessary formatting text in MOOCs in order to facilitate the study and handling of a learning activity such as:

1. Short texts.
2. Maximum length of each line about 60-80 characters.
3. Use short paragraphs or columns.
4. Keep rules of electronic typography as consistent colors, leading, left-aligned etc. and avoid bold across the body text or underlining which refers for existence of a link.
5. Compliance with web design guidelines by strengthening the principle of UX perspicuous in order to avoid wrong expectations, for example, elements like buttons must be buttons etc.
6. Visualization of text information whenever is possible.
7. Keep reading habits by focus in screen from top to bottom and from left to right, although societies with opposite reading and lack of experience in computers can find it difficult (Dorian, 2013; Oppermann, 2002).
8. Popup text blocks that do not overlap the content

Design Guideline 3: Visualized Information

Following the UX design principles attractiveness and satisfaction and engaging them with Gamification technics aesthetics and abstract concepts of reality, the interface of MOOC will become more attractive and exciting. At the same time the visual elements not only for beauty but will create symmetry in space and can replace concepts that would take many words to express themselves. Thus strengthened and other attributes of usability as clarity, perception, effectiveness and efficiency so as information visualization principles proposed:

1. Use abstract casual models to help learners understanding complex concepts, processes and activities.
2. Use icons and visualized learning tools already known from web surfing.
3. Visualized elements simplified deduction, aiming to transmit feelings and meanings.
4. Avoid photorealistic images.
5. Use visual indicators, different colors, and proportionate check to pending or complete missions, unread comments etc.

In the design proposal (Figure 2) has created in profile to every learner stylized avatar likely to change color and expression if not properly perform a task, a virtual book with the learning content, an interactive map, otherwise check the learning materials have downloaded, visual and audible indication to tasks learner etc.

Figure 2. Interactive map and Material page with the optional and sourced learning materials. The learning content of this design proposal was based on course Gamification of Kevin Werbach at Coursera (Werbach, 2014)

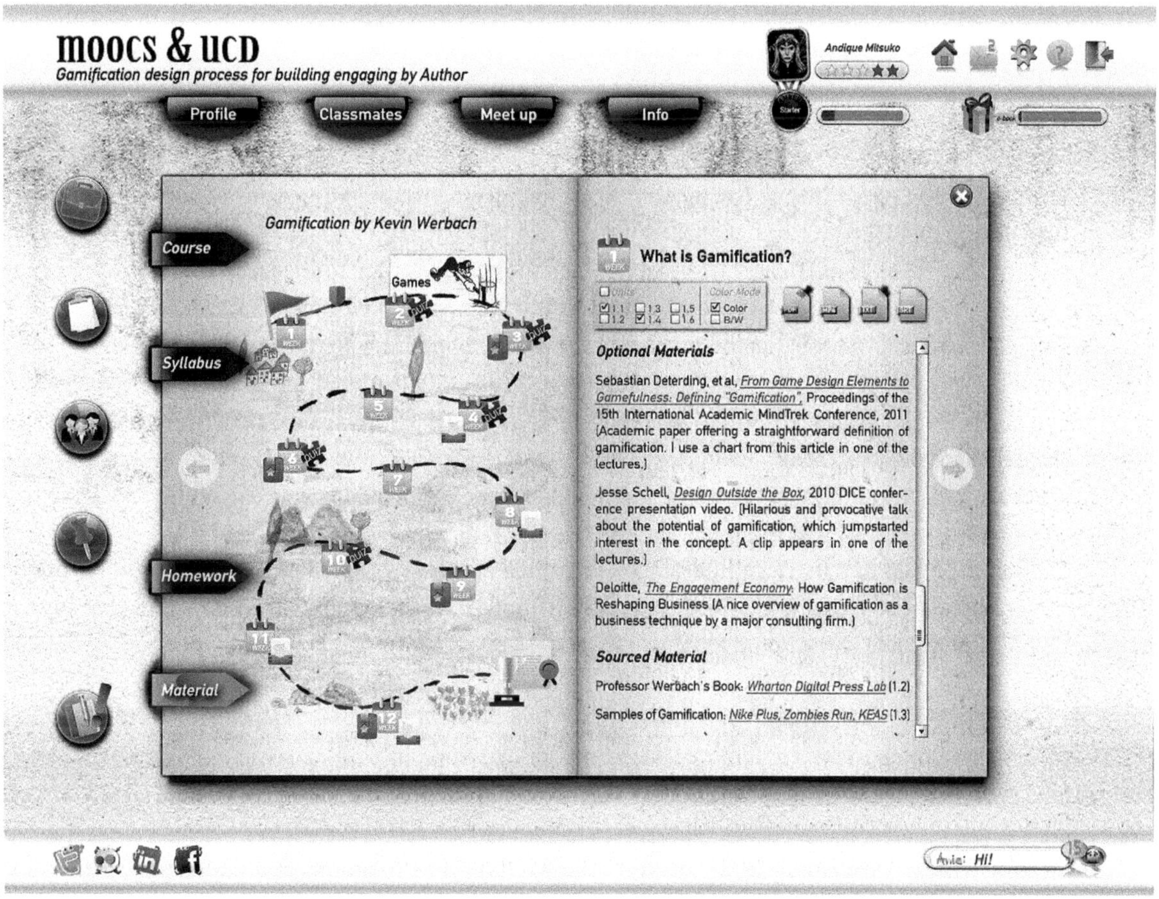

Design Guideline 4: Create Challenges and Determining the Expected Results

The significance of the objectives, missions and the expected results have extensively analyzed in the background section. Therefore proposed:

1. Separate the course into individual targets - short missions with different difficulty that are required to complete a course.
2. The structure of each lesson should follow the below hierarchical tree that should be adapted to analogous cognitive area (Domínguez et al., 2013)

MOOC Course

a. Lesson 1 - Unit Title

1st Challenge - Title

Level 1: Basic thematic basic skills exercises
Level 2: Optional exercises and connection with prior knowledge
Level 3: Specific tasks for rewards and medals
Level 4: Additional detailing activities and specific steps to complete the MOOC and get trophy, certificate etc.

3. Descriptive titles, according to learners interests and giving to them the sense of solving a problem or fulfilling a mission.
4. Gradually increase the difficulty of levels and challenges in order to increase motivation without the risk of losing the learners interest because it is either too easy or too difficult.
5. Notify precise objectives, expected results and rewards to learners so that each learner knows what to do, why it is important, the degree of difficulty and set their own aims to achieve.
6. Leave some levels unlocked so that the learner can proceed with his own rhythm learning and be responsible for own learning.
7. In contrast lock the challenges as an obstacle to the acquisition of the award and the certificate.

This design proposal has used an interactive map into a virtual book which contains the structure of the course, objectives, levels, etc. (Figure 3) and virtual containers of medals and prizes that inform analytically how they obtain the achievements (Figure 4).

Design Guideline 5: Definition of Rules

Create rules according to the needs of the course that ensure actions of the learners be reduced. There are:

1. **Function Rules:** Describing how "played" the MOOC. For example you cannot go to the next section if you do not deliver the work or by collecting 2.000 points you can win an e-book etc.
2. **Implicit Rules:** Or rules of conduct that govern the social contract between two or more learners such as cooperativity, team spirit, as if not respected in a group, can be the cause to exclude a learner from the group.
3. **Educational Rules:** Belong in the learning process such as if learner win if chooses a correct answer.

Design Guideline 6: Provide Feedback with Counters Completion

Replace grades with completion counters in order to have learner's direct feedback and be motivated of competition while reduce the pressure and the stress of evaluation. More specifically, the degree of complete work can be converted to performance measurement of the learner, in relation to the others learners performance, their own performance or with a template that has been provided by the instructional design. This design proposal suggested:

- **Counter Completion of Course:** Where the grades are represented with stars which going up the level of learners and gives to them a sense of evolution.

Figure 3. Homework page with counters completion of missions

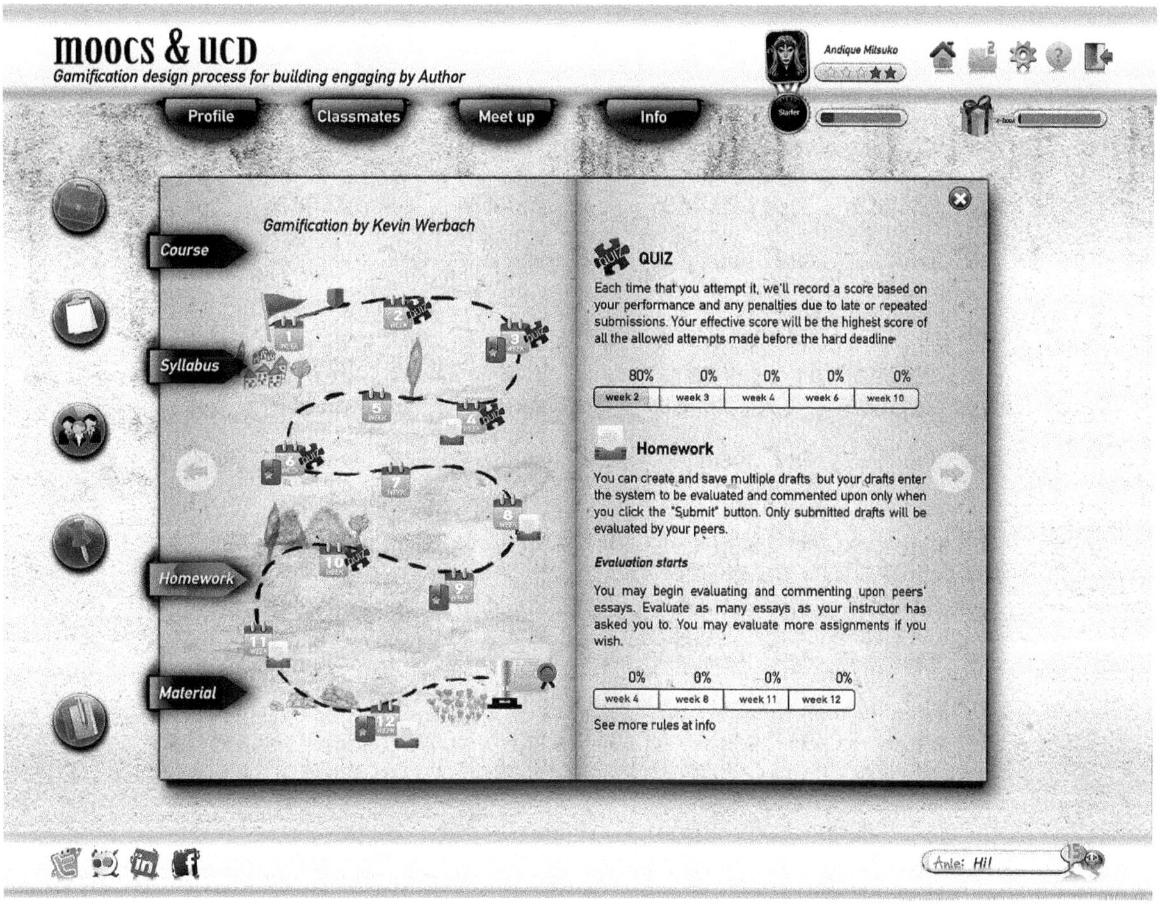

- **Counter Completion of Modules:** Where the grades are represented with percentages experience- XP that shows how well learners executed the mission and earn analogous badges and medals.
- **Counter Completion of Socialization:** Where their contribution converted into XP experience levels and earn analogs gifts.

Design Guideline 7: Provide Rewards for Successful Completion

As in traditional teaching is necessary the use of digital rewards at MOOC in order to increase the motives of learners to learn and change their behavior and attitude. However the excessive use of rewards, may reduce the intrinsic motivation of learners as well as their autonomy, so they should be used restrictively to essential challenging tasks that have been completed. Proposed:

1. Specify rewards according to the structure of the hierarchical tree MOOC and the course objectives.
2. Supplied rewards upon completion of modules, tasks and quiz of the MOOC but also for the cooperatively and team spirit of the learner such as free access at libraries or special offers - discounts, medals, trophies, features, and even a virtual assistant.

Figure 4. Explanation of the prize and how it wins

3. Provide the reason each time to enable learners (and teachers) to recapitulate what they did and won in order to realize and feel they did something important.
4. Provide the option to repeat a mission in order to improve the experience rates XP.
5. Never rewarded every small achievement or only very difficult because in the process the learners will not be aware of and will feel a disappointing experience.

In particular design proposal (Figure 5) indicative proposed seminar certificate, gifts (analyzed in Design guideline #8), medals with features by completing every 20 percent of the course (Starter, Develop-Bronze, Expert-Silver, Super Star-Gold) and trophies Bronze, Silver, Gold depending on the successful completion of MOOC.

Design Guideline 8: Enhancing Teamwork Learning

The learning theories should be combined with gamification techniques especially to enhance the self-organized teamwork learning in a mass level. The aim is the learners to actively participate and be encouraged to share their ideas, their perceptions and knowledge by creating a social network that requires at Connentivist approach. Therefore proposed:

Figure 5. Medal case of MOOC, with lighted medal to be acquired upon completion

1. Provide tools for direct and for indirect communication with interactive, visual and auditory indications.
2. Provide links and social networks, which will take learners in provider learning community to enroll with groups for discussion and study. The links should open in a separate web browser so the learning process does not interrupt.
3. Integrate the gifts that offered at MOOCs to the forum by depending from learners behavior and from votes of peers while their acquisition will characterize the social features which pass in their profile.
4. Integrate leaderboard of learners that provides social recognition with the appearance of the achievements to other learners. Probably the observation of evolution of the others learners will bring a positive impact on their performance with increasing motivations, improve self-efficacy and encourage them to complete the MOOC. Also will be increase competitiveness, cooperation - teamwork and is an instrument of direct feedback. As a design principle of leaderboard proposed.

a. Providing as a CV form with all necessary information such as the learners avatars their names, their achievements, their social features and the courses that enrolled.
b. Gives the opportunity to communicate with each other by e-mail and the ability of friend request, if the learner recognize common interests and wants to cooperate with them.
c. Create group activities with assigning roles without selected members and use blended learning approach into creation of them.

In this design proposal have been created:

- Tools for direct communication-chat with other learners (Figure 6) and for indirect communication-forum that contains all discussions, categorized, with visual and audible indications with the possibility of like, dislike, follow etc.
- Creation of five levels cooperation of learner and analogous social features and gifts (Figure 7)
    - **Level 1-Social:** The learner actively participates in the forum, send e-mail and make friendships with peers.
    - **Level 2-Liked:** The peers vote "like" to post of learner. Otherwise, if they dislike it, learner would be characterized as Rude and losing XP from the counter. If the dislike increase there is a possibility to be excluded from the team.

Figure 6. Maximizing post area of forum by learner and possibility vote by others learners.

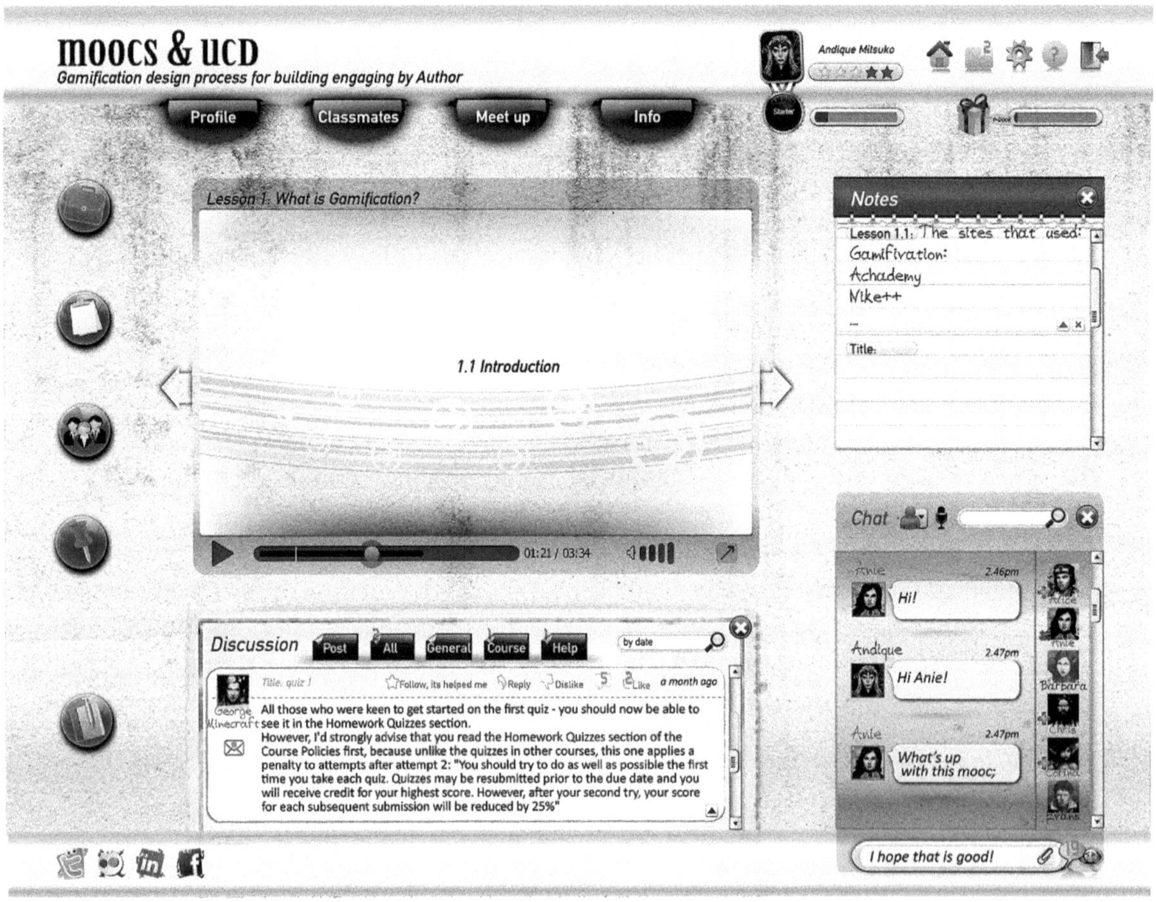

Figure 7. Gift case with lighted gift that the learners will gain soon

- ◦ **Level 3-Friendly:** Actively involved with "Reply" on forum and helps other learners.
- ◦ **Level 4-Helpful:** The peers follow the learner because it's helped.
- ◦ **Level 5-Genius:** The learner actively participates with the others and suggest games, tools, blogs and other resources. Also learner has gained all the gifts, medals and one of the trophy and reward with the opportunity to choose whichever MOOC desires free.
    - ▪ Leaderboard with CV form etc. (Figure 8).
    - ▪ Menu with a Meet up link and buttons for Facebook, twitter etc.

Design Guideline 9: Fostering Learning with Interactive Tools and Resources

1. Enrich interface with interactive learning tools such as glossaries, devices, sources, etc.
2. Provide tools to learners in order to create their own missions and competitions for other learners and to define the aims and rewards.
3. Integrate in the weekly e-mail newsletter, personal information's of the individual performance, statistics compared with the average of other learners, pending missions, rewards which will earn when they have completed the level, so as to increase the motivations and exists continuous self-improvement.

Figure 8. Integration of profile and classmate to leaderboard

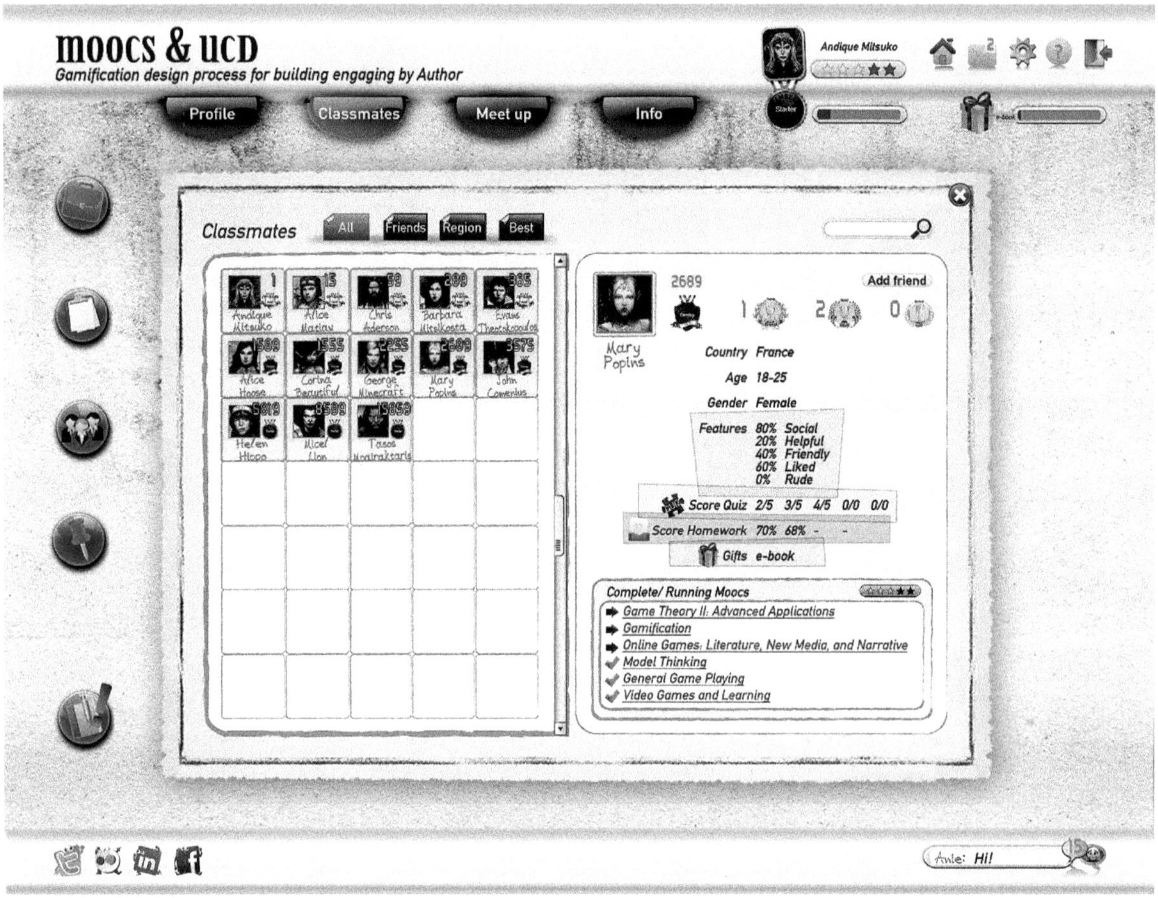

This design proposal has been enhanced with an electronic notepad and a sticker which indicates points in the video probably the learner will want to watch again (Figure 9-Figure 10).

Design Guideline 10: Strengthening Confidence

Often attend MOOCs learners with inadequate knowledge and reduced self-confidence which are not feel confidence for their abilities and want guidance.

1. Create a guide and a narrative fun video with the objectives, rules, presentation of the learning environment etc. to enhance the experience and guiding the learners.
2. Give the choice to learners for prescriptive learning or self-learning by strengthening the interface with popup information at points which they chooses.
3. Invite learners to produce their own educational material either individually or in group and expand a topic from their own perspective. In this way, all the learners feel important while also learning becomes attractive and amplified to maintain knowledge

Figure 9. Sticker to mark the important points on video conference

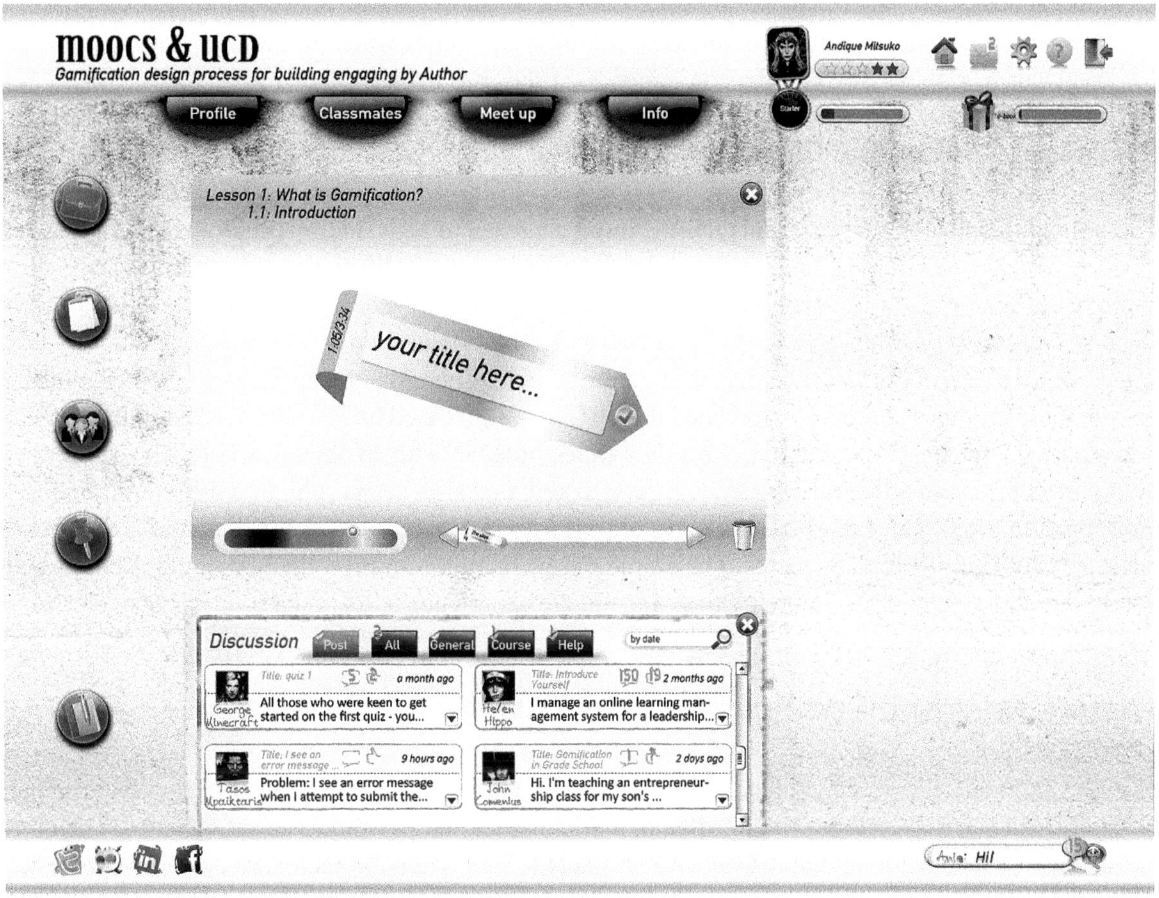

Figure 10. Sticker which indicate a point on progress bar of video and a creation of a new post at forum.

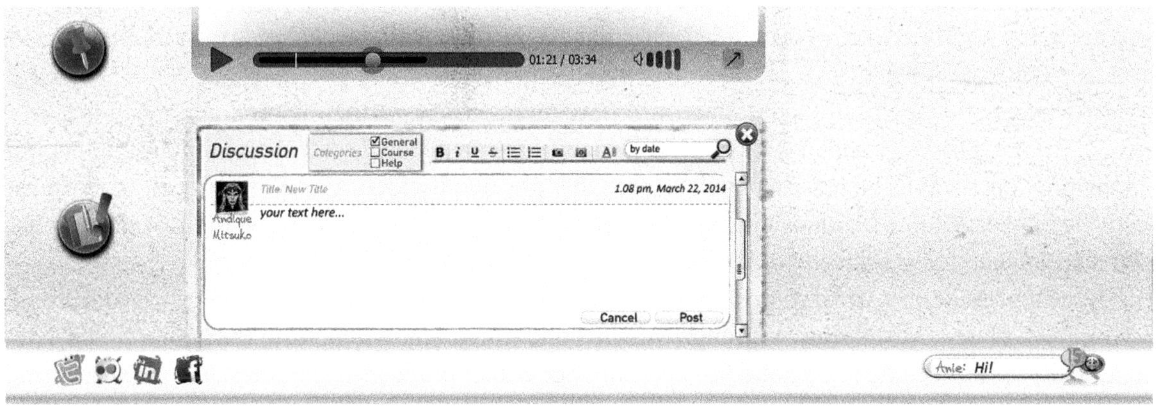

4. Provided a variety of interactive activities so learners can choose their study according to their preferences.
5. Integrate fantastic activities, simulations, role-playing games where knowledge will apply in the real world, without worry of the consequences if they are wrong.

5th Stage: Continuous Pilots Testing

Throughout the planning process and until the interface reach to high fidelity prototype must evaluated by users with a combination of qualitative and quantitative methods, by means of formative user-centric iterative evaluation at various stages of design, in order to similarly redesign the interface to improve it. Usually evaluation based on a scenario of tasks which with observation or interviews or usability testing, research learners from different age and culture. This will provide feedback and comments for the design of the interfaces to check beforehand if interface design based on learners needs, if the visualization passes the message of the object, what they expect interact with an objects, what their feelings and their views, if it's attractive, etc. Finally, it is good to note that after each evaluation the interface needed redesign to improve and reassessment until to achieved the desired outcomes in relation to UX and with integration of Gamification elements. The aim in the evaluation is to meet the learning objectives with the mechanics of game and offer more than a moderate experience to learners.

FUTURE RESEARCH DIRECTIONS

From the literature review we conclude that, in today's society, it is necessary to develop various forms of flexible educational systems, which will aim to lifelong learning in multicultural societies. Therefore the next few years e-learning through MOOCs, is likely to bring the solution to the problem of providing adequate and effective, mass and open education.

In order for the learners to be satisfied and to achieve their learning objectives easily, is not needed only quality in the content of learning resources. It is necessary to emphasize at humanistic design of interfaces of Moocs, in order to gain the interest of learners, increase the motivation for meaningful engagement, in a highly aesthetic educational environment, by introducing techniques to mobilize behavior such as gamification that engage learners to completion of the learning process.

Furthermore the design of the interface may have an impact on further dissemination and improvement of MOOCs services and in the diffusion of knowledge on a global scale. Foreseen the competition among providers will be increase and will be probably prevail providers as their interfaces are designed aesthetically beautiful, with innovative graphic ideas, offering interactive learning tools, with personalized learning and focus basically on the needs and experiences of learners.

The design guidelines and design proposal of these chapter is a first attempt to change the educational environment of distance education through MOOCs and it was impossible from the author to reach the high fidelity prototype that is required to approach the actual product. If the interfaces integrated in a real environment of MOOC and used by learners for a certain period to completed a course, it will be possible to evaluate the results that support the author and many researchers, such as to increase the participation and the motivation to the learners, to lead them to desired learning behaviors and generally solve critics of MOOCs.

However they lead to the assumption of new research into the educational design of interfaces which must be improved the experience that offered to the learners. It is proposed similar research and redesign in the first level of an educational design of interface that is the learning content which provided by MOOCs, to accord the experience of the learner and Gamification techniques. Besides, in an educational environment with gamification techniques, the content shall be convey the same feelings. Learners must feel in each course that they have a mission to "solve", to "win", and "gain" awards with their friends Therefore, the design should not only focus on style of the interface, but also in the learning content in order to solve the criticisms to MOOCs, that provide the same subject that it provided in traditional teaching merely is posted online. At the same time should be investigated for the learning materials and tools that prefers the variform population of learners, as well as how to study and solve their problems. Finally, it should be immediately conducted a more systematic comparative research to learners whether they prefer the new educational environment interface that created or the present MOOCs their look more manageable and more functional.

CONCLUSION

Until nowadays the design of interfaces and the construction of the educational environment of MOOCs, are incomplete also in terms of study, but also in practical terms. Specifically the research found that in the majority of MOOCs interfaces, are lack both educational and graphic design, as well as the user experience they provide. As a result not only digitally illiterate learners but also demanding users can not complete the courses and end up disappointed.

According to the above, author believes that it is crucial for the design of the interface to create a model that it will engaged principals of UCD and UX with the Gamification. So this chapter proposes a framework that must be followed starting from the roots of education, relying on pedagogical, sociological and educational theories, combining them with the knowledge of computing and visualization, to generate an interactive gamify educational interface. The design guidelines for interfaces of MOOCs were choosing as to promote self-organized cooperation learning at mass level with the specific objectives:

- Anyone must be able to use these interfaces regardless of the degree of familiarity with the MOOCs educational environments.
- The learning content must be perceived in a practical and enjoyable way.
- The interfaces should satisfy and attract the learners aesthetically.
- The interfaces are designed so as to increase the motivation to learn.

These design proposal of MOOCs, was validate by taking learners' perspective and the research showed that it is possible to design usable interfaces for MOOCs. Nevertheless, this work is an ongoing project and they are subject to further empirical tests for integration and validation.

For a conclusion the dissemination and continuous evolution of e-learning through MOOCs and the demand of modern society for lifelong learning, require from the competent to adopt and to implement innovative practices and do not allowed to the designers of educational systems will be lulled. The objectives, the strategies and the assessment methods must be constantly redefined in order to ensure that the educational applications and interfaces follow the standards of the time. In particular time must be redesigned with emphasis on instructional design and user experience with the introduction of elements from Gamification, so that even the learners who have reduced information literacy can manage them, while also meeting the requirements of Digital Natives and participants feel pleasant as well as fun during their engagement in the learning process.

REFERENCES

Anderson, T., & Dron, J. (2011). Three generations of distance education pedagogy. *International Review of Research in Open and Distance Learning*, *12*(3).

Baggaley, J. (2013). MOOC rampant. *Distance Education*, *34*(3), 368–378. doi:10.1080/01587919.2013.835768

Bartle, R. A. (2004). *Designing virtual worlds*. New Riders.

Bruce, A., Manuel Dodero, J., Doran, R., Kouzov, O., Lazonder, A., Leemkuil, H., . . . Rattasepp, K. (2014). White paper on the adoption and use of elearning resources across Europe, *Open discovery space*. Retrieved from http://www.opendiscoveryspace.eu/sites/ods/files/wp1-t1.1-white_paper_final_version.pdf

Buley, L. (2013). *The user experience team of one*. Rosenfeld Media.

Cassidy, S. (2004). Learning styles: An overview of theories, models, and measures. [Taylor & Francis]. *Educational Psychology*, *24*(4), 419–444. doi:10.1080/0144341042000228834

Clarà, M., & Barberà, E. (2013). Learning online: Massive open online courses (MOOCs), connectivism, and cultural psychology. *Distance Education*, *34*(1), 129–136. doi:10.1080/01587919.2013.770428

Colman, D. (2013). MOOC interrupted: Top 10 reasons our readers didn't finish a massive open online course. Retrieved from http://www.openculture.com/2013/04/10_reasons_you_didnt_complete_a_mooc.html

Conole, G. (2014). *MOOCs as disruptive technologies: Strategies for enhancing the learner experience and quality of MOOCs*. University of Leicester.

Daniel, J. (2012). *Making sense of MOOCs: Musings in a maze of myth, paradox and possibility. Journal of Interactive Media in Education*. Korea National Open University.

De Freitas, A. A., & De Freitas, M. M. (2013). Classroom live: A software-assisted gamification tool. [Taylor & Francis]. *Computer Science Education*, *23*(2), 186–206. doi:10.1080/08993408.2013.780449

De Waard, I., Koutropoulos, A., Özdamar Keskin, N., Abajian, S. C., Hogue, R., Rodriguez, C. O., & Gallagher, M. S. (2011). Exploring the MOOC format as a pedagogical approach for mLearning. *Proceedings from mLearn,*

Deterding, S. (2014). (Forthcoming). The lens of intrinsic skill atoms: A method for gameful design. *Human-Computer Interaction, Special Issue. HCI and Digital Games*.

Deterding, S., Dixon, D., Khaled, R., & Nacke, L. (2011). From game design elements to gamefulness: Defining gamification. *Proceedings of the 15th International Academic MindTrek Conference: Envisioning Future Media Environments*, Tampere, Finland (pp. 9-15). ACM doi:10.1145/2181037.2181040

Domínguez, A., Saenz-de-Navarrete, J., De-Marcos, L., Fernández-Sanz, L., Pagés, C., & Martínez-Herráiz, J. (2013). Gamifying learning experiences: Practical implications and outcomes. *Computers & Education, 63*, 380–392. doi:10.1016/j.compedu.2012.12.020

Dorian, P. (2013). *Interface design for learning: Design strategies for learning experiences*. New Riders.

Downes-Le Guin, T., Baker, R., Mechling, J., & Ruyle, E. (2012). Myths and realities of respondent engagement in online surveys. *International Journal of Market Research, 54*(5), 1–21. doi:10.2501/IJMR-54-5-613-633

Farzan, R., & Brusilovsky, P. (2011). Encouraging user participation in a course recommender system: An impact on user behavior. *Computers in Human Behavior, 27*(1), 276–284. doi:10.1016/j.chb.2010.08.005

Forni, K. (2012). 62 tips on graphic design, UI/UX design, and visualization for eLearning (The eLearning Guild ed.)

Gardner, H. (1985). *Frames of mind: The theory of multiple intelligences*. Basic books.

Grünewald, F., Meinel, C., Totschnig, M., & Willems, C. (2013). Designing MOOCs for the support of multiple learning styles. Scaling up learning for sustained impact (pp. 371-382). University of Potsdam, Germany: Springer.

Hamari, J., Koivisto, J., & Sarsa, H. (2014). Does gamification work?--A literature review of empirical studies on gamification. *Proceedings of the 2014 47th Hawaii International Conference on System Sciences (HICSS)* (pp. 3025-3034). IEEE

Jennings, C. (2013). Human design for engagement and critical thinking. Retrieved from http://www.learningsolutionsmag.com/articles/1314/human-design-for-engagement-and-critical-thinking

Johnson, J. (2010). *Designing with the mind in mind: Simple guide to understanding user interface design rules*. Morgan Kaufmann.

Kalogeraki, A. (2014). *Design interfaces for massive open online courses*. Cyprus: Open University of Cyprus.

Kapp, K. M. (2012). *The gamification of learning and instruction: Game-based methods and strategies for training and education*. John Wiley & Sons.

Koper, R., & Tattersall, C. (2005). *Learning design-A handbook on modelling and delivering networked education and training*. Heidelberg: Springer Verlag.

Lane, J., & Kinser, K. (2012). MOOC's and the McDonaldization of global higher education. [Commentary from globetrotting higher-education thinkers]. *Education, 30536*, 1.

Laszlo, A., Rowland, R., Johnston, T., & Taylor, G. (2012). Virtual learning in a socially digitized world. *World Futures, 68*(8), 575–594.

Legon, R. (2014). MOOCs do not represent the best of online learning (essay), *Inside higher ed*. Retrieved from http://www.insidehighered.com/views/2013/04/25/moocs-do-not-represent-best-online-learning-essay

Malone, T. W. (1980). What makes things fun to learn? heuristics for designing instructional computer games. *Proceedings of the 3rd ACM SIGSMALL Symposium and the First SIGPC Symposium on Small Systems* (pp. 162-169). ACM. doi:10.1145/800088.802839

Malone, T. W. (1982). Heuristics for designing enjoyable user interfaces: Lessons from computer games. *Proceedings of the 1982 Conference on Human Factors in Computing Systems* (pp. 63-68). ACM Management Services, I & J. doi:10.1145/800049.801756

Australian government. (n. d.). E-learning benchmarking survey – final report. Retrieved from http://flexiblelearning.net.au/wp-content/uploads/2011_e-arning_benchmarking_survey_final_report.pdf

McAuley, A., Stewart, B., Siemens, G., & Cormier, D. (2010). The MOOC model for digital practice.

McGonigal, J. (2011). *Reality is broken: Why games make us better and how they can change the world*. Penguin.

Meisel, S. (2012). Adaptive learning in concept and implementation. *Organizational Management Journal*, *9*(1), 20–21. doi:10.1080/15416518.2012.666947

Morrison, D. (2014). The ultimate student guide to xMOOCs and cMOOCs, *Mooc news and reviews*. Retrieved from http://moocnewsandreviews.com/ultimate-guide-to-xmoocs-and-cmoocso/

Nolan, J., & McBride, M. (2014). Beyond gamification: Reconceptualizing game-based learning in early childhood environments. Information, Communication & Society, (17(5), 594-608.

Ong, M. (2013). Gamification and its effect on employee engagement and performance in a perceptual diagnosis task. University of Canterbury. *Psychology (Savannah, Ga.)*.

Oppermann, R. (2002). *User-interface design. Handbook on information technologies for education and training* (pp. 233–248). Germany: Springer. doi:10.1007/978-3-662-07682-8_15

Öztürk, E. (2013). The new trend in education: Gamification [Abstract]. Muğla University; Anadolu University.

Reece. (2013). MOOC: What about content design? Retrieved from http://transmoder.com/2013/02/06/mooc-what-about-content-design/

Reece. (2014). Feedback is the indispensable ingredient in elearning The transmoder project. Retrieved from http://transmoder.com/2012/06/11/feedback-is-the-indispensable-ingredient-in-elearning/

Reeves, B., & Read, J. L. (2013). *Total engagement: How games and virtual worlds are changing the way people work and businesses compete*. Harvard Business Press.

Riechmann, S. W., & Grasha, A. F. (1974). A rational approach to developing and assessing the construct validity of a student learning style scales instrument. *The Journal of Psychology*, *87*(2), 213–223. doi:10.1080/00223980.1974.9915693

Ring, G. (1993). Interface designs considerations for educational multimedia. *Proceedings of the 3rd International Interactive Multimedia Symposium*, Australia Western (pp. 355-361).

Siemens, G. (2005). Connectivism: A learning theory for the digital age. *International Journal of Instructional Technology and Distance Learning*, *2*(1), 3–10.

Siemens, G. (2006). Connectivism: Learning theory or pastime of the self-amused? Manitoba, Canada: Learning Technologies Centre, e-learn space

Werbach, K. (2014). Gamification. Retrieved from https://class.coursera.org/gamification-003/wiki/Syllabus

Zichermann, G., & Linder, J. (2010). *Game-based marketing: Inspire customer loyalty through rewards, challenges, and contests*. John Wiley & Sons.

ADDITIONAL READING

Bass, S. A. (2014). Simple Solutions to Complex Problems—MOOCs as a Panacea? *The Journal of General Education*, *63*(4), 256–268. doi:10.1353/jge.2014.0023

Flynn, J. (2013). MOOCS: Disruptive innovation and the future of higher education. *Christian Education Journal*, *10*(1), 149–162.

Konstan, J. A., Walker, J. D., Christopher Brooks, D., Brown, K., & Ekstrand, M. (2014) Teaching recommender systems at large scale: evaluation and lessons learned from a hybrid MOOC. *Proceedings of the first ACM conference on Learning @ scale conference*, Edinburgh, UK, (pp. 61-70). ACM Press. doi:10.1145/2556325.2566244

Kumbhar, R. M. (2014). Academic Library's Responses to the Emerging Trends in Higher Education. *DESIDOC Journal of Library & Information Technology*, *34*(6), 477–485. doi:10.14429/djlit.34.6.6878

Milligan, C., & Littlejohn, A. (2014). Supporting Professional Learning in a Massive Open Online Course. *International Review of Research in Open and Distance Learning*, *15*(5), 197–213.

Martin, F. G. (2012). Will massive open online courses change how we teach? *Communications of the ACM*, *55*(8), 26–28. doi:10.1145/2240236.2240246

Murray, M., Pérez, J., Geist, D., & Hedrick, A. (2012). Student Interaction with Online Course Content: Build It and They Might Come. *Journal of Information Technology Education*, *11*(1), 125–142.

KEY TERMS AND DEFINITIONS

Design of Interface: Composed of three basic levels which often overlap each other. First the system design that deals with system architecture, interaction, elements that will be displayed etc., second the interface styling that deals with the appearance, feels that transfer, adaptability and information design and third multimedia content that deals with the graphics, video, sound, animation, interactivity etc.

Design Principles and Guidelines: Although the definitions is very board, is usually based on deep research about learning process and it defined instructions in order to create educational environment usable to all students, without the need for adaptation or specialized design.

Gameful Design: The creation of an object in educational environment which intended to specific goals and satisfying the learners.

Gamification of Learning: Include elements and technics in education environment, which belongs in games in order to engage learners in learning process with pleasure, fun and increase the motivations.

Instructional Design: The design of curricula, of courses and of learning activities. Also encompasses the evaluation of instructional and non-instructional processes to improve the learning process.

User Experience: The perceptions and prior knowledge of learners will interact when use a new technology. It concerned from all the elements of interface, including layout, visual design, sound, text, learning content and interaction.

Visual-Graphic Design: The design of multimedia objects, of resources and of environment that will support the activities to allow interaction with the learner. The designer will convert ideas, words etc. into images, shapes, colors that will pass messages, emotions and often resolve communication problems.

APPENDIX

Table 3. Summary of pedagogical methods at distance education (Anderson & Dron, 2011)

Categories of Pedagogical Methods	Cognitive Behavioral	Social Constructivism	Connectivist
Technology	Mass media: print, television, internet etc., one-to-one communication with teleconference direct or indirect communication, practice and drilled learning systems (tutorials), Praise etc. "Good job!".	Multimedia such as audio, video, web, etc., many to many communication with wikis, chat rooms, 3-D virtual worlds etc.	Web 2.0 and Social Networks
Educational activities	Reading and Writing	Discussion, creation, construction	Discovery, connection, creation and evaluation
Learner	Personal	Groups	Online
Analyze of content	Good: Scenario and instructional design from scratch	Medium: Support ideological and placement, educational guidance	General: Mainly at the level of objects and persons, self-creation
Evaluation	Recall	Composition and insertion	Creative construction
Educational role	Content creator and a wise	He guides the discussion, stands	Friendly criticism and fellow traveler
Extensibility instructional design	High	Medium	Low

Table 4. Howard Gardner, Frames of mind: The theory of multiple intelligences, 1983

Intelligence Type	Characteristics	Multimedia Features
Linguistic: effective use of words	Uses language or written language to express feelings and to communicate.	Text, sounds, recordings
Logical mathematical: use of numbers and scientific thought	Uses the analytical capacity for discovering thinking models and correlations. Productive and inductive syllogism.	Graphics, animation, video lectures
Visual / Spatial: conception of space accurately	Creates mental images, learns through pictures maps or videos.	Graphics, videos, tables, photographs, color labeling
Bodily - Kinesthetic: using the body to express feelings and ideas	Uses his body as an athlete, surgeon or actor in solving or creating problems. Learns better through activities that uses body and senses such as dance and sport.	Graphics, sounds and charts
Existential	Raises questions about the meaning of life and death.	Organigrammes, concept maps
Intrapersonal: self-knowledge, perception of moods, feelings and motivations	Recognizes their abilities and the limits of. Works with aims. Maintain control of their emotions. Resourceful.	Concept maps
Interpersonal: perception of moods, feelings and motivations of other people	Understands and cooperative well with others. Teamwork.	Videos, tables
Music - Rhythmic: recognition production and conversion of music forms	Thinking in musical terms. Able to discover types and relationships. It usually astute listeners.	Sounds, animation
Naturalistic: distinction between phenomena of the natural world and their evaluation	It derives pleasure from contact with nature. It has capability classification.	Tables, charts, lists, video

Chapter 15
Use of Augmented Reality a New Vision on the Massive Open Online Courses

Julio Ponce
Universidad Autonoma de Aguascalientes, México

Francisco Álvarez
Universidad Autonoma de Aguascalientes, México

Francisco Ornelas
Universidad Politecnica de Aguascalientes, México

Beatriz Toscano
Universidad Autonoma de Nayarit, México

ABSTRACT

This study explains the importance of use Augmented Reality in education and how it can be used on the Massive Open Online Courses (MOOCs) in order to improve specific advantages. Augmented reality (AR) is an area that mixes real-world images, whose elements are augmented by computer-generated sensory input such as sound, video, graphics or GPS data. This study further shows the development tools, application areas, and results obtained through augmented reality in the education, as a support tool to achieve the primary objective of education, which is learning through the use of MOOCs, making it a more attractive with the use of information and communication technologies. Currently there is a great variety of applications that use the augmented reality in areas such as medicine, military, education, among others.

INTRODUCTION

Massive Open Online Courses (MOOCs)

The new education era requires greater use of the Information and Communication Technologies (ICT). In some countries there are politics about the incorporation of the technology on the Education System, new technologies have allowed us to extend the teaching and learning environments. New learning models have been implemented such as e-learning, b-learning, m-learning in order to develop interactive environments by using different educational resources that allow us to achieve learning goals. Because

DOI: 10.4018/978-1-4666-9743-0.ch015

of this, educational tools have been developed to support the courses and training programs using ICT, such as Learning Objects (digital resources that are considered as a minimum unit of learning), augmented reality (environments real elements that coexist with the virtual), etc. This technology is used to create teaching resources that can include and display the information in a way that is attractive and interactive for people to use technology.

Thus, making use of the potential of these tools, the aim is to reach the primary goal in the education process, that of which students easily learn specific knowledge to be conveyed. This may provide new educational tools available to the student community at any level of education (Ponce, et. al 2015).

In early days, the use of information technology focused on learning was only used for electronic presentations, video and audio resources, among others. However, throughout time new methodologies emerged and converged into one tool by taking advantage of all technological resources mentioned above resulting in learning resources (Area, 2009).

Nevertheless, the gradual development in the information technologies as well as the availability to these resources by a growing amount of users and the use of internet generated new trends in the education and its scope. E-learning mainly appeared as a supporting tool to education. And, currently it is widely used in higher education, continuing education, special education to vulnerable learners, businessmen, occupational group of learners, among others. E-learning is a type of teaching-learning method that it is based on multimedia material design, use of learning platform, and learning evaluation through the use of computer nets which allows users to be linked everywhere. Another innovation is that this type of education does not depend on a specific time in order to participate in the online course; neither does it depend on a teacher-specialist in the study area which is being taken.

This type of education has grounded the actual development and implementation of Massive Open Online Courses (MOOCs). A relatively new addition to the world of online education is the MOOCs. These are a revolutionary new concept in higher education by which course content is delivered online, and it is aimed at unlimited participation and open access via the web.

The first MOOCs emerged from the open educational resources (OER) movement. This term was coined in 2008 by Dave Cormier.

The original concept of MOOCs is to offer free and open access courses for massive number of learners. However, there are some problems with the quality learning of the students, like escalability issues and low completion rates, (less than 10% of students registered in most of the offered MOOCs complete the course) which constantly concerns the MOOC providers (Brown, 2013).

MOOCs have been offered in conjunction with academic institutions and independently by facilitators: to date, topics have remained within the E-learning and educational technologies fields. Some MOOCs have had more than 2,000 registrations (McAuley, 2010). Some MOOCs elements are showed in the Figure 1.

Describe the general perspective of the chapter. End by specifically stating the objectives of the chapter.

There is a number of websites where you can find courses. Some sites of massive open online courses are as follows:

- **Coursera** (https://www.coursera.org/)**:** Is a social entrepreneurship company that partners with the top universities (Stanford, Duke University, Illinois, Georgia Institute of Technology, John Hopkins University, Rice University, University of California San Francisco, University of Edinburgh, University of Pennsylvania, University of Michigan, University of Toronto, others) in the world to offer courses online.

Figure 1. Key Elements of Moocs (Yousef, 2014)

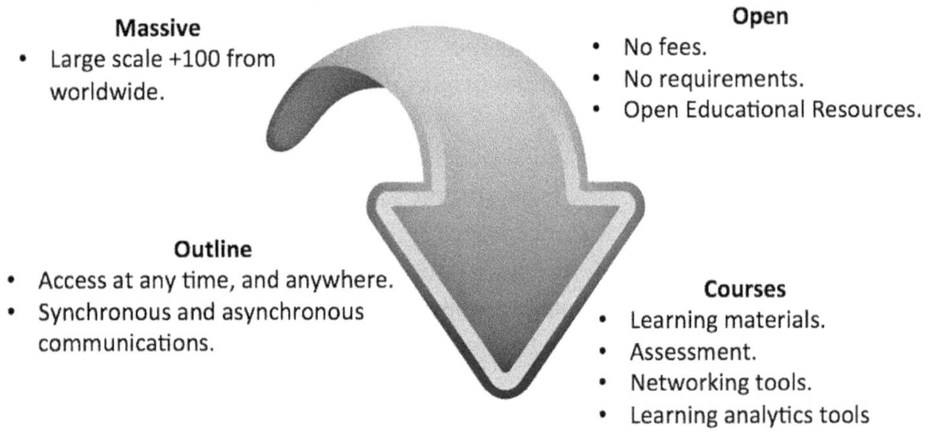

- **Edx** (www.edx.org)**:** Is a partnership between the Massachusetts Institute of Technology and Harvard University to offer online learning to all people around the world.
- **FutureLearn** (www.futurelearn.com)**:** Is a private company, wholly owned by the UK's Open University. Futurelearn will bring together a range of free, open, online courses from leading UK Universities, in the same place and under the same brand.
- **Iversity** (https://iversity.org/)**:** It is a German alternative. Open Courses Education for everyone we make online learning interactive, scalable and social.
- **Miriada X** (https://www.miriadax.net/)**:** Founded by Universia and Telefonica Learning Services. Working with more than 18 universities of Spain and Latin America.
- **NovoED** (https://novoed.com/)**:** This presents more MOOCs from Stanford University. Courses focus on: "Crash Course in Creativity" to "Mobile Health without Borders" to "Technology Entrepreneurship" to "Sustainable Design & Product Management" and others.
- **OpenLearning** (www.openlearning.com)**:** Site users have the option to "Start Teaching" or "Start Learning". Site markets itself as a place for people to teach and/or learn online. You can create a public or private online course, or take free open courses. This site was founded in Sydney Australia by University of New South Wales senior lecturer.

The Figure 2 shows an example of the students distribution of MOOCs users; this case was particularly related to edX platform.

With the use of MOOC, it is possible to add and distribute a diversity of contents which not are not only provided by an expert but by a large group of experts, instructors, teachers in a specific field of study. In this case, both materials and courseware can be open-coded and free accessed. The main purpose of a MOOC is that all participants can administer their own learning process, and thus, participants are able to generate their own knowledge. Evidently, this signals a change of paradigm in the teaching-learning process.

According to the literature review, various advantages can be listed (Montero García, 2015), (The New Media Consortium y Universitat Oberta de Catalunya, 2012), (Fossatti, 2015), (Aranda, Creus, & Sánchez-Navarro, 2014):

Figure 2. An example of edX reach. Every point in the map represents one of 2100 fellow learners of a current MOOC student. Courtesy of (Ralston, 2013)

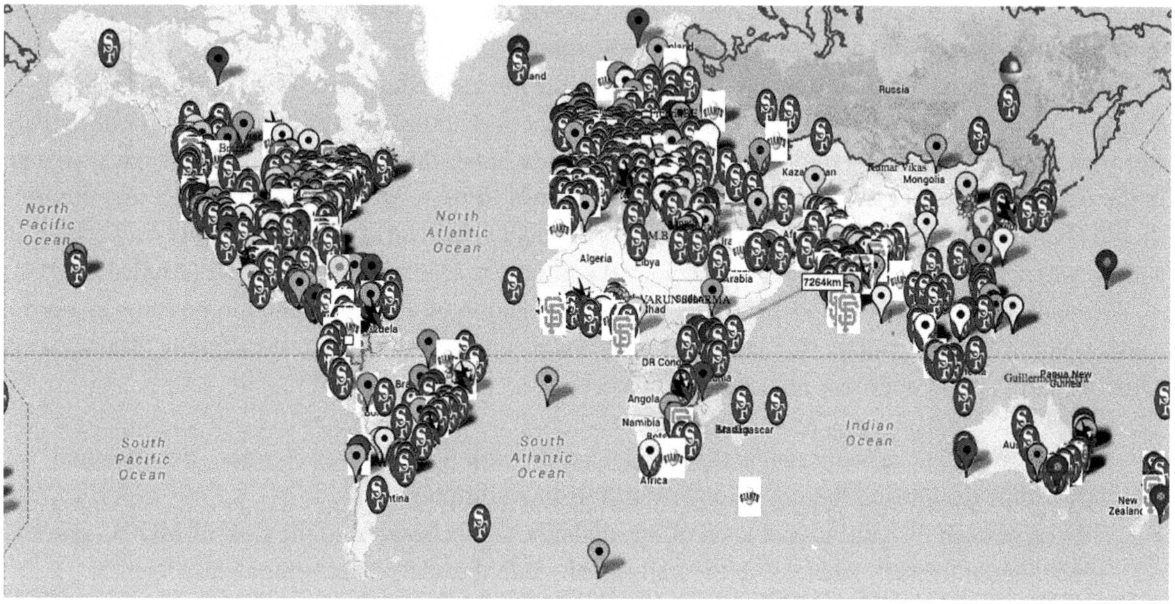

- Materials can surpass the advantages over the open educational contents, particularly when these materials are free and the process itself.
- Materials facilitate training as these provide learning opportunities which are not necessarily part of the institutions' equipment.
- Learning becomes student-centered approach in the sense that learners choose what he or she is really interested regarding the contents provided by the experts.
- The MOOCs can be an affordable source of income for the universities. This is because they are not only an asset for learning, but also MOOCs mean an important point of employability since companies may focus on the candidates' solved problems. This would provide useful information about their capacity previous to their hiring contracts.
- Materials allow the building of subjects which means the possibility of getting a certification. According to the statistics obtained by the educational platform Coursera, such data shows that 20% of the active users opt for the certificate; however, this amount may vary drastically when we refer to colleges with a great capacity of fidelity or other initiatives such as edX, MIT, and Harvard.
- Even though when colleges fail to have the technological capacity for the implementation of MOOC, external service management may be hired to business companies (external suppliers). This helps to cut down costs to colleges.
- MOOC encourage the creation of learning communities in the global village. This further promotes the achievement of collaborative projects among multi-disciplinary groups.
- MOOC does not occur in only one virtual space. The course is composed by a diversity of spread elements that is evident in the social nets, blogs, postings and a wide variety of links with valuable contents.

With the use of MOOC, teacher-student interaction is secondary as it is more relevant peer interaction and the instructional contents. According to Anglada (2014), MOOCs are disruptive in that they are expensive and because they are based on new knowledge about learning psychology. Furthermore, they need to be adapted to new social needs in education.

MOOCs are based on their disruptive potential in the inverted education. This is because learning is achieved by the learner within an independent and self-access approach. Thus, discussion is done in pairs and with the course administrator (teacher). On the other hand, the use of MOOCs demands a change in the traditional colleges where the library system needs to be re-structured. That is to say, libraries should abandon the obsolete physical space for storing books. Instead of this, they should be working as a place where the information use is available and configured around the work flows (Anglada, 2014).

Although it is easy to misunderstand the conceptualization of a traditional course versus an online course, and a MOOC course, this latter has its particular issues that make it different (Martinez de Rituerto, 2014) point out some important differences.

- The arrangement of work teams that participate in various phases of creation, development, instructional design and the execution of the course are different.
- The origin and the educational level of the students, this is because in the case of MOOC space is global and universal, whereas, in the traditional mode the space is geographically local.
- The learner's personal attention is scarce in the MOOC courses.
- The evaluation system is different. This is because in the MOOC courses, personal attention cannot be provided, therefore, learners have to work on self-evaluation or peer evaluation activities.

In a MOOC course, coherence is not an element in course management as opposed to traditional courses where instructors decide on the knowledge domain which learners have to explore by providing the coursebook, readings, and tests. On the contrary, in the MOOC courses, instructors give their viewpoints about how different elements are related, but in the end, students explore, review and work further on their stories, opinions, or additional comments.

It is important to point out that the concept of MOOC courses has been changing over time since it emerged. In these changes some errors have occurred which were detected and corrected based on the initial model. This way, two important currents have gained relevance (though there are more models) such as cMOOX and cMOOC.

The xMOOC (x stands for the platforms Edx, Coursera, Miridiax,..), tend to be e-learning university traditional courses that can be adapted to the characteristics of MOOC platforms, even though their structure is sort of rigid as they focus on Web pages that administer all participants' activities. In this proposal, the teacher's role is an expert that not only selects the contents to be taught to his or her students but also designs standardized and automated test items. This is fundamental for the student's course credits in order to achieve the certification. As it is evident, the assessment model that is being used it is very similar to traditional online courses (Cabrero Almenara, Lorente Cejudo & Vazquez Martínez, 2014).

As for cMOOC (c stands for connectivist), and it is based on the philosophy of conectivist learning approach proposed by George Siemen and Stephen Downes). The cMOOC allow a great interaction among participants. This is due to various resources such as online document exchange, collaborative blogs, and to send and receive FEEDS RSS in order to strengthen learning experiences and students' course feedback. The evaluation system in this model is more open and responds to formative and personal needs. This system furthers facilitates the creation of Personal Learning Nets (PNL –Spanish initials) in which results are not verifiable vis a vis objective tests. On the other hand, the system goes beyond and it turns into an extension of capacities by allocating external nodes that will serve as resources in the future (MOOC.es, 2015).

Which of these environments is the most convenient? Obviously, this depends on the facilitator who will finally decide on which MOOC course best suits the learners' specific needs. Some specific issues, challenges and questions in the MOOCs include:

- The capacity to support deep enquiry and the creation of sophisticated knowledge.
- The breadth versus the depth of participation.
- Whether and under what conditions successful participation can be extended beyond those with technology access and skills in the use.
- Specific strategies to maximize the effective contribution of facilitators in particular and more advanced participants in general.

Augmented Reality

Virtual reality has many meanings but a definition can be: A 3D Space Environment, generated by computer in which the user can interact in real time. One way to see Virtual Reality is like a magic window that overlooks other worlds. Virtual Reality can cause in the coming decades, the reality disappears behind a screen (See Figure 3).

Some features of Virtual Reality (VR) are:

- **Immersion:** The ability of abstraction of the actual environment in which the system user is located. In the (VR) one can try to do this by stimulation of the senses so that the user feels to be inside the new reality.

Figure 3. Virtual Reality Example. Courtesy of (RtoVR, 2015)

- **Presence:** To enable the user to interact within the (VR) must be able to be inside. Thus it becomes an essential feature to be present within the system and this is achieved through different input devices. (Motion Sensors, dimensions, gloves, goggles, and the like).
- **Interactivity:** The VR system should allow the user to perform actions in which the system will modify it and the user gets answers through his or her senses.
- **Virtual Reality Systems Desktop:** These systems use visual information to display a large computer monitor or a projection system. Some of such systems allow the user to view a three-dimensional image on their monitors, but using lenses or LCD or liquid crystal displays.
- **Simulation Cabs:** The most common example of this type of cabin simulator is to train aviators. Generally, it recreates the cabin inside the device or machine to be simulated (for example, a car, an airplane, a tank). The windows are replaced by computer screens with high resolution, and there are stereo speakers that deliver surround sound and can be placed on fixed or movable axes. The program is designed to respond in real time to stimuli that sends you through the controls inside cabins time.
- **Virtual Reality in Second Person:** Unlike immersion systems in the second person (or unencumbered systems) involve perceptions and responses in real time to the actions of the humans involved, who are released or are not subject to the use of helmets, gloves while, HMD's, wires or any other intrusive interface.
- **Telepresence System:** Term created by Marvin Minsky which means remote presence. It is a medium that provides the person the feeling of being physically elsewhere through a scene created by a computer. It is a psychological experience that occurs when simulation technology works well enough to convince the user that it is in a virtual world.
- **Immersed Systems (Immersive):** The more sophisticated virtual reality systems allow the user to feel "immersed" into the virtual world. These immersive systems are generally equipped with a helmet-visor HMD. This device is equipped with a helmet or mask containing visual resources, as both to produce stereoscopic vision and resources acoustic displays thumbnails dimensional effects.
- **Augmented Reality (AR):** This is achieved when a person chooses to trust the real world as a baseline, but viewers use transparent glass or other means to increase immersive reality, overlaying schematics, diagrams, texts, references and so on. As an example of this, Boeing is exploring the possibility to use this system in the engineering of airplanes, in such a way that their technicians and engineers are not going to see a manual to solve a problem, because the augmented reality system schematics show them lists of parts of the airplane, without the operator having to move his chair

Augmented Reality is a field in constant growing. The applications are many and so are the advantages. Our interest is the study in the use of this technology in education in the different education levels but there are augmented reality systems applied to medicine, army, and others. The necessity to have a better perception of the reality and improve activities accomplished by the humans have led to develop the Augmented Reality. The virtual objects that interact with the real world show certain aspects that are not easy to perceive by the human senses, or simply, they don't exist anymore.

Augmented Reality is considered a variation of Virtual Environments (VE), or Virtual Reality (VR). The big difference is that in VE, the user doesn't see the real objects while it is immerse in the virtual world, while in AR, the user can see the real objects and the virtual ones that are superimposed in the reality. Then, the Augmented Reality supplements the reality and the VE replaces it. (Azuma, 1997). It is a technology that integrates real-world signals captured with the computer-generated signals mapped to build new worlds consistent, complemented and enriched –that makes coexist real world objects and virtual world objects. Augmented reality is a new branch of interfaces where real elements coexist with the virtual, which serve to provide additional information to the elements.

Thus, Augmented Reality is an information system that manages to incorporate virtual reality by overlaying data layers related to a pre-existing image. The concept and operation of augmented reality is based on the superimposition of virtual information on a particular object or image digitally, using optimized devices with specific applications to develop these types of tasks. In Figure 4 the evolution of AR shown. To apply augmented reality solutions may be required specific equipment, as transparent screens and touch, special glasses or mobile phones.

There are some definitions about Augmented Reality, but the three characteristics that distinguish it are as follows (Azuma, 1997):

- Combines real and virtual
- Interactive in real time
- Registered in 3-D

To use this technology, many devices and applications have been developed. PCs, smart phones, tablets, touch screens have been used and others created especially for Augmented Reality like eyeglass,

Figure 4. Augmented Reality Throughout History. Courtesy of ("Using APA," 2015)

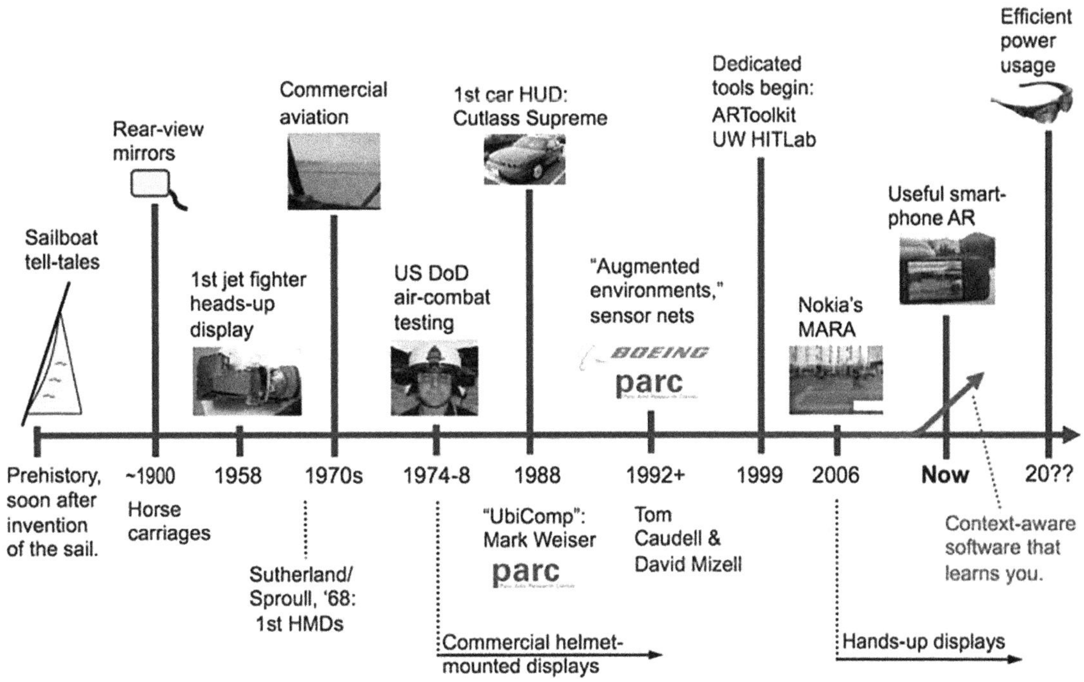

Figure 5. An example of an Augmented Reality Device. Courtesy of (VRT, 2015)

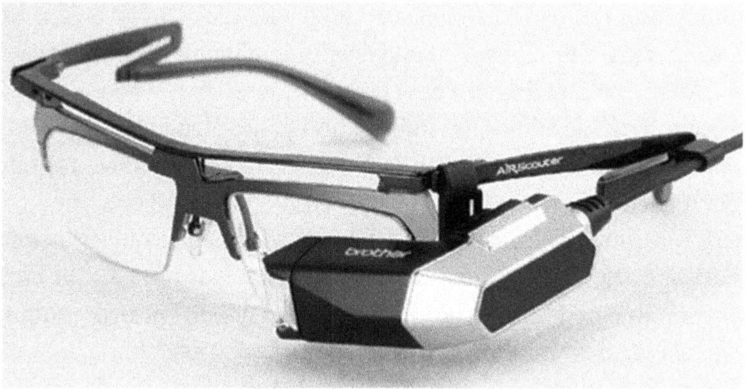

transparent screens and books (see Figure 5). Moreover, Augmented Reality can be considered like an example of Intelligence Amplification defined by Fred Brooks (Brooks, 1996) where the use of a computer as a tool can help to perform the task in an efficient way by humans.

The same author provides a more complete definition which reduces the emphasis on graphical objects, and mentions the term “mediated reality” (Azuma et al., 2001).

Recent research work has contributed to complement definitions that take into account all the type of data which is possible to use in the Augmented Reality. This includes the fusion of any digital information within real world settings considering text, video, audio and haptic overlays (FitzGerald, 2012).

Augmented reality can expand the different means by which humans perceive the world, that is, increase the reality not only for the eyes but also for touch, hearing, smell and even taste. We can see that the human has sought to “complement” the reality with certain elements that can help both to realize basic tasks like to explain what is going on around them.

In the nineties, due to new technological capabilities and the search for alternatives to facilitate and make more productive interaction between people and computers, both research and development in augmented reality have increased enormously (Azuma et al., 2001).

We have mentioned that the objective of Augmented Reality is to help someone to make an activity or task in an efficient way but also it could be used for entertainment, business and others.

The objectives can be grouped in:

- Visualization.
- Training.
- Control.
- Teaching.
- Learning.
- Hearing.
- Enjoying.

It is possible to define other groups, according to the research, but for this chapter these ones are relevant.

Augmented Reality has now been applied in various areas and applications. In the next paragraphs, we will mention some of these areas (see Figure 6).

1. **Educational:** Augmented Reality is particularly relevant for education because it aligns well with Constructivist concepts and situated learning. Augmented Reality is learner-based, allowing the learner to direct their course of discovery in a rich environment that allows for experimentation and making mistakes with no major consequences. The learner is engaged in a dynamic process that provides visual and interactive forms of authentic learning. Augmented Reality can be used in several ways in Education like: Training, Discovery Based Learning, Augmented Books, Augmented Reality to Model Objects and Game Based Learning, among others. Dunleavy, Dede and Mitchell provide a diagrammatic conceptual framework for the process of AR in the learning environment (Dunleavy et. al, 2008).
2. **Medical:** The AR is used to ease the surgeon where the doctor can visualize the internal body's patient in real time and improve the results, by employing a less invasive procedure. It is also used for the training aid for surgery that can be achieved for the internal images of the patient obtained by Magnetic Resonance Imaging and Computed Tomography scans (Azuma, 1997).
3. **Entertainment:** The AR is a funny way to enjoy singers and actors that are not real. In some events like the SIGGRAPH, have shown advances in these areas (Azuma, 1997). And presently, there are virtual singers that could fill stadiums.
4. **Military:** In this area the augmented reality has the potential to significantly impact on training. As dismounted warrior systems become more sophisticated, the need for detailed, precise, and advanced training and simulation has become paramount (Livingston et al., 2002).
5. **Music:** Augmented Reality has been used to modify the interface on video music.

Figure 6. Examples of Augmented Reality Application. Courtesy of ("Using APA," 2013)

BACKGROUND

Augmented Reality Tools

Today there is a great variety of computational tools that can be used for developing applications using augmented reality in various ways. Some of the tools that can be found are:

- ARToolKit was originally developed by Dr. Hirokazu Kato, and its ongoing development is being supported by the Human Interface Technology Laboratory (HIT Lab) at the University of Washington, HIT Lab NZ at the University of Canterbury, New Zealand, and ARToolworks, Inc, Seattle (ARToolKit, 2013).
- Atomic Authoring Tool is a type of software for the development of augmented reality scenes; the program detects the pattern of the marker and displays the object in 3D. One of its advantages is that it is cross-platform, but makes use of the ARToolKit for the recognition and video output. It has a variant, Atomic Web Authoring Tool whose peculiarity lies in creating augmented reality applications for the web.
- Aurasma is augmented reality platform. It is available as an SDK or as a free app for iOS and Android mobile devices. Aurasma's image recognition technology uses a smartphone's or tablet's camera to recognize real world images and then overlay rich media form of animations, videos, 3D models and web pages.
- Aumentaty is a program that allows you to associate your 3D models to classic markers by dragging the name of the model on the marker. Aumentaty Author uses fiducial markers technology to recognize the three-dimensional space shown by the webcam and position the content generated without programming.
- Osgart is a library, which mixes with OpenSceneGraph ARToolkit to try to simplify the development of AR applications (Osgart, 2013).
- SDK to augmented reality of Qualcomm is a development kit for mobile operating systems Android and iOS.

MAIN FOCUS OF THE CHAPTER

Issues, Controversies, Problems

Augmented Reality on the Massive Open Online Courses

Education now requires further implementation of the Technologies of Information and Communication. Incorporating technology has enabled environments extend teaching and/or learning, in order to develop interactive environments by using different multimedia teaching materials that allow achieving the goals of education. Because of this, educators has developed tools to support the courses and training programs using ICTs, such as Learning Objects (digital resources considered minimal learning unit).

The development of Learning Objects using augmented reality (real environments with virtual elements coexist), thus, the application can include and display information in a way that is engaging and interactive for students to use technology as proposed vanguard. For example, the use of the potential of Learning Objects and Augmented Reality that is used for ensuring the reach of the primary objective in the education process, which means that students learn easily specific knowledge to be conveyed.

As mentioned above, a key feature of the AR has to do with its capacity to respond to the user's actions. Such interactivity allows both learning and evaluation to become more dynamic due to MOOC that demonstrate a change in the instructional framework. This would actually be the perfect combination.

One of the features of MOOC, which was previously cited in this study, "the learner plays the role as in a learner-centered approach (independent work) by choosing what appeals to him or her in terms of content course designed by the experts". AR allows applications that provide more surrender value to the user as well as a different form to browse and find information. Furthermore, AR allows learners to reinforce learning in course contents by linking the former to the real world. AR is a new way to learn and gain knowledge through interaction in the physical environment as the study object. This, consequently, fosters learner's autonomy which is ultimately the purpose of MOOC.

Online teaching environments, such as MOOC should utilize various creative ways in educational technologies and emerging teaching approaches. Such teaching approaches are an array of approaches and teaching ideas that are not systematized, but they have emerged in the communication and technology era. And, yet these teaching approaches intend to make use of their potentially communicative, informational, collaborative, interactive, creative and innovating richness.

AR, as it has already been mentioned in this study, is a type of emerging technology that has been introduced in some disciplines in the academic world. However, given this feature, its use and applicability in some teaching environments is still minimum. Thus, experience on this study field is scarce.

AR facilitates practical learning in E-learning environments. This is because AR allows the access to remote laboratories and augmented reality applications that can be utilized in practice and simulations. Given the fact that this provides a contextual learning environment where learners are able to develop new skills.

As an example of this, it has been observed through the Project VISIR (Figure 7) developed by the University of Deusto, learners can access via internet to a remote laboratory which allows learners use a smartphone and a remote AR application. This further helps both teacher and learners to promote real experimentation with electronic basic analogical circuits. The VISIR environment allows learners to set up a circuit everywhere as well as to connect self-control and feeding devices so that there is full adjustment with the experiment. This way, learners are able to study at home and still catch the image for practice in his or her phone in order to achieve the exercise given. This, of course, is possible by using a screen and superimposed images from the coursebook, instruments and laboratory materials with the corresponding results (García Zubia et al., 2010).

SOLUTIONS AND RECOMMENDATIONS

The American expert and the Director of the Consulting Company eLearning 24/7 Craig Weiss identifies the augmented reality as one of the three key tendencies in the future of e-Learning. With this, in the past months, it has been developed and implemented a number of software applications in this field. Weiss thinks that the augmented reality or he calls it "a-learning", would add additional capacity that is not available at this time. "Employees could walk around the building, in the meantime, on the screens

Figure 7. Access Web Page to VISIR (http://visir-network.eu/trends/augmented-reality/)

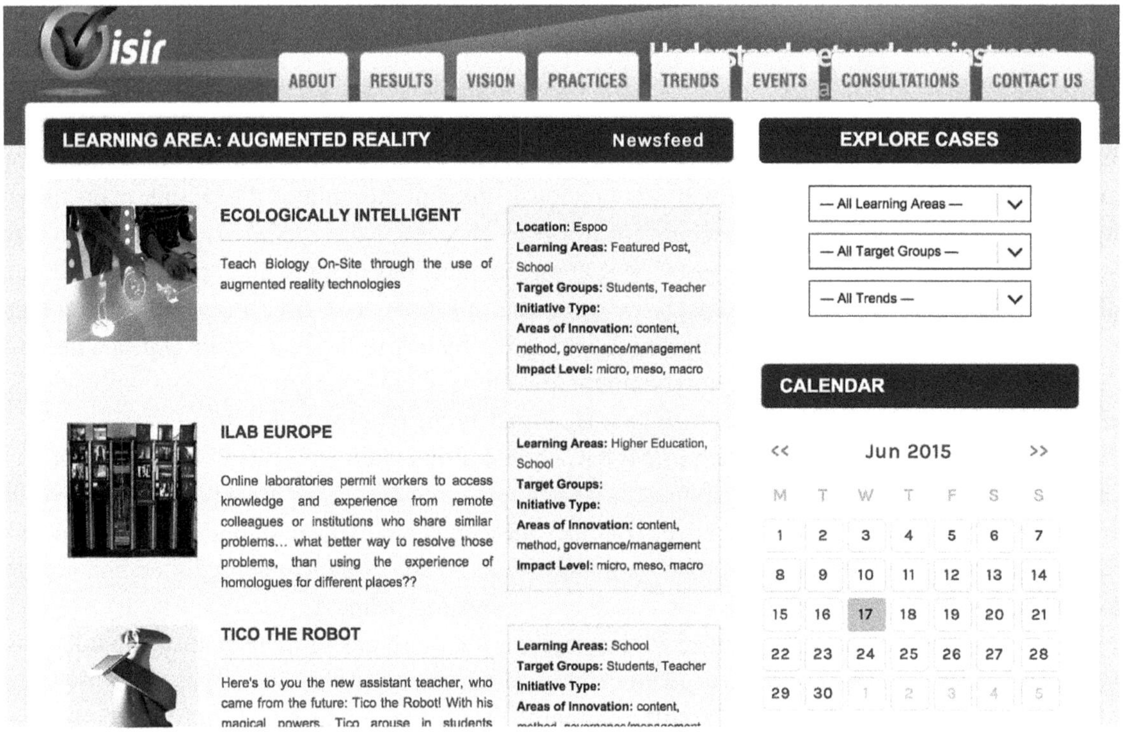

would appear in every key area: video clips with information, commentaries, information, and the like. For example, they could also sit down comfortably and learn on how to use the computer without the help of someone to operate it. This is in order to exemplify the utility of this tool (Weiss, 2015).

Some experts in this field of study such as Bruno Uzzan, co-founder & CEO of Total Immersion, emphasize on AR as an efficient learning tool because it is easily adapted to any learning style (kinesthetic, auditory, or visual). Uzzan highlights: "Augmented Reality is able to promote an active formation not only in the physical sense but also in the psychological sense. AR further helps and fosters diverse thought perspectives on the part of the users, which the former allows them to prepare themselves in a better way day by day. As for the companies, results are given more rapidly, and these are more relevant and profitable as opposed to training based on laboratory practice and documentation" (America Learning & Media, 2015).

Susan Trabaldo, Net-learning Director (Argentina), points out that the augmented reality contributes very importantly in using different levels of information of objects. "AR is used in games, texts and situated information and its richness is based on the response capacity vis a vis the user's input. This is the feature, which transforms AR as a very important tool for situated learning and for evaluation purposes" (America, Learning & Media, 2015).

And, regarding the use of AR and its digital contents, MOOC, indeed, emphasizes more on the interaction among learners and his or her academic peers and with the instructional contents. Thus, these should be not only interactive but also motivating in a real environment with learning transmission. In this sense, Zaloa Urrutikoetxea, Ialcubo CEO, advises to restructure the formation processes that have been worked until the present time. Then, he proposes to think in real structured contents for augmented reality. He further points out that in order for the capacity to be effective the teaching materials should be planned. For this reason, he suggests to know the potential elements that this technology provides. Moreover, he recommends concentrating efforts in order to generate contents which can be adapted to our needs (America Learning & Media, 2015).

An evident and successful experience in the use of AR and Virtual Reality in online training has been developed by the Foundation for training and employment from Andalucia (FOREM-A –spanish initials). The main objective of this foundation is to satisfy the Andalucia's employees' needs in terms of training and employment. In this sense, as part of different actions in the manufacture and experimentation of products, techniques and/or tools which are innovative and interesting in the improvement of professional training for employment have been executed by the project named "Teaching Quality and RA Technology. This has been a solid basis in the design of a tele-training platform based on the RV and AR techniques, an execution system of formative contents of Virtual Reality and AR around the Web environment for the purpose of remote learners training.

The use of AR in MOOC's is not solely from other countries. In the case of Mexico, the Tecnológico de Monterrey offers a wide variety of online bachelor's degree, graduate programs and continuing education that involve the engineering field. This institution employs technology focused on the teaching-learning process in both face-to-face and blended learning. Some innovative and educational online projects are related to the teaching of engineering such as: MOOCs, blended learning courses, simulators, virtual and remote laboratories, among other relevant projects in corporative universities and executive continuing education (Escamilla, 2013).

Thus, regarding the professional training, AR is a type of tool that can facilitate the acquisition of practical learning in training virtual or e-learning processes. Of course, in this field MOOC courses are included.

FUTURE RESEARCH DIRECTIONS

It is important to examine the impact of use Augmented Reality on society, evaluate the implications for process education, and explore his integration on applications into teaching and learning environments. To learn more about its potentials and future in teaching and learning process.

As future work is increasingly creating mobiles, best of applications augmented reality oriented education through both markers such simulations, the making of books and magazines that implement the RA.

CONCLUSION

As it can be seen Augmented Reality (AR) is an area that has been growing in recent years, but it is still awaiting potential users, although there has been a boom in use due to new mobile devices such as smartphones, tablets, and other gadgets that are currently available to most people, but there are new devices such as glasses, gloves, among others that will take a little more time to be available for people.

On the other hand, there are a number of free or commercial tools, which allow the development of augmented reality applications in an easy form, both for various platforms such as Windows, Linux, Mac OS X, SGI and even for systems of mobile devices.

In education and training, AR has the potential to make ubiquitous learning a reality, allowing learners to gain immediate access to a wide range of location-specific information from various sources. It is expected that the use of AR in education will be widely spread and that it will be more common within a few years.

It is clear that there are currently various AR applications oriented to education such as books with markers, the representation of the solar system, geometric Figures, among others, but they are rarely compared to all levels of education, and knowledge areas.

In Mexico, educational innovation needs to increase the use of information technologies and communications, and the use of AR can be a viable option to start having more attractive and interactive applications and to give greater use the equipment that is currently in a lot of schools due to the projects that have been implemented previously. And, it is a tool to achieve meaningful learning in students.

REFERENCES

Adell, J., & Castañeda, L. (2012). Tecnologías Emergentes. ¿Pedagogías Emergentes? Tendencias Emergentes. Proceedings of Educación Con Tic. Barcelona, España. Asociación Espiral, Educación Y Tecnología. Espacio Ciemem.

Alkhamisi, A., & Monowar, M. (2013). Rise of Augmented Reality: Current and Future Application Areas. *International Journal of Internet and Distributed Systems*, *1*(4), 25–34. doi:10.4236/ijids.2013.14005

America, Learning & Media. (2015). *America, Learning & Media. Tendencia - Innovación - Tecnología Cultura*. Retrieved from http://www.americalearningmedia.com/component/content/article/118-tendencias/846-realidad-aumentada-mas-alla-de-la-formacion

Anglada, L. (2014). Los MOOCs: Viables, Inquietantes y Consistentes. In J. Guallar, E. Orduña-Malea, & I. Olea, Thinkepi, A. (Eds.), Análisis De Tendencias En Información Y Documentación (pp. 41-55). Barcelona, España: Editorial UOC.

Aranda, D., Creus, A., & Sánchez-Navarro, J. (2014). Educación, Medios Digítales Y Cultura De La Participación. Barcelona, España: UOC Press.

Artoolkit. (2013). *Artoolkit Home-Page*. Retrieved from http://www.hitl.washington.edu/artoolkit/

Azuma, R. (1997). A Survey of Augmented Reality. *Presence (Cambridge, Mass.)*, *6*(4), 55–385.

Azuma, R., Baillot, Y., Behringer, R., Feiner, S., Julier, S., & Macintyre, B. (2001). Recent Advances In Augmented Reality. *IEEE Computer Graphics and Applications*, *21*(6), 34–47. doi:10.1109/38.963459

Basogain, X., Olabe, M., Espinosa, K., Roueche, C., & Olabe, J. (2007). *Realidad Aumentada En La Educación: Una Tecnología Emergente*. Retrieved from http://www.anobium.es/docs/gc_fichas/doc/6CFJNSalrt.pdf

Billinghurst, M. (2002). *Augmented Reality In Education, New Horizons For Learning*. Retrieved from http://www.newhorizons.org/strategies/technology/billinghurst.htm

Brooks, F. (1996). The Computer Scientist as Toolsmith Ii. *Communications of the ACM*, *39*(3), 61–68. doi:10.1145/227234.227243

Brown, S. (2013). Back to the Future with MOOCs. *Proceedings of the International Conference on Information Communication Technologies in Education* (pp. 237-246), UNESCO.

Cabero, J., Lorente, M., & Vázquez, A. (2014). Las Tipologías de Mooc: Su Diseño e Implicaciones Educativas. *Profesorado*, 13-26.

Cook, J. (2010). Mobile Phones as Mediating Tools within Augmented Contexts for Development. *International Journal of Mobile and Blended Learning*, *2*(3), 1–12. doi:10.4018/jmbl.2010070101

Dunleavy, M., Dede, C., & Mitchell, R. (2008). Affordances and Limitations of Immersive Participatory Augmented Reality Simulations for Teaching and Learning. *Journal of Science Education and Technology*, *18*(1), 7–22. doi:10.1007/s10956-008-9119-1

Escamilla, J. G. (2013). Avances en la Enseñanza a Distancia de la Ingeniería. *Revistad de Ingeniería*, 67-72.

Fitzgerald, E., Adams, A., Ferguson, R., Gaved, M., Mor, Y., & Thomas, R. (2012). Augmented Reality And Mobile Learning: The State Of The Art. *Proceedings of The 11th World Conference On Mobile And Contextual Learning*, Helsinki, Finland

Fossatti, M. (2015). *Sinergianet-In latina*. Retrieved from http://sinergianet.org/moocs-el-modelo-de-los-cursos-masivos-abiertos/

García, J., Gustavsson, I., Hernández, U., Orduña, P., Angulo, I., & Ruiz De Garibay, I. (2010). *El Proyecto VISIR en la Universidad de Deusto: Laboratorio Remoto para Electrónica Básica*. Retrieved from http://e-spacio.uned.es/fez/eserv.php?pid=taee:congreso-2010-1063&dsID=S10A04.pdf

Horizon (2010). *Two to Three Years: Simple Augmented Reality*. Retrieved from http://wp.nmc.org/horizon2010/chapters/simple augmented-reality/

Kaufmann, H., & Papp, M. (2006). Learning Objects For Education With Augmented Reality. *Proceedings of the European Distance and E-Learning Network Conference*, Vienna Austria (160-165).

Lara, L. Y., & Villareal, J. (2004). *La Realidad Aumentada: Una Tecnología en Espera de Usuarios, Revista Digital Universitaria, 7(7)*. Universidad Autonoma de Mexico.

Livingston, M., Rosenblum, L., & Julier, S. Brown D., Baillot Y., Swan Ii J., Gabbard J. Hix D. (2002). An Augmented Reality System For Military Operations In Urban Terrain. Proceedings of Interservice / Industy Training, Simulation & Education Conference, Orlando, Florida (p. 89). I/ITSEC.

Machado, E. (2005). *Spatially Adaptive Augmented Reality. (Unpublished doctoral dissertation)*. Georgia Institute of Technology.

Martínez De Rituerto, P. (2014). Figura de los Facilitadores en los Cursos Online Masivos y Abiertos (Coma/Mooc). Nuevo Rol Profesional para los Educativos en Abierto. *Revista Iberoamericana de Educación a Distancia*, *17*(1), 35–67.

Mcauley, A., Stewart, B., Siemens, G., & Cormier, D. (2010). *The Mooc Model For Digital Practice*, Retrieved from http://www.elearnspace.org/Articles/MOOC_Final.pdf

Mehigan, T. J. (2009). Harnessing Accelerometer Technology For Inclusive Mobile Learning. *Proceedings of the 11th International Conference on Human-Computer Interaction with Mobile Devices and Services*, New York, NY (pp. 1-2) ACM. doi:10.1145/1613858.1613973

Montero García, S. (2015). *Universidad Autónoma de Madrid*. Retrieved April 10, 2015, from: http://www.uam.es/gruposinv/dim/assets/sergiomonterouned.pdf

Mooc.Es. (2015). *Mooc.Es*. Retrieved from http://Mooc.Es/Cmoox-Vs-Xmooc/

Osgart. (2013). *Home Page*. Retrieved from http://www.artoolworks.com/community/osgart/

Plan de Estudios de 2009. (2009). *Educación Básica Primaria*, Secretaria de Educación Pública, México.

Ponce, J., Oronia, Z., Silva, A., Muñoz, J., Ornelas, F., & Alvarez, F. (2015). Incremento del Interés de Alumnos en Educación Básica en los Objetos de Aprendizaje Usando Realidad Aumentada en las Matemáticas. *Proceedings of Conferencias LACLO*, *5*(1).

Poupyrev, I., Berry, R., Billinghurst, M., Kato, H., Nakao, K., Baldwin, L., & And Kurumisawa, J. (2001). Augmented Reality Interface For Electronic Music Performance. *Proceedings of HCI* (pp. 805-808).

Ralston Consulting. (2013). An example of edX reach. Retrieved from http://ralstonconsulting.com/

Rto, V. R. (2015). Road to Virtual Reality. Retrieved from http://www.roadtovr.com/

The New Media Consortium y Universitat Oberta de Catalunya. (2012). *Perspectivas Tecnológicas: Educación Superior en Iberoamérica 2012-2017. Un Análisis Regional Del Informe Horizon del NMC y la UOC*. The New Media Consortium y Universitat Oberta de Catalunya.

Using APA. (2013). Week 5: Augmented Reality Hits the Real Estate Market. Retrieved from https://annabellearts3091.wordpress.com/

Using APA. Augmented Reality Throughout History, Retrieved from http://www.crystalinks.com/

Van Der Linden, J., Braun, T., Rogers, Y., Oshodi, M., Spiers, A., Mcgoran, D., & O'dowd, P. et al. (2012). Haptic Lotus: A Theatre Experience For Blind And Sighted Audiences. *Proceedings of The 2012 ACM Annual Conference - Extended Abstracts on Human Factors in Computing Systems,* New York (pp. 1471-1472). ACM. doi:10.1145/2212776.2212491

VRT. (2015) Augmented Reality Devices. Retrieved from http://www.augmentedrealitytrends.com/

Weiss, C. (2015). Elearninfo247.Com. Retrieved from http://elearninfo247.com/2011/08/27/fast-forward-e-learning-in-2013/

Yousef, F., Chatti, M. A., Schroeder, M. A., Wosnitza, U., & Jakobs, M., & Harald (2014). Moocs: A Review Of The State-Of-The-Art. *Proceedings Of The 6th International Conference On Computer Supported Education*, Barcelona, Spain (pp. 9-20).

ADDITIONAL READING

Daniel, J. (2012). Making sense of MOOCs: Musings in a maze of myth, paradox and possibility. *Journal of Interactive Media in Education*, 3.

Sprock, A. M. S. & Ponce J. (2014). Development Model of Learning Objects Based in the Instructional Techniques Recommendation. *International journal of learning, teaching and educational research, 4*(1).

Wu, H. K., Lee, S. W. Y., Chang, H. Y., & Liang, J. C. (2013). Current status, opportunities and challenges of augmented reality in education. *Computers & Education*, *62*, 41–49. doi:10.1016/j.compedu.2012.10.024

Yuan, L., Powell, S., & Cetis, J. (2013). *MOOCs and open education: Implications for higher education*. White Paper. Retrieved from http://publications.cetis.org.uk/wp-content/uploads/2013/03/MOOCs-and-Open-Education.pdf

Yuen, S., Yaoyuneyong, G., & Johnson, E. (2011). Augmented reality: An overview and five directions for AR in education. *Journal of Educational Technology Development and Exchange*, *4*(1), 119–140.

KEY TERMS AND DEFINITIONS

Augmented Reality: It refers to the incorporation of virtual reality by overlaying data layers related to a pre-existing image. The concept and operation of augmented reality is based on the superimposition of virtual information on a particular object or image digitally, using optimized devices with specific applications to develop these types of tasks.

E-Learning: This has to do with courses based on a learner-centered approach that utilize audio-visuals for fostering significant learning. The main characteristic is that these courses are designed by using web resources. One of the main contributions is that given to their structure these courses allow suitable settings for learning, thus, they are not subject to the teacher's availability and they are equipped with evaluation tools.

MOOCs: The original concept of MOOCs is to offer free and open access courses for a large number of learners.

Virtual Reality: This refers to 3D Space Environments that are generated by computers in which the user can interact in real time.

Chapter 16

Therapy Reports through a Supervision Model using MOOCs

Raúl Alejandro Gutiérrez García
Universidad Politecnica de Aguascalientes, Mexico

Karina Elizeth Armas de Santos
Universidad Politecnica de Aguascalientes, Mexico

Kalina Isela Martínez Martínez
Universidad Autonoma de Aguascalientes, Mexico

José Antonio Saldivar Cervantes
Universidad Politecnica de Aguascalientes, Mexico

María Abigail Paz Pérez
Universidad Politecnica de Aguascalientes, Mexico

ABSTRACT

This chapter has the purpose of analyzing the PIBA supervision on the MOOC by a group of clinical psychologists of UNEME- CAPA, by sending reports to counselors' sessions in moodle platform. 95 participating clinical psychologists who applied for the adolescents program were advised on a case of an alcohol users and other drugs. Qualitative methodology was used to collect the information techniques and instruments. Each of the reports was analyzed and the dimension regrouped to classify them into four: This process allowed them to know the four aspects considered as essential for the PIBA implementation which are 1) Users approximation, 2) Session Development, 3) Therapist strategies, and 4) Contradictory speeches. It was found that they mainly describe how users are, which mainly are sent by schools. And how well the session and developing therapeutic channeling strategies worked over the users. This is important because therapists seemed to have used, as main MOOC strategies, technology techniques to promote readiness to change among adolescents.

DOI: 10.4018/978-1-4666-9743-0.ch016

INTRODUCTION

MOOCs

An increasing number of universities around the globe produce and conduct Massive Open Online Courses (MOOCs). (Janssen & Stohr, 2015). The literature study highlighted the rapid growth in interest in understanding MOOCs and seeking to understand the most relevant pedagogic frameworks to their adoption and the importance of the concept of openness embodied within them. More recently a new emphasis has been emerging where institutional factors, particularly those concerned with financial viability, certification and retention have been highlighted. (Martínez et al, 2014).

The MOOC aim to increase the learners' capacity to appreciate the complexity of sustainability issues and to apply thinking and critical reflection systems on the information flow in public media. The pedagogical approach attempts to emphasize interactivity among learners with a minimum of teacher involvement.

The character of the mass is one of the characteristics that defines MOOC, and is precisely what differentiates you from other experiences of e-Learning. In fact, Siemens (2012) indicates that when he and Downes got 2,300 students in their course network was when he really began to speak of courses in not only open, but also massive online.

The massive nature of the MOOC contribute some advantages to the learning process: 1. Interactivity with other learners. This is a traditional feature of teaching but in network is multiplied in the MOOC. The larger network participants, occur more possibilities for enriching connections for other students from anywhere in the world. How come, says the report Scopeo June 2013 (Vega Cruz, et al., 2013), MOOC allow you to connect with people who share the same interests or professional profiles, and from there to create new groups and to generate new ideas for future undertaken projects. 2. Promote the institution itself. One of the reasons for large Universities designing and implementing MOOC is that they can assume a kind of framework facing advertising potential students. (Sánchez, León & Hugs, 2015).

Rethinking the curriculum. As Yuan and Powell indicate (2013), the MOOC popularity can be assumed by universities in order to rethink how to develop the curriculum for more open and flexive models due to the massive nature of the courses. It's important to highlight that an institution may go through a particular risk to face when designing a MOOC, with the possible failure of it, therefore, it is a concern for the quality and innovation that can be positive to improve educational quality of resources and educational processes.

But MOOC are also a critized phenomenon precisely because of the massive character and what this implies. Some of the problems that can occur are:

The triumph of "package content". In the previously cited Innovation Department report in United Kingdom (2013) discusses how those most critical cases with MOOC indicate that the triumph of the MOOC imply a return to the early 90's when education models were based in the "packaged content" network such as including digital content and good quality resources, but not transforming the educational process.

The problems of evaluation. With thousands of students, the evaluation may tend to be carried out through multiple choice tests. In other areas time is carried by trying to relax foster education online as "peer assessment" as in connective MOOC views, however, this strategy is also questionable and as Toole (2013) indicated, they are usually provided to enrolling students to evaluate a student, so more than Peer-assessment it should be nominated "peer- grading".

The procedural evaluation is complicated when a high volume of students is evaluated. The difficulties of learning manage the provision of a course in network with thousands of students are not easy, as feedback becomes complicated with so many students participating in various tools (Prendergast & Sánchez, 2014)

Stated earlier, the mass registration is a characteristic of the MOOC, but it is also a Descent Participation what is Clow (2013) as "the funnel Participation", explaining paragraph students loss process from those who are enrolled until the end who are rated between 5% and 15%, as the first research (Jordan, 2013; UTHSC, 2013; Daradounis et al., 2013).

Drugs Dependence

Drug use is a health phenomenon that affects mostly teenagers from all regions of this country. In the National Survey of Addictions (ENA) it was found that more than one million adolescents have indicators of dependence on alcohol and other drugs, the figures also indicate that a significant population of adolescents have problems related to their consumption (ENA, 2011). However, there have been some efforts to address this public health problem as the National Information Campaigns for a New Life, in addition to the academic preparation of therapists of UNEME-CAPA coordinated by the National Autonomous University of Mexico (UNAM), coupled with health institutions seeking improving clinical outcomes and methods of diagnosis and treatment (Berwick, 2003).

The programs implemented in care centers are different, one is the Brief Intervention Program for Adolescents who began drinking alcohol and taking other drugs (PIBA), which aims to reduce the consumption pattern of adolescents, and related problems. This program has shown its effectiveness through case studies and comparisons among groups (Martinez & Medina-Mora, 2013). The PIBA, is derived from Brief Intervention (IE) models, which have been applied in different environments; primarily in adolescent and young people who recently attended a health care center.

The PIBA has a preventive purpose, directed not only to teenagers but also to therapists who apply this program, so it is required to find alternatives for this program to be disseminated into these groups and online training can be an alternative.

In this vein, the Information and Communication Technologies (TIC) are tools that are extended globally, especially with greater access and used among adolescents and youth, it is necessary to use them for training, where they have demonstrated their major achievements in reducing costs (Ramos, Fuentes, Flores & Ruiz, 2014). It should be noted that approximately one third of the population in the world connects virtually, so the importance of such strategies in the field of health is major.

The digital and online revolution has provided opportunities for formal training for professionals, including psychologists where experts of adolescent development and youth have been linked profoundly in order to apply the knowledge that would be underpinned in their work. In Mexico the contribution that UNAM had to develop training strategies for therapists of UNEME - CAPA stands.

In a qualitative study done in Costa Rica (Marin, 2006) recounted the user visits from records stored on an educational platform, arguing that one of the advantages of online training is to update immediately information and to meet the needs of different professional fields. In addition, training tends to be more personalized because there is a synchronized involvement with the student advisor and vice versa.

In another interesting study, it was found that PIBA therapists report the success of the intervention is related to knowledge of the theoretical basis, the commitment to the program, positive belief in the possibilities of change in adolescents and therapeutic skills (Pacheco & Martinez, 2013).

Following this vein, a study online training qualitative analysis of 237 online interventions that have information on the effectiveness of these interventions in social problems of adolescents and youth in Latin America, where it was found that some programs addressed to different levels of intervention and oriented to diverse populations (Abad & Gomez, 2008).

In Mexico, an effort was made to train therapists in UNEME-CAPA for them to study a specialty called "Health promotion and prevention of addictive behavior" where first the PIBA theory is extended for one month, after as part of the certification process, therapists had a case of a teenager attending health centers, where the couple sent the reports of the sessions to the counselor during monitoring in order to provide continuous monitoring of the form in which PIBA is applied.

The PIBA session reports were reviewed in each of the phases of the intervention program (Martinez Salazar, Pedroza, Ruiz & Ayala, 2009) described as below:

1. Detection of cases, where mainly made by channeling educational institutions, but also teenagers attended by their own.
2. Session intake for the purpose of evaluating the young was identified to determine if they were candidates for intervention or not. The POSIT was used to identify problems that adolescents had.
3. Evaluation session in order to know the pattern of consumption through the retrospective baseline (180 days) and evaluation of the perception of the severity of consumption, which is measured by indicators of the initial interview.
4. Induction treatment session to promote the entry into treatment through the use of techniques proposed by the motivational interview.
5. Treatment, which consisted of five weekly sessions individually.
6. Follow-ups, which aim was to measure the consumption pattern of adolescents, self-efficacy and related problems to alcohol and other drugs over a period of 30 days.

Thus, it is thought that another perspective on the training of professionals -may be remote- with the aim of addressing drug problems and effective interventions development. The aim of this paper is to analyze online monitoring of PIBA in a group of therapists of UNEME-CAPA, through reports sent to session counselors.

BACKGROUND

Method

This work was focused on analyzing the therapists reports sent to session advisors. This process yielded information on the way the PIBA is applied and through this analysis the strategies are used by therapists in sessions. Therefore, it is considered that the method to explore the complexity of this process is the qualitative paradigm (Guba & Lincoln, 1994), under an Interpretive comprehensive-interpretative method (Ulin, Robinson & Tolley, 2006).

Participants

This analysis was conducted with 95 session therapists' reports session who participated in the monitoring module Brief Intervention Program for Adolescents (PIBA) during the year 2013 and supervision of 6 experts of the intervention program.

These cases, which include the following criteria, were selected: a) be a student of Specialization health promotion and prevention of addictive behavior of the National Autonomous University of Mexico (UNAM), b) Sessions reports submission to the counselor during supervision specialty, and c) must have applied the PIBA in the sessions.

Procedure

To supervise therapists, reports were asked from each of the PIBA sessions, through the moodle platform in coordination with the UNAM http://www.cuaed.unam.mx/esp_adicciones/moodle/escritorio/

The data analysis was carried out in two phases, 1) Firstly, advisers of health promotion and prevention of addictive behavior Specialization gathered information from a case monitoring module, each of the groups. 2) After that, the information analysis stage began which consisted in reviewing each of the reports to their respective sessions.

Following Castro (1999), in order to conduct a deep analysis of the reports of therapists, the first task was to identify the themes in which information was structured and organized. Developing this analysis allowed a preliminary identification of findings based on the story of each of the sessions, gathering the sentences and paragraphs of text in specific categories.

Thus, the analysis categories were developed to classify information from the reports of session and the study objectives. These categories were clustered using the technique of categorization of meanings given by Kvale (1996) which consists in coding each interview in a series of mutually exclusive categories, allowing structuring large and complex narratives in units of information to facilitate understanding of a phenomenon; and their occurrence along the sessions.

The next step was finding subcategories that allowed a more precise analysis of the information. This process was carried out through the successive reading of each session. Thus it was possible to manage and clarify the meaning and significance of what it was said by therapists and possible convergences and divergences among them, in order to understand since the reality of each. The generated categories were analyzed together with two researchers who corroborated the information. The process for carrying out this phase of the study was as follows:

1. Identifying and defining the general categories.
2. A color was assigned to each category in order to be distinguished among them and regardless of what the annotation identifies the relevant part of the paragraph was made.
3. A pseudonym will be awarded to each of the reports to identify each report.
4. Subsequently, a dialog frame concentration was prepared with each of the categories, which sought to find the differences and similarities among them.
5. Finally, the interpretation was worked out in order to obtain the information.

SOLUTIONS AND RECOMMENDATIONS

Results

The results were grouped into four sections.

1. Users approaching.
2. Therapists strategies.
3. Sessions development.
4. PIBA execution contradictions.

Analysis categories were designed through the coding stage and they are presented in Figure 1.

It was found that some therapists mentioned how the first contact is through an institutional channel and at the request of parents in this first category.

Channeling

In general it was found that at the beginning of reporting the evaluation session, some therapists mentioned how the approaching was with users. Channeled cases were reported mainly by educational institutions and group counselors.

"They realized he's using drugs at school, that's why he is sent to this institution" (Jenny)

"13-year-old male user accompanied by his aunt is presented .... Arriving to the center by the recommendation of the school psychologist because the user commented on marijuana use. In an interview, the user explains that smoking marijuana was easy to be told to the psychologist, I never thought I would be sent here if I hardly smoke"(Anayanci).

Figure 1. Analysis categories

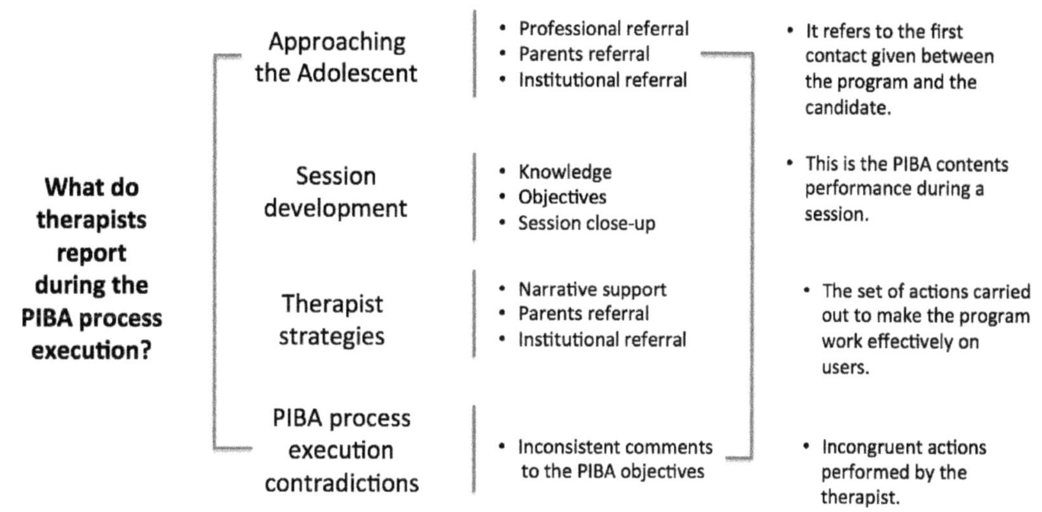

Parents Request

The second category is the demand reported by parents, therapists report that it is important for parents that children receive care because they identify it is a problem that needs a solution because it's reported to have negative consequences such as: low school performance, school reports or long-term fear consequences.

"Minor User, he went to his initial assessment appointment with his mama, is not entirely convinced he requires assistance. However, he does because her mom has pressed him to keep the appointment with the psychologist" (Giovanni).

"The mother says she recently caught him smoking marijuana at home but she already knew that he smoked cigarettes and drank beer so she had already had several arguments but what it happened recently was the last straw so she decided to put her into treatment"(Mariana).

Although these two categories were the most reported, there were found other two ways to approach users which were by means of the institution (case detection process by institution).

"First, the information spread is done by teachers and community schools. Second step is performed by applying the POSIT (V. Gr. in the week from 8 to 12 October contacting educational institution, a school TV, which allows the application POSIT is made with the entire student community and carried out this group application, subsequently they are scored and it yields a list of potential candidates. Then the target students are called to be interviewed to those who look like to be prospectives."(Javier).

Sessions Development

It is the execution of the activities of the PIBA session reported by therapists in monitoring documents (session reports).

Sessions Knowledge

It is defined as the knowledge that the therapist has on the PIBA, the phases and objectives.

"The user meets inclusion criteria to the program if he is 16 years old, if he attends high school, if he presents indicators of alcohol abuse. Risk level of abuse has 6 glasses per drinking occasion" (Javier).

It was also noted that therapists explained key situations for change in the delivered reports:

"Something that is very important to take into account Alex, relapsing is part of the changing process" (Sandra).

It was also found that therapists give feedback from the previous session and explained the objectives of it.

Objectives of the Session

It is understood how to explain objectives of the session when the therapist guides and explains what each of the activities will be about.

The therapist reported:

"Assessment instruments were applied: POSIT, LIBARE, DSM-IV and CBCS, explaining the purpose of each instrument" (Marcela)

"The session starts by explaining the purpose of it which is to analyze the impact of alcohol in achieving short, medium or long term user life goals (school, family, economic, recreational, etc.); thus clarifying the user wants to achieve in the future which is currently assessing if his consumption at this time hurts the goals he wants to achieve"(Gavino).

Session Close-up

One element related to the above two axes is regarding the skills applied. It was found that the dialogue with the user and his companions (at the beginning and end of the process), the therapist reported to establishes rapport, makes open questions and gives sessions feedback. These factors favours the change in adolescent and where the PIBA training module focuses on. For example, one of the therapists refers:

"I establish rapport ... I ask him questions so he analyzes consequences ... I make the close-up by summarizing all the revised points" (Guadalupe).

Strategies Therapist

Within this category the narrative support and motivation to change is mainly found, empathy was found only in few reports. Moreover, it was also found that contacting the user and doing role play was important.

Narrative Support

It was found that therapists reported narrative support to users; a preamble was found for change motivation in users.

"The user attends on time and punctually at the scheduled time, I appreciate punctuality and responsibility to arrive on time for the for the session; he is being asked how he has been during the week and how he has felt. He mentions he's fine and feels comfortable" (Javier).

"After analyzing the self-registration, the previous session is reviewed with the user. For example, a summary of the decisional balance and consumption target setting is analyzed, the set target is remembered and the consumption behavior changes advantages" (Juan Carlos).

Other identified issues spotted into the reports were that therapists do aggregations about what it was seen during session and summarize and retake important points from that session or before ones to motivate the user's change.

"Important points of the initial interview were retaken such as the risk factors teenager has for consuming as health professional as the self user refers to" (Maria Guadalupe).

"Ulises mother asks me if there was anything wrong with the results of her child, then I explained the PIBA purpose in a general way and the early detection of substance abuse importance" (Sara).

Also, rapport was generally present in all reports as essential part of the meetings. The main issues are: school, weather, and family among others. An example of these speeches is "To establish rapport, I start asking about the time taken to reach the Center for Primary Care Addiction, then I ask them who sent them" (Emiliano).

Conducting open-ended questions were also found as:

"I will question those things that concern their consumption plus feedback is also located within the sessions, which were very important in reports because therapists do much emphasis on these, usually at the beginning and end each session" (Sara).

Motivation Change

In clarifying this category was defined to strengthen the resolve of the user to change. As seen in the following examples of two therapists:

"He commented that decide to reduce the frequency is a good start to initiate change and motivation for football can help you achieve it" (Dew).

Another example in the review of the reports was as follows:

"Wanted a positive feedback to the user and highlight their achievements and efforts" (Giovanny).

In general within the reporting one of the elements that is highlighted is the motivation to change, it becomes visible within the reports as pointed therapists.

"I remark that is admirable determination has taken to remain abstinent" (Karla).

"I was congratulated by not consuming and recognizing that although not consumed, sported no problem" (Mariana).

"The awareness and motivate you to stop using drugs has been positive and has led to a change in his life" (Elmer).

It is noted that therapists motivated to change, and that fluctuates from one moment to another and from one session to another, and may be influenced by many factors. In the speeches the following were found:

Strengthen the change of a session and at the end of this, helps the teen feel they are advancing in the process, since in some reports is reported.

"Go encouraging the change to be continued" (Guadalupe).

"Recognize that your change is happening" (Elmer).

It was also noted that therapists emphasized the advantages of the change in consumption and continue with the goal to avoid the negative consequences raised above so that the user could reflect on their consumption.

Another aspect that was found when therapists reinforce the user with congratulations, the term motivation is unclear in some reports as therapists only mention that they contribute to motivation but do not explain how.

Contradictions in the Implementation of PIBA

It was found in the reports, some therapists do not apply sessions as indicated by the PIBA handbook, but apply different instruments or materials to the program for example.

"You said his parents sent him to the meeting, it is good to take note that your consumer does not like your parents and live in their home, must obey and abide by its rules" (Selena).

"Recommending abstinence to it being Teenager" (Dew). "User is presented in a subsequent referring, have no desire to return so he was questioned as part of rapport on the reasons for this thought" (Marcela).

We also found that therapists report having family sessions and invite parents to observe sessions with users, implement relaxation techniques, suggest punishments, give orders, suggest, issuing external causal attributions and judgments of value to users.

"We worked with the youth's family based on the observations of Luis, and its connection with the fact that parents drink alcohol, have constant arguments, they have no defined rules and regulations, lack of parental and fraternal" (Herlinda).

"It was suggested to the mother of the user that puts punishment in proportion to the disruptive behavior of the child" (Selena).

"He was told the user that would teach breathing techniques do not notice as annoying in session" (Sara).

CONCLUSION AND FUTURE WORK

Session reports analyzed here provide insight into the perspective of therapists on how their knowledge are interwoven, skills and attitudes in the application of a brief intervention program for adolescents and reported perceptions and experiences regarding care an adolescent consumers of alcohol and other drugs. Moreover, computational resources and technological tools in this model online monitoring, where the aim is that the advisor and the healthcare team to participate in the benefit of the knowledge construction process and where it enables communication highlights how to implement the model (Marin, 2006). The above data are consistent with the findings of a study of Pacheco and Martinez (2013) performed with 8 PIBA therapists and two project leaders, where the clinical variables that in view of the participants, are associated with the success of the intervention and that relate to the categories of knowledge, attitudes and skills.

With regard to knowledge of the program coincides providing Ally (2009) where the trainees hope to develop a learning applied in their job performance and the acquisition of specialized skills of a therapist in the field of addictions. This is closely related with input from health professionals to have an understanding of how to apply the program and topic axis, which are addictions, considering the various axes of analysis that are at stake in this area of health.

The results of other research supports the above, in the sense that interventions are targeted to different populations (Abad & Gómez, 2008), at different levels and with different care strategies, this study found that therapists UNEMA -layer give better care to the extent that he is empathetic and emphasize the confidentiality of information in which various factors associated with respect for the patient and the care taken with the information provided by the adolescent combine.

The reports also show that therapists speak directly to their abilities, and when they do, have helped in changing adolescent consumption. This is perhaps related to the foundation of motivational interviewing, offering a dynamic perspective and broad vision of psychosocial factors that help to possible change.

The analysis of current practice showed that many of the concerns in the academic literature were absent from not only the practices embodied in current MOOC-based learning experiences but seem to have been ignored in the conceptual phase of implementing a MOOC-based teaching model.

The digital and online revolution have provided opportunities for formal training for professionals, including psychologists where experts of adolescent development and youth have been linked profoundly apply the knowledge that underpin their work. In Mexico the contribution that had the UNAM to develop training strategies for therapists of UNEME - CAPA stands.

For example, in UNAM, an effort was made to train therapists in UNEME-CAPA for them to study a postgraduate by a specialty "Health promotion and prevention of addictive behavior" where it is first Brief Intervention Program for adolescents (PIBA) studied theoretically for a month. Then, as part of the certification process, therapists had a case of a teenager attending health centers where the couple sent reports to the advisory sessions during supervision in order to provide continuous monitoring on how the PIBA is applied.

The purspose of this paper is to analyze the supervision of MOOC the PIBA in a group of therapists of Uneme - CAPA, through sent reports to counselors' sessions in moodle platform. 95 participating therapists who applied the program for adolescents, who were advised on a case of a user of alcohol and other drugs. This work focused on analyzing the reports sent therapists session advisors.

REFERENCES

Abad, M., & Gómez, J. (2008). ¡Preparados, Listos, Ya! Una síntesis de intervenciones efectivas para la prevención de violencia que afecta a adolescentes y jóvenes. Retrieved from http://iris.paho.org/xmlui/handle/123456789/2498

Ally, M. (2009). *Mobile learning: Transforming the delivery of education and training*. Athabasca, AB: Athabasca University Press.

Bentley, P., Crump, H., Cuffe, P., Gniadek, B. J., Macneill, S., & Mor, Y. (2014). Signals of Success and Self-Directed Learning. *Proceedings of the European MOOCs Stakeholder Summit*, Lausanne, Switzerland (pp. 5-10). École Polytechnique Fédérale de Lausanne (EPFL) and P.A.U. Education.

Berners-Lee, T., Weitzner, D. J., Hall, W., O'Hara, K., Shadbolt, N., & Hendler, J. A.Berners -L Ee. (2006). A Framework for Web Science. *Foundations and Trends in Web Science*, *1*(1), 1–130. doi:10.1561/1800000001

Berwick, D., James, B., & Coye, J. (2003). Connections between quality measurement and improvement. *Medical Care*, *41*(Supplement), 30–38. doi:10.1097/00005650-200301001-00004 PMID:12544814

Buendía, L., Colás, P., & Hernández, F. (1998). *Métodos de investigación en psicopedagogía*. Madrid: McGraw Hill.

Burkle, M. (2004). El aprendizaje on-line: Oportunidades y retos en instituciones politécnicas. *Comunicar*, *37*(19), 45–53.

Chainé, S. M., Martínez, K. I. M., Venegas, C. C., López, A. A. C. C., & Ruíz, M. J. M. (2013). Evaluación de habilidades de consejo breve en el ámbito de las adicciones. *Health and Addictions Journal*, *13*(2), 109–116.

Clow, D. (2013). MOOCs and the Funnel of Participation. *Proceedings of the 3rd Conference on Learning Analytics and Knowledge* (185-189), Leuven. Belgium. doi:10.1145/2460296.2460332

Daradounis, T., Bassi, R. X., Hafa, F., & Caballé, S. (2013). A Review of Massive e-learning (MOOCs), In *Proceedings of Design, Delivery and Assessment. Eight International Conference on P2P* (pp. 208-213), Compiegne, France, IEEE Press.

Davis, H., & Ickens, D., K., L Eón, M., S Ánchez -V Era, M.M. & W Hi - Te, S. (2014). MOOCs for Universities and Learners an Ana lysis of Motivating Factors. *Proceedings of the 6th International Conference on Computer Supported Education*, Barcelona, Spain: SCITEPRESS Digital Library.

Dirección General de Epidemiología, Secretaría de Salud México. (2011). *Encuesta Nacional de Adicciones 2011*. México, DF: SSA. Retrieved from http://www.conadic.salud.gob.mx/pdfs/ENA_2011_DROGAS_ILICITAS_.pdf

Guba, E., & Lincoln, Y. (1994). Competing paradigms in qualitative research. In N. K. Denzin & Y. S. Lincoln (Eds.), *Handbook of qualitative research (105 - 117)*. London: Sage Publications.

Kearney, M. H. (2014). Be a Responsible Co-Author. *Research in Nursing & Health*, *37*(1), 1–2. doi:10.1002/nur.21580 PMID:24414937

Kvale, S. (1996). *InterWiews: An introduction to qualitative research interviewing*. London, England: Sage Publications.

Lira, L. R., de Iturbe, P. F., Celis, K. F., & Cortés, E. R. (2014). Evaluación de una intervención en línea para prevenir la violencia en población juvenil y adolescente. Resultados preliminares sobre su efectividad con profesionales de la salud. *Salud Mental*, *37*(3), 195–204.

Mak, S., Williams, R., & Mackness, J. (2010). Blogs and Forums as Communication and Learning Tools in a MOOC. *Proceedings of Networked Learing Conference*, University of Lancaster (pp.275-285).

Marín, C. (2005). Capacitación a distancia (CapDis) y el uso de plataformas virtuales. La experiencia del Centro Centroamericano de Población. *Población y Salud en Mesoamérica*, *3*(2), 1–13.

Martínez, K., & Medina-Mora, M. (2013). Transferencia tecnológica en el área de adicciones: El programa de intervención breve para adolescentes, retos y perspectivas. *Salud Mental*, *36*(6), 505–512.

Martínez -Abad, F., Rodríguez -Conde, M.J. & G Arcía -Peñalver, F.J. (2014). Evaluación del impacto del término MOOC Vs eLearning en la literatura científica y de divulgación. *Profesorado*, *18*(1), 1–17.

Mcguire, R. (2013). *Building a Sense of Community in MOOCs*. Retrieved from http://campustechnology.com/articles/2013/09/03/building-a-sense-of-community-in-moocs.aspx

Pacheco, A. Y., & Martínez, K. I. (2012). El arte de ser terapeuta. ¿Qué hace efectiva una intervención en el consumo de drogas? *Enseñanza e Investigación en Psicología*, *18*(1), 159–176.

Siemens, G. (2012). *What is the Theory that Underpin our MOOCs?* Retrieved from http://goo.gl/nHhCOJ

Stake, R. (1994). Case studies. In N. K. Denzi & Y. S. Lincoln (Eds.), *Handbook of Qualitative Research. Thousand Oaks*. London: Sage Publications.

Ulin, P., Robinson, E., & Tolley, E. (2006). *Investigación aplicada en salud pública. Métodos cualitativos* (Technical Report). Retrieved from http://iris.paho.org/xmlui/bitstream/handle/123456789/729/9275316147.pdf

University Of London. (2013). Massive Online Open Courses (MOOCs). London: The University of London.

Vargas, E., Martínez, K., Pedroza, F., & Morales, S. (2012). Incursión del programa de intervención breve para adolescentes en el E-learning: Resultados del piloteo. *Investigacion y Ciencia*, *20*(55), 42–47.

Vega Cruz, P., Almaraz Menéndez, F., Pinto Escribano, J., & Martín Hernández, S. (2013), *MOOC: Estado de la situación actual, posibilidades, retos y futuro. Scopeo*, Reporte Técnico. Retrieved from http://scopeo.usal.es/wp-content/uploads/2013/06/scopeoi002.pdf

ADDITIONAL READING

Breslow, L. B., Pritchard, D. E., DeBoer, J., Stump, G. S., Ho, A. D., & Seaton, D. T. (2013). Studying learning in the worldwide classroom: Research into edX's first MOOC. *Research & Practice in Assessment*, 8, 13-25.

Chorianopoulos, K., & Giannakos, M. N. (2013, June). Usability design for video lectures. *Proceedings of the 11th European conference on Interactive TV and video* (pp. 163-164). ACM Press. doi:10.1145/2465958.2465982

Conole, G. (2013). MOOCs as disruptive technologies: strategies for enhancing the learner experience and quality of MOOCs. *RED - Revista de Educación a Distancia, 39*, 1-17

Covadonga, R., & Iniesto, F. (2015) Holistic vision for creating accessible services based on MOOCs. *Proceedings of the Open Education Global Conference*, Banff Calgary, Alberta, Canada, Open Education Consortium

Fox, A. (2013). From MOOCs to SPOCs, *Communications of the ACM. Communications of the ACM, 56*(12), 38–40. doi:10.1145/2535918

Guàrdia, L., Maina, M., & Sangrà, A. (2013). MOOC Design Principles. A Pedagogical Approach from the Learner's Perspective. *eLearning Papers, 33*(May), 1–6

Hall, O., Jr. (2014). Future Trends in MOOCs and SOOCs in Management Education. *Proceedings of Society for Information Technology & Teacher Education International Conference* (p. 192). Chesapeake, VA, Association for the Advancement of Computing in Education (AACE).

Milligan, C., Littlejohn, A., & Margaryan, A. (2013). Patterns of Engagement in Connectivist MOOCs. *MERLOT Journal of Online Learning and Teaching, 9*(2), 149–159.

Ramirez, M. S. (2014) Guidelines and success factors idebntified in the first MOOCs in Latin America. *Proceedings of the 6th International Conference on Education and New Learning Technologies*, Barcelona, Spain (pp. 3042-3051). EDULEARN.

Rodriguez, C. O. (2012). MOOCs and the AI-Stanford like Courses: Two Successful and Distinct Course Formats for Massive Open Online Courses. *European Journal of Open, Distance and E-Learning*, 2012.

Yousef, A. M. F., Chatti, M. A., Schroeder, U., & Wosnitza, M. (2015). A usability evaluation of a blended MOOC environment: An experimental case study. *The International Review of Research in Open and Distributed Learning, 16*(2).

KEY TERMS AND DEFINITIONS

Drug Dependence: A state in which an organism functions normally only in the presence of a drug, manifested as a physical disturbance when the drug is removed.

MOOCs: A massive open online course is an online course aimed at unlimited participation and open access via the web. In addition to traditional course materials such as filmed lectures, readings, and problem sets, many MOOCs provide interactive user forums to support community interactions between students, professors, and teaching assistants. MOOCs are a recent and widely researched development in distance education, which was first, introduced in 2008 and emerged as a popular mode of learning in 2012.

Online Training: Can occur in or out of the classroom. It can be self-paced, asynchronous learning or may be instructor-led, synchronous learning. It is suited to distance learning and in conjunction with face-to-face teaching, which is termed blended learning. Learners and educators in homes, schools, businesses, and other settings use educational technology.

Therapy Report: It could be represented as a document or format that resume results and progress from Therapy. Therapy (often abbreviated tx or Tx) is the attempted remediation of a health problem, usually following a diagnosis. In the medical field, it is usually synonymous with treatment (also abbreviated tx). Among psychologists and other mental health professionals, including psychiatrists, psychiatric nurse practitioners, and clinical social workers, the term may refer specifically to psychotherapy or talking therapies.

Compilation of References

Abad, M., & Gómez, J. (2008). ¡Preparados, Listos, Ya! Una síntesis de intervenciones efectivas para la prevención de violencia que afecta a adolescentes y jóvenes. Retrieved from http://iris.paho.org/xmlui/handle/123456789/2498

Abedin, B., Daneshgar, F., & D'Ambra, J. (2013). Do non-task interactions matter? The relationship between non-task sociability of computer supported collaborative learning and learning outcomes. *British Journal of Educational Technology*, *43*(3), 385–397. doi:10.1111/j.1467-8535.2011.01181.x

Aboshady, O., Radwan, A., Eltaweel, A., Azzam, A, & Aboelnaga, A. (2015). Perception and use of massive open online courses among medical students in a developing country: multicentre cross-sectional study. *BMJ open*. Retrieved from http://bmjopen.bmj.com/content/5/1/e006804.short

Acosta, E. S. MOOC (2013). Resultados reales. Retrieved from http://revistaeducacionvirtual.com/mooc-resultados-reales/

Adams, C., Yin, Y., Vargas, L., & Mullen, C. (2014). Snapshots from the Lived World of Massive Open Online Courses (MOOCs): A phenomenological study of learning large.*Proceedings of the 9th International Conference on Networked Learning*.

Adell, J., & Castañeda, L. (2012). Tecnologías Emergentes. ¿Pedagogías Emergentes? Tendencias Emergentes. Proceedings of Educación Con Tic. Barcelona, España. Asociación Espiral, Educación Y Tecnología. Espacio Ciemem.

Adelsköld, G., Alklett, K., Axelsson, R., & Blomgren, G. (1999). Problem- based distance learning of energy issues via computer network. *Distance Education*, *20*(1), 129–143. doi:10.1080/0158791990200110

Agarwal, A. (2013). Online universities: It's time for teachers to join the revolution. *The Guardian*. Retrieved from http://www.theguardian.com/education/2013/jun/15/university-education-online-mooc

Agrawal, P., Kumar, A., & Agrawal, A. (2015). Massive Open Online Courses: EdX.org, Coursera.com and NPTEL, A Comparative Study Based on Usage Statistics and Features with Special Reference to India. *Proceedings of the 10th International CALIBER,* Shimla, Himachal Pradesh, India (pp. 390-403). INFLIBNET.

Ahmad, N., Tasir, Z., Kasim, J., & Sahat, H. (2013). Automatic Detection of Learning Styles in Learning Management Systems by Using Literature-based Method. *Procedia: Social and Behavioral Sciences* (Vol. *103*, pp. 181–189). doi:10.1016/j.sbspro.2013.10.324

Al Faraj, K., Mojahid, M., & Vigouroux, N. (2009). BigKey: A Virtual Keyboard for Mobile Devices. *Proceedings Of The 13th International Conference, HCI International*, San Diego, CA, USA, LNCS (Vol. 5612, pp. 3-10). Springer. doi:10.1007/978-3-642-02580-8_1

Alkhamisi, A., & Monowar, M. (2013). Rise of Augmented Reality: Current and Future Application Areas. *International Journal of Internet and Distributed Systems*, *1*(4), 25–34. doi:10.4236/ijids.2013.14005

Ally, M. (2009). *Mobile learning: Transforming the delivery of education and training*. Athabasca, AB: Athabasca University Press.

Al-Mouh, N., Al-Khalifa, A., & Al-Khalifa, H. (2014) A First Look into MOOCs Accessibility. *Proceedings of the 15th International Conference on Computers Helping People with Special Needs ICCHP* (pp. 145-152). Springer. doi:10.1007/978-3-319-08596-8_22

Al-Saedi, I. (2014). Implementation of Terrain Height Detection and Collision Check Systems in a 3-Dimensional Environment. *American Journal of Intelligent Systems*, *4*(4), 148–153.

Alwi, N., & Fan, I. (2010). E-learning and information security management. *International Journal of Digital Society*, *1*(2), 148–156.

Al-Zoube, M. (2009). E-Learning on the Cloud. *Int. Arab J. e-Technol, 1*(2), 58-64.

America, Learning & Media. (2015). *America, Learning & Media. Tendencia - Innovación - Tecnología Cultura*. Retrieved from http://www.americalearningmedia.com/component/content/article/118-tendencias/846-realidad-aumentada-mas-alla-de-la-formacion

Anderson, T., & Dron, J. (2011). Three generations of distance education pedagogy. *International Review of Research in Open and Distance Learning*, *12*(3).

Angeli, C., Valanides, N., & Bonk, C. (2003). Communication in a web-based conferencing system: The quality of computer- mediated interactions. *British Journal of Educational Technology*, *34*(1), 31–43. doi:10.1111/1467-8535.00302

Anglada, L. (2014). Los MOOCs: Viables, Inquietantes y Consistentes. In J. Guallar, E. Orduña-Malea, & I. Olea, Thinkepi, A. (Eds.), Análisis De Tendencias En Información Y Documentación (pp. 41-55). Barcelona, España: Editorial UOC.

APA. (2014). *Diagnostic and Statistical Manual of mental disorders (DSM) 5*. Arlington, VA: American Psychological Association.

Aranda, D., Creus, A., & Sánchez-Navarro, J. (2014). Educación, Medios Digítales Y Cultura De La Participación. Barcelona, España: UOC Press.

Arnim, D., Piuzzi, B. S., Nam, C. S., & Chung, D. (2007), Guidelines for the Development and Improvement of Universal Access Systems for Blind Students. *Proceedings of The 4th International Conference on Universal Access in Human-Computer Interaction,*Beijing, China, LNCS (Vol. 4554, pp. 603-612). Springer. doi:10.1007/978-3-540-73279-2_67

Artoolkit. (2013). *Artoolkit Home-Page*. Retrieved from http://www.hitl.washington.edu/artoolkit/

Atman, N., Inceoğlu, M., & Aslan, B. (2009). Learning styles diagnosis based on learner behaviors in web based learning. *Computational Science and Its Applications*, LCNS (Vol. 5593, pp. 900-909).

Australian government. (n. d.). E-learning benchmarking survey – final report. Retrieved from http://flexiblelearning.net.au/wp-content/uploads/2011_e-arning_benchmarking_survey_final_report.pdf

Austrian Science and Research Liaison Office (ASRLO). (2007). *Bridging the Digital Divide in South-Eastern Europe (SEE)*. Retrieved from www-it.fmi.uni-sofia.bg/cist/bridge/index.htm

Azuma, R. (1997). A Survey of Augmented Reality. *Presence (Cambridge, Mass.)*, *6*(4), 55–385.

Azuma, R., Baillot, Y., Behringer, R., Feiner, S., Julier, S., & Macintyre, B. (2001). Recent Advances In Augmented Reality. *IEEE Computer Graphics and Applications*, *21*(6), 34–47. doi:10.1109/38.963459

Baggaley, J. (2013). MOOC rampant. *Distance Education*, *34*(3), 368–378. doi:10.1080/01587919.2013.835768

Baggaley, J. (2014). MOOCs: Digesting the facts. *Distance Education*, *35*(2), 159–163. doi:10.1080/01587919.2014.919710

Baguma, R., Stone, R. G., Lugega, J. T., & van der Weide, Th. P. (2009). A Framework for Filtering Web Accessibility Guidelines. *Proceedings of International Cross-Disciplinary Conference on Web Accessibility W4A'09*, Madrid, Spain (pp. 46-49). ACM Press. doi:10.1145/1535654.1535663

Bahr, P. (2010). The bird's eye view of community colleges: A behavioral typology of first-time students based on cluster analytic classification. *Research in Higher Education*, *51*(8), 724–749. doi:10.1007/s11162-010-9180-5

Bajraktarevic, N., Hall, E., & Fullick, P. (2013). *Incorporating learning styles in hypermedia environment: Empirical evaluation.*

Bardac, M., Deaconescu, R., & Florea, A. M. (2010). Scaling peer-to-peer testing using linux con-tainers.*Proceedings of the 9th Roedunet International Conference,*Sibiu, Romania, (pp. 287–292). IEEE Press.

Bartle, R. (2004). *Designing Virtual Worlds*. Indianapolis, IN: New Riders Publishing. Bowman.

Basogain, X., Olabe, M., Espinosa, K., Roueche, C., & Olabe, J. (2007). *Realidad Aumentada En La Educación: Una Tecnología Emergente*. Retrieved from http://www.anobium.es/docs/gc_fichas/doc/6CFJNSalrt.pdf

Bentley, P., Crump, H., Cuffe, P., Gniadek, B. J., Macneill, S., & Mor, Y. (2014). Signals of Success and Self-Directed Learning. *Proceedings of the European MOOCs Stakeholder Summit*, Lausanne, Switzerland (pp. 5-10). École Polytechnique Fédérale de Lausanne (EPFL) and P.A.U. Education.

Berners-Lee, T., Weitzner, D. J., Hall, W., O'Hara, K., Shadbolt, N., & Hendler, J. A.Berners -L Ee. (2006). A Framework for Web Science. *Foundations and Trends in Web Science*, *1*(1), 1–130. doi:10.1561/1800000001

Berwick, D., James, B., & Coye, J. (2003). Connections between quality measurement and improvement. *Medical Care*, *41*(Supplement), 30–38. doi:10.1097/00005650-200301001-00004 PMID:12544814

Billinghurst, M. (2002). *Augmented Reality In Education, New Horizons For Learning*. Retrieved from http://www.newhorizons.org/strategies/technology/billinghurst.htm

Binghamton University. (2011). *Bridging the Digital Divide Project*. Retrieved from www.binghampton.edu/cce/digitaldivide/home.html

Bohnsack, M., & Puhl, S. (2014). Accessibility of MOOCs. *Proceedings of the 15th International Conference on Computers Helping People with Special Needs ICCHP. Springer International Publishing,* 141-144. doi:10.1007/978-3-319-08596-8_21

Bonk, C., Lee, M. M., Reeves, T., & Reynolds, T. (2014). MOOCs and Open Education around the World: Recapping the Past Year, Mapping the Road Ahead.*Proceedings of World Conference on E-Learning in Corporate, Government, Healthcare, and Higher Education 2014*, Chesapeake, VA (pp. 238-241). Association for the Advancement of Computing in Education (AACE).

Bonwell, C., & Eison, J. (1991). *Active Learning: Creating Excitement in the Classroom AEHE-ERIC Higher Education Report No. 1*. Washington, D.C.: Jossey-Bass.

Bosse, T., & Stam, S. (2011). A Normative Agent System to Prevent Cyberbullying. *Proceedings of the IEEE/WIC/ACM International Conferences on Web Intelligence and Intelligent Agent Technology*, Lyon, France (pp. 425-430). IEEE Computer Society Press. doi:10.1109/WI-IAT.2011.24

Bouzidi, L., & Jaillet, A. (2009). Can online peer assessment be trusted? *Journal of Educational Technology & Society*, *12*(4), 257.

Boyle, T., & Ravenscroft, A. (2012). Context and deep learning design. *Computers & Education*, *59*(4), 1224–1233. doi:10.1016/j.compedu.2012.06.007

Bradley, J. (2010). Promoting and Supporting Authentic Online Conversations - Which Comes First - The Tools or Instructional Design? *International Journal of Pedagogies*, *5*(3), 20–31. doi:10.5172/ijpl.5.3.20

Brady, K. P., Holcomb, L. B., & Smith, B. V. (2010). The Use of Alternative Social Networking Sites in Higher Educational Settings : A Case Study of the E-Learning Benefits of Ning in Education. *Journal of Interactive Online Learning*, *9*(2), 151–170.

Breslow, L. B., Pritchard, D. E., DeBoer, J., Stump, G. S., Ho, A. D., & Seaton, D. T. (2013). Studying learning in the worldwide classroom: Research into edX's first MOOC. *Research & Practice in Assessment* (pp. 13-25).

Breslow, L., Pritchard, D. E., DeBoer, J., Stump, G. S., Ho, A. D., & Seaton, D. T. (2013). Studying learning in the worldwide classroom: Research into edX's first MOOC. *Research & Practice in Assessment*, *8*(1), 13–25.

Brinton, C. G., Chiang, M., Jain, S., Lam, H., Liu, Z., & Wong, F. M. F. (2013). Learning About Social Learning in MOOCs: From Statistical Analysis to Generative Model. *IEEE Transactions on Learning Technologies*, *7*(4), 346–359. doi:10.1109/TLT.2014.2337900

Brooks, F. (1996). The Computer Scientist as Toolsmith Ii. *Communications of the ACM*, *39*(3), 61–68. doi:10.1145/227234.227243

Brown, S. (2013). Back to the Future with MOOCs.*Proceedings of the International Conference on Information Communication Technologies in Education* (pp. 237-246), UNESCO.

Bruce, A., Manuel Dodero, J., Doran, R., Kouzov, O., Lazonder, A., Leemkuil, H., . . . Rattasepp, K. (2014). White paper on the adoption and use of elearning resources across Europe, *Open discovery space*. Retrieved from http://www.opendiscoveryspace.eu/sites/ods/files/wp1-t1.1-white_paper_final_version.pdf

Bruckman, A. (2004). Co-Evolution of Technological Design and Pedagogy in an Online Learning Community. In S. Barab, R. Kling, & J. Gray (Eds.), *Designing Virtual Communities in the Service of Learning (Learning in Doing: Social, Cognitive and Computational Perspectives)*. Cambridge: Cambridge University Press. doi:10.1017/CBO9780511805080.013

Brusilovsky, P., & Millán, E. (2007). User models for adaptive hypermedia and adaptive educational systems. *The adaptive web*, LCNS (Vol. 4321, pp. 3-53).

Brusilovsky, P. (1996). Methods and techniques of adaptive hypermedia. *User Modeling and User-Adapted Interaction*, *6*(2-3), 87–129. doi:10.1007/BF00143964

Brusilovsky, P. (2001). Adaptive hypermedia. *User Modeling and User-Adapted Interaction*, *11*(1/2), 87–110. doi:10.1023/A:1011143116306

Buck, D., Diethelm, I., & Sheneman, S. (2013). Objektgraph: why code when mvc applications can be generated with uml-based diagrams?*Proceedings of the 2013 Companion Publication for Conference on Systems, Programming, & Applications: Software for Humanity*, Indianapolis, IN, (pp. 25–26). ACM Press. doi:10.1145/2508075.2514576

Buendía, L., Colás, P., & Hernández, F. (1998). *Métodos de investigación en psicopedagogía*. Madrid: McGraw Hill.

Buley, L. (2013). *The user experience team of one*. Rosenfeld Media.

Burgos Aguilar, J. V., Cox, G., Czerniewicz, L., D'Antoni, S., Diallo, B., Downes, S., . . . Lane, A. (Eds.), (2013). Perspectives on Open and Distance Learning: Open Educational Resources: Innovation, Research and Practice, Athabasca, Alberta, Canada. Commonwealth of Learning.

Burgstahler, S. (2002). Real connections: Making distance learning accessible to everyone. Retrieved from https://www3.cac.washington.edu/doit/Brochures/PDF/distance.learn.pdf

Burkle, M. (2004). El aprendizaje on-line: Oportunidades y retos en instituciones politécnicas. *Comunicar*, *37*(19), 45–53.

Buschmann, F., Maunier, R., Rohnert, H., Sommerlad, P., & Stal, M. (1999). *A System of Patterns. Pattern-Oriented Software Architecture*. Siemens Ag, Germany: Wiley.

Buzzi, M. C., Buzzi, M., Leporini, B., & Mori, G. (2012). Designing E-Learning Collaborative Tools for Blind People. In E. Pontes, A. Silva, A. Guelfi & S.T. Kofuji (Eds.), E-Learning - Long-Distance and Lifelong Perspectives, Rijeka, Croatia. InTech Open Access.

Buzzi, M. C., Buzzi, M., Leporini, B., & Mori, G. (2012). Designing E-Learning Collaborative Tools for Blind People. In E. Pontes (Ed.), *E-Learning - Long-Distance and Lifelong Perspectives* (pp. 125–144). Rijeka, Croatia: InTech.

Cabero, J., Lorente, M., & Vázquez, A. (2014). Las Tipologías de Mooc: Su Diseño e Implicaciones Educativas. *Profesorado*, 13-26.

Calle-Jimenez, T., Sanchez-Gordon, S., & Luján-Mora, S. (2014) Web Accessibility Evaluation of Massive Open Online Courses on Geographical Information Systems.*IEEE Global Engineering Education Conference EDUCON* (pp. 680-686). doi:10.1109/EDUCON.2014.6826167

Carbunescu, R., Devarakonda, A., Demmel, J., Gordon, S., Alameda, J., & Mehringer, S. (2014). Architecting an autograder for parallel code.*Proceedings of the 2014 Annual Conference on Extreme Science and Engineering Discovery Environment,*Atlanta, GA, (pp. 68:1–68:8). ACM Press.

Carr, N. (2012). *The crisis in higher education. MIT Technology Review.* Retrieved from http://www.technologyreview.com/featuredstory/429376/the-crisis-in-higher-education/

Cassidy, S. (2004). Learning styles: An overview of theories, models, and measures.[Taylor & Francis]. *Educational Psychology*, *24*(4), 419–444. doi:10.1080/0144341042000228834

Castronova, E. (2004). *Synthetic Worlds*. Chicago, IL: The University of Chicago Press.

CDDH. (2014). *The Center for Developmental Disability Health Victoria Fact Sheet*. Retrieved from http://www.cddh.monash.org/assets/documents/working-with-people-with-intellectual-disabilities-in-health-care.pdf

Cha, H., Kim, Y., Park, S., Yoon, T., Jung, Y., & Lee, H. (2006). Learning Styles Diagnosis Based on User Interface Behaviors for the Customization of Learning Interfaces in an Intelligent Tutoring System. *Intelligent Tutoring Systems*, 513-524.

Chainé, S. M., Martínez, K. I. M., Venegas, C. C., López, A. A. C. C., & Ruíz, M. J. M. (2013). Evaluación de habilidades de consejo breve en el ámbito de las adicciones. *Health and Addictions Journal*, *13*(2), 109–116.

Chamberlin, L., & Parish, T. (2011). MOOCs: Massive Open Online Coursesor Massive and Often Obtuse Courses? *E- learn Magazine*, 2011(8).

Chaqfeh, M. A., & Mohamed, N. (2012). Challenges in middleware solutions for the internet of things.*Proceedings of the International Conference on Collaboration Technologies and Systems,*Denver, CO, (pp. 21–26). IEEE Press. doi:10.1109/CTS.2012.6261022

Chauveau Brañes, D., & Vergara Sánchez, E. (2009). Proyecto piloto de Escuelas Rurales de Informática y Ciudadanía: un modelo de transformación social en Chile (Technical Report). Ministerio de Agricultura, y Comité para la Democratización de la Informática, Santiago, Chile.

Chen, X. D., Barnett, R., & Stephens, C. (2013, September). Fad or Future: The Advantages and Challenges of Massive Open Online Courses. *Paper Presented at theResearch-to Practice Conference in Adult and Higher Education*, St. Charles Missouri.

Chen, C. Y., Pedersen, S., & Murphy, K. L. (2011). Learners' perceived information overload in online learning via computer-mediated communication. *Research in Learning Technology*, *19*(2), 101–116. doi:10.1080/21567069.2011.586678

Chittaro, L., & Ranon, R. (2007). Special issue on Web3D technologies in learning, education and training. *Computer & Education, 49*(1), 3–18. doi:10.1016/j.compedu.2005.06.002

Choi, S., Lim, C., & Leem, J. (2002). Effects of Different Types of Interaction on Learning Achievement, Satisfaction and Participation in Web-Based Instruction. *Innovations in Education and Teaching International*, 39(2), 153-162.

Choudaha, R., Chang, L., & Kono, Y. (2013). International Student Mobility Trends 2013: Towards Responsive Recruitment Strategies. *World Education News & Reviews, 26*(2)

Christensen, S. (2001). How We Work to Make the Web SPEAK. *Computers in Libraries*, *21*(9), 30–34.

Christopher, B. (2013). Learning about social learning in MOOCs: From statistical analysis to generative model.

Christopher, B., Mung Chiang, Jain, S., Lam, H., Zhenming Liu, & Wong, F.M.F. (2013). Learning about social learning in MOOCs: From statistical analysis to generative model, *IEEE Transactions on Learning Technologies, 7*(4), 346-359.

Clarà, M., & Barberà, E. (2013). Learning online: Massive open online courses (MOOCs), connectivism, and cultural psychology. *Distance Education*, *34*(1), 129–136. doi:10.1080/01587919.2013.770428

Claros, I., Cobos, R., Guerra, E., De Lara, J., Pescador, A., & Sánchez-Cuadrado, J. (2013). Integrating open services for building educational environments.*Proceedings of the Global Engineering Education Conference,*Berlin, Germany (1147-1156). IEEE. doi:10.1109/EduCon.2013.6530253

Clow, D. (2013, April). MOOCs and the funnel of participation.*Proceedings of the Third International Conference on Learning Analytics and Knowledge* (pp. 185-189). ACM. doi:10.1145/2460296.2460332

Collazos, C. A., González, C. S., & García, R. (2014). Computer Supported Collaborative MOOCs: CSCM.*Proceedings of the IDEE Conference* (pp. 1-5), Albacete, Spain. ACM Press.

Colman, D. (2013). MOOC interrupted: Top 10 reasons our readers didn't finish a massive open online course. Retrieved from http://www.openculture.com/2013/04/10_reasons_you_didnt_complete_a_mooc.html

Colombia, I. C. D. L. (2015). *Ciudadano Digital.* Retrieved from www.ciudadanodigital.org.co

Comeaux, P., & McKenna-Byington, E. (2003). Computer-mediated communication in online and conventional classroom: Some implications for instructional design and professional development programmes. *Innovations in Education and Teaching International*, *40*(4), 348–355. doi:10.1080/1470329032000128387

Connell, B., Jones, M., Mace, R., Mueller, J., Mullick, A., Ostroff, E., & Sanford, J. (1997). *The Center for Universal Design- North Carolina State University.* Retrieved from http://www.ncsu.edu/ncsu/design/cud/

Conole, G. (2013). MOOCs as disruptive technologies: strategies for enhancing the learner experience and quality of MOOCs *Revista de Educación a Distancia*, 39.

Conole, G., (2013). MOOCs as disruptive technologies: strategies for enhancing the learner experience and quality of MOOCs. *RED - Revista de Educación a Distancia, 39*, 1-17.

Conole, G. (2014). *MOOCs as disruptive technologies: Strategies for enhancing the learner experience and quality of MOOCs*. University of Leicester.

Cook, J. (2010). Mobile Phones as Mediating Tools within Augmented Contexts for Development. *International Journal of Mobile and Blended Learning*, *2*(3), 1–12. doi:10.4018/jmbl.2010070101

Cooper, S., & Sahami, M. (2013). Education reflections on Stanford's MOOCs: New possibilities in online education create new challenges. *Communications of the ACM*, *56*(2), 28–30. doi:10.1145/2408776.2408787

Correa, C. (2013). *Why Video Games are More Addictive and Bigger than Movies Will Ever Be*. Retrieved October 20, 2014, from: ttp://www.forbes.com/sites/christophercorrea/2013/04/11/why-video-games-are-addic¬tive-and-bigger-than-movies-will-ever-be/.

Coursera -. *Free Online Courses From Top Universities*. (n. d.). Retrieved from https://www.coursera.org/specialization/mobilecloudcomputing2/36

Coursera. (2012). *Coursera*. Retrieved from https://www.coursera.org/

Covadonga, R., & Iniesto, F. (2015). Holistic vision for creating accessible services based on MOOCs. *Proceedings of the Open Education Global Conference*, Banff Calgary, Alberta, Canada, Open Education Consortium.

Cruz, P. V. (2013). *SCOPEO*. Obtenido de SCOPEO: Retrieved from http://scopeo.usal.es/wp-content/uploads/2013/06/scopeoi002

Dadvar, M., & de Jong, F. (2012). Cyberbullying Detection: A Step Toward a Safer Internet Yard *Proceedings of the World Wide Web Companion WWW*, Lyon, France (Vol. *12*, pp. 121–125). ACM Press.

Dadvar, M., de Jong, F., Ordelman, R., & Trieschnigg, D. (2012). Improved Cyberbullying Detection Using Gender Information.*Proceedings of the 12th -Dutch-Belgian Information Retrieval Workshop DIR'12*, Ghent, Belgium.

Daniel, J. (2012). *Making sense of MOOCs: Musings in a maze of myth, paradox and possibility. Journal of Interactive Media in Education*. Korea National Open University.

Daniel, J. (2012). Making Sense of MOOCs: Musings in a Maze of Myth, Paradox and Possibility. *Journal of Interactive Media in Education*, *2012*(3), 18. doi:10.5334/2012-18

Daniel, J. (2012). Making sense of MOOCs: Musings in a maze of myth, paradox and possibility. *Journal of Interactive Media in Education*, *2013*(3).

Daniel, J., Vázquez-Cano, E., & Gisbert, M. (2015). The Future of MOOCs: Adaptive Learning or Business Model? *Universities and Knowledge Society Journal*, *12*(1), 64–74. doi:10.7238/rusc.v12i1.2475

Daradounis, T., Bassi, R. X., Hafa, F., & Caballé, S. (2013). A Review of Massive e-learning (MOOCs), In *Proceedings of Design, Delivery and Assessment. Eight International Conference on P2P* (pp. 208-213), Compiegne, France, IEEE Press.

Dasarathy, B., Sullivan, K., Schmidt, D. C., Fisher, D. H., & Porter, A. (May de 2014). The past, present, and future of MOOCs and their relevance to software.*Proceedings of the on Future of Software Engineering* (pp. 212-224). doi:10.1145/2593882.2593897

Davis, H., & Ickens, D., K., L Eón, M., S Ánchez -V Era, M.M. & W Hi - Te, S. (2014). MOOCs for Universities and Learners an Ana lysis of Motivating Factors. *Proceedings of the 6th International Conference on Computer Supported Education*, Barcelona, Spain: SCITEPRESS Digital Library.

Davis, P. (2003). *Including Children with Visual Impairment in Mainstream Schools: A Practical Guide*. London, England: David Fulton Publishers.

de Figueiredo, A. D., & Afonso, A. P. (2006). *Managing Learning in Virtual Settings: The Role of Context*. Hershey, PA: IGI Global. doi:10.4018/978-1-59140-488-0

De Freitas, A. A., & De Freitas, M. M. (2013). Classroom live: A software-assisted gamification tool.[Taylor & Francis]. *Computer Science Education*, *23*(2), 186–206. doi:10.1080/08993408.2013.780449

De Raedt, L. (2008). *Logical and relational learning*. Berlin: Springer. doi:10.1007/978-3-540-68856-3

De Raedt, L., Kimmig, A., & Toivonen, H. (2007). ProbLog: A Probabilistic Prolog and Its Application in Link Discovery.*Proceedings of the 20th international joint conference on Artifical intelligence*, Hyderabad, India (pp. 2468-2473). Morgan Kaufmann Publishers.

De Santana, V. F., De Oliveira, R., Almeida, L. D. A., & Baranauskas, M. C. C. (2012). Web accessibility and people with dyslexia: a survey on techniques and guidelines.*Proceedings of the International Cross-Disciplinary Conference on Web Accessibility*. doi:10.1145/2207016.2207047

De Waard, I., Koutropoulos, A., Özdamar Keskin, N., Abajian, S. C., Hogue, R., Rodriguez, C. O., & Gallagher, M. S. (2011). Exploring the MOOC format as a pedagogical approach for mLearning. *Proceedings from mLearn,*

Deane, P., & Sheehan, K. (2003). *Automatic item generation via frame semantics: Natural language generation of math word problems (Unpublished work)*. Princeton, NJ: Educational Testing Service.

Deterding, S. (2014). (Forthcoming). The lens of intrinsic skill atoms: A method for gameful design. *Human-Computer Interaction, Special Issue. HCI and Digital Games.*

Deterding, S., Dixon, D., Khaled, R., & Nacke, L. (2011). From game design elements to gamefulness: Defining gamification.*Proceedings of the 15th International Academic MindTrek Conference: Envisioning Future Media Environments*, Tampere, Finland (pp. 9-15). ACM doi:10.1145/2181037.2181040

Dewiyanti, S., Brand-Gruwel, S., Jochems, W., & Broers, N. J. (2007). Students' experiences with collaborative learning in asynchronous computer-supported collaborative learning environments. *Computers in Human Behavior*, *23*(1), 496–514. doi:10.1016/j.chb.2004.10.021

Diez, E., Alonso, A., Verdugo, M.A., Campo, M., Sancho, I., & Sánchez, S. (2011). European Higher Education Area: standards and indicators of good practices for the attention of college students with disabilities. Retrieved from http://sid.usal.es/libros/discapacidad/26032/8-1/espacio-europeo-de-educacion-superior.aspx

Digital Divide Network (DDN). (2015) *Digital Divide*. Retrieved from www.digitaldivide.net

Dirección General de Epidemiología, Secretaría de Salud México. (2011). *Encuesta Nacional de Adicciones 2011*. México, DF: SSA. Retrieved from http://www.conadic.salud.gob.mx/pdfs/ENA_2011_DROGAS_ILICITAS_.pdf

Dix, A., Finlay, J., Aboud, G. D., & Beale, R. (2004). *Human – Computer Interaction* (3rd ed.). Essex, England: Pearson / Prentice Hall.

Dix, A., Finlay, J., Abowd, G. D., & Beale, R. (2003). *Human Computer Interaction* (3rd ed.). New York, USA: Pearson-Prentice Hall.

Dix, A., Finlay, J., Abowd, G., & Beale, R. (2004). *Human-Computer Interaction* (3rd ed.). London, England: Pearson Prentice Hall.

Docker Inc. (2013) *Doker official site*. (n. d.). Retrieved from http://docker.com

Domingos, P., & Lowd, D. (2009). Markov logic: An interface layer for artificial intelligence. In R. Brachman, W. Cohen, & P. Stone (Eds.), *Synthesis Lectures on Artificial Intelligence and Machine Learning* (pp. 1–155). Los Angeles, CA: Morgan & Claypool Publishers. doi:10.2200/S00206ED1V01Y200907AIM007

Domingos, P., & Richardson, M. (2007). Markov Logic: A Unifying Framework for Statistical Relational Learning. *Proceedings of the Workshop on Statistical Relational Learning and its Connections to Other Fields*, Banff, Canada.

Domínguez, A., Saenz-de-Navarrete, J., De-Marcos, L., Fernández-Sanz, L., Pagés, C., & Martínez-Herráiz, J. (2013). Gamifying learning experiences: Practical implications and outcomes. *Computers & Education*, *63*, 380–392. doi:10.1016/j.compedu.2012.12.020

Dorian, P. (2013). *Interface design for learning: Design strategies for learning experiences.* New Riders.

Dorsey, M. (2011). *Pearson Assignments: Quizzes, Tests, and Homework Explained.* Retrieved from http://www.myaccountinglabcommunity.com/custom/scripts/google-search-init.js

Doug, A. (2001). An Introduction to 3-D User Interface Design. *Presence (Cambridge, Mass.)*, *10*(1), 96–108. doi:10.1162/105474601750182342

Downes-Le Guin, T., Baker, R., Mechling, J., & Ruyle, E. (2012). Myths and realities of respondent engagement in online surveys. *International Journal of Market Research*, *54*(5), 1–21. doi:10.2501/IJMR-54-5-613-633

Downes, S. (2012). *Connectivism and connective knowledge: essays on meaning and learning networks.* Canada: National Research Council.

Dow, S. P., Fortuna, J., Schwartz, D., Altringer, B., Schwartz, D. L., & Klemmer, S. R. (2012). Prototyping dynamics: sharing multiple designs improves exploration, group rapport, and results. In H. Plattner, C. Meinel, & L. Leifer (Eds.), *Design Thinking Research: Measuring Performance in Context* (pp. 47–70). Berlin, Heidelberg: Springer. doi:10.1007/978-3-642-31991-4_4

Du, Y. (2014). Massive Open Online Course: The Implication to iSchool Education. Proceedings of iConference, Berlin, Germany (884–888).

Dunleavy, M., Dede, C., & Mitchell, R. (2008). Affordances and Limitations of Immersive Participatory Augmented Reality Simulations for Teaching and Learning. *Journal of Science Education and Technology*, *18*(1), 7–22. doi:10.1007/s10956-008-9119-1

edX, (2013). *How It Works.* Retrieved from https://www.edx.org/how-it-works

edX. (2012). *edX.* Retrieved from http://www.edxonline.org/

Escamilla, J. G. (2013). Avances en la Enseñanza a Distancia de la Ingeniería. *Revistad de Ingeniería*, 67-72.

Escudeiro, P. (2007). X-Tec Model and QEF Model: A case study. *Proceedings of World Conference on E-Learning in Corporate, Government, Healthcare, and Higher Education*, Quebec City, Canada (pp. 258-265).

Ezen-Can, A., Grafsgaard, J. F., Lester, J. C., & Boyer, K. E. (2015). Classifying student dialogue acts with multimodal learning analytics *Proceedings of the Fifth International Conference on Learning Analytics And Knowledge*, Poughkeepsie, NY, USA (280-289). ACM Press. doi:10.1145/2723576.2723588

Farzan, R., & Brusilovsky, P. (2011). Encouraging user participation in a course recommender system: An impact on user behavior. *Computers in Human Behavior*, *27*(1), 276–284. doi:10.1016/j.chb.2010.08.005

Fasihuddin, H. A., Skinner, G. D., & Athauda, R. I. (2013). Boosting the Opportunities of Open Learning (MOOCs) through Learning Theories. *Journal on Computing*, 3(3), 112-117.

Felder, R. M., & Spurlin, J. (2005). Applications, reliability, and validity of the index of learning styles. *International journal of Engineering Education,* 21(1), 103-112.

Felder, R. M. (2002). Author's preface to learning and teaching styles in engineering education. *Engr. Education*, Volume, 674–681.

Felder, R. M., & Silverman, L. K. (1988). Learning and teaching styles in engineering education. *Engr. Education*, Volume, 674–681.

Fini, A. (2009). The technological dimension of a massive open online course: The case of the CCK08 course tools. *International Review of Research in Open and Distance Learning*, *10*(5), 1–15.

Fitzgerald, E., Adams, A., Ferguson, R., Gaved, M., Mor, Y., & Thomas, R. (2012). Augmented Reality And Mobile Learning: The State Of The Art.*Proceedings of The 11th World Conference On Mobile And Contextual Learning*, Helsinki, Finland

Flinn, C.E., Jr. (2012). *MOOCs in Size Small, Please*. Retrieved from http://educationnext.org/moocs-in-size-small-please/

Følstad, A., Lai-Chong Law, E., & Hornbæk, A. (2010). Analysis in Practical Usability Evaluation: A Survey Study. *Proceedings of the ACM SIGCHI Conference on Human Factors in Computing Systems CHI'12*, Austin, Texas, USA (pp. 2127-2136). ACM Press.

Forni, K. (2012). 62 tips on graphic design, UI/UX design, and visualization for eLearning (The eLearning Guild ed.)

Fossatti, M. (2015). *Sinergianet-In latina*. Retrieved from http://sinergianet.org/moocs-el-modelo-de-los-cursos-masivos-abiertos/

Fox, A. (2013). From MOOCs to SPOCs. *Communications of the ACM*, *56*(12), 38–40. doi:10.1145/2535918

Francisco, J. M. (2013). Learning in collaborative settings: Students building on each other's ideas to promote their mathematical understanding. *Educational Studies in Mathematics*, *82*(3), 417–438. doi:10.1007/s10649-012-9437-3

Frosini, G., Lazzerini, B., & Marcelloni, F. (1998). Performing automatic exams. Computers & Education, p. 281-300. *Computers & Education*, *31*(3), 281–300. doi:10.1016/S0360-1315(98)00042-6

Future Learn. (2013). *Future learn launches*. Retrieved from http://futurelearn.com/feature/futurelearn-launches

Gaebel, M. (2013). MOOCs: Massive Open Online Courses. European University Association Occasional Papers. Retrieved from http://www.eua.be/Libraries/Publication/EUA_Occasional_papers_MOOCs.sflb.ashx

Gaebel, M. (2013). MOOCs: Massive Open Online courses. European University Association. Retrieved from http://www.eua.be/news/13-02-25/Massive_Open_Online_Courses_MOOCs_EUA_to_look_at_development_of_MOOCs_and_trends_in_innovative_learning.aspx

Gaf, S., Kinshuk, & Tzu-Chien, L. (2008). Identifying Learning Styles in Learning Management Systems by Using Indications from Students' Behaviour. *Proceedings of the 8th IEEE ICALT '08* (pp. 482-486).

Gamma, E., Helm, R., Johnson, R., & Vlissides, R. (1994). *Design Patterns: Elements of Reusable Object-Oriented Software*. United States: Addison-Wesley Professional Computing.

García, J., Gustavsson, I., Hernández, U., Orduña, P., Angulo, I., & Ruiz De Garibay, I. (2010). *El Proyecto VISIR en la Universidad de Deusto: Laboratorio Remoto para Electrónica Básica*. Retrieved from http://e-spacio.uned.es/fez/eserv.php?pid=taee:congreso-2010-1063&dsID=S10A04.pdf

Gardner, H. (1985). *Frames of mind: The theory of multiple intelligences*. Basic books.

Garrison, D. R., & Anderson, T. (2005). *El e-learning en el siglo xxi: Investigación y práctica*. Barcelona: Octaedro.

Getoor, L., & Taskar, B. (2007). *Introduction to statistical relational learning*. Cambridge Massachusetts, MA: MIT press.

Gilliani, N. (2013). Learner Communications in Massively Open Online Courses. Retrieved from http://oxcheps.new.ox.ac.uk/MainSite%20pages/Resources/OxCHEPS_OP53.pdf

Githens, R. (2007). Older Adults and E-learning: Opportunities and Barriers. *The Quarterly Review of Distance Education, 8*(4), 329–338.

Glance, D., Frosey, M., & Riley, M. (2012). *The pedagogical foundation of massive online courses*. First Monday Journal.

Goldrick-Rab, S. (2010). Challenges and opportunities for improving community college student success. *Review of Educational Research, 80*(3), 437–469. doi:10.3102/0034654310370163

Goldwasser, D., & Roth, D. (2011). Learning from natural instructions. *Procedings of the International Joint Conference on Artificial Intelligence* IJCAI, Beijing, China. doi:10.1007/s10994-013-5407-y

Google. (2013). *Kubernetes by Google*. Retrieved from http://kubernetes.io/

Graf, S. (2007). *Adaptivity in Learning Management Systems Focusing on Learning Styles* [Ph.D. Thesis]. Vienna University of Technology.

Graf, S., & Kinshuk, K. (2007). Providing Adaptive Courses in Learning Management Systems with Respect to Learning Styles. *Proceedings of theWorld Conference on E-Learning in Corporate, Government, Healthcare, and Higher Education.*

Graf, S., & Viola, S. (2009). Automatic student modelling for detecting learning style preferences in learning management systems. *Proceedings of theInternational Conference on Cognition and Exploratory Learning in Digital Age* (pp. 172-179).

Graf, S. (2014). *Kinshuk. Adaptive Technologies. Handbook of Research on Educational Communications and Technology*(pp. 771–779).

Graf, S., & Tzu-Chien, L. (2009). Supporting Teachers in Identifying Students' Learning Styles in Learning Management Systems: An Automatic. *Journal of Educational Technology & Society*, 12(4), 3–14.

Griffin, P., Care, E., Bui, M., & Zoanetti, N. (2013). Development of assessment design and delivery of collaborative problem solving in the assessment of teaching of 21st century skills project. In E. McKay (Ed.), *ePedagogy in online learning: new developments in web mediated human computer interaction* (pp. 55–73). Hershey, PA: IGI Global. doi:10.4018/978-1-4666-3649-1.ch004

Grillo, M., Zúñiga, M., Esquivel, W., González, M., & Fonseca, E. (2007). *Modelo TecnoBus Inducción en la Cultura Tecnológica para Adolescentes de Comunidades en Desventaja Social. Una intervención costo efectiva y replicable para enfrentar la brecha digital que afecta a su población meta, Paper presented in the X Reunión de la Red de Popularización de la Ciencia y la Tecnología en América Latina y el Caribe (RED POP - UNESCO), IV Taller "Ciencia.* San José, Costa Rica: Comunicación y Sociedad.

Grünewald, F., Meinel, C., Totschnig, M., & Willems, C. (2013). Designing MOOCs for the support of multiple learning styles. Scaling up learning for sustained impact (pp. 371-382). University of Potsdam, Germany: Springer.

Guàrdia, L., Maina, M., & Sangrà, A. (2013). MOOC Design Principles. A Pedagogical Approach from the Learner's Perspective. *eLearning Papers, 33*(May), 1–6.

Guardia, L., Maina, M., & Sangrá, A. (May de 2013). *MOOC Design Principles. A Pedagogical Approach from the Learner's Perspective*. Retrieved from http://elearningeuropa.info/sites/default/files/asset/Indepth_33_4_0.pdf

Guba, E., & Lincoln, Y. (1994). Competing paradigms in qualitative research. In N. K. Denzin & Y. S. Lincoln (Eds.), *Handbook of qualitative research (105 - 117)*. London: Sage Publications.

Guermazi, R., Hammami, M., & Ben Hamadou, A. (2007). Combining Classifiers for Web Violent Content Detection and Filtering. *Proceedings of the 7th International Conference on Computational Science*, LCNS (Vol. 4489, pp. 773-780). Springer. doi:10.1007/978-3-540-72588-6_126

Gunawardena, C. (1995). Social Presence Theory and Implications of Interaction and Collaborative Learning in Computer Conferencing. *International Journal of Educational Telecommunications*, *1*, 147–166.

Gunawardena, C. N., & Zittle, F. J. (1997). Social presence as a predictor of satisfaction within a computer-mediated conferencing environment. *American Journal of Distance Education*, *11*(3), 8–26. doi:10.1080/08923649709526970

Guo, P., & Reinecke, K. (2014). Demographic differences in how students navigate through MOOCs.*Proceedings of the first ACM Conference on Learning @ Scale* (pp. 21-30). doi:10.1145/2556325.2566247

Gustafson, D. H., Mc Tavish, F. M., William, S., Ballard, D., Jones, E., Julesberg, K., & Hawkins, R. et al. (2005). Reducing the Digital Divide for Low-incomeme Women with Breast Cancer: A Feasibility Study of a Population-Based Intervention. *Journal of Health Communication: International Perspectives*, *10*(1), 173–193. doi:10.1080/10810730500263281 PMID:16377607

Gutierrez-Rojas, I., Alario-Hoyos, C., Pérez-Sanagustin, M., Leony, D., & Delgado-Kloos, C. (2014). Scaffolding Self-learning in MOOCs. Proceedings of European MOOCs Stakeholders Summit Lausanne, Switzerland (pp. 43-49).

Hall, O., Jr. (2014). Future Trends in MOOCs and SOOCs in Management Education. *Proceedings of Society for Information Technology & Teacher Education International Conference* Chesapeake, VA, (pp. 192). Association for the Advancement of Computing in Education (AACE).

Hamari, J., Koivisto, J., & Sarsa, H. (2014). Does gamification work?--A literature review of empirical studies on gamification. *Proceedings of the 2014 47th Hawaii International Conference on System Sciences (HICSS)* (pp. 3025-3034). IEEE

Handigol, N., Heller, B., Jeyakumar, V., Lantz, B., & McKeown, N. (2012). Reproducible network experiments using container-based emulation.*Proceedings of The 8th International Conference on Emerging Networking Experiments and Technologies,*Nice, France, (pp. 253–264). ACM Press. doi:10.1145/2413176.2413206

Hartson, R., & Pyla, P. (2012). *The UX Book: Process and Guidelines for Ensuring a Quality User Experience*. Burlington, MA: Morgan Kaufman.

Hasselbring, T., & Williams, C. (2000). Use of computer technology to help students with special needs. *The Future of Children*, *10*(2), 102–122. doi:10.2307/1602691 PMID:11255702

Hernández - Rizzardini., R., Gütl, C., Chang, V, & Morales, M. (2013). MOOC in Latin America: Implementation and Lessons Learned. *Proceedings of the 2nd International Workshop on Learning Technology for Education in Cloud*, Kaohsiung, Taiwan (pp. 147-158). Springer.

Hillman, D. C., Willis, D. J., & Gunawardena, C. N. (1994). Learner-interface interaction in distance education: An extension of contemporary models and strategies for practitioners. *American Journal of Distance Education*, *8*(2), 30–42. doi:10.1080/08923649409526853

Holcomb, T., & Kreeft, J. (1992). ESL Literacy for a Linguistic Minority: The Deaf Experience. Retrieved from http://www.cal.org/caela/esl_resources/digests/ESLlit.html

Horizon (2010). *Two to Three Years: Simple Augmented Reality*. Retrieved from http://wp.nmc.org/horizon2010/chapters/simple-augmented-reality/

Horton, S., & Leventhal, L. (2008). Universal Usability. In S. Harper, & Y. Yesilada (Eds.), Web Accessibility: A Foundation for Research (pp. 346-355). Berlin, Germany: Springer-Verlag.

Horton, S., & Sloan, D. (2014). Accessibility in Practice: A Process-Driven Approach to Accessibility. In Inclusive Designing (pp. 105-115). Springer International Publishing. doi:10.1007/978-3-319-05095-9_10

http://www.engr.ncsu.edu/learningstyles/ilsweb.html

Huang, J., Piech, C., Nguyen, A., & Guibas, L. (2013). Syntactic and Functional Variability of a Million Code Submissions in a Machine Learning MOOC. *Proceedings of the Workshop on Massive Open Online Courses,* Memphis, Tennessee, USA, LCNS (pp. 25-32), , Springer Verlag.

Huerta, M. (2014). Why your Kids Should MOOCs. Retrieved from http://www.kars4kids.org/blog/why-kids-should-mooc/

Hu, R., Feng, J., Lazar, J., & Kumin, L. (2013). Investigating input technologies for children and young adults with Down syndrome. *Universal Access in the Information Society*, *12*(1), 89–104. doi:10.1007/s10209-011-0267-3

IDSCEA. (2015) *Instituto para el Desarrollo de la Sociedad del Conocimiento del Estado de Aguascalientes.* Retrieved from http://www.aguascalientes.gob.mx/idscea/vagones.aspx

Instituto Jaliscience de Tecnologías de la Información (IJTI). (2013). Agenda Digital Jalisco 2013. Retrieved from http://www.bajacalifornia.gob.mx/agendadigitalbc/doctos/AGENDA_DIGITAL_JALISCO.pdf

Instituto para el Desarrollo de la Sociedad del Conocimiento del estado de Aguascalientes. (n. d.).

International Development Research Center (IDRC). (2002) *Bridging the Digital Divide: Electronic Networking for Rural Asia/Pacific (ENRAP).* Retrieved from www.ifad.org/evaluation/public_html/eksyst/doc/profile/pi/enrap.htm

International Society for Technology in Education (ISTE). (2008). *National Educational Technology Standards for Teachers* (2nd ed.). United States: ISTE.

ISO. (2012). ISO 9241-171 Ergonomics of human system interaction – Guidance on software accessibility.

Jan, A. G. M., & Van, D. (2006). Digital Divide Research, Achievements, and Shortcomings. *Poetics*, *34*(4-5), 221–235. doi:10.1016/j.poetic.2006.05.004

Jennings, C. (2013). Human design for engagement and critical thinking. Retrieved from http://www.learningsolutionsmag.com/articles/1314/human-design-for-engagement-and-critical-thinking

Johnson, J. (2010). *Designing with the mind in mind: Simple guide to understanding user interface design rules.* Morgan Kaufmann.

Jones, C., Reichard, C., & Mokhtar, K. (2003). Are students' learning styles discipline specific? *Community College Journal of Research and Practice*, *27*(5), 363375. doi:10.1080/713838162

Jones, S. (2007). Online Discourse: Encourage active student participation in large classes. In E. McKay (Ed.), *Enhancing learning through Human-computer interaction.* Hershey: Idea Group Reference. doi:10.4018/978-1-59904-328-9.ch005

Kainda, R., Flechais, I., & Roscoe, A. W. (2010). Two Heads are Better Than One: Security and Usability of Device Associations in Group Scenarios.*Proceedings of the Symposium on Usable Privacy and Security SOUPS'10,* Redmond, Washington, United States. ACM Press. doi:10.1145/1837110.1837117

Kalogeraki, A. (2014). *Design interfaces for massive open online courses.* Cyprus: Open University of Cyprus.

Kalyvioti, K., & Mikropoulos, T. (2013). A Virtual Reality Test for the Identification of Memory Strengths of Dyslexic Students in Higher Education. *J. UCS*, *19*(18), 2698–2721.

Kanuka, H., & Anderson, T. (1998). Online social interchange, discord, and knowledge construction. *Journal of Distance Education*, *13*(1), 57–74.

Kanuka, H., & Anderson, T. (1998). Online Social Interchange, Discord, and Knowledge Construction. *Journal of Distance Education*, *13*(1), 57–74.

Kapp, K. M. (2012). *The gamification of learning and instruction: Game-based methods and strategies for training and education*. John Wiley & Sons.

Karam, M. (2010). The Coffee Lab: Developing a Public Usability Space.*Proceedings of the ACM SIGCHI Conference on Human Factors in Computing Systems CHI'10*, Atlanta, Georgia, USA (pp. 2671-2680). ACM Press. doi:10.1145/1753846.1753850

Karsenti, T. (2013). What the research says. *International Journal of Technologies in Higher Education*, *10*(2), 23–37.

Kaufmann, H., & Papp, M. (2006). Learning Objects For Education With Augmented Reality. *Proceedings of the European Distance and E-Learning Network Conference*, Vienna Austria (160-165).

Kay, J., Reinmann, P., Diebold, E., & Kummerfeld, B. (2013). MOOCs: So Many Learners, So Much Potential.... *IEEE Intelligent Systems*, *28*(3), 2–9. doi:10.1109/MIS.2013.66

Kearney, M. H. (2014). Be a Responsible Co-Author. *Research in Nursing & Health*, *37*(1), 1–2. doi:10.1002/nur.21580 PMID:24414937

Kehrwald, B. (2008). Understanding social presence in text-based online learning environments. *Distance Education*, *29*(1), 89–106. doi:10.1080/01587910802004860

Khalil, H., & Ebner, M. (2013). How satisfied are you with your MOOC? - A Research Study on Interaction in Huge Online Courses. *Proceedings of World Conference on Educational Media and Technology,* Victoria, Canada (pp. 830-839). Association for the Advancement of Computing in Education (AACE).

Khalil, H., & Ebner, M. (2013, June). How satisfied are you with your MOOC?-A Research Study on Interaction in Huge Online Courses. *Proceedings of theWorld Conference on Educational Multimedia, Hypermedia and Telecommunications* (Vol. 1, pp. 830-839).

Khalil, H., & Ebner, M. (2013). Interaction Possibilities in MOOCs – How Do They Actually Happen?*International Conference on Higher Education Development* (pp. 1-24).

Kim, JI. (2015). A Study on the K_MOOC Platform Standardization Measures. *International Journal of Software Engineering and its Applications, 9*(1), 221-236.

Kinash, S., & Paszuk, A. (2007). *Accessible Education for Blind Learners: Kindergarten Through Postsecondary*. Charlotte, North Carolina, USA. Information Age Publishing.

Kizilcec, R. F., Schneider, E., Cohen, G. L., & McFarland, D. A. (2014). Encouraging Forum Participation in Online Courses with Collectivist, Individualist, and Neutral Motivational Framings. In Proceedings of European MOOCs Stakeholders Summit, Lausanne, Switzerland (pp. 80-87).

Klemmer, S., Hartmann, B., & Takayama, L. (2006). How bodies matter: five themes for interaction design. In *Proceedings of the 6th conference on Designing Interactive systems* (pp. 140-149), University Park, PA, USA, ACM Press. doi:10.1145/1142405.1142429

Knox, J., Ross, J., Sinclair, C., Macload, H., & Bayne, S. (2013). MOOC Feedback: Pleasing All the People? In S. D. Krause & C. Lowe (Eds.). Invasion of the MOOCs: The Promise and Perils of Massive Open Online Courses (98-104), San Francisco, CA: Parlor Press

Kok, S., & Domingos, P. (2005). Learning the structure of Markov logic networks.*Proceedings of the 22nd international conference on Machine learning*, Bonn, Germany (pp. 441-448). ACM Press. doi:10.1145/1102351.1102407

Kolb, D. A. (1984). *Experiential learning: Experience as the source of learning and development.* Upper Saddle River, New Jersey: Prentice Hall.

Kolb, D. A., & Fry, R. E. (1975). Toward an applied theory of experiential learning. In C. Cooper (Ed.), *Theories of group processes.* London: Wiley Press.

Koller, D. (2012). What we're learning from online education. *TED Talk.* Retrieved from http://www.ted.com/talks/daphne_koller_what_we_re_learning_from_online_education/

Koller, D., Ng, A., Do, C., & Chen, Z. (2013). Retention and intention in massive open online courses: In depth. *EDUCAUSE Review.*

Könings, K. D., Brand-Gruwel, S., & Merriënboer, J. J. G. (2010). An approach to participatory instructional design in secondary education: An exploratory study. *Educational Research, 52*(1), 45–95. doi:10.1080/00131881003588204

Koper, R., & Tattersall, C. (2005). *Learning design-A handbook on modelling and delivering networked education and training.* Heidelberg: Springer Verlag.

Koster, R. (2004). *Raph Koster's writings on game design.* Retrieved on January 20, 2015 from: http://www.legendmud.org/raph/gaming/index.html

Kotturi, Y., Kulkarni, C., Berstein, M. S., & Klemmer, S. (2015) Structure and Messaging Techniques for Online Peer Learning Systems that Increase Stickiness. *Proceedings of L@S*, Vancouver, Canada (pp. 31-38). ACM Press. doi:10.1145/2724660.2724676

Kumin, L., Lazar, J., Feng, J., Wentz, B., & Ekedebe, N. (2012). Usability Evaluation of Workplace-Related Tasks on a Multi-Touch Tablet Computer by Adults with Down Syndrome. *Journal of Usability Studies, 7*(4), 118–142.

Kvale, S. (1996). *InterWiews: An introduction to qualitative research interviewing.* London, England: Sage Publications.

Lane, J., & Kinser, K. (2012). MOOC's and the McDonaldization of global higher education.[Commentary from globetrotting higher-education thinkers]. *Education, 30536*, 1.

Lara, L. Y., & Villareal, J. (2004). *La Realidad Aumentada: Una Tecnología en Espera de Usuarios, Revista Digital Universitaria, 7(7).* Universidad Autonoma de Mexico.

Laszlo, A., Rowland, R., Johnston, T., & Taylor, G. (2012). Virtual learning in a socially digitized world. *World Futures, 68*(8), 575–594.

Lave, J., & Wenger, E. (1991). *Situated learning: Legitimate peripheral participation. Learning in doing* (p. *95*, p. 138). Retrieved from http://books.google.com/books?id=CAVIOrW3vYAC&pgis=1

LeClair, J., & Ferrer, T. (2014). A case for MOOCs. *Proceedings of the ASEE Gulf-Southwest Conference,*New Orleans, Louisiana, USA (pp. 1-8). American Society for Engineering Education.

Legon, R. (2014). MOOCs do not represent the best of online learning (essay), *Inside higher ed.* Retrieved from http://www.insidehighered.com/views/2013/04/25/moocs-do-not-represent-best-online-learning-essay

Legros, G., Havet, I., Bruce, N., & Bonjour, S. (2009). *The energy access situation in developing countries*. United Nations Development Programme and World Health Organization.

Lemire, D. (2002). Brief report: What developmental educators should know about learning styles and cognitive styles. *Journal of College Reading and Learning*, *32*(2), 177–182. doi:10.1080/10790195.2002.10850296

Lewin, T. (2015). Harvard and MIT are sued over lack of closed captions. *The New York Times*. Retrieved from http://www.nytimes.com/2015/02/13/education/harvard-and-mit-sued-over-failing-to-caption-online-courses.html

Lewis, R. J. (1993). *IBM Computer Usability Satisfaction Questionnaires: Psychometric Evaluation and Instructions for Use*. Boca Raton, FL: Human Factors Group.

Lim, S., Coetzee, D., Hartmann, B., Fox, A., & Hearst, M. A. (2014). Initial Experiences with Small Group Discussions in MOOCs.*Proceedings of the L@S Conference*, Atlanta, GA, (pp. 151-152). ACM Press. doi:10.1145/2556325.2567854

Lira, L. R., de Iturbe, P. F., Celis, K. F., & Cortés, E. R. (2014). Evaluación de una intervención en línea para prevenir la violencia en población juvenil y adolescente. Resultados preliminares sobre su efectividad con profesionales de la salud. *Salud Mental*, *37*(3), 195–204.

Liu, C.-L., Wang, C.-H., Gao, Z.-M., & Huang, S.-M. (2005). Applications of lexical information for algorithmically composing multiple-choice cloze items.*Proceedings of the second workshop on Building Educational Applications Using NLP,*Ann Arbor, MI (pp. 1-8). ACM Press. doi:10.3115/1609829.1609830

Livingston, M., Rosenblum, L., & Julier, S. Brown D., Baillot Y., Swan Ii J., Gabbard J. Hix D. (2002). An Augmented Reality System For Military Operations In Urban Terrain. Proceedings of Interservice / Industy Training, Simulation & Education Conference, Orlando, Florida (p. 89). I/ITSEC.

Liyanagunawardena, T., Williams, S., & Adams, A. (2013). The impact and reach of MOOCs: A developing countries' perspective. *eLearning Papers*, 33.

Lowdermilk, T. (2013). *User Centered Design: A Developer's Guide to Building User – Friendly Applications. Sebastopol*. CA: O'Reilly.

Lowdermilk, T. (2013). *User Centered Design: A Developer's Guide to Building User-Friendly Applications*. Sebastopol, CA: O'Reilly.

Mace, R. L., Hardie, G. J., & Place, J. P. (1996). *Accessible Environments: Toward Universal Design*. The Center for Universal Design, North Carolina State University.

Machado, E. (2005). *Spatially Adaptive Augmented Reality. (Unpublished doctoral dissertation)*. Georgia Institute of Technology.

Mahenthiran, S., & Rouse, P. J. (2000). The impact of group selection on student performance and satisfaction. *International Journal of Educational Management*, *14*(6), 255–264. doi:10.1108/09513540010348043

Mak, S., Williams, R., & Mackness, J. (2010). Blogs and Forums as Communication and Learning Tools in a MOOC. *Proceedings of Networked Learing Conference*, University of Lancaster (pp.275-285).

Mak, S., Williams, R., & Mackness, J. (2010). Blogs and Forums as Communication and Learning Tools in a MOOC. *Proceedings of the 7th International Conference on Networked Learning* (pp. 275-284).

Mak, S., Williams, R., & Mackness, J. (2010). Blogs and Forums as Communication and LearningTools in a MOOC. *Proceedings of the 7th International Conference on Networked Learning* (pp. 275-284).

Malone, T. W. (1982). Heuristics for designing enjoyable user interfaces: Lessons from computer games. *Proceedings of the 1982 Conference on Human Factors in Computing Systems* (pp. 63-68). ACM Management Services, I & J. doi:10.1145/800049.801756

Malone, T. W. (1980). What makes things fun to learn? heuristics for designing instructional computer games.*Proceedings of the 3rd ACM SIGSMALL Symposium and the First SIGPC Symposium on Small Systems* (pp. 162-169). ACM. doi:10.1145/800088.802839

Manjunatha, A., Ranabahu, A., Sheth, A., & Thirunarayan, K. (2010). Power of clouds in your pocket: An efficient approach for cloud mobile hybrid application development.*Proceedings of The Second International Conference on Cloud Computing Technology and Science* (Indianapolis, IN, pp. 496–503). IEEE Press. doi:10.1109/CloudCom.2010.78

Mannadiar, R., & Vangheluwe, H. (2010). Modular synthesis of mobile device applications from domain-specific models. *Proceedings of The 7th International Workshop on Model-Based Methodologies for Pervasive and Embedded Software*, Antwerp, Belgium, (pp.21–28). IEEE/ACM Press. doi:10.1145/1865875.1865879

Mao, J., Vredenburg, K., Smithh, P. W., & Carey, T. (2005). The State of User-Centered Design Practice. *Communications of the ACM*, *48*(3), 105–109. doi:10.1145/1047671.1047677

Marín, C. (2005). Capacitación a distancia (CapDis) y el uso de plataformas virtuales. La experiencia del Centro Centroamericano de Población. *Población y Salud en Mesoamérica*, *3*(2), 1–13.

Markow, D., & Pieters, A. (2011). *The MetLife Survey of Preparing Students for College and Careers.*

Martínez -Abad, F., Rodríguez -Conde, M.J. & G Arcía -Peñalver, F.J. (2014). Evaluación del impacto del término MOOC Vs eLearning en la literatura científica y de divulgación. *Profesorado*, *18*(1), 1–17.

Martínez De Rituerto, P. (2014). Figura de los Facilitadores en los Cursos Online Masivos y Abiertos (Coma/Mooc). Nuevo Rol Profesional para los Educativos en Abierto. *Revista Iberoamericana de Educación a Distancia*, *17*(1), 35–67.

Martinez-Cruz, C. (2014). An experience using a Massive Open Online Course at the University of El Salvador.*Proceedings of the 5th International Conference on Quality and Accessibility of Virtual Learning CAFVIR* (pp. 536-538).

Martínez, K., & Medina-Mora, M. (2013). Transferencia tecnológica en el área de adicciones: El programa de intervención breve para adolescentes, retos y perspectivas. *Salud Mental*, *36*(6), 505–512.

Martin, F. G. (2012). Will massive open online courses change how we teach? *Communications of the ACM*, *55*(8), 26–28. doi:10.1145/2240236.2240246

Martin-Monje, E., Barcena, E., & Ventura, P. (2013). Peer - to - peer interaction in Professional English MOOCs: A proposal for effective feedback. *The European Conference on Language Learning*. Retrieved from http://www.iafor.org/offprints/ecll2013-offprints/ECLL2013_Offprint_0220.pdf

Martin-Monje, E., Bárcena, E., & Read, T. (2014). *Peer-to-peer interaction and linguistic feedback in foreign language MOOCs. Revista Profesorado, 18(1).* Universitat de Oberta de Catalunya.

McAuley, A., Stewart, B., Siemens, G., & Cormier, D. (2010). Massive Open Online Courses Digital ways of knowing and learning. *The MOOC model For Digital Practice.*

Mcauley, A., Stewart, B., Siemens, G., & Cormier, D. (2010). *The Mooc Model For Digital Practice*, Retrieved from http://www.elearnspace.org/Articles/MOOC_Final.pdf

McAuley, A., Stewart, B., Siemens, G., & Cormier, D. (2010). The MOOC model for digital practice.

McAuley, A., Stewart, B., Siemens, G., & Cormier, D. (2010). *The MOOC model for digital practice*. Retrieved from http://www.elearnspace.org/Articles/MOOC_Final.pdf

McAuly, A., Bonnie, S., Siemens, G., & Cormier, D. (2010). The MOOC Model for Digital Practice, Knowledge Synthesis Grants on the Digital Economy, *University of Prince Edward Island*. Retrieved from http://www.elearnspace.org/Articles/MOOC_Final.pdf

McGonigal, J. (2011). *Reality is broken: Why games make us better and how they can change the world*. Penguin.

Mcguire, R. (2013). *Building a Sense of Community in MOOCs*. Retrieved from http://campustechnology.com/articles/2013/09/03/building-a-sense-of-community-in-moocs.aspx

McInnerney, J. M., & Roberts, T. S. (2004). Online learning: Social interaction and the creation of a sense of community. *Journal of Educational Technology & Society*, *7*(3), 73–81.

Mehigan, T. J. (2009). Harnessing Accelerometer Technology For Inclusive Mobile Learning.*Proceedings of the 11th International Conference on Human-Computer Interaction withMobileDevices and Services*, New York, NY (pp. 1-2) ACM. doi:10.1145/1613858.1613973

Meisel, S. (2012). Adaptive learning in concept and implementation. *Organizational Management Journal*, *9*(1), 20–21. doi:10.1080/15416518.2012.666947

Menage, P. B. (2007). Adding generic process containers to the Linux kernel. *Proceedings of the Linux Symposium*, Ottawa, Canada (Vol. 2, pp. 45–57). Kernel.org.

Menchaca, R., & Ballares, B., Quintero & Carreto,C. (2005). Software Engineering, HCI Techniques and Java Technologies Joined to Develop Web-Based 3D Collaborative Virtual Environments. *Proceedings of the Latin American conference on Human-computer interaction*, Cuernavaca, México, (pp. 40-51). ACM Press doi:10.1145/1111360.1111365

Mendoza-González, R., Muñoz Arteaga, J., & Álvarez Rodríguez, F. J. (2010). Designing Usable Security Feedback for Web Filtering Systems. In M. Vargas Martin, M. García-Ruíz, & A. Edwards (Eds.), *Technology for Facilitating Humanity and Combating Social Deviations* (pp. 230–248). Hershey, PA: IGI Global. doi:10.4018/978-1-60960-094-5.ch013

Milligan, C., Littlejohn, A., & Margaryan, A. (2013). Patterns of Engagement in Connectivist MOOCs. *MERLOT Journal of Online Learning and Teaching*, *9*(2), 149–159.

Möckel, C. (2011). Usability and Security in EU E-Banking Systems - Towards an Integrated Evaluation Framework. *Proceedings of the 2011 IEEE/IPSJ International Symposium on Applications and the Internet SAINT'11*, Munich, Germany, (pp. 230-233). IEEE Computer Society. doi:10.1109/SAINT.2011.42

Moe, R. (2015). The Brief & Expansive History (and Future) of the MOOC: Why two divergent models share the same name. *Current Issues in Emerging eLearning*, 2(1), 2-24.

Molina, R. (2010). Higher education for disabled students. *The R Journal*, *34*(70), 95–115.

Montero García, S. (2015). *Universidad Autónoma de Madrid*. Retrieved April 10, 2015, from: http://www.uam.es/gruposinv/dim/assets/sergiomonterouned.pdf

Mooc.Es. (2015). *Mooc.Es*. Retrieved from http://Mooc.Es/Cmoox-Vs-Xmooc/

Moore, M. G. (1989). Editorial: Three types of interaction. *American Journal of Distance Education*, *3*(2), 1–6. doi:10.1080/08923648909526659

Morales, A. (2007). White Paper on University and Disability. *Royal Board on Disability*.

Mordini, E., Wright, D., Wadhwa, K., De Hert, P., Mantovani, E., Thestrup, J., & Vater, I. (2009). Senior citizens and the ethics of e-inclusion. *Ethics and Information Technology*, *11*(3), 203–220. doi:10.1007/s10676-009-9189-7

Morgado, L., Spilker, M., & Silva, P. (2013). Novos Ambientes de Aprendizagem PLE, MOOC, Mobile Learning. *Proceedings of the 2nd Encontro de Bibliotecas do Ensino Superior*, Aveiro, Portugal.

Morrison, D. (2014). The ultimate student guide to xMOOCs and cMOOCs, *Mooc news and reviews*. Retrieved from http://moocnewsandreviews.com/ultimate-guide-to-xmoocs-and-cmoocso/

Mossberger, K., Tolbert, C. J., & McNeal, R. S. (2008). *Digital Citizenship*. Cambridge, Massachusetts: MIT Press.

Muñoz, J., Mendoza, R., Vargas Martin, M., Vanderdonckt, J., & Álvarez, F. J. (2009). A Methodology for Designing Information Security Feedback Based on User Interface Patterns. *Advances in Software Engineering*, *40*(12), 1231–1241. doi:10.1016/j.advengsoft.2009.01.024

Murphy, K. L., & Cifuentes, L. (2001). Using web tools, collaborating, and learning online. *Distance Education, 22*(2), 285-305. Retrieved from http://search.proquest.com/docview/217782583?accountid=14667

Murray, M., Pérez, J., Geist, D., & Hedrick, A. (2012). Student Interaction with Online Course Content: Build It and They Might Come. *Journal of Information Technology Education*, *11*(1), 125–142.

Nasjonalt Fagorgan for Kompetansepolitikk (NFK). (2008). The Digital Citizen: An analysis of digital competence in the Norwegian population. Oslo, Norway.

National Association of the Deaf. (2015). NAD Sues Harvard and MIT for Discrimination in Public Online Content. Retrieved from http://nad.org/news/2015/2/nad-sues-harvard-and-mit-discrimination-public-online-content

Navarro, P., & Shoemaker, J. (2000). Performance and perceptions of distance learners in cyberspace. *American Journal of Distance Education*, *14*(2), 15–35. doi:10.1080/08923640009527052

Neil, T. (2014). *Mobile Design Pattern Gallery: UI Patterns for Smartphone Apps* (2nd ed.). Sebastopol, CA: O'Reilly Media.

Nelimarkka, M., & Vihavainen, A. (2015). Alumni & Tenured Participants in MOOCs: Analysis of Two Years of MOOC Discussion Channel Activity.*Proceedings of the L@S Conference*, Vancouver, BC, (pp. 85-93). ACM Press. doi:10.1145/2724660.2724671

Neubaum, G., Wichmann, A., Eimler, S., & Krämer, N. (2014). Investigating Incentives for Students to Provide Peer Feedback in a Semi – Open Online Course: An Experimental Study.*Proceedings of International Symposium on Open Collaboration*. Berlin, Germany, ACM press. doi:10.1145/2641580.2641604

Nielsen, J. (1999). *Designing Web Usability*. United State, New Riders.

Nieuwenhuijsen, E. (2014). *Using game based learning as an approach for teaching kids how to program* (Forum).

Nolan, J., & McBride, M. (2014). Beyond gamification: Reconceptualizing game-based learning in early childhood environments. Information, Communication & Society, (17(5), 594-608.

North, C. (2013). Ontario Online Learning Portal for Faculty and Instructors. Retrieved from http://contactnorth.ca/home

Northrup, P. T. (2002). Online learners' preferences for interaction. *The Quarterly Review of Distance Education*, *3*(2), 219–226.

Notess, M., & Lorenzen-Huber, L. (2007). Online learning for seniors: barriers and opportunities. *eLearn*, 2007(5). Retrieved from http://doi.acm.org/10.1145/1266885.1266893

Notten, N., Peter, J., Kraaycamp, G., & Valkenburg, P. M. (2009). Digital Divide Across Borders –A Cross-National Study of Adolescents' Use of Digital Technologies. *European Sociological Review*, *25*(5), 551–560. doi:10.1093/esr/jcn071

Núñez, M. M., Oriol, G., & Ángel, B. (2014). Social community in MOOCs: practical implications and outcomes. *Proceedings of the Second International Conference on Technological Ecosystems for Enhancing Multiculturality*. Salamanca, Spain. ACM Press.

Nurmela, K., Palonen, T., Lehtinen, E., & Hakkarainen, K. (2003). Developing tools for analyzing CSCL process. In B. Wasson, S. Ludvigsen, & U. Hoppe (Eds.), *Designing for change in networked learning environments* (pp. 333–342). Dordrecht, The Netherlands: Kluwer. doi:10.1007/978-94-017-0195-2_41

O'Donnel, E., Mulwa, C., Sharp, M., & Wade, V. (2013). Web mediated education and training environments: a review of personalised interactive eLearning. In E. McKay (Ed.), *ePedagogy in online learning: new developments in web mediated human computer interaction* (pp. 188–208). Hershey, PA: IGI Global. doi:10.4018/978-1-4666-3649-1.ch012

Ong, M. (2013). Gamification and its effect on employee engagement and performance in a perceptual diagnosis task. University of Canterbury. *Psychology (Savannah, Ga.)*.

Oppermann, R. (2002). *User-interface design. Handbook on information technologies for education and training* (pp. 233–248). Germany: Springer. doi:10.1007/978-3-662-07682-8_15

Oreilly, M., Lefoe, G., Philip, R., & Parrish, D. (2010). Designing for user engagement: The ALTC Exchange for higher education. *International Journal on E-Learning*, *9*(2), 251.

Osgart. (2013). *Home Page*. Retrieved from http://www.artoolworks.com/community/osgart/

Osman-Schlegel, L., Fluker, G., & Cheng, S. T. (2011). Working collaboratively in a group assignment using MediaWiki for an architecture and construction management undergraduate unit. *Paper presented at the Ascilite*.

Öztürk, E. (2013). The new trend in education: Gamification [Abstract]. Muğla University; Anadolu University.

Pacheco, A. Y., & Martínez, K. I. (2012). El arte de ser terapeuta. ¿Qué hace efectiva una intervención en el consumo de drogas? *Enseñanza e Investigación en Psicología*, *18*(1), 159–176.

Palin, A. (2014). Moocs: Young students from developing countries are still in the minority. *Financial Times - Online learning*. Retrieved from http://www.ft.com/cms/s/2/8a81f66e-9979-11e3-b3a2-00144feab7de.html#axzz3T66iShyI

Palmer, S., & Holt, D. (2012). Trajectories of engagement: A repeated cross-sectional investigation of student perceptions of an online learning environment. *Research in Learning Technology*, *20*(3), 253–265.

Parr, C. (2013). *Mooc Creators Criticise Courses' Lack of Creativity*. Retrieved from http://www.timeshighereducation.co.uk/news/mooc-creators-criticisecourses-lack-of-creativity/2008180.fullarticle

Parr, C. (2013). MOOC makes Oxford online dictionary. *Times Higher Education*. Retrieved from http://www.timeshighereducation.co.uk/news/mooc-makes-oxford-online-dictionary/2006838.article

Perez-Gonzalez, D., Soto-Acosta, P., & Popa, S. (2014). A Virtual Campus for E-learning Inclusion: The Case of SVC-G9. *J. UCS*, *20*(2), 240–253.

Perna, L., Ruby, A., Boruch, R., Wang, N., Scull, J., Evans, Ch., & Ahmad, S. (2013). The Life Cycle of a Million MOOC Users. Retrieved from http://www.gse.upenn.edu/pdf/ahead/perna_ruby_boruch_moocs_dec2013.pdf

Piech, C., Huang, J., Chen, Z., Do, C., Ng, A., & Koller, D. (2013). Tuned Models of Peer Assessment in MOOCs. *Proceedings of The 6th International Conference on Educational Data Mining*, Memphis, Tennessee, United States.

Piemonte, C. S. I. (CSIP) (2013) Satellite systems to Slash Digital Divide in Europe, Retrieved from www.csipiemonte.it/en/newsroom/497-satellite-systems-to-slash-digital-divide-in-europe.html

Pierre Dillenbourg, P., & Self, J. (1992). A computational approach to socially distributed cognition. *European Journal of Psychology of Education*, *7*(4), 252–373.

Plan de Estudios de 2009. (2009). *Educación Básica Primaria*, Secretaria de Educación Pública, México.

Playa, J. (2013) *Los cursos on line y gratuitos obligan a las universidades a replantear su modelo*. Retrieved from http://www.lavanguardia.com/vida/20130205/54366352711/ cursos-on-line-gratuitos-universidades-replantear-modelo.html

Ponce, J., Oronia, Z., Silva, A., Muñoz, J., Ornelas, F., & Alvarez, F. (2015). Incremento del Interés de Alumnos en Educación Básica en los Objetos de Aprendizaje Usando Realidad Aumentada en las Matemáticas. *Proceedings of Conferencias LACLO*, *5*(1).

Popescul, A., & Lyle, H. (2003). Statistical Relational Learning for Link Prediction. *Proceedings of the 2nd Workshop on Learning Statistical Models from Relational Data* Amherst, MA (pp. 109-115). UMass Press.

Porter, A., Schmidt, D. C., & White, J. (2014). *Mobile Cloud Computing with Android, Coursera Specialization*. Retrieved from www.coursera.org/specialization/mobilecloudcomputing/2

POST. (2006). ICT in Developing Countries. Parliamentary Office of Science and Technology Postnote, 261.

Pouncey, I. (2010). Web accessibility for cognitive disabilities and learning difficulties. Retrieved from http://dev.opera.com/articles/view/cognitive-disability-learning-difficulty/

Poupyrev, I., Berry, R., Billinghurst, M., Kato, H., Nakao, K., Baldwin, L., & And Kurumisawa, J. (2001). Augmented Reality Interface For Electronic Music Performance.*Proceedings of HCI* (pp. 805-808).

Preece, J., Rogers, Y., Sharp, H., Benyon, D., Holland, S., & Carey, T. (1994). *Human-computer interaction*. Addison-Wesley Longman Ltd.

Price, M., Handley, K., Millar, J., & O'Donovan, B. (2010). Feedback: All the effort, but what is the effect? *Assessment & Evaluation in Higher Education*, *35*(3), 277–289. doi:10.1080/02602930903541007

Prougestaporn, P. (2010). Development of a web accessibility model for visually-impaired students on Elearning websites. *International Conference on Educational and Network Technology ICENT* (pp. 20-24). doi:10.1109/ICENT.2010.5532117

Public Policy Exchange (PPE). (2013). *Europe 2020: Bridging the Digital Divide: Securing Equal Access to High-Speed Internet*. Retrieved from www.publicpolicyexchange.co.uk

Ralston Consulting. (2013). An example of edX reach. Retrieved from http://ralstonconsulting.com/

Raschick, M., Maypole, D. E., & Day, P. A. (1998). Improving field education through Kolb's learning theory. *Journal of Social Work Education*, *34*(1), 31–42.

Raza, M. (2014). MobiSOOCs for In-Service Teacher Education: Design Considerations for Developing Countries. *Proceedings of the e-Skills for Knowledge Production and Innovation Conference*, Cape Town, South Africa (pp. 371-381).

Reece. (2013). MOOC: What about content design? Retrieved from http://transmoder.com/2013/02/06/mooc-what-about-content-design/

Reece. (2014). Feedback is the indispensable ingredient in elearning The transmoder project. Retrieved from http://transmoder.com/2012/06/11/feedback-is-the-indispensable-ingredient-in-elearning/

Reeves, B., & Read, J. L. (2013). *Total engagement: How games and virtual worlds are changing the way people work and businesses compete*. Harvard Business Press.

Reis, R., Escudeiro, P., & Escudeiro, N. (2010) Comparing Social Virtual Worlds for Educational Purposes.*Proceedings of the 10th IEEE International Conference on Advanced Learning Technologies*, Sousse, Tunisia (186-190). IEEE Press. doi:10.1109/ICALT.2010.57

Ribble, S. M., Gerald, D., Bailey, D., & Ross, T. W. (2004). Digital Citizenship, addressing appropriate technology behavior. *Learning and Leading with Technology*, *1*(32), 6.

Richards, L. (2002). Rigorous, rapid, reliable and qualitative? Computing in qualitative method. *American Journal of Health Behavior*, *26*(6), 425–430. doi:10.5993/AJHB.26.6.3 PMID:12437017

Richardson, J. C., & Swan, K. (2003). Examing social presence in online courses in relation to students' perceived learning and satisfaction.

Riechmann, S. W., & Grasha, A. F. (1974). A rational approach to developing and assessing the construct validity of a student learning style scales instrument. *The Journal of Psychology*, *87*(2), 213–223. doi:10.1080/00223980.1974.9915693

Riel, A., & Lawless, K. A. (2014). Massive Open Online Courses (MOOCs) and the Technologies That Support Learning with Them. In M. Khosrow-Pour (Ed.), *Encyclopedia of Information Science and Technology* (3rd ed., pp. 7529–7535). Hershey, PA: IGI Global Publishing.

Ring, G. (1993). Interface designs considerations for educational multimedia. *Proceedings of the 3rd International Interactive Multimedia Symposium*, Australia Western (pp. 355-361).

Roberts, J. J., & O'Loughlin, J. (2013). The Season of the MOOC. *Universitas*, 8.

Rodriguez, C. O. (2012). MOOCs and the AI-Stanford like courses: Two successful and distinct course formats for massive open online courses. *European Journal of Open, Distance and E-Learning*, 2012.

Rodriguez, C. O. (2012). MOOCs and the AI-Stanford like Courses: Two Successful and Distinct Course Formats for Massive Open Online Courses. *European Journal of Open, Distance and E-Learning*, 2012.

Rodriguez, C. (2012). *MOOCs and the ai-standord like courses: Two successful and distinct course formats for massive open online courses*. Learning.

Rodriguez, O. (2013). *The concept of opennes behind a and x-moocs (massive open online courses)*. Open Praxis.

Rose, C. P., Ferschke, O., Tomar, G., Yang, D., Howley, I., Aleven, V., & Baker, R. et al. (2015). Challenges and Opportunities of Dual-Layer MOOCs: Reflections from an edX DeploymentStudy.*Proceedings of the 11th International Conference on Computer Supported Collaborative Learning* (Vol. 2). Gothenburg, Sweden: International Society of the Learning Sciences

Rosenberg, M. (2001). *E-Learning: Strategies for Delivering Knowledge in the Digital Age*. New York, NY, United States: McGraw-Hill.

Rto, V. R. (2015). Road to Virtual Reality. Retrieved from http://www.roadtovr.com/

Rubin, J., & Chisnell, D. (2008). Handbook of Usability Testing: How to Plan, Design, and Conduct Effective Tests (2nd ed.). Indianapolis, IN: Wiley Publishing.

Sadigh, D., Seshia, S. A., & Gupta, M. (2012). Automating Exercise Generation: A Step towards Meeting the MOOC Challenge for Embedded Systems.*Proceedings of The Workshop on Embedded and Cyber-Physical Systems Education*, Tampere, Finland, (p. 2). ACM Press.

Saenz, V., Hatch, D., Bukoski, B., Kim, S., Lee, K., & Valdez, P. (2011). Community college student engagement patterns a typology revealed through exploratory cluster analysis. *Community College Review*, *39*(3), 235–267. doi:10.1177/0091552111416643

Sanchez-Gordon, S., & Luján-Mora, S. (2013b). Web accessibility of MOOCs for elderly students.*Proceedings of the 12th International Conference on Information Technology Based Higher Education and Training ITHET* (pp. 1-6). doi:10.1109/ITHET.2013.6671024

Sanchez-Gordon, S., & Luján-Mora, S. (2014a). Web Accessibility Requirements for Massive Open Online Courses. *Proceedings of the 5th International Conference on Quality and Accessibility of Virtual Learning CAFVIR* (pp. 530-5350.

Sanchez-Gordon, S., & Luján-Mora, S. (2014b). MOOCs Gone Wild.*Proceedings of the IEEE 8th International Technology, Education and Development Conference INTED* (pp. 1449-1458).

Satharasinghe, A. (2004). Computer Literacy of Sri Lanka. Retrieved from http://www.statistics.gov.lk/CLS/index.htm

Schmidt, D. C., & McCormick, Z. (2013). Creating and Teaching a MOOC on Pattern-Oriented Software Architecture for Concurrent and Networked Software.*Proceedings of the WaveFront Forum at the SPLASH 2013 conference*, Indianapolis, IN.

Shah, W. (2014). MOOCs in 2014: Breaking Down the Numbers. *edSurge*. Retrieved from https://www.edsurge.com/n/2014-12-26-moocs-in-2014-breaking-down-the-numbers/

Sharma, K., Jerman, P., & Dillenburg, P. (2014). How Students Learn Using MOOCs: An Eye-Tracking Insight. In Proceedings of European MOOCs Stakeholders Summit Lausanne, Switzerland (pp. 80-87).

Shatnawi, S., Gaber, M., & Cocea, M. (2014). Automatic Content Related Feedback for MOOCs Based on Course Domain Ontology. *Proceedings of the Intelligent Data Engineering and Automated Learning,*Wroclaw, Poland, Springer International Publishing (pp. 27-35). doi:10.1007/978-3-319-10840-7_4

Shipyard. (2014). *Shipyard*, Retrieved from http://shipyard-project.com/

Short, J., Williams, E., & Christie, B. (1976). The social psychology of telecommunications.

Shulman, S., Beisser, S., Larson, T., & Shelley, M. (2002). Digital Citizenship: Lessons Learned as Service-Learning Meets the Digital Divide. *Proceedings of the Annual Conference on Digital Government Research,* Santorini, Greece, ICPS (pp. 1-7). ACM press.

Siemens, G. (2005). Connectivism: A Learning Theory for the Digital Age. *International Journal of Instructional Technology & Distance Learning* .

Siemens, G. (2006). Connectivism. Retrieved from http://www.elearnspace.org/Articles/connectivism.htm

Siemens, G. (2006). Connectivism: Learning theory or pastime of the self-amused? Manitoba, Canada: Learning Technologies Centre, e-learn space

Siemens, G. (2008). *Learning and knowing in networks: changing roles for educators and designers.* Retrieved from: http://itforum.coe.uga.edu/Paper105/Siemens.pdf

Siemens, G. (2012). George Siemens on Massive Open Online Courses (MOOCs) and recent useful resources. Retrieved from http://facultyecommons.org/george-siemens-on-massive-open-online-courses-moocs-and-recent-useful-resources/

Siemens, G. (2012). *What is the Theory that Underpin our MOOCs?* Retrieved from http://goo.gl/nHhCOJ

Siemens, G. (2014). *The Future of MOOCs*. Retrieved from http://www.educause.edu/blogs/gbayne/george-siemens-future-moocs-0

Siemens, G., & Downes, S. (2008). *Connectivism & connective knowledge*. Retrieved from http://ltc.umanitoba.ca/connectivism

Siemens, G. (2005). Connectivism: A learning theory for the digital age. *International Journal of Instructional Technology and Distance Learning*, *2*(1), 3–10.

Siemens, G. (2013). Massive Open Online Courses: Innovation in Education? *Commonwealth of learning, Perspectives on Open Educational Resources: Innovation, Research and Practice*, 5.

Simpson, C., & Du, Y. (2004). Effects of learning styles and class participation on students' enjoyment level in distributed learning environments. *Journal of Education for Library and Information Science*, *45*(2), 123–136. doi:10.2307/40323899

Singh, R., Gulwani, S., & Solar-Lezama, A. (2013). Automated feedback generation for introductory programming assignments. *Proceedings of the 34th ACM SigPlan Conference on Program-Ming Language Design and Implementation,* New York, NY (pp. 15–26). ACM Press. doi:10.1145/2491956.2462195

Skillings, M. J., & Ferrell, R. (2000). Student-generated rubrics: Bringing students into the assessment process. *The Reading Teacher*, 53(6), 452–455.

Sloan, D., Atkinson, M., Machin, C., & Li, K. (2010). The potential of adaptive interfaces as an accessibility aid for older web users.*Proceedings of the International Cross Disciplinary Conference on Web Accessibility*. doi:10.1145/1805986.1806033

Smith, M. (2012). Application of the ADA to Websites: Congress Should Rely on the Standards Created by the World Wide Consortium. Retrieved from http://works.bepress.com/marad_smith/1

Soloman, B. A., & Felder, R. M. (2013). *Index of Learning Styles Questionnaire*. Retrieved April 20, 2015 from:

Soltesz, S., Pötzl, H., Fiuczynski, M. E., Bavier, A., & Peterson, L. (2007). Container-Based Operating System Virtualization: A Scalable, High-Performance Alternative to Hypervisors. *Operating Systems Review*, *41*(3), 275–287. doi:10.1145/1272998.1273025

Spada, D., Sánchez-Montañés, M., Paredes, P., & Carro, R. (2008). Towards Inferring Sequential-Global Dimension of Learning Styles from Mouse Movement Patterns. *Adaptive Hypermedia and Adaptive Web-Based Systems* (pp. 337-340).

Stacey, P. (2014). Pedagogy of MOOCs. *INNOQUAL-International Journal for Innovation and Quality in Learning, 2*(3).

Stacey, E. (2007). Collaborative learning in an online environment. *International Journal of E-Learning & Distance Education*, *14*(2), 14–33.

Stake, R. (1994). Case studies. In N. K. Denzi & Y. S. Lincoln (Eds.), *Handbook of Qualitative Research. Thousand Oaks*. London: Sage Publications.

Stephanidis, C., ... (1998). Adaptable and adaptive user interfaces for disabled users in the AVANTI project. Intelligence in Services and Networks: Technology for Ubiquitous Telecom Services, 153-166.

Stephanidis, C. (2001). Adaptive techniques for universal access. *User Modeling and User-Adapted Interaction*, *11*(1-2), 159–179. doi:10.1023/A:1011144232235

Stephanidis, C. (2001). User Interfaces for All: New perspectives into Human-Computer Interaction. In C. Stephanidis (Ed.), *User Interfaces for All - Concepts, Methods, and Tools* (pp. 3–17). Mahwah, NJ: Lawrence Erlbaum Associates.

Stewart, B. (2013). Massiveness + Openness = New Literacies of Participation? *MERLOT Journal of Online Learning and Teaching*, *9*(2), 228–238.

Stiggins, R. J. (1998). *Classroom Assessment for Student Success. Student Assessment Series*. NEA Professional Library.

Subba Rao, S. (2005). Bridging the Digital Divide: Efforts in India. *Telematics and Informatics*, *22*(4), 361–375. doi:10.1016/j.tele.2005.01.007

Suen, H. K. (2014). Peer assessment for massive open online courses (MOOCs). *International Review of Research in Open and Distance Learning*, *15*(3), 312–327.

Swan, K. (2001). Virtual interaction: Design factors affecting student satisfaction and perceived learning in asynchronous online courses. *Distance Education*, *22*(2), 306–331. http://search.proquest.com/docview/217782729?accountid=14667 doi:10.1080/0158791010220208

Sylvester, D. E., & McGlynn, A. J. (2010). The Digital Divide, Political Participation and Place. *Social Science Computer Review*, *28*(1), 64–74. doi:10.1177/0894439309335148

Taibi, T. (2006). Formalising design patterns composition. *IEE Proceedings. Software Engineering*, *153*(3), 127–136. doi:10.1049/ip-sen:20050072

Terry, M. (2001). Translating learning style theory into university teaching practices: An article based on Kolb's experiential learning model. *Journal of College Reading and Learning*, *32*(1), 68–85. doi:10.1080/10790195.2001.10850128

The European Computer Driving Licence Foundation (TECDLF). (2014). *Syllabus Guide e-Citizen*. Retrieved from http://www.icdl.org.za/ktml2/files/uploads/Syllabus%20Guide%20SWGP1eC1.pdf

The New Media Consortium y Universitat Oberta de Catalunya. (2012). *Perspectivas Tecnológicas: Educación Superior en Iberoamérica 2012-2017. Un Análisis Regional Del Informe Horizon del NMC y la UOC*. The New Media Consortium y Universitat Oberta de Catalunya.

Thiele, J. E. (2003). Learning patterns of online students. *The Journal of Nursing Education*, *42*(8), 364–367. PMID:12938899

Tiffin, J., & Rajasingham, L. (2003). *The Global Virtual University*. London, New York, Canada: Routledge. doi:10.4324/9780203464670

Top-Ten Reviews. (2012). Internet Filter review. Retrieved from http://internet-filter-review.toptenreviews.com/

Triglianos, V., & Pautasso, C. (2013). ASQ: Interactive Web Presentations for Hybrid MOOCs. *Proceedings of the WWW Conference*Rio de Janeiro, Brazil (pp. 209-210). ACM Press.

Tsai, H., Shillair, R., & Cotten, S. (2014). Social Support and 'Playing Around': An Examination of How Older Adults Acquire Digital Literacy with Tablet Computers.*Proceeding of the 42nd Research Conference on Communication, Information and Internet Policy*.

Tullis, T., & Stetson, J. (2004, June). *A Comparison of Questionnaires for Assessing Website Usability*. Paper presented at the Usability Professionals Association Conference, Minneapolis, MN.

Turati, A., Cerizza, D., Celino, I., & Della Valle, E. (2009) Analyzing User Actions within a Web 2.0 Portal to Improve a Collaborative Filtering Recommendation System. *Proceedings of the IEEE/WIC/ACM International Conference on Web Intelligence and Intelligent Agent TechnologyWI'09*, Milan, Italy (pp. 65-68). IEEE Computer Society. doi:10.1109/WI-IAT.2009.232

Udacity. (2012). *Udacity*. Retrieved April 20, 2015 from http://www.udacity.com/

Ulin, P., Robinson, E., & Tolley, E. (2006). *Investigación aplicada en salud pública. Métodos cualitativos* (Technical Report). Retrieved from http://iris.paho.org/xmlui/bitstream/handle/123456789/729/9275316147.pdf

UNESCO. (2002). *UNESCO*. Retrieved from http://www.unesco.org/education/news_en/080702_free_edu_ress.shtml

UNESCO. (2005). *Hacia las Sociedades del Conocimiento*. Ediciones UNESCO.

UNESCO. (2008). *Estándares de Competencia en TIC para Docentes*. Retrieved from www.eduteka.org/pdfdir/UNESCOEstandaresDocentes.pdf

United Nations. (2008). *Convention on the Rights of Persons with Disabilities and Optional Protocol.* Retrieved from http://www.un.org/disabilities/documents/convention/convoptprot-e.pdf

United Nations. (2015). *United Nations ENABLE Rights and Dignity of Persons with Disabilities*. Retrieved from http://www.un.org/disabilities/

University Of London. (2013). Massive Online Open Courses (MOOCs). London: The University of London.

Using APA. (2013). Week 5: Augmented Reality Hits the Real Estate Market. Retrieved from https://annabellearts3091.wordpress.com/

Using APA. Augmented Reality Throughout History, Retrieved from http://www.crystalinks.com/

Van Der Linden, J., Braun, T., Rogers, Y., Oshodi, M., Spiers, A., Mcgoran, D., & O'dowd, P. et al. (2012). Haptic Lotus: A Theatre Experience For Blind And Sighted Audiences.*Proceedings of The 2012 ACM Annual Conference - Extended Abstracts on Human Factors in Computing Systems,*New York (pp. 1471-1472). ACM. doi:10.1145/2212776.2212491

Van, D., & Hacker, K. (2003). The Digital Divide as a Complex and Dynamic Phenomenon. *The Information Society*, *19*(4), 315–326. doi:10.1080/01972240309487

Vanderheiden, G. (n. d.). *Application Software Design Guidelines: Increasing the Accessibility of Application Software to People with Disabilities and Older Users*. Retrieved from http://trace.wisc.edu/docs/software_guidelines/software.htm

Vargas, E., Martínez, K., Pedroza, F., & Morales, S. (2012). Incursión del programa de intervención breve para adolescentes en el E-learning: Resultados del piloteo. *Investigacion y Ciencia*, *20*(55), 42–47.

Vega Cruz, P., Almaraz Menéndez, F., Pinto Escribano, J., & Martín Hernández, S. (2013), *MOOC: Estado de la situación actual, posibilidades, retos y futuro. Scopeo*, Reporte Técnico. Retrieved from http://scopeo.usal.es/wp-content/uploads/2013/06/scopeoi002.pdf

Velasco, R. (2011). *Health and Longevity I: Aging*. CODEU, 14-16.

Velásquez, T. MOOCS (2013). *Un mundo gratuito de conocimientos a um clic de distancia*. Retrieved from http://nochesdemedia.com/2013/01/27/moocs-un-mundo-gratuito-de-conocimientos-a-un-clic-de-distancia/

Vie, S. (2008). Digital Divide 2.0: Generation M and Online Social Networking Sites in the Composition Classroom. *Computers and Composition*, *25*(1), 9–23. doi:10.1016/j.compcom.2007.09.004

Villalobos, L. (2012). *Orientación y movilidad. Notes from the Course "Orientación y Movilidad"*. Universidad Popular de Veracruz.

Vizoso, M. (2013). ¿Serán los COMA (MOOC), el futuro del e-learning y el punto de inflexión del sistema educativo actual? Retrieved from http://scopeo.usal.es/seran-los-coma-mooc-el-futuro-del-e-learning-y-el-punto-de-inflexion-del-sistema-educativo-actual/

VOX Norway. (2012). The Digital Citizen: An analysis of digital competence in the Norwegian population. Retrieved from http://www.vox.no/PageFiles/15123/The_Digital

VRT. (2015) Augmented Reality Devices. Retrieved from http://www.augmentedrealitytrends.com/

Vygotsky, L. S. (1978). Mind and society: The development of higher mental processes.

Vygotsky, L. S. (1978). *Mind in society: The development of higher psychological processes*. Cambridge, MA: Harvard University Press.

W3C. (1999). Weaving the Web Berners Lee. Retrieved from http://www.w3.org/People/Berners-Lee/Weaving/glossary.html

W3C. (2014). Website Accessibility Conformance Evaluation Methodology (WCAG-EM) 1.0. Retrieved from http://www.w3.org/TR/WCAG-EM/

Waard, L. (2011). *Explore a New Learning Frontier – MOOCs*. Retrieved from http://www.cedmaurope.org/newsletter%20articles/eLearning%20Guild/Explore%20a%20New%20Learning%20Frontier%20-%20MOOCs%20(Jul%2011).pdf

Waard, L. (2011, July). *Explore a New Learning Frontier – MOOCs*. Retrieved from http://www.cedma-europe.org/newsletter%20articles/eLearning%20Guild/Explore%20a%20New%20Learning%20Frontier%20-%20MOOCs%20(Jul%2011).pdf

WAI. (2014). WAI: Web Accessibility Initiative. Retrieved from http://www.w3.org/WAI/

Waldmeir, P. (2014). China's elderly flock back to university. *Financial Times*. Retrieved from http://www.ft.com/cms/s/0/aa918952-7ac8-11e4-8646-00144feabdc0.html#axzz3RrTJjcZW

Warbuton, S. (2009). Out of control-Managing our digital reputations. Retrieved from: http://www.slideshare.net/stevenw/out-of-managing-our-digital-reputations

WebAIM. (2015). Constructing a POUR website. Retrieved from http://webaim.org/articles/pour/perceivable

Wei, L., & Hindman, D. B. (2011). Does the Digital Divide Matter More? Comparing Effect of New Media and Old Media Use on the Education-Based Knowledge Gap. *Mass Communication & Society*, *14*(2), 216–235. doi:10.1080/15205431003642707

Weiss, C. (2015). Elearninfo247.Com. Retrieved from http://elearninfo247.com/2011/08/27/fast-forward-e-learning-in-2013/

Werbach, K. (2014). Gamification. Retrieved from https://class.coursera.org/gamification-003/wiki/Syllabus

Whitelock, D., Gilbert, L., & Wills, G. (2013). Feedback Generators: Providing Feedback in MOOCs. *Proceedings of the Computer Applications and Quantitative Methods in Archaeology,* Western, Australia (pp. 1-6). CAA Publishing.

WHO. (2001). *International classification of functioning, disability and health: ICF, World Health Organization*. Retrieved from http://www.who.int/classifications/icf/en/

Willging, P. A., & Johnson, S. D. (2009). Factors that Influence Students' Decision to Dropout of Online Courses. *Journal of Asynchronous Learning Networks*, *13*(3), 115–127.

Williams, J. J. (2013). Improving learning in MOOCs with Cognitive Science. *Proceedings* of *AIED 2013 Workshops* (p. 49).

Willings, C. (2015). *Interpreting the Eye Report*, Retrieved April 01, 2015, from: http://www.teachingvisuallyimpaired.com

Woll, R., Buschbeck, S., Steffens, T., Berrang, P., & Loviscach, J. (2014). A Platform that Integrates Quizzes into video. Proceedings of European MOOCs Stakeholders Summit, Lausanne, Switzerland (pp. 80-87).

World Bank. (2014). World Development Indicators: Internet users. 2013. Retrieved from http://data.worldbank.org/indicator/IT.NET.USER.P2

World Health Organization. (2011). *Word Report on Disability*. Retrieved from http://www.who.int/disabilities/world_report/2011/en/

Wu, M., Baecker, R., & Richards, B. (2007). Designing Cognitive Help for and with People Who Have Anterograde Amnesia. In J. Lazar (Ed.), *Universal Usability*. Hoboken, NJ: John Wiley and Sons.

Xavier, M. G., Neves, M. V., Rossi, F. D., Ferreto, T. C., Lange, T., & De Rose, C. A. (2013). Performance Evaluation of Container-Based Virtualization for High Performance Computing Environments. *Proceedings of the21st EUROMICRO International Conference on Parallel, Distributed and Network-based Processing*, Belfast, Northern Ireland (pp.233–240). IEEE Press. doi:10.1109/PDP.2013.41

Xin, C., Barnett, D. R., & Stephens, C. (2013). Fad or Future: The Advantages and Challenges of Massive Open Online Courses (MOOCs).*Proceedings of the 32nd Research-to-Practice Conference in Adult and Higher Education*, St. Charles, Mo., Lindenwood University Press.

Yadav, K., Shrivastava, K., Prasad, M. P., Arsikere, H., Patil, S., Kumar, R., & Deshmukh, O. (2015). Content-driven Multi-modal Techniques for Non-linear Video Navigation. *Proceedings of the 20th International Conference on Intelligent User Interfaces*, Atlanta, GA, United States (pp. 333-344). ACM Press. doi:10.1145/2678025.2701408

Yair, Y. (2014). Did You Let a Robot Check My Homework? *ACM Inroads*, *5*(2), 33–34. doi:10.1145/2614512.2614522

Yi, M. (2004). *They Got Game / Stacks of New Releases for Hungry Video Game Enthusiasts Mean It's Boom Time for an Industry Now Even Bigger than Hollywood*. Retrieved from http://www.sfgate.com/news/article/THEY-GOT-GAME-Stacks-of-new-releases-for-hungry-2663371.php

Young, A. (2008). Structuring asynchronous discussions to incorporate learning principles in an online class: One professor's course analysis. *MERLOT Journal of Online Learning and Teaching*, *4*(2), 218–224.

Young, G. (1997). *Adult development, therapy, and culture: A postmodern synthesis*. Springer Science & Business Media. doi:10.1007/978-1-4757-9015-3

Yousef, F., Chatti, M. A., Schroeder, M. A., Wosnitza, U., & Jakobs, M., & Harald (2014). Moocs: A Review Of The State-Of-The-Art. *Proceedings Of The 6th International Conference On Computer Supported Education*, Barcelona, Spain (pp. 9-20).

Yuan, L., & Powell, S. (2013). MOOCs and Open Education: Implications for Higher Education. *Proceedings of CETIS JISC*, 2013.

Zheng, S., Rosson, M. B., Shih, P. C., & Carroll, J. M. (2015). Understanding Student Motivation, Behaviors and Perceptions in MOOCs.*Proceedings of the 18th ACM Conference on Computer Supported Cooperative Work & Social Computing*, Vancouver, Canada (pp. 1882-1895) ACM Press. doi:10.1145/2675133.2675217

Zhou, Y., Singh, N., & Kaushik, P. D. (2011). The Digital Divide in Rural South Asia: Survey Evidence from Bangladesh, Nepal, and Sri Lanka. *IIMB Management Review*, *23*(1), 15–19. doi:10.1016/j.iimb.2010.12.002

Zichermann, G., & Linder, J. (2010). *Game-based marketing: Inspire customer loyalty through rewards, challenges, and contests*. John Wiley & Sons.

Zikmund, W. G. (2003). *Business Research Methods* (7th ed.). Mason, Ohio: Thomson Learning.

About the Contributors

Ricardo Mendoza-Gonzalez is a Researcher/Professor at the Instituto Tecnológico de Aguascalientes (Mexico). He holds a Ph.D. in Computer Science (Universidad Autónoma de Aguascalientes, México, 2009), a Master's degree in Computer Science (Universidad Autónoma de Aguascalientes, México, 2007), and a Bachelor of Computer Science (Instituto Tecnológico de Aguascalientes, México, 2004). Dr. Mendoza-González has reported his work in journals such as Advances in Engineering Software, and prestigious international conferences such as IEEE-CCECE, CADUI, ICIMP, and IASTED-CNIS. He collaborates with researchers of the University of Ontario Institute of Technology (UOIT, Canada), and Universidad Autónoma de Aguascalientes (Mexico). His current research interests include several topics on: human-computer interaction, information security, usability, artificial intelligence, and software engineering.

***

Ren Atkins Researcher Professor, Social Learning Community Manager, Senior Education Analyst, Future Student and Admissions Coordinator, and Student Communications Coordinator at Open Universities Australia, Australia. She holds a Master degree of Education, from Queensland University of Technology.

Juanita Avila is a Social Worker at the government dependency Procuraduria General de Justicia de Aguascalientes, Mexico. She has almost 15 years of experience in research on children violence and its consequences in learning process. Currently, She has been attending cases on cyber bullying and cyber abuse in social networks among pre-adolescents and adolescents in Aguascalientes.

Mandi Axmann Researcher Professor, Social Learning Community Manager, at Open Universities Australia, Australia. She is current completing her PhD (Bus Info Systems) at RMIT University in Melbourne, Australia. Her research topic is 'An exploration of the human-dimensions of human-computer interaction within web-based higher education.' She holds a Master degree in Information Science, Specialization, Instructional Design, Learning Theories for Instructional Technology, Modalities for Instructional Technology for Teaching and Development, Information Science and Knowledge Management. She has Postgraduate Diploma in Adult Education, Psychology of Andragogics, Tertiary, Didactics, Theoretical Frameworks in Adult Education, Educational Research, Temporal Andragogics, Educational Management.

Stein Brunvand is an associate professor in the Department of Education at the University of Michigan-Dearborn. He teaches courses in educational technology. His research interests include the effective integration of technology and online teaching and learning.

Paula Escudeiro is a professor of the Department of Computer Engineering of the Engineering School of the Porto Polytechnic (ISEP). Member of the Board of the Department of Computer Engineering, Director of the Multimedia Laboratory of the Department of Computer Science.

Alma Rosa García Gaona, is Professor in Computer Science at Universidad Veracruzana. She holds a Ph.D. in International Education (Autonomous University of Tamaulipas, México, 2004), Dr. Alma Rosa is senior research professor in Statistics and Informatics faculty, lead-member of the PhD. program in Computer Science and lead member of MSc. In User Centered Interactive Systems. Her work is focused in User Centered Design systems for education. She has reported her work in journals, book chapters, conference papers, and technical reports.

Alfredo Mendoza González is an Associate Professor of Computer Science in the Autonomous University of Aguascalientes. He received a MS in Computer Science from this institution in 2012 and he is currently enrolled in a Ph.D. program in Computer Science. He has participated in international conferences of IEEE and ACM. Most of his research centers on Human-Computer Interaction specifically with moderate intellectual disabled users and mobile devices. His most recent research is about the use of mobile gestural interfaces by Down syndrome children.

Nina Grgić-Hlača was born in 1993, in Rijeka, where she finished elementary school and high school. In 2011 she enrolled in the Faculty of Humanities and Social Sciences of the University of Zagreb, where she obtained her bachelor's degree in Information Sciences with a thesis in Logic and Machine learning under the title "Evaluacija dvaju modela klasifikatora formula propozicijske logike" [Evaluation of two classification models of well-formed formulas of propositional logic], and where she is currently pursuing her bachelor's degree in Philosophy. In 2012 she enrolled in the Faculty of Science of the University of Zagreb, where she is pursuing her bachelor's degree in Mathematics. She has been serving as a demonstrator of Logic since 2012. She is the co-author of the book "Logika I. – Riješeni zadaci iz logike sudova" [Logic I – solved exercises on propositional logic].

Raul Alejandro Gutierrez B.A.in Psychology at Universidad Autónoma de Aguascalientes (UAA) and Ph. D. in Social Sciences focused on Psychology at UAA. Internactional Research Stay at Universidad de Oviedo and in Uruguay by Consejo Latinoamericano de Ciencias Sociales (CLACSO). Posdoctoral Stay at Instituto Nacional de Psiquiatría Ramón de la Fuente (INPRFM). Sistema Nacional de Investigadores (SNI) level (C). Research Full Time Professor at Universidad Politécnica de Aguascalientes (UPA). Journals Peer-reviewer for specialized magazines. Research lines: Youth who do not study nor work, identity, mental health and drug consumption.

Sandra Jiménez-González earned her Career of Strategic Information Systems in 2014 and currently she studies her Master Degree in Networks and System from the Universidad Politécnica de Aguascalientes. Sandra´s research interest focus on the Human-Computer interaction oriented in Massive Online Open Courses (MOOCs).

Aikaterini Kalogeraki holds a Master's degree in Information and Communication Systems with specialization in Education Technology and her dissertation was on UI design for Massive Open Online Courses (MOOCs). Also she has degrees in Technology of Graphics Arts and Pedagogy with specialization in students with disabilities. She works since 1997 as a graphic designer for digital and print productions and since 2001 as an instructor of graphic design and visualization in all levels of education and also in training centers. Particular she specializes in concept visualization using 2D and 3D computer graphics with emphasis on usability and overall user experience.

Davor Lauc Born in 1971, in Osijek, where he finished the mathematical high school. In 1990, he enrolled in the Faculty of Humanities and Social Sciences of the University of Zagreb, with a major in Information Sciences and Philosophy. He graduated in 1994 with a thesis in Logic. From 1995 he worked as a research assistant on the project "Modeli znanja i obrada prirodnoga jezika" [Models of knowledge and natural language processing], while attending the graduate program in Philosophy at the Faculty of Humanities and Social Sciences of the University of Zagreb. He obtained his MA degree in 1997 by defending a thesis in the field of logic under the title "Formalizacija pojma relevantnosti u okviru teorije situacije" [The formalization of the concept of relevancy in the framework of situation theory]. Since 2000, he works as a teaching assistant at the chair for Logic, department of Philosophy, Faculty of Humanities and Social Sciences of the University of Zagreb. He attained his PhD in Logic in 2004 under the title "Problem logičkog zaključivanja o promjenama i djelovanjima" [The problem of logical reasoning about change and action], when he became a senior research assistant, and afterwards Assistant Professor. From 1995 to 2004 he was in Barcelona, Prague, Aix en Provance, Birmingham, Helsinki and Stanford for professional development. During his undergraduate studies he served as demonstrator, and after graduating he was involved in teaching courses as a teaching assistant, and subsequently he taught and conducted courses independently at the undergraduate, graduate and postgraduate levels. He is the author of over twenty papers in books and international peer-reviewed journals, among others: "An Logical Reconstruction of Programming Languages Paradigms", "Logička analiza pojma relevantnosti" [The logical analysis of the concept of relevance], "Elementi simboličke logike" [Elements of symbolic logic], "Current Methods for Statistical and Logical Estimation of Significance of Genetic Matches Might Not Always be Appropriate".

Sergio Luján-Mora is Lecturer of the Department of Software and Computing Systems, University of Alicante. He earned his Ph.D. in Computer Engineering at the University of Alicante (Spain) in 2005. His main research topics include web accessibility and usability, web applications and business intelligence, data warehouse design, analysis and object-oriented design with UML, MDA, etc. He teaches the courses "Programming and Data Structures" and "Internet Programming" on computing qualifications. He has taught several courses in web programming, web application development and web usability and accessibility, both in Spain and in other countries like Mexico and Poland. He has published several research papers in various conferences and high-impact journals both nationally and internationally. Among them, the Congress ER, UML or DOLAP. Among the international journals indexed in the JCR include DKE, JCS or JDBM. He has also published several books related to programming and web design. He has participated in several research projects funded by public entities, such as "hypermedia environment for code migration and development", financed by the Ministry of Science and Technology, "Development of a methodology for ensuring usability and accessibility of Web Interfaces (Demeter) "funded by the Department of Education of the Generalitat Valenciana. Finally, it has been a visiting professor at universities in Algeria, Kyrgyzstan, Mexico, Moldova and Poland.

Huizilopoztli Luna-García is a Researcher/Professor in the Department of Electrical Engineering, Campus Jalpa at the Universidad Autónoma de Zacatecas, México. Currently he is a Ph.D. student in Computer Science at Instituto Tecnológico de Aguascalientes; he holds a Master's degree in Sciences and Information Systems (Universidad Autónoma de Aguascalientes), and a Bachelor in Computer Systems Engineering (Instituto Tecnológico de Zacatecas). His research interests are educational technology, design patterns, mobile technology, human-computer interaction, usability and user centered design.

Kalina Isela Martínez B.A. in Psychology at Universidad Autónoma de Aguascalientes (UAA). Ph. D. in Psychology at Universidad Nacional Autónoma de México (UNAM). National and International speaker. Author of more than 30 scientific journals and books on Drug Consumption Prevention and Model for a Brief Intervention for Adolescents of her own authorship. This model is being used by Centro de Atención de las Adicciones in Mexico. She has been a national and international research coordinator on this major topic. Currently she participates in an international research network focused on studying Complex Behaviour in coordination to Universidad de Colombia and Universidad de Guadalajara.

Francisco Javier Ornelas PhD in Computer Science, specializing in Artificial Intelligence. Research Professor at the Polytechnic University of Aguascalientes and the Autonomous University of Aguascalietes. Main lines of research: Genetic Algorithms, Education and Logistics.

Maria Abigail Paz B.A. in Psychology at Universidad Autónoma de Aguascalientes (UAA) and Masters in Family Education at Universidad Panamericana. She currently works for Universidad Politécnica de Aguascalientes. Main study area on Youth Drug Consumption.

Julio Cesar Ponce PhD in Computer Science from the Autonomous University of Aguascalientes (2010). Master in Computer Science from the Autonomous University of Aguascalientes (2007). Full professor at the Autonomous University of Aguascalientes since 2003, has published 5 books, 15 book chapters, 15 journal articles and more than 50 publications in national and international conferences in the areas of Artificial Intelligence, Evolutionary Computation, Software Engineering, Data Mining, Parallel Programming with GPUs, Augmented Reality and Information Technologies in Education.

Mario A. Rodríguez-Díaz earned his M.Sc. in 2009 and his Ph.D. in 2015 both in Exact Sciences, Systems and Information from the Universidad Autónoma de Aguascalientes. Currently, he works at Instituto Tecnológico de Aguascalientes, where he teaches undergraduate courses in computer programming and image processing, he also works at Traffic System developing software for the broadcasting industry. His main interests are image processing, computer vision, pattern recognition, information theory, automata theory, video games and artificial intelligence.

Laura C. Rodriguez-Martinez earned her Ms. in Computing Sciences in 2006 and her Ph.D. in Computing Sciences in 2009 from the Autonomous University of Aguascalientes, Mexico. She is a full-time Professor and Researcher in Institute of Technology of Aguascalientes (ITA) since 2010. Before joining ITA she worked as Software Engineer in Mexican Private Enterprises since 1992 to 2006. Her current teaching and research interest include Service-Oriented Software Engineering, Software-System Development Life Cycle and Graphical User Interface Processes Design.

Rosa Maria Reis teaches at IPP- ISEP in the Computer Engineering Department. She has a PhD on Informatics at the University UTAD-Tras-os-Montes and Alto Douro, Vila Real. She is a researcher at GILT- Graphic Interaction & Learning Technologies and her area of research is related to the application of techniques of software engineering in the design of educational collaborative virtual environments. She has been involved in several National and European research projects and is presently a regular reviewer of several conferences and scientific journals. She is author/co-author of book chapters, 50 papers and more than 15 communications in scientific meetings.

Teresita de Jesús Álvarez Robles is a prominent last year student of Master of Science in User Centered Design Interactive Systems hold by the University of Veracruz in Mexico. Her main research topic focuses in Interactive Mobile Systems for blind users, in both Software Engineering and Artificial Intelligence. She has extended her research across Mexican territory; enriching it with congress presentations and books chapters in Brazil, Spain and Portugal.

Francisco Alvarez Rodriguez, is Professor in Computer Science at Universidad Autónoma deAguascalientes. He holds a Ph.D. in Engineering (UNAM, México, 2004), He has a number of collaborations with very important researches in prestigious universities around the world. Dr. Álvarez Rodriguez has reported his work in journals, book chapters, conference papers, and technical reports, and so far has supervised almost 30 students at the graduate and undergraduate level. His current research interests include software engineering (methodologies, metrics, among others), and distance education (educational internet technologies, learning environments, learning objects, among others.

Jose Antonio Saldivar Universidad Politécnica de Aguascalientes full time Language Department professor and investigator. Ph.D. Social Sciences student at Universidad Autónoma de Aguascalientes. Bilingual Education is his main research stream. International congress participation at Oaxaca (2013) and Aguascalientes (2013 and 2012).

Sandra Sanchez-Gordon is a PhD Student at University of Alicante, Spain and professor of the Department of Informatics and Computer Sciences, National Polytechnic School of Ecuador. She has a Master's degree in Software Engineering by Drexel University, USA in 2001. Her main research topics include web accessibility, software engineering, requirements engineering, testing engineering, IT governance. She has twenty years of experience in teaching graduate and undergraduate courses. Currently, she teaches the course "Software Engineering Quality". She has published several research papers in various international conferences. She has 23 years of experience in development and implementation of software solutions in Ecuador, Panama and USA.

Douglas C. Schmidt is a Full Professor in the Department of Electrical Engineering & Computer Science of the Vanderbilt University in Nashville, Tennessee. He holds a PhD in Computer Science by the University of California at Irvine. He has over one hundred publications among Journals, books, chapters, and conference papers. He leads the Distributed Object Computing (DOC) Group in collaboration with the Computer Science and Engineering department at Washington University. The DOC Group also includes members at Remedy IT, Riverace Corporation, PrismTech, and Object Computing Inc. The purpose of the DOC group is to support advanced R&D on patterns, middleware, and modeling tools using an open source software development model, which allows academics, developers, and end-users to participate in leading-edge R&D projects driven by the free market of ideas, requirements, and resources. Hi has more than one hundred publications among journals, book-chapters, and conference papers.

Sandro Skansi Born in Zagreb in 1985. He graduated in 2009 at the Centre for Croatian Studies of the University of Zagreb in Philosophy and Croatian Studies with a thesis in logic under the name "ZFC and the Russellian nonstandard set theory MP". He received his Ph.D. at the Faculty of Humanities and Social Sciences with a thesis in logic under the title "Cut elimination and structural proof theory for second order logic".

Beatriz Angélica Toscano de la Torre has a Degree in Computer Sciences and Statistics from the Autonomous University of Nayarit, where she has held positions of academic management, the latter as a Coordinator of the Academic Program of Computer Science from 2008 to 2014. Full time researcher and professor of the Area of Economic and Administrative Sciences in the Academic Program of Informatics in the Autonomous University of Nayarit. She has 15 articles in indexed journals, publications in national and international seminars in the areas of Total Quality in Education; Some of the titles of her works are Augmented Reality and ICT in education, data mining, and educational assessment, Augmented Reality as a Tool for the Development of Mathematical Skills; Video games as a strategy to improve reading and writing skills. Exploratory study; Quality of the educational programes in ICT in Mexico from the perspective of the CONAIC; Learning objects for mobile devices, and some others.

Michael A Walker Is a Graduate Research Assistant at Institute for Software Integrated Systems Vanderbilt University from August 2011 – Presently a member of the team working on 2 Coursera MOOC Specializations comprising of 12 month long courses in Android mobile development from introductory courses up to concurrency, cloud synchronization, and mobile security.

Jules White is an assistant Professor at Vanderbilt University. He holds a PhD in Computer Sciences by Vanderbilt University. He has almost ninety publications among journals, paper conferences, and book-chapters. His research interest include but not limited to Mobile Security, Mobile Augmented Reality, Cyber-physical Systems, Deployment and Configuration Optimization Distributed Systems, and Cloud Computing.

Index

H

I

L

M

O

P

S

T

U

V

W

X

www.ingramcontent.com/pod-product-compliance
Ingram Content Group UK Ltd.
Pitfield, Milton Keynes, MK11 3LW, UK
UKHW050951290926
15470UKWH00005B/1766